"Kat is the master of free-from recipes!"
MATT ADLARD,
author of *Bake it Better*

"This is so much more than a cookbook,
it's a baking science bible!"
TESSA ARIAS,
creator of *Handle the Heat*

"Katarina's recipes are delicious, foolproof and you'd
simply not know that they're 'without' in any way."
MARK DIACONO,
author of *Spice: A Cook's Companion*

"A deliciously authoritative guide to creating
the gluten-free, dairy-free, egg-free, and
vegan baked treats of our dreams."
ZOË FRANÇOIS,
author of *Zoë Bakes Cookies* and host of *Zoë Bakes*

"*The Elements of Baking* practically and
beautifully shares a wonderful message –
baking is truly for everyone."
ERIN JEANNE MCDOWELL,
author of *The Book on Pie* and host of *Happy Baking*

"Brilliantly smart and poised to become
the essential baking guide for folk who
want to learn or love to bake."
NIK SHARMA,
James Beard finalist, author of *Veg-Table*

# The Elements of Baking

Making any recipe gluten-free,
dairy-free, egg-free or vegan

## Katarina Cermelj

For my parents, who dealt with my almost daily questions of "Does this taste gluten-free?" and "Can you tell that there are no eggs in this?" with shocking amounts of patience.

Love you so much.

# Contents

# Introduction

Imagine this: you come across the most mouth-watering recipe for a chocolate cake. It looks amazing – moist and terribly decadent; it's the chocolate cake of your dreams. And then you look at the ingredient list and realize that you can't actually make this recipe. Because you can't eat eggs. Or gluten. Or dairy. Or a combination of them.

If this sounds familiar, I'm sorry, I know exactly how frustrating that can be. Now, let's change it.

Of course, there are numerous truly marvellous free-from recipes out there (be they gluten-, dairy- or egg-free, or vegan or gluten-free vegan), but this doesn't quite solve your problem if you have your heart set on one specific recipe, or something as close to it as possible. Or maybe you want to recreate a family favourite that's been handed down through generations. You don't want a pale approximation – you want *that* recipe. Just without the gluten, or the eggs, or the dairy.

Most free-from recipes come without much explanation as to why they work. This means that when you then come across a recipe you'd want to prepare but it doesn't fit your dietary needs, you're left with two choices: (a) don't make the recipe at all, or (b) blindly try to adapt the recipe and hope you don't end up with a disaster.

This book provides a third option: (c) adapt the recipe in a systematic, scientifically grounded way, armed with a thorough understanding of the science of baking and of the individual ingredients – with guaranteed success. It's the encyclopedia of adapting recipes, regardless of your specific dietary needs – your constant companion in the kitchen, the book that you refer to every time you want to translate a recipe to fit your lifestyle and your diet.

I won't give you just vague, general advice about modifying recipes. Instead, I'll give you a list of quantitative rules that tell you exactly how you need to adjust the amounts of the existing ingredients and exactly how much of a new ingredient you need to add when you want to modify a recipe to be X-free (where X = gluten, eggs, dairy or a combination of these).

That said, this cookbook isn't just for those who have to follow a particular diet. It's also for home cooks and bakers who love to host dinner parties and want to tailor their menu to the dietary needs of their guests, but who don't have time to check numerous cookbooks and websites for the different free-from possibilities. It's for food bloggers and recipe developers who are asked about whether their recipes can be made without this or that. And it's for anyone who just wants to geek out over the endlessly fascinating science of free-from baking.

Regardless of which of these groups you belong to and why you've picked up this book, one thing's for certain: in it you'll find endless baking inspiration, numerous mouth-watering recipes and a generous pinch of approachable, fun science sprinkled on to every page.

# First: Understand the Ingredients

My own interest in allergy-friendly or free-from baking started when I had to eliminate gluten and dairy from my diet to solve a host of health problems. Like most people, I struggled with finding recipes that I could make that actually tasted like the gluten- and dairy-filled delicacies I was used to. Over time, I started developing my own reliable, delicious recipes, which went beyond just gluten- and dairy-free. Once I started experimenting, I simply couldn't stop. And in no time, I was tinkering with egg-free and vegan recipes, as well.

Along the way, there were numerous failures: rock-hard cookies, cakes so dry they would crumble away into nothing and gloopy brownies that looked like strange brown soup. But with each failure – just like with each success – I developed a better understanding of the individual ingredients, their properties and the role they played in each bake as a whole.

Of course, I had an ace up my sleeve: my knowledge of science and Chemistry, honed first through my undergraduate studies and later refined during my Inorganic Chemistry PhD, both at the University of Oxford. I am a self-professed nerd – I like numbers and trends and detailed Excel spreadsheets. And while there's something wonderfully freeing about being creative in the kitchen, I firmly believe that in order for that creativity to be successful (in a reproducible manner that doesn't rely on sheer dumb luck), it needs to be based on science.

So, over time, I started thinking of each of the fundamental ingredients (the flour, the butter, the eggs, and so on) not as an indivisible whole, but rather in terms of its individual components and the properties that each ingredient brings to the bakes.

For example, we should always consider an egg as two ingredients: an egg white and an egg yolk. The white plays the crucial role of binder (giving bakes some elasticity and preventing them from being too crumbly) and a source of structure, moisture and fluffiness (that is, it provides some lift and aeration to the bakes). The yolk adds moisture, fat and flavour. Overall, their many important roles make eggs the trickiest ingredient to replace in a bake.

You can apply this change in mindset to all other ingredients, too – from regular wheat flour to dairy butter – and this new approach is crucial if you want to become a confident and successful adapter of recipes. What's more, it's not restricted to adapting recipes to exclude this or that. Even when you want to make a seemingly negligible or easily administered change, like halving a recipe, the *role* of an ingredient is as important as its quantity.

Consider a recipe that includes one egg – say, a recipe for twelve cookies. You want to halve it to make just six, but how exactly do you halve an egg? Many would say that you just whisk up the egg, and measure out half of it. But, how do you know that the mixture you've measured out contains the egg yolk and the egg white in the right proportions, so as to be representative of the egg as a whole? You don't, not really. Instead, think back to the egg as a composite of a yolk and a white – this tells you what to do next. Separate the egg into the yolk and the white and measure out half of each (Ideally with a digital scale, for absolute precision.) Voilà! You can now make only six cookies, knowing that they will have the perfect texture and flavour and will be indistinguishable from the cookies you'd have made if you'd made the full recipe of twelve.

## "You'd Never Know It's X-free!"

The truly amazing thing about my approach to baking is that it can achieve free-from results (whether that's gluten-, dairy-, egg–free, or any combination of those) that are pretty much indistinguishable from the original "regular" recipe. And you don't even need any super unusual or inaccessible ingredients! Honestly, the most exotic ingredients in this book are xanthan gum and psyllium husk, which are pretty commonplace in gluten-free baking now.

That said, I'll try to keep exclamations along the lines of, "You'll never guess that this is X-free!" to a minimum... because this is true for every recipe in these pages and things would get very repetitive very quickly. But I just know that I won't be able to help myself in some cases (honestly, even I am still astonished that you can make perfectly soft, squishy cinnamon rolls without any gluten, eggs or dairy, and I developed the recipe!) – so bear with me.

## This Isn't a "Healthy Eating" Book

Many people equate free-from cooking and baking with "healthy eating" – whatever that may be. This book isn't about that. Don't expect these recipes to be about wholesome ingredients or low sugar or low carb or low fat... or whatever else the current (totally subjective, forever changing and always somewhat dubious) definition of "healthy eating" is.

I'm also not here to try to convince you about the superiority of any one free-from diet, or to convert you to a particular way of eating or baking. (I am, though, trying to convert you to start using a kitchen scale.) My only aim is to give you the tools to enjoy truly spectacular free-from alternatives that are packed full of flavour and just as delicious as the "regular" equivalents.

## One Book, Endless Recipes

There are more than 150 recipes in this book, counting the fundamental recipes in the case studies' chapter (Chapter 4, including both the original regular and all the free-from versions), the recipes in the individual free-from chapters, and all the frostings and so on in Chapter 10.

But here's the thing: you can use the rules for adapting recipes in Chapter 3 to take any one of these recipes and transform it into whatever other free-from version you fancy. And then you can go beyond the pages of this book, armed with these same rules, and use them to create free-from variations of other recipes that you found online or in other cookbooks, or of those that have been in your family for generations.

So, while the number of recipes in this cookbook is finite (there was a page limit), the information *within* the book enables you to adapt and modify countless recipes to suit your diet. The options are quite literally endless.

# How this Book Is Organized

This is an enthusiastically nerdy cookbook. It's so much more than just a collection of recipes – there is also science and there are case studies and even more science. Use the following information to direct you where to go depending on what information you want to find.

Importantly, you can find bake recipes in two places: at the end of each case study in Chapter 4 and in the individual free-from chapters (Chapters 5-9).

## CHAPTER 1

### Everything you need to get started

This is your starting point: Chapter 1 contains all the information about the ingredients and tools you'll need to get the best possible result on your X-free baking journey (where X = gluten, dairy, eggs or a combination of these). Here, you'll find a detailed list of all the essential ingredients, including how to choose the best possible shop-bought options and how to make your own homemade versions.

## CHAPTER 2

### The science of ingredients & recipe modification

This chapter contains all the crucial science about free-from baking that everything else in the book is based on. If you want to eliminate gluten, dairy or eggs from your baking, you first need to understand what role they play in a recipe, both in and out of the oven. This chapter gives you an overview of their properties, and also provides insight into how you can swap them with other ingredients to achieve an end result that's pretty much indistinguishable from the original.

## CHAPTER 3

### The rules for adapting recipes

Chapter 3 contains all the quantitative rules that will help you to adapt any recipe to be X-free (where X = gluten, dairy, eggs, or a combination of these). The rules are organized by the type of recipe or bake you want to adapt, and then further by the specific free-from diet. You can also combine the rules as needed, or even work in reverse and take a specific free-from recipe and adapt it to work in a regular (non-free-from) way!

## CHAPTER 4

### The case studies

This is probably the most unique part of this cookbook and it's an idea that I borrowed from maths and science textbooks. The chapter is made up of "worked examples" that show you how the rules from the previous chapter work within the context of an actual recipe, and also demonstrate how I derived the rules in the first place. The case studies span a huge range of different recipes, from myriad types of cake and cookie to brownies and pastry. In each case study, I'll take you, in turn, from the original "regular" recipe that contains gluten, eggs and dairy to each free-from version.

## CHAPTERS 5–9

### The individual free-from chapters

Each of these chapters is devoted to one specific dietary requirement: gluten-free, dairy-free, egg-free, vegan and gluten-free vegan. Here, you'll find in-depth science and show-stopping recipes that focus on just that one free-from variation. And the great part is that you can take any recipe from any of these chapters and use the rules from Chapter 3 to modify it to create any other free-from bake, too!

# Choose Your X-free Adventure

I am a science nerd. Making Excel spreadsheets to track how the ingredient ratios change between different free-from versions of the same recipe is my idea of a fun evening. However, I'm fully aware that you, as my reader, might fall on the science keenness scale anywhere between "I have nightmares about high-school Chemistry" to "I read about different shapes of salt crystals in my free time."

While this is obviously a very science-forward cookbook, you don't have to read about the science (although I totally recommend it – it's fun *and* useful, I promise!). There are several levels at which you can use and interact with this book.

## LEVEL 1
### "Just give me the recipes"

You just want to follow a set of instructions with all the ingredient quantities already figured out – you don't want any pesky maths standing between you and the perfect slice of cake, please and thank you.

**HAVE A LOOK AT:**

• the recipes in the case-study chapter (Chapter 4)

• the recipes in the individual free-from chapters (Chapters 5–9)

## LEVEL 2
### "I want to dip my toes into adapting my own recipes"

You don't want to know all the science, but you have some favourite recipes (online, in cookbooks, among family hand-me-downs...) that you want to adapt to become free-from.

**HAVE A LOOK AT:**

• the recipes in the case-study chapter (Chapter 4)

• the recipes in the individual free-from chapters (Chapters 5–9)

• the rules for adapting recipes (Chapter 3)

## LEVEL 3
### "I'm a total science nerd"

You not only want to know the rules of recipe modification but also understand the "why" behind them – you love reading and learning about the Chemistry that happens in bakes both in and out of the oven, and baker's percentages (see page 272) are basically your love language.

**HAVE A LOOK AT:**

• all the fundamentals of recipe modification and the science of the individual ingredients (Chapter 2)

• the rules for adapting recipes (Chapter 3)

• the recipes in the case-study chapter (Chapter 4)

• the introduction sections to all the free-from chapters (Chapters 5–9), and the recipes themselves

• the footnotes with the individual recipes

## "But I only want gluten-free (or dairy-free, or vegan...)!"

Even if you're interested in only one free-from version (be that gluten-, dairy- or egg-free or vegan), I recommend you have a look through Chapter 2, because it will help you to develop a deeper understanding of the roles and interactions of various ingredients in a bake.

Using the rules for adapting recipes in Chapter 3 is easy: just use whichever you need. Then, focus on the relevant sections of the case studies in Chapter 4. For example, if you're interested in only gluten-free recipes, have a look at the gluten-free sections. But if you're vegan, look at not only the vegan section but also at the dairy-free and the egg-free – simply because the vegan versions usually build on (or are a combination of) dairy- and egg-free.

Finally, have a thorough look at whichever free-from chapter is relevant to you (plus the egg-free and dairy-free, if you're vegan). Of course, if you're interested in gluten-free vegan baking, I recommend that you read through everything, to gain a thorough understanding.

## A note on measurements

I'm all about precision and reproducibility when it comes to my recipes – and I'm a big believer in the superiority of using metric gram measurements and of weighing your ingredients if you want to get the best possible result every single time.

That said, you will find volume measurements (cups and tablespoons) in this book. I admit, I was hesitant to include them. But, I do want the book to be as accessible as possible... so, rather begrudgingly, I included conversions, too. Keep in mind, though, that if you're using volume measurements and you have trouble with a recipe or a set of rules for adapting recipes to your chosen variation, it's possible that the cups and tablespoons are to blame. This is especially true if you're making gluten-free recipes (more on that on page 270).

## Gluten-free flour blend: the gram-to-cup conversion

Whenever a gluten-free (or gluten-free vegan) recipe in this book uses a "plain gluten-free flour blend", I use a gram-to-US-cup conversion that assumes that 1 cup ~ 120g. Over the years, I've found that this works well for the majority of shop-bought gluten-free flour blends.

However, gluten-free flour blends can vary widely in density, especially if homemade. For example, the general homemade gluten-free flour blend on page 24 with the suggested composition made up of tapioca starch, millet flour and sorghum flour, has a density such that 1 cup ~ 120g. However, if you substituted tapioca starch with potato starch, its density would change so that 1 cup ~ 150g. And if you replaced millet flour with finely ground brown rice flour, then the conversion would be 1 cup ~ 130g. And so on. And then there's also the issue that different brands of the same gluten-free flour (such as buckwheat flour, tapioca starch or sorghum flour) can vary in terms of how finely they're milled and therefore their density.

As you can see, using volume measurements with gluten-free flours and blends leaves much room for error; it's probably the number-one reason why many people struggle with gluten-free baking. That's why I always recommend using a scale when it comes to gluten-free recipes. Come over to the we-weigh-everything side... trust me, we have much better cookies.

## Measure everything in grams (and never millilitres)

When I say that I weigh everything... I do mean absolutely everything, including liquid ingredients. That's because measuring out, for example, 105g of water is much easier than measuring out 105ml of water – unless, of course, you're using a laboratory-grade measuring cylinder, in which case, carry on.

# Chapter

# 1

# Xf

## X-free

## Baking Basics

# Before You Begin

Before you dive into the science and the recipes in the rest of the book, here are some important notes that apply to all the recipes and will help to guarantee success in the kitchen.

**Use a digital food scale** I know I've said this before, and I'll say it again (many times) – for the most consistently delicious and reliable results, nothing beats weighing your ingredients.

**Check your oven temperature** An oven thermometer is one of your best friends in the kitchen. Most ovens aren't perfectly calibrated and, in reality, they can be shockingly hotter or colder compared to the temperature you set them to. So, get an oven thermometer and check your oven temperature and then adjust your oven dial as needed.

**Use a conventional (non-fan) oven** The oven temperatures in this book are for a conventional oven, not a fan/fan-assisted/convection oven. In general, I prefer to use the conventional oven setting for all of my baking – but if you have only a fan oven, reduce the recipe's given temperature by about 20°C/25°F.

**Use level spoon measurements** All spoon measurements in the recipes are level, not heaped or rounded. For example, if you measure out 1 teaspoon of baking powder, level it off with your finger or the back of a knife to get the correct amount.

**Volume measurements** Cups, tablespoons and teaspoons, and sticks of butter refer to the US measuring system. This means that 1 cup = 240ml, 1 tablespoon = 15ml, 1 teaspoon = 5ml and 1 stick (½ cup or 8 tablespoons) of butter ~ 115g (true for regular and vegan butter).

**The gluten-free flour blend gram-to-cup conversion** This assumes that 1 US cup ~ 120g. See page 15 for more info on this important point!

**Use fine sea salt (table salt), unless otherwise specified** Fine sea salt or table salt has very small, fine grains, which are quick to dissolve in liquids and batters.

> In the US, you'd frequently use Morton kosher or Diamond Crystal salt rather than table salt. The density (weight per unit volume) of Morton kosher salt is actually quite similar to table salt, so you can use the same volume – that is, use 1 teaspoon of Morton salt for each teaspoon of table salt or fine sea salt. Diamond Crystal kosher salt has larger, flakier crystals and therefore a lower density. In this case, use double the volume given in a recipe – that is, use 2 teaspoons for every 1 teaspoon of table salt or fine sea salt. (Note that if you're weighing your salt, you'll use the same weight regardless of the type of salt – it's just the density and therefore the volume that's changing.)

**Use UK medium eggs (equivalent to US large eggs)** The average weight of one whole egg is about 60g with the shell or about 50–52g without the shell. One egg yolk weighs about 15–16g and one egg white weighs about 35–36g.

**Read the whole recipe before you start baking** That way, you'll know exactly what ingredients you need at every stage of the recipe and how best to organize your time.

**Check your ingredients for allergens** While all the recipes in this cookbook use only ingredients suitable for the relevant diet, allergens can sneak in to the manufacture of some baking foods. Always double check the labels before you buy or use.

# Essential Ingredients

All baking starts with choosing the correct ingredients. And that's even more important when it comes to free-from baking. Knowing how to choose the best gluten-free flours and blends, what kind of vegan butter to go for, or which dairy-free milk alternatives are best avoided is half the battle when it comes to free-from success.

To make your life easier, I've compiled some of my recommendations over the following pages, including a few ingredients that you can make yourself if you can't find good alternatives in shops or online. This section isn't about giving you a list of specific brands or anything like that (which will depend on where in the world you are). Instead, I want to give you all the information you might possibly need so that you can choose the best option based on the selection of products available to you. And I definitely encourage you to test out a few different brands until you find your favourite.

With that in mind, I've tested all the recipes in the book both with shop-bought ingredients and with homemade versions that are either difficult to find in some regions or that many people have told me they prefer to prepare themselves. As vegan butter, milk, cream, yogurt and cream-cheese alternatives are widely available nowadays, I haven't included homemade versions for those.

## Gluten-free flours

- Use finely ground (finely milled) gluten-free flours with a powdery texture. Gluten-free flours that are too coarse can interfere with moisture absorption.

- You'll need at least three different gluten-free flours to mix up your own gluten-free flour blend (see page 24) or to make gluten-free bread. You need one from each of the following groups: starchy flours, "lighter" protein flours and "heavier" protein flours (see also page 260). My go-to are tapioca starch, millet flour and sorghum flour (but there are many other options).

## Gluten-free flour blends

- As for the individual gluten-free flours, use a finely ground (finely milled) gluten-free flour blend (see above).

- Different shop-bought gluten-free flour blends can vary widely in terms of moisture absorption and flavour. If your batters and doughs turn out very dry when using the gluten-free recipes in this book, it's possible that your gluten-free flour blend absorbs a lot of moisture, in which case try reducing the amount you add by about 10–15g (1–2 tablespoons) per 120g (1 cup) of gluten-free flour blend.

- All the recipes in this book use a plain gluten-free flour blend (it doesn't contain any baking powder or bicarbonate of soda/baking soda) rather than a self-raising one. This gives you the best control over the amount of lift and aeration in your bakes.

- Some gluten-free flour blends have xanthan gum already added to them. That will affect how much xanthan gum you need to add separately – I've covered this in the recipes and on page 263. If you have the option, use a gluten-free flour blend without any xanthan gum added, as that gives you the most control over the amount of binder in your bakes.

- To make your own gluten-free flour blend, use the recipe on page 24. It offers lots of customization, depending on which flours you can find and any other dietary requirements you might have.

## Xanthan gum

- Xanthan gum (widely available in stores and online) acts as a binder – it's essentially a gluten substitute that gives gluten-free bakes some elasticity and prevents them from being too crumbly. You can read more about it on page 263.

## Psyllium husk

- Like xanthan gum, psyllium husk acts as a gluten substitute, but it's best suited for gluten-free bread, where it gives the dough elasticity, flexibility and extensibility. Read more about it on page 265.

- There are two psyllium husk forms to choose from: whole husk and the powder form. I recommend using whole husk, as it's less likely to form clumps when you mix it with water to make psyllium gel, and so it's easier to incorporate into your dough. If you use powder, use 15% less than is listed in the recipe – the powder has a larger surface area and so absorbs more moisture, forming a firmer gel.

- Psyllium husk should be the only ingredient in whichever brand of it you choose – there shouldn't be any additives.

- It's best to use the "blond" psyllium husk variety, as that won't add any colour or flavour to your bakes (some non-blond varieties can impart a greyish-purple or brown hue). Many brands don't specify the variety, in which case have a look at the reviews, if they're available, and avoid brands that are reviewed as turning the bakes a strange colour.

### Dairy-free (vegan) butter

- Use a firm dairy-free (usually labelled "vegan") butter block, not a soft spread.

- Use unsalted vegan butter for baking, to get the best control over the amount of salt in your bakes.

- Ideally, use a vegan butter with a high fat content of around 75–80% and also a high saturated fat content of 40% or higher. This composition is as close as it gets to the composition of regular dairy butter, and it will give the best results. Look at the nutritional information on the packaging or the relevant brand's website for the data you need.

- Choose a brand whose flavour you like best. This is especially important in bakes with a high butter content, such as cookies or pastry.

- While most cake, cupcake, muffin and brownie recipes are quite forgiving when it comes to which vegan butter you choose, cookies and pastry (especially laminated flaky pastry with discrete pieces of butter in the dough) are more sensitive. Test a few brands to find the one that performs best, if need be.

### Dairy-free milks

- Most dairy-free milks, such as almond, soy, rice and oat milk, will work great as a dairy milk substitute. It's best to use unsweetened dairy-free milk for baking.

- Unless otherwise specified in the recipe, avoid using canned coconut milk, as it can make bakes heavy, dense and greasy owing to its high fat content.

### Vegan yogurt

- Most shop-bought vegan yogurts work well. It's best to use unsweetened (and unflavoured) plain or Greek-style vegan yogurt for baking.

- In some recipes, Greek-style vegan yogurt will give the best results owing to its lower water content – if that's the case, I've said so in the recipe.

### Vegan buttermilk

- Use the recipe on page 25 to make your own.

### Vegan double (heavy) cream

- Especially if you're using it for any kind of frosting, the vegan double (heavy) cream should be whippable (so that you can achieve a stiff, firm peak) and hold its shape after you've piped it or spread it on to your bake, even if it stands at room temperature for an hour or two. Similarly, it should create a firm, stable foam that can handle the weight of another sponge on top without squishing or oozing out.

- While coconut cream is a popular vegan cream, in this book I use it only to make the homemade condensed coconut milk on page 26. That's because different brands of coconut cream can vary widely in terms of their composition. Consequently, coconut cream can give rather unreliable and inconsistent results. Furthermore, while it is possible to use it to make chocolate ganache, whipped or in frosting, it's not stable enough to hold its shape.

$\rightarrow$

### Vegan cream cheese

- Use a fairly firm dairy-free (or vegan) cream cheese with a texture that's as close as possible to that of regular dairy (full-fat) cream cheese.

- Choose a brand that has a low water content. If you can only find one that's softer and looser in texture, though, strain it through a cheesecloth (see page 316) until it is noticeably thicker.

### Vegan condensed milk

- All shop-bought varieties of vegan condensed milk (such as condensed coconut or oat milk) tend to work well. If you can't find one, though, you can make your own using the recipe on page 26 or 27.

You don't need any special additional ingredients when it comes to egg-free baking, just your usual pantry staples are enough. There are no flax or chia "eggs" in this book – nor any apple sauce nor mashed banana to act as (rather dubious) egg replacements. Read more about avoiding one-size-fits-all egg replacements in Chapter 2, in the case studies in Chapter 4, and in the egg-free chapter (see page 345).

The vegan essential ingredients list is the same as that for dairy-free.

The gluten-free vegan essential ingredients list is a combination of the gluten-free and dairy-free ones.

# Homemade Gluten-free Flour Blend

Makes 1kg / Prep time 5 mins

500g starchy flour, such as
   arrowroot starch, cornflour
   (cornstarch), potato starch
   or tapioca starch
250g "lighter" protein flour, such
   as superfine brown rice flour
   or millet flour
250g "heavier" protein flour,
   such as light buckwheat
   flour, oat flour, sorghum flour
   or white teff flour

**My go-to gluten-free
flour blend**

Makes 1kg (about 8⅓ cups,
where 1 US cup ~ 115–120g)

500g (4⅓ cups)
   tapioca starch
250g (1¾ cups +
   2 tablespoons)
   millet flour
250g (1¾ cups +
   3 tablespoons)
   sorghum flour

**The great thing about this recipe is that it's incredibly versatile. It's less of an exact recipe and more of a general formula that gives you the proportions of the different types of gluten-free flour, enabling you to tailor the exact composition as you need – for example, if you have a nightshade allergy or you don't want to use rice flour.**

**You can use this blend in all recipes that call for "plain gluten-free flour blend". The exact density (weight per unit volume, or the weight per cup) of this blend will vary depending on which exact flours you use – and it can even vary with the same flour composition, depending on how finely the particular brand has been ground or milled. That's why I recommend using a digital food scale to weigh your ingredients, especially when it comes to gluten-free baking – and it's also why I haven't specified the volume for 1kg of the general blend formulation.**

**As well as the general formula, I've included the recipe for my own favourite go-to gluten-free flour blend (see box, left) in the ratios given by the general formula. This blend gives me the flavour I prefer, which I think actually comes really close to the flavour you'd get with wheat plain (all-purpose) flour.**

1. Add all the gluten-free flours to a large bowl and whisk well until thoroughly combined.

2. Transfer the gluten-free flour blend to an airtight container.

3. Shake the container before using in case any of the gluten-free flours have settled unevenly, then use as directed in the recipe. Keeps well in an airtight container in a cool, dry place for several months.

# Homemade Vegan Buttermilk

Makes about 360g (1½ cups)  /  Prep time 5 mins

230g (1 cup) unsweetened plain
    or Greek-style vegan yogurt
120g (½ cup) dairy-free milk,
    such as almond, soy, rice or
    oat milk (not canned coconut
    milk), plus extra if needed
15g (1 tablespoon) apple cider
    vinegar or 20g (4 teaspoons)
    lemon juice

**Making your own homemade vegan buttermilk alternative is incredibly straightforward, and it works great in any recipes that call for buttermilk. Use it as a simple 1:1 substitution – that is, you can easily replace regular buttermilk in a recipe with an equal weight or volume of this dairy-free version.**

**While many homemade buttermilk recipes use only milk and an acid (usually vinegar or lemon juice), I prefer to use a mixture of yogurt and milk in a 2:1 ratio, in addition to the acidic component. This will give you a homemade (dairy-free) buttermilk that's much closer in consistency to the shop-bought regular version. You can easily adjust the consistency by adding more milk, as necessary.**

1. Whisk all the ingredients together until well combined, adding a small amount of extra dairy-free milk to make the buttermilk runnier, if necessary, then use as directed in the recipe. Keeps well in an airtight container in the fridge for up to 3 days.

# Homemade Condensed Coconut Milk

Makes 300g (1 cup)  /  Prep time 5 mins  /  Cook time 35 mins

400g (1¾ cups) full-fat canned coconut milk (from one 400ml/14oz can), mixed to fully combine the cream and water, if separated

150g (¾ cup) caster (superfine) or granulated sugar

¼ teaspoon salt

**Condensed coconut milk is a great alternative to regular, dairy-containing condensed milk. Transforming coconut milk into condensed coconut milk reduces the coconut flavour, making it less prominent in a finished bake.**

**Use a full-fat canned coconut milk with minimal additives and gums, such as xanthan gum, guar gum or similar. There will always be some, but if they're present in very large quantities, they can make your condensed coconut milk almost gummy and strangely elastic in texture. A good indicator that the coconut milk doesn't contain too many stabilizers is that it separates into thick coconut cream and coconut water over time or if it's placed in the fridge. If your coconut milk doesn't separate under these conditions, then it probably contains too many stabilizers to give you a good condensed milk.**

1. Add the coconut milk, sugar and salt to a saucepan. Dip a toothpick or skewer into the liquid so that it touches the bottom of the pan. Mark the depth of the liquid with a line on the toothpick or skewer – this will help you to determine when the volume has reduced by half later on.

2. Cook on a medium–high heat, stirring frequently, until the sugar is fully dissolved and the mixture comes to a simmer.

3. Reduce the heat to low and simmer for 35–45 minutes, with occasional stirring, until the mixture has thickened, reduced by half and darkened in colour to a light greyish-brown. You can spoon a small amount of the mixture on to a plate and put it in the fridge for a few minutes to check the consistency – it should be thick, sticky and viscous, but still pourable.

4. Pour the condensed coconut milk into a heatproof container and allow it to cool to room temperature. It will be fairly runny while hot but it will thicken as it cools down. Don't worry if you get some oil separation initially – the mixture will emulsify as the condensed coconut milk cools, just give it a good stir.

5. Once cooled, transfer the condensed milk to an airtight container and store it in the fridge for up to 2 weeks.

# Homemade Vegan & Coconut-free Condensed Milk

Makes 300g (1 cup)  /  Prep time 5 mins  /  Cook time 45 mins

600g (2½ cups) dairy-free milk, such as soy, almond, rice or oat milk

150g (¾ cup) caster (superfine) or granulated sugar

¼ teaspoon salt

20g (1½ tablespoons) vegan butter block (optional but recommended)

**Vegan condensed milk made with dairy-free milks such as soy, rice, almond or oat milk (rather than coconut milk; see opposite) will result in a slightly looser, runnier consistency. Depending on the exact dairy-free milk you're using, you'll need to reduce it by anywhere from one half to two thirds.**

**I recommend adding a small amount of vegan butter to the reduced mixture after you've removed it from the heat to give the richness you'd expect.**

1. Add the dairy-free milk, sugar and salt to a saucepan. Dip a toothpick or skewer into the liquid so that it touches the bottom of the saucepan and mark the depth of the liquid – this will help you to determine when the volume has been sufficiently reduced later on.

2. Cook on a medium–high heat, stirring frequently, until the sugar is fully dissolved and the mixture comes to a simmer.

3. Reduce the heat to low and simmer for 45–60 minutes, with occasional stirring, until the mixture has thickened and darkened in colour and the volume of liquid has reduced by anywhere from one half to two thirds (so, the final depth of the liquid will be between one half and one third of the initial depth). The consistency of the liquid is more important than its exact volume; and the exact colour and reduction will depend on the dairy-free milk you're using. You can spoon a small amount of the mixture on to a plate and put it in the fridge for a few minutes to check the consistency – it should be thick, sticky and viscous but still pourable.

4. Remove the condensed milk from the heat and stir in the vegan butter, if using, until it's fully melted and the condensed milk is perfectly smooth.

5. Pour the vegan condensed milk into a heatproof container and allow it to cool to room temperature. It will be fairly runny while hot but it will thicken as it cools.

6. Once cooled, transfer the condensed milk to an airtight container and store it in the fridge for up to 2 weeks.

# Kitchen Tools

While it's true that you need certain equipment to produce some mouth-watering bakes, I appreciate those simple recipes that require only a large bowl and a whisk to whip up (and a rubber spatula to scrape all the delicious bits into the baking tin). With that in mind, I tried to minimize the number of tools and baking tins used for my recipes – for example, if I use a 23cm (9in) square baking tin for the gluten-free brown butter chocolate chip blondies on page 291, then I'll also use it to make the dairy-free blueberry meringue bars on page 331 and the simple gluten-free vegan strawberry cake on page 435. Below is a list of the indispensable general equipment that you'll need for the recipes in this book. Then, over the following pages, I've given the equipment that is helpful, but not essential, and the bakeware that means you can achieve perfect results, every time.

## Indispensable general equipment

### Digital food scale
Yes, this is the very first item on the list. With the exception of ingredients like baking powder, bicarbonate of soda (baking soda), xanthan gum and salt (which I usually measure with teaspoons), I weigh pretty much everything – including liquids like water, milk, oil and lemon juice (see page 15). For absolutely best results, use a digital kitchen scale that shows decimal places – I use one with a ±0.1g resolution.

### Measuring spoons
In most of my recipes, I measure ingredients like baking powder, bicarbonate of soda (baking soda), xanthan gum and salt with teaspoons. You'll need a measuring spoon set that includes 1, ½ and ¼ teaspoon measures. The calibration of such sets is sometimes questionable, so I recommend checking their precision with a scale: 1 teaspoon of water should weigh 5g.

### Oven thermometer
Ovens can be unpredictable. Keep an oven thermometer in your oven (or, if you're a baking control freak like yours truly, you can go crazy and have two oven thermometers in there) and adjust the oven dial to allow for any discrepancy as necessary. My current oven is about 10°C out of sync, so I have to set the dial to 190°C/375°F if I want to bake something at 180°C/350°F.

### Digital instant-read food thermometer
This is crucial if you want to make things like chewy caramel or Swiss meringue with any sort of accuracy. It's also very useful when tempering chocolate or if you want to determine the internal temperature of a pie filling or a loaf of bread.

### Mixing bowls
When it comes to bowls, consider three things: their size, the material they're made from and whether or not they're heatproof. A variety of different sizes comes in handy, and I prefer heatproof, sturdy and durable bowls made from stainless steel or from microwaveable Pyrex glass.

### Whisks, wooden spoons and rubber spatulas
Small and medium whisks are great for preparing icings, glazes and smallish amounts of pastry cream or curd; a large balloon whisk helps you to whip up perfectly smooth cake batter or cheesecake filling. Wooden spoons are great for preparing stiffer mixtures, like cookie dough; and rubber spatulas are useful for everything from carefully folding dry ingredients into wet to scraping every last bit of frosting or batter from your bowl.

# Helpful tools to make life easier

### Electric stand or hand mixer

While you could make most of the recipes in this book by hand, you'll be very thankful for an electric mixer when you're faced with a bowl of aquafaba that needs to be whipped to stiff peaks (trust me, that's painful to attempt armed with just a balloon whisk). I use a stand mixer, as it's more versatile and suitable for everything from cake batter or meringue to kneading a large batch of bread dough. A hand-held mixer also comes in useful, but (even if yours comes with dough hooks) it's not suitable for preparing bread dough.

### Food processor

The usefulness of a food processor goes beyond just grinding nuts and finely crushing biscuits for cheesecake crusts – you can also use it to prepare shortcrust pastry and creamy pie fillings.

### Bench scraper and bowl scraper

A bench scraper is a straight-edged piece of metal with a handle on one end and you can use it for cutting and dividing dough or pastry, for decorating cakes with a smooth coating of frosting, or for scraping every stubborn piece of dough off your work surface. A bowl scraper is curved, flexible and usually made from silicone or plastic. It's the perfect tool for scraping dough off the sides and bottom of a bowl and also for managing sticky bread dough.

### Standard grater and fine rasp-style grater (zester)

I used to use a standard grater to zest lemons and other citrus – but getting an actual zester (Microplane or other fine rasp-style grater) has been a total gamechanger. It makes zesting so much easier and you get much more zest off each individual fruit. A box grater, on the other hand, is useful for grating ingredients like carrots and apples.

### Ice-cream or cookie scoops

These are incredibly useful not only for scooping individual portions of cookie dough, but also for easily and quickly dividing cupcake or muffin batter between the paper liners. The scoop sizes are usually described by the tablespoon volume measurement: you'll need a 2-tablespoon and a 3-tablespoon ice-cream/cookie scoop for my recipes.

### Small offset spatula

Small but mighty, the small offset spatula is an incredibly versatile kitchen tool that will spread batters into an even layer, swirl frostings, icings, ganache or meringue on top of bakes, lift hot cookies off a baking sheet, loosen cakes from the sides of baking tins – and so, so much more.

### Fine-mesh sieve

There are two main uses for a sieve in baking. First, to sift dry ingredients to remove any stray clumps and so ensure that your final batter is perfectly light and airy. Second, to pass wet mixtures through to remove any solids (for example, to remove lemon zest from lemon curd or seeds from a berry reduction).

### Ruler

This might be an unexpected addition to your kitchen arsenal, but you'll need it whenever the recipe requires you to portion out and shape any dough or pastry, and also if you want to cut your finished bake (such as brownies) into precisely equal portions.

# Bakeware

I recommend using metal bakeware, unless otherwise specified. Metal is the best at conducting heat – it will heat up and cool down quickly, which ensures that your bakes are perfectly and evenly baked. Avoid glass and silicone bakeware, as they tend to give disappointing results. I've used the following bakeware in this book.

### Large baking sheets
Both light- and dark-coloured baking sheets work great – just keep in mind that dark baking sheets will result in more pronounced browning on the bottom of cookies and other, similar bakes.

### 25x38cm (10x15in) rimmed baking sheet
While you can use this to bake cookies and similar, I use one primarily for baking Swiss roll sponges – the dimensions are absolutely perfect if you want to achieve a generous swirl when you roll them up.

### 20cm (8in) and 23cm (9in) cake tins (at least 5cm/2in deep)
To minimize the browning and doming of your cakes and sponges, it's best to use light-coloured cake tins – the ones that I use are made from anodized aluminium.

### 20cm (8in) springform tin (at least 7cm/2¾in deep)
Springform tins are useful for bakes such as cheesecakes, or cakes baked with a topping that makes it impossible to invert them to remove them from the tin.

### 23cm (9in) square and 23x33cm (9x13in) rectangular baking tins (at least 5cm/2in deep)
Use light-coloured baking tins to ensure a more even bake with no excessive browning around the edges.

### 23cm (9in) pie dish (about 4cm/1½in deep)
For a perfectly crisp, golden bottom crust, I recommend using a metal pie dish (pie plate). Metal is much better at conducting heat than glass or ceramic, which means that it heats up in no time and starts baking the crust straight away, which greatly reduces the likelihood of a soggy bottom, no matter how juicy the filling.

### 23cm (9in) loose-bottom tart tin with a fluted edge (about 3.5cm/1⅜in deep)
A loose bottom makes it straightforward to remove a tart shell (or an assembled tart) from the tin. To ensure even baking and a crisp, golden pastry, choose metal.

### 900g (2lb) loaf tin (measuring 23x13cm/9x5in across the top)
The colour of your loaf tin will greatly affect how much caramelization and browning you get on the edges of your loaf cakes – the darker the loaf tin, the more caramelization. Either is great, it's just a matter of preference.

### 12-hole muffin tin
All the cupcake and muffin recipes in this book use a 12-hole muffin tin with about 100ml (about 3.5fl oz or about 6½-tablespoon) holes that fit paper liners that are 7cm (2¾in) wide on the top, 5cm (2in) wide on the bottom and about 3.5cm (1⅜in) tall.

### Cast-iron Dutch oven, combo cooker or skillet
Cast iron is the best material for baking crusty loaves of artisan-style bread (like the gluten-free honey and sesame loaf on page 297) because it's excellent at absorbing, retaining and radiating heat. The closed environment of a Dutch oven or a combo cooker traps the steam released by the loaf, which helps with oven spring – but you can achieve a similar effect by adding a steam source to your oven if you're using a cast-iron skillet (and my recipes include instructions for both options).

# Other baking equipment

## Pastry brush

A pastry brush (I prefer natural bristles over silicone) is most useful for glazing your bakes before baking, but also for brushing excess flour off your dough or pastry.

## Rolling pin

Choose a rolling pin according to how it feels in your hands and how much control it gives you over how thinly and evenly you can roll out dough or pastry. Make sure it's sturdy and at least 24cm (9½in) long, so that it'll be able to handle large amounts of pastry and dough. My favourites are wooden rolling pins with handles that don't spin independently (revolving rolling pins are something of a pet peeve of mine).

## Pizza cutter

This is great for quickly and cleanly slicing dough and pastry. You can also use it to trim the rolled-out pie crust or shortcrust pastry into a more perfectly round shape before you transfer them into a pie dish or tart tin, respectively.

## Baking beans (or dried beans or rice)

These are crucial if you want to properly blind bake a tart shell or a pie crust without it puffing up and slumping down the sides of the tart tin or pie dish, respectively.

## Baking paper

While many prefer to use silicone baking mats, I've always used baking paper for my baking, which you can cut to fit the size and shape of whatever container you're using. If you're used to silicone baking mats, keep in mind that some recipes might give slightly different results (for example, your cookies might spread a bit more).

## Kitchen (aluminium) foil

The main use for foil in my kitchen is to cover bakes in the oven if they start browning too much or too quickly before they're fully baked through. Placing a sheet of foil, shiny side up, over a bake blocks out some of the radiative heat, which slows down the rate of browning.

## Cling film (plastic wrap; or reusable alternative)

In addition to wrapping dough or pastry so that it doesn't dry out as it chills in the fridge, I use cling film as a rolling surface to roll out pie crust and shortcrust pastry. This makes it easy to transfer the rolled-out pastry into the pie dish or tart shell without the risk of tearing or breaking.

## Toothpicks, skewers or cake tester

The "toothpick test" is crucial for determining when your cakes, brownies – and more – are perfectly baked. Insert the toothpick, skewer or cake tester into the centre of your bake for about 2 seconds and see how it comes out. For most cakes, cupcakes and muffins you're looking for a clean stick, possibly with a few moist crumbs attached. For fudgy or gooey brownies, you want it to come out with some half-baked batter and many moist crumbs (see also page 135).

## Wire cooling racks

When you cool your bakes to room temperature, it's important that you ensure proper air circulation around them. This achieves two things: first, it speeds up the cooling process and, second, it prevents any condensation build-up, which could make your bakes soggy or otherwise spoil their texture. I'm firmly convinced that there's no such thing as too many wire racks.

## Kitchen blow torch

While it's not the most frequently used tool in my kitchen, a blow torch is incredibly useful if you want to make a tart, cake or other bake that's topped with a small mountain of perfectly toasted meringue (whether it's egg-based as on page 331, or vegan aquafaba-based as on page 375). And if you want to use a hot knife for cutting a bake (for example, to achieve neat, clean slices of a cheesecake or tart), you can (carefully!) use a kitchen blow torch to heat it up instead of dipping it into hot water.

## 25cm (10in) oval proving basket (banneton)

There are numerous different sizes and shapes of proving basket available, but the gluten-free honey and sesame loaf (see page 297) uses a 25cm (10in) oval one that's 7.5cm (3in) deep, which gives a quite generously large artisan-style loaf. You'll need to use it with the cloth cover because of the sesame seed crust – or, if you don't have a cloth cover, a clean tea towel works just as well.

## Reusable piping bags and nozzles

For my recipes, you'll need a simple round nozzle, a large French star nozzle and a medium open star nozzle.

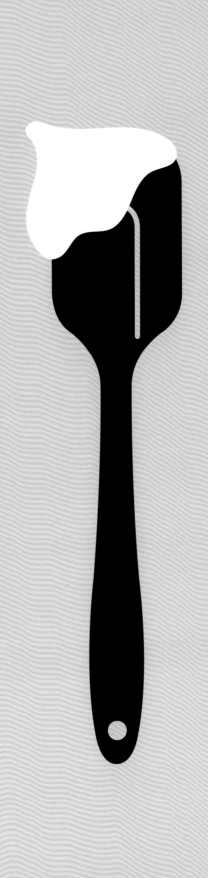

Chapter
2

# Sci

## The Science
## of Ingredients

**Modifying recipes to be X-free (where X = gluten, eggs, dairy or a combination of these), primarily needs us to focus on two groups of ingredients.**

**First, there are the ingredients that we're substituting: plain (all-purpose) wheat flour, eggs, and dairy (butter, milk, yogurt, cream cheese, double/heavy or whipping cream, and so on). Then, second, there are the ingredients we can use as replacements: gluten-free flours and blends, binders (xanthan gum and psyllium husk), dairy-free alternatives (vegan butter, milks, yogurt, cream and so on), and raising agents.**

**If you want to successfully modify any recipe to suit your dietary requirements, you need to understand the properties of each of these ingredients and the roles that they play in the various bakes. This understanding actually makes the process of recipe modification much easier than you might expect.**

# Understanding Ingredient Properties

Modifying recipes is all about being systematic and analytical – two words that are very near and dear to my nerdy, science-loving heart.

So, when it comes to the crucial ingredients, I don't want you to think of them as "just flour" or "just eggs". Instead, I want to break them down into their individual components and into the properties that they bring to a bake.

**Regular plain (all-purpose) wheat flour** There are two main things flour does in a bake: it absorbs moisture (it's a dry ingredient) and it provides structure. With the exception of a flourless chocolate cake or a flourless brownie cookie, pretty much all bakes rely on some sort of flour for their structure and texture. Even gluten-free flours provide some degree of structure, despite lacking gluten.

**Eggs** As I've said before, an egg is essentially two ingredients in one: an egg white and an egg yolk. The white acts as a binder (giving bakes structure and a degree of flexibility, preventing them from being too crumbly), as well as being a source of moisture and fluffiness (that is, it provides some lift and aeration). The yolk adds moisture, fat and richness.

**Dairy butter** Like eggs, dairy butter is a composite: it is about 80% fat, 15% water and 5% milk solids. In comparison, the ratio of fat to water in vegan alternatives can vary. This means that if you want to convert a recipe to dairy-free with a simple 1:1 swap, it's important to choose an alternative that has a similar fat content to dairy butter.

**Milk and yogurt** The main purpose of milk and yogurt in a bake is to provide moisture. Yes, they can also affect the flavour and add a small amount of richness – but at their core, they're wet ingredients that prevent bakes from being too dry.

There's lots more to learn about these and other ingredients (and we'll come to it all later in the book), but I hope that for now this is enough to illustrate how I want you to think about your ingredients. In Chapter 4 you'll see this approach put into practice, and once you've used it yourself over and over, it will become instinctual.

What really lies at the heart of this cookbook, though, and what we will return to time and again, is how you can easily group all these ingredients into four categories, according to their properties and functions. These categories then provide a simple, logical roadmap for modifying pretty much any recipe to suit any dietary requirement you want.

# The Four Ingredient Categories

Here's the amazing part. Realizing this was a huge "Eureka!" moment for me and it completely revolutionized how I approach converting and developing free-from recipes. You can group all of the relevant ingredients that I've mentioned on the previous page into just four categories (note that some ingredients, like eggs, fall into more than one category).

### 1.
#### Structure-providing ingredients

These are: egg whites, flour (both wheat flour and gluten-free flours and blends), and binders (xanthan gum and psyllium husk).

### 2.
#### Tenderizing (structure-destroying) ingredients

These are: butter (both dairy butter and vegan alternatives, such as vegan butter block and vegetable shortening), oil, and egg yolks (to a smaller extent).

### 3.
#### Aerating (lift-providing) ingredients

These are: raising/leavening agents (baking powder and bicarbonate of soda/baking soda, and yeast for bread), and egg whites.

### 4.
#### Moisture sources

These are: milk (both dairy milk and dairy-free alternatives), water, yogurt (both dairy yogurt and dairy-free alternatives), egg whites, and egg yolks.

All successful baking (regular but especially free-from) is about getting the right balance between these ingredient categories. Specifically, in free-from baking, we want to replace the ingredients that we want to eliminate with other ingredients from the same category.

So, for example, when you convert a regular cake to be egg-free, you're removing a structure-providing ingredient – egg whites. To make up for this, you need to increase the amount of the other structure-providing ingredients (flour and/or binders) to achieve the same texture. Because eggs also add moisture, you must also add or increase the amount of other moisture sources, such as milk or yogurt. And, finally, as the egg whites also act as an aerating ingredient, you need to compensate for them with another aerating ingredient, typically by increasing the amount of raising agents.

There are, though, differences between ingredients within the same category. I don't mean the obvious differences between, say, egg whites and baking powder, but between ingredients that are similar at first glance. These differences mean that you sometimes need to tweak the ingredient quantities when making substitutions so that's it's not just a simple 1:1 replacement, even if you're just swapping one flour (wheat flour) for another (a gluten-free flour blend). At other times, these differences can mean that you need to adjust the preparation method. The two main differences between ingredients in the same category are:

- **The different moisture and fat responses of regular wheat flour and gluten-free flours and blends.**
- **The different melting points of dairy butter and vegan butters.**

You can read more about this on pages 42 and 43, as well as in the case studies in Chapter 4.

Of course, there are other types of ingredient in a recipe, each with its own properties. Sugar, for example, not only adds sweetness but also drastically affects the texture and appearance of a bake. Flavourings (like vanilla, citrus zest and juices, cocoa powder, ground nuts, and so on) affect not only the flavour, but also the specific chemistry of bakes.

However, everything that relates to these other ingredients is true regardless of whether you're dealing with a regular or a free-from bake. As such, I'll mention them here or there (both because the associated science is endlessly fascinating and it makes my inner nerd very happy, and because it's important to understand it), but, in general, they're not that relevant to the process of modifying and creating free-from recipes.

Now, let's have a closer look at each of the four ingredient categories.

# 1. Structure-providing ingredients

These ingredients provide structure (a framework) to a bake that prevents it from collapsing into a dense, stodgy mess or, in the case of a cookie or pastry, from losing its shape during baking and becoming too crumbly. In this category, you'll find egg whites, wheat flour, gluten-free flours and blends, and binders, among which xanthan gum and psyllium husk are the most important.

To get a better understanding of the role of these types of ingredient, consider two examples: cakes, and cookies or shortcrust pastry. First, cakes: cake batter rises in the oven owing to the presence of raising agents and/or egg whites. However, without the structure-providing ingredients, there wouldn't be anything that keeps the cake in that fluffy, aerated state. Instead, it would just puff up in the oven and then collapse.

In the case of cookies or pastry, structure-providing ingredients prevent the bakes from spreading out too much and melting into a puddle in the oven. Again, they provide a framework that helps a bake to maintain its shape.

To some extent these ingredients also provide varying degrees of flexibility and elasticity – with the exception of most gluten-free flours, which are pretty inefficient at this. This flexibility is especially important when it comes to bread (you need the dough to be flexible and extensible so that you can knead and shape it, and also so that it proves effectively) and also with bakes that need to be malleable in some way – Swiss rolls (page 113) and flaky pie crusts (page 187), for example.

## 2. Tenderizing (structure-destroying) ingredients

These ingredients are the very opposite of structure-providing ingredients. They work against the framework created by the flour and the egg whites, to give bakes a more tender, delicate texture – hence the name "tenderizing". However, these ingredients do have a tendency to make bakes stodgy or pudding-y if present in quantities that are too large (especially in free-from baking) – hence the name "structure-destroying". The main tenderizing ingredients are fats: butter (both dairy and vegan butter) and oil. Egg yolks are also a tenderizing ingredient, but their effect is negligible compared with fats in most cases (I'll point out any exceptions as we come across them).

Now, purely based on what I've told you so far, you might think that tenderizing ingredients are "negative" or undesirable in some way – but that's not the case at all! These are the ingredients that give richness and that wonderful, tantalizing melt-in-the-mouth quality to bakes. They prevent cakes from being too doughy, they ensure that cookies aren't tooth-breakingly hard and they prevent pastry from being leathery.

But the truth of the matter is that when it comes to modifying recipes, tenderizing ingredients can sometimes cause problems. In such cases, we need to adjust their quantities (usually reduce them) to ensure the perfect texture of the bake, while still preserving the best possible flavour and just the right degree of richness.

## 3. Aerating (lift-providing) ingredients

These are all the usual suspects that make bakes light, fluffy and airy: chemical raising agents (baking powder and bicarbonate of soda/baking soda), other leavening agents that are mainly relevant in bread baking (yeast and sourdough starter), and egg whites. First, it's important to understand the difference between bicarbonate of soda (baking soda) and baking powder.

| Bicarbonate of soda (baking soda) | Baking powder |
|---|---|
| Bicarbonate of soda (chemical name: sodium bicarbonate; chemical formula: $NaHCO_3$) is a base or an alkaline compound that reacts with acids to release a gas (carbon dioxide, $CO_2$) and that's what makes your bakes fluffy. In the context of baking, this means that bicarbonate of soda needs an acidic ingredient present in order to "activate" it. This acidic ingredient can be anything from vinegar and lemon juice to yogurt, buttermilk, sour cream, or even chocolate (as it has an acidic pH). | Baking powder is not a chemically pure substance. Instead, it's a mixture of bicarbonate of soda (baking soda), an acidic component (cream of tartar, a phosphate or a sulphate) and an anti-caking agent, such as rice flour or cornflour (cornstarch). As it already contains an acidic component, baking powder doesn't need an external acidic ingredient to react and release the carbon dioxide. In fact, you can simply put some baking powder into water and you'll see the mixture start bubbling and frothing – that's the gas, carbon dioxide, being released (this is also the best way to check whether your baking powder has expired). |

Owing to their different compositions, baking powder and bicarbonate of soda (baking soda) don't have the same strength or activity. Bicarbonate of soda is much, much stronger than baking powder – about three to four times as strong, in fact. That means that you can't simply just 1:1 substitute baking powder for bicarbonate of soda or vice versa (even if you have fulfilled any requirements for acidic ingredients).

When you want to make a bake even fluffier (or when you want to replace another aerating ingredient, for example eggs in an egg-free or vegan recipe), you have two options. First, you can simply just increase the amount of the baking powder and/or bicarbonate of soda (baking soda) in the recipe. Or, you can add an acidic ingredient or increase the amount of an acidic ingredient already present – this boosts the activity of the raising agents even further.

As it goes, you'll find that I often use both options to get the best possible result. For example, when making the egg-free version of a buttery vanilla cake (see page 98), per egg removed, I add ¼ teaspoon of extra baking powder and also ½ teaspoon of apple cider vinegar. This makes the egg-free cake just as soft and fluffy as the regular version (and you can't taste the vinegar in the final baked cake either).

Egg whites are another important aerating ingredient – and that's not just the case when you whip them up until fluffy before incorporating them into a bake. Even egg whites in their as-is, "un-whipped" state provide a degree of lift and fluffiness – although admittedly not to the extent that they would if you whip them.

## 4. Moisture sources

The ingredients in this category make sure that your bakes are moist and that there's enough moisture in the batter or dough so that all the flour is sufficiently hydrated. Moisture sources also help to bring together cookie dough, pastry, bread dough and so on.

Most often the ingredients in this category are milk (or alternatives), water, yogurt (both dairy and dairy-free), egg whites and egg yolks.

It's worth noting that not all moisture sources are created equal, and there are differences between them in terms of their composition and consistency (consider, for example, the different texture and consistency of milk compared with yogurt). Consequently, you'll often find that a recipe will have one moisture source that will outperform all others to give you the best possible result. More on that in Chapter 4.

# GF vs Wheat Flour: Moisture & Fat Response

While gluten-free flours and blends belong to the same ingredient category as wheat flour (they're all structure-providing ingredients; see page 38), there are some important differences (other than whether or not they have gluten) between them. That often means that you can't simply substitute one with an equal weight of the other – or, if you do, you have to tweak the quantities of the other ingredients instead. These flours exhibit differences in their moisture and fat responses.

- **Moisture response** refers to how flours interact with the moisture in the recipe – how well they absorb it and how well they hold on to it.

- **Fat response** looks at how flours interact with the fat in the recipe (usually either butter or oil) – how well they absorb it and how much fat they can essentially "take on" before the bake turns stodgy, pudding-y, dense or, usually in the case of cookies or shortcrust pastry, too crumbly.

Interestingly, while gluten-free flours absorb more moisture than wheat flour, they can actually tolerate a smaller amount of fat. So, the moisture and the fat response of gluten-free flours essentially work in opposite directions when it comes to adapting regular recipes to be gluten-free: while the moisture response suggests that you'd have to reduce the amount of flour (or increase the amount of moisture/liquid), the fat response requires that you increase it instead (or reduce the amount of fat).

In practice, either the moisture or the fat response plays the more important role in a recipe and therefore determines the adjustments you need to make when going from regular to gluten-free. Which of the two is the more important varies from recipe to recipe – sometimes they can even cancel each other out, like when making brownies (page 136).

The table below sets out a few broad generalizations, based on the hundreds of experiments I've done as part of writing this book. These generalizations should provide a helpful starting point (but will always have exceptions).

| | |
|---|---|
| **Cakes, cupcakes and muffins** | The moisture response is more important. |
| **Brownies** | The moisture and the fat response cancel each other out, except when making egg-free or vegan brownies – in that case, the fat response is more important. |
| **Cookies and shortcrust pastry** | The fat response is more important (except with cakey cookies, where the moisture response is more important). |
| **Flaky pastry (pie crust and puff pastry)** | The moisture response is more important (for these kinds of pastry, the fat is present in discrete pieces or layers, and isn't fully incorporated into the pastry/dough). |
| **Bread** | The moisture response is more important. |

When you adapt a regular recipe to be gluten-free:

1. If the moisture response is more important, reduce the amount of flour *or* increase the amount of wet ingredients (you need to reduce the flour-to-moisture ratio).

2. If the fat response is more important, increase the amount of flour *or* reduce the amount of fat (you need to increase the flour-to-fat ratio).

# Preparation & Baking Methods

Modifying recipes and making them free-from doesn't stop at choosing the correct ingredients and ingredient quantities. Selecting the appropriate preparation and baking methods is just as important.

You need the preparation and baking methods that minimize or balance out the absence of the relevant ingredients. This includes the form of the ingredients (for example, using softened rather than melted butter in chocolate chip cookies; see page 164), the way in which the ingredients are combined and incorporated (such as the creaming method when making a buttery vanilla cake; see pages 98–9), and the baking temperature. Another very important example is the different preparation method required when making any sort of laminated pastry or dough with vegan butter (especially if you're also using gluten-free flour).

# Laminated Pastry & Butter Melting Point

One of the most important differences between vegan and regular butter is the melting point. Vegan butters melt at a slightly lower temperature than dairy butter – and this can cause problems when you're making any sort of laminated bake, where the butter exists in discrete pieces or layers in a dough matrix, such as with flaky pie crust (see page 187) or American-style flaky buttermilk biscuits (page 215). (Note that I'm talking about firm vegan butter blocks here, not soft vegan spreads; see page 22.)

When making such recipes with dairy butter, you'd typically keep the butter pieces fairly large to give the final bake its flaky texture and "puff" (as the moisture content in the butter rapidly evaporates and turns to steam, and pushes the dough layers apart). However, owing to its lower melting point and different composition (especially its large proportion of unsaturated fats that are naturally liquid at room temperature, such as rapeseed/canola and sunflower oil), vegan butter has a greater tendency to leak out during baking. This can result in a greasy, hard pastry or tough buttermilk biscuits and a smoky mess in your oven.

To prevent this, first, make sure that your laminated pastry or dough is cool at all times and give it a long and thorough chill in the fridge (or even the freezer) before baking to really minimize the butter leakage. This is even more important in free-from baking than in regular baking.

Second, it'll sometimes be necessary to work the vegan butter into your dry ingredients to a greater extent, so that your final butter pieces are smaller. This is less important when using plain (all-purpose) wheat flour, as its strong gluten framework acts as something of a failsafe against excessive butter leakage. However, when making a dairy- and gluten-free version, you absolutely need the butter pieces to be much smaller, as the gluten-free flour blend won't give you much help. So, for example, if the butter pieces in a regular flaky pie crust should be the size of walnut halves, they need to be about pea-sized when making a gluten- and dairy-free (or gluten-free vegan) version (see page 195).

Finally, keep in mind that while you can achieve a similar degree of flakiness when using vegan butter, the amount of "puff" you'll get in the oven can vary significantly with the brand of vegan butter you use and might also be reduced compared to versions using dairy butter. That means that your vegan flaky pastry might not puff up as much and your vegan buttermilk biscuits might not be quite as tall. But don't worry, they'll still be just as delicious.

# Four-step Recipe Conversion Formula

All the recipe modifications in this book follow the same simple step-by-step formula.

| | |
|---|---|
| **STEP 1** | Determine which ingredients you need to eliminate or replace and which ingredient categories they belong to: structure-providing, tenderizing (structure-destroying), aerating (lift-providing) or moisture sources. |

| | |
|---|---|
| **STEP 2** | Select alternative ingredients from the same ingredient categories that will achieve the same final effect. If they're already present in the recipe, increase their quantity. If they're not already present, add them. |

| | |
|---|---|
| **STEP 3** | If you're converting a regular recipe to gluten-free (or vice versa), consider the moisture and fat responses of the gluten-free flours, and determine which is more important (or if they cancel each other out). Then, adjust the amounts of the flour, liquid and/or fat. |

| | |
|---|---|
| **STEP 4** | Adjust the preparation and baking methods, if necessary. |

But don't worry – you won't have to go through this formula every time you want to adapt a recipe and you won't have to guess how to adjust the ingredient quantities. I've done all the experiments for you, and it's all summarized in the next chapter in the form of really handy, quantitative rules for adapting recipes. These rules will tell you exactly what quantity adjustments you need to make for all the relevant ingredients, depending on the type of bake and the free-from variation you're interested in. But, before we get to that, here are my top ten tips for successful recipe modification.

# Top 10 Tips for (Stress-free & Successful) Recipe Modification

The rules for modifying recipes in the next chapter cover a huge range of recipes – from cakes, cookies and brownies to pastry, pancakes and even cheesecakes. It is, of course, impossible for me to cover every single type of bake out there, but if you use these rules together with the underlying science, I'm sure there's hardly any recipe that you can't successfully modify yourself.

To help you get started, I've summarized my top tips for recipe modification below. These are all the things that I keep in mind when developing new recipes. Many of these are "best practices" for baking in general, while others are relevant specifically to free-from recipe modification.

Just note that these apply to when you start out with a completely new recipe, not one that's already been optimized for whatever free-from version you need (like the ones in this book). If you're just following an existing, fully optimized recipe without making any changes, make sure to read it in full before you start, and follow it to the letter.

1. **Start with a reliable recipe**
   Even if you follow the science and have a good understanding of the role of the different ingredients in a bake – if you start off with a bad recipe, then your free-from recipe will be equally disappointing.

2. **Give yourself time**
   The process of adapting and perfecting a recipe can take a bit of time and you might have to go through a few test batches before you're 100% happy with the final result. Don't rush it and don't try to adapt a new recipe last minute before an important event.

3. **Test a small batch first**
   For example, if I want to make a three-layer 20cm (8in) cake, I'll make a single 15cm (6in) sponge first. That cuts down on food waste and doesn't leave me with a mountain of cake by the end of a few rounds of testing.

4. **Take notes as you go**
   Note everything down – from the ingredients you've used and their quantities to the preparation method, oven temperature, baking time and any other useful details like the texture or appearance of the final bake, and even other ideas you want to try out next time.

5. **Don't eyeball your ingredient quantities**
   If you want to be able to recreate the recipe, always measure your ingredients, ideally with a digital food scale. Precision matters in baking!

6. **Use good-quality ingredients**
   Quality matters. For example, using gluten-free flours that aren't milled finely enough can interfere with moisture absorption and completely change the batter or dough texture. Same goes for dairy-free milks and everything else in your bake. So, if your recipe fails (especially if it's worked for you previously), consider if anything about your ingredients has changed.

7. **Think about the ingredient properties and roles**
   Keep referring to the four ingredient categories on page 38. Also, don't forget to consider the different moisture and fat responses of gluten-free flours and blends as compared to regular wheat flour (page 42) and the different melting points of vegan butter alternatives when compared to that of dairy butter (page 43).

8. **Use the rules for adapting recipes in Chapter 3**
   I've tested the rules on various recipes that I've found in other cookbooks and online, and they've all proven to be reliable and consistent. In fact, these rules are one of the most important parts of this book, so use them!

9. **Accept that some recipes will flop**
   Baking failures are inevitable, especially in the realm of recipe modification. But learn from the failures! Every failure presents a new opportunity to learn something about the recipe or one (or several) of the ingredients. Don't get discouraged – and remember point 4: make notes!

10. **Practice makes perfect**
    While I've tried to pack as much helpful information and advice into these pages as possible, the simple truth is that when it comes to mastering the art and science of adapting recipes, nothing beats doing it yourself. Over time, and hopefully with the help of this book, you'll find that thinking about the ingredients in terms of their properties and what they bring to a bake will become almost intuitive. So, get baking and have fun!

# Chapter
# 3

# R

## The Rules

In this book, I'm not just giving you the recipes and a general, qualitative understanding of how free-from recipe modification works. I'm also giving you actual quantitative rules that will help you to adapt any recipe to be X-free. This means that if you want to take a regular cake recipe and make it gluten-free, these rules will enable you to work out exactly how much gluten-free flour blend you need to use and exactly how much xanthan gum you need to add. Or, if you want to convert a regular cookie recipe to be egg-free, these rules will give you exact numbers for how you should change the quantities of the other ingredients to get the best possible result that's nearly indistinguishable from your starting point.

The modification rules are summarized in this chapter, and they're organized first by the type of recipe or bake you want to adapt, and then further by the specific diet (gluten-free, dairy-free, egg-free, vegan and gluten-free vegan) you want to follow. To make things easier, there's a flowchart on the following pages that will direct you to the rules you need quickly and efficiently.

## Who made the rules?

Science! These rules are the culmination of my years of experiments and trial and error. I've actually derived them based on individual recipes (see Chapter 4) – but the really, *really* important thing is that while they're based on a few bakes, they apply so much more widely.

For example, I devised the rules for adapting buttery cakes (see page 52) based on the buttery vanilla cake case study (page 95). However, those rules don't apply just to that one specific vanilla cake. Instead, they apply more widely to other vanilla cake recipes and also to other types of cake, like banana bread, pound cakes and other layer cakes. To avoid any confusion, I've included a list of all the other types of bake to which the rules do and don't apply with each set of rules.

---

### How to use this chapter

1.   Use the flowchart on pages 50–51 to find the rules you need.

2.   Use the "apply to/don't apply to" list at the top of the relevant rules to check they're suitable for your bake.

3.   Select the rules that apply to your dietary requirement(s).

4.   Keep an eye out for any exceptions and extra tips.

5.   Combine the rules if you need to (see opposite).

---

## How (and when) to combine the rules

It's perfectly possible to combine rules for multiple free-from baking, but it's important to do so in the correct way, considering what is already in – or not in – the recipe. Here are a few examples so that you can see what I mean:

- **If you're starting with a regular recipe and you want to make it gluten- and egg-free**, you need to combine the gluten-free and the egg-free modification rules for the relevant bake.
- **If you're starting with a gluten-free recipe and you want to make it gluten-free vegan**, you need to use the vegan modification rules – not the gluten-free vegan ones!
- **If you're starting with a dairy-free recipe and you want to make it vegan**, you need to use the egg-free rules – not the vegan ones!

## "Reversing" the rules

Yes, you can work in reverse! For example, you could take a gluten-free cake recipe and adapt it for plain (all-purpose) wheat flour. The gluten-free modification rules for buttery cakes (see page 52) require you to reduce the amount of flour by 10% and add ¼ teaspoon of xanthan gum per 120g (1 cup) of gluten-free flour blend. To make that gluten-free cake with wheat flour, you need to increase the amount of flour by 10% and omit the xanthan gum.

## Going one step further

Sometimes, the recipe you'll get with the help of these rules will be just a (very good) starting point. That often happens to me in the process of recipe development: you get an outcome that's delicious but not quite there – you might want a cake to be a bit fluffier, cookies to spread a tiny bit less or muffin tops to be even taller. That's okay – that's when you start tweaking it, adding or removing a tablespoon or so of flour, increasing or decreasing the amount of baking powder by ¼ teaspoon, or swapping yogurt for buttermilk. And the great thing is that if you read through this book, you'll have all the knowledge necessary to make the right changes to take your recipes from really good to absolutely 100% spot on.

Note also that sometimes, after you've adjusted a recipe (and especially if you're making it egg-free, vegan or gluten-free vegan), you might need to adjust the total amount of batter or dough to make it fit perfectly into the baking tin you're using. To do this, just multiply all the ingredient quantities by the same factor. This step might be necessary because eliminating and/or replacing ingredients will often result in a slightly different volume of batter or dough.

## The tricky ones

When you're choosing your starting point for an egg-free, vegan or gluten-free vegan recipe, avoid flourless recipes, such as a flourless chocolate cake. These recipes usually rely on eggs for their structure in the absence of flour... so removing the eggs usually results in a chocolate soup with no structure whatsoever (unless you make very drastic changes).

Furthermore, I tried to keep these modification rules as simple and small in number as possible. Unfortunately, that's not always possible. Primarily that's that case for the eggless (egg-free, vegan and gluten-free vegan) Swiss rolls: there, the rules are quite complex simply because you need to change so many different things.

In such instances, it might be easier (and less time consuming) to start with the already optimized free-from recipes in the case-studies chapter (Chapter 4; pages 120–22) and then tweak them slightly by adding whatever flavourings and add-ins you fancy.

**AND REMEMBER...**

At first glance, the rules can seem a bit abstract. So, if you want to understand where they come from and how they work within the context of an actual recipe, read the case studies in Chapter 4.

In all of the rules, I use a gram-to-US-cup conversion for the gluten-free flour blend that assumes that 1 cup ~ 120g. You can read more about that on page 15.

**WHAT ARE YOU MAKING?**

**BANANA BREAD** — Rules for adapting buttery cakes (page 52)

**BREAD & YEASTED BAKES** — Rules for adapting bread & yeasted bakes (page 84)

**BROWNIES** — Rules for adapting brownies (page 62)

**CAKE** — Does the batter include melted chocolate?
- yes → Rules for adapting chocolate cakes (page 55)
- no → Is it a cake with a high butter or oil content, a loaf cake or a pound cake? → Rules for adapting buttery cakes (page 52)
- no → Is it a Swiss roll or a sponge cake based on whipped eggs/ egg whites? → Rules for adapting Swiss rolls & sponge cakes (page 58)

**BAKED CHEESECAKE** — Rules for adapting baked cheesecake (page 82)

**COOKIES** — Are they cakey cookies (or biscotti)?
- yes → Rules for adapting cakey cookies (page 68)
- no → Do the cookies spread in the oven? → Rules for adapting cookies that spread (page 66)
- no → Do the cookies hold their shape in the oven? → Rules for adapting cookies that hold their shape (page 64)

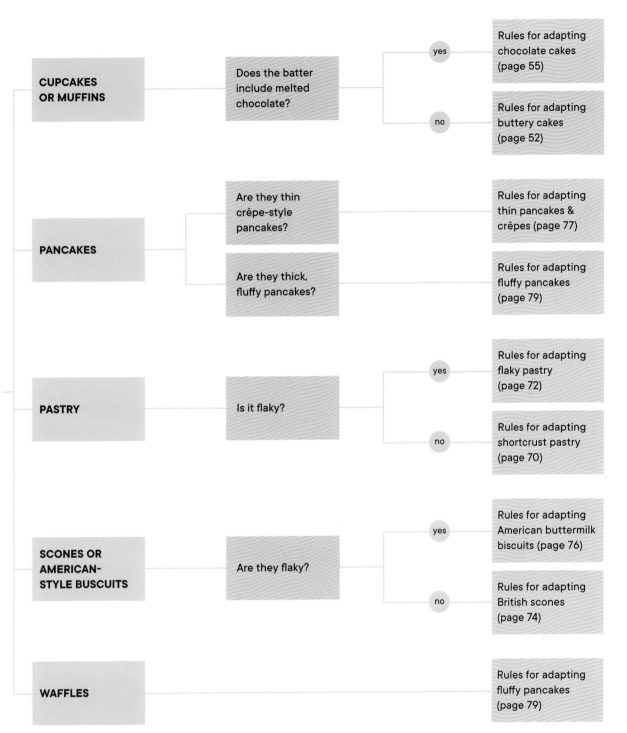

# Rules for Adapting Buttery Cakes

## To make gluten-free

- Use a gluten-free flour blend and reduce the amount of flour by 10% by multiplying the weight of the flour by 0.9, or by reducing its volume by 1½ tablespoons for each cup of flour in the recipe.

- **For cakes and cupcakes:** Add ¼ teaspoon xanthan gum per 120g (1 cup) of gluten-free flour blend (omit if your blend already contains binders).

- **For muffins:** Add ½ teaspoon xanthan gum per 120g (1 cup) of gluten-free flour blend (or ¼ teaspoon if your blend already contains binders).

*If you're starting with a vegan bake without any ground nuts or cocoa powder in the batter: add 20g (3½ tablespoons) of almond flour per 120g (1 cup) of gluten-free flour blend (if you have a nut allergy, use an equal weight of finely ground sunflower seeds).*

## To make dairy-free

- Replace the dairy milk with an equal weight or volume of a dairy-free milk, such as almond, rice, soy or oat milk, but avoid canned coconut milk.

- Replace the dairy butter with an equal weight or volume of a firm vegan butter block (not a soft spread). Or, replace the dairy butter with 80% of a neutral-tasting oil, like sunflower or vegetable, and 15% of dairy-free milk. Multiply the weight of the butter by 0.8 to get the weight of the oil and 0.15 to get the weight of the dairy-free milk. In terms of volume, use 7 tablespoons of oil and 1 tablespoon of dairy-free milk for each stick of butter.

- Replace the dairy yogurt or sour cream with an equal weight or volume of unsweetened plain or Greek-style vegan yogurt.

- Replace the dairy buttermilk with an equal weight or volume of homemade vegan buttermilk (see page 25).

## To make egg-free

- Use melted instead of softened butter for the best texture (see pages 98–9).

- **For each egg or egg white removed:**

  » Add 20g (2½ tablespoons) of flour (true for wheat flour and gluten-free flour blend).

  » Add 30g (2 tablespoons) of whole milk or unsweetened plain or Greek-style yogurt (true for dairy and dairy-free ingredients).

  » Add ¼ teaspoon of baking powder and ½ teaspoon apple cider vinegar.

### APPLY TO

- layer cakes, traybakes (sheet cakes), loaf cakes and pound cakes

- chocolate cakes made with cocoa powder and no melted chocolate in the batter

- banana bread, lemon drizzle cake, carrot cake

- cupcakes and muffins without melted chocolate in the batter

### DON'T APPLY TO

- foam or sponge cakes that rely on whipped eggs (or whipped egg whites) for their texture, including Swiss rolls and roulades (for those, see page 58)

- chocolate cakes, cupcakes and muffins with melted chocolate in the batter (for those, see page 55)

- Replace the dairy milk with an equal weight or volume of a dairy-free milk, such as almond, rice, soy or oat milk, but avoid canned coconut milk.

- Replace the dairy yogurt or sour cream with an equal weight or volume of unsweetened plain or Greek-style vegan yogurt.

- Replace the dairy buttermilk with an equal weight or volume of homemade vegan buttermilk (see page 25).

- Replace the dairy butter with an equal weight or volume of a firm vegan butter block (not a soft spread). Use melted (not softened) butter for the best texture (see pages 98–9). Or, replace the dairy butter with 80% of a neutral-tasting oil like sunflower or vegetable oil and 15% of dairy-free milk. Multiply the weight of the butter by 0.8 to get the weight of the oil and 0.15 to get the weight of the dairy-free milk. In terms of volume, use 7 tablespoons of oil and 1 tablespoon of dairy-free milk for each stick of butter replaced.

- **For each egg or egg white removed:**

  » Add 20g (2½ tablespoons) of flour (true for wheat flour and gluten-free flour blend).

  » Add 30g (2 tablespoons) of dairy-free milk or unsweetened plain or Greek-style vegan yogurt.

  » Add ¼ teaspoon of baking powder and ½ teaspoon apple cider vinegar.

*If you're starting with a gluten-free bake without any ground nuts or cocoa powder in the batter: add 20g (3½ tablespoons) of almond flour per 120g (1 cup) of gluten-free flour blend (if you have a nut allergy, use an equal weight of finely ground sunflower seeds).*

Continued overleaf →

- Use a gluten-free flour blend and reduce the amount of flour by 10% by multiplying the weight of the flour by 0.9, or by reducing its volume by 1½ tablespoons per cup of flour in the recipe.

- **For cakes and cupcakes:** Add ¼ teaspoon xanthan gum per 120g (1 cup) of gluten-free flour blend (omit if your blend already contains binders).

- **For muffins:** Add ½ teaspoon xanthan gum per 120g (1 cup) of gluten-free flour blend (or ¼ teaspoon if your blend already contains binders).

- Replace the dairy milk with an equal weight or volume of a dairy-free milk, such as almond, rice, soy or oat milk, but avoid canned coconut milk.

- Replace the dairy yogurt or sour cream with an equal weight or volume of unsweetened plain or Greek-style vegan yogurt.

- Replace the dairy buttermilk with an equal weight or volume of homemade vegan buttermilk (see page 25).

- Replace the dairy butter with an equal weight or volume of a firm vegan butter block (not a soft spread). Use melted instead of softened butter for the best texture (see page 102). Or, you can replace the dairy butter with 80% of a neutral-tasting oil like sunflower or vegetable oil and 15% of dairy-free milk. Multiply the weight of the butter by 0.8 to get the weight of the oil and 0.15 to get the weight of the dairy-free milk. In terms of volume, use 7 tablespoons of oil and 1 tablespoon of dairy-free milk for every stick of butter.

- **If the regular recipe you're starting with doesn't contain any ground nuts or cocoa powder in the batter:** add 20g (3½ tablespoons) of almond flour per 120g (1 cup) of gluten-free flour blend used (if you have a nut allergy, use an equal weight of finely ground sunflower seeds).

- **For each egg or egg white removed:**

  » Add 20g (2½ tablespoons) of the gluten-free flour blend.

  » Add 30g (2 tablespoons) of dairy-free milk or unsweetened plain or Greek-style vegan yogurt.

  » Add ¼ teaspoon of baking powder and ½ teaspoon apple cider vinegar.

**For all the science**

↓

**Case Study 1: Buttery Vanilla Cake (p.95)**

# Rules for Adapting Chocolate Cakes with Melted Chocolate in the Batter

**To make gluten-free**

- Use a gluten-free flour blend and reduce the amount of flour by 10%, by multiplying the weight of the flour by 0.9, or by reducing its volume by 1½ tablespoons per cup of flour used in the recipe.
- Add ½ teaspoon xanthan gum per 120g (1 cup) of gluten-free flour blend (or ¼ teaspoon if your blend already contains binders).

*If you're starting with an egg-free or vegan cake: add 1 teaspoon of xanthan gum per 120g (1 cup) of gluten-free flour blend instead (or ¾ teaspoon if your blend already contains binders).*

**To make dairy-free**

- Replace the dairy milk with an equal weight or volume of a dairy-free milk, such as almond, rice, soy or oat milk, but avoid canned coconut milk.
- Replace the dairy butter with an equal weight or volume of a firm vegan butter block (not a soft spread). Or, replace the dairy butter with 80% of a neutral-tasting oil like sunflower or vegetable oil and 15% of dairy-free milk. Multiply the weight of the butter by 0.8 to get the weight of the oil and 0.15 to get the weight of the dairy-free milk. In terms of volume, use 7 tablespoons of oil and 1 tablespoon of dairy-free milk for each stick of butter.
- Replace the dairy yogurt or sour cream with an equal weight or volume of unsweetened plain or Greek-style vegan yogurt.
- Replace the dairy buttermilk with an equal weight or volume of homemade vegan buttermilk (see page 25).

**To make egg-free**

- **For each egg or egg white removed:**
  » Add 20g (2½ tablespoons) of flour (true for wheat flour and gluten-free flour blend).
  » Add 30g (2 tablespoons) of whole milk or unsweetened plain or Greek-style yogurt (true for dairy and dairy-free ingredients).

*If you're starting with a gluten-free cake: add 1 teaspoon of xanthan gum per 120g (1 cup) of gluten-free flour blend (or ¾ teaspoon if your blend already contains binders).*

## APPLY TO

- **layer cakes, traybakes (sheet cakes), loaf cakes and pound cakes with melted chocolate in the batter**
- **cupcakes or muffins with melted chocolate in the batter**

## DON'T APPLY TO

- **foam or sponge cakes that rely on whipped eggs (or whipped egg whites) for their texture, including Swiss rolls and roulades (for those, see page 58)**
- **chocolate cakes, cupcakes and muffins with only cocoa powder and no melted chocolate in the batter (for those, see page 52)**

Continued overleaf →

To make vegan

- Replace the dairy milk with an equal weight or volume of a dairy-free milk, such as almond, rice, soy or oat milk, but avoid canned coconut milk.

- Replace the dairy yogurt or sour cream with an equal weight or volume of unsweetened plain or Greek-style vegan yogurt.

- Replace the dairy buttermilk with an equal weight or volume of homemade vegan buttermilk (see page 25).

- Replace the dairy butter with an equal weight or volume of a firm vegan butter block (not a soft spread). Or, replace the dairy butter with 80% of a neutral oil and 15% of dairy-free milk. Multiply the weight of the butter by 0.8 to get the weight of oil and 0.15 to get the weight of dairy-free milk. For volume, use 7 tablespoons of oil and 1 tablespoon of dairy-free milk for each stick of butter.

- **For each egg or egg white removed:**

  » Add 20g (2½ tablespoons) of flour (true for wheat flour and gluten-free flour blend).

  » Add 30g (2 tablespoons) of dairy-free milk or unsweetened plain or Greek-style vegan yogurt.

*If you're starting with a gluten-free cake: add 1 teaspoon of xanthan gum per 120g (1 cup) of gluten-free flour blend (or ¾ teaspoon if your blend contains binders).*

---

To make gluten-free vegan

- Use a gluten-free flour blend and reduce the amount of flour by 10% by multiplying the weight of the flour by 0.9, or by reducing its volume by 1½ tablespoons per cup of flour in the recipe.

- Add 1 teaspoon of xanthan gum per 120g (1 cup) of gluten-free flour blend (or ¾ teaspoon if your blend already contains binders).

- Replace the dairy milk with an equal weight or volume of a dairy-free milk, such as almond, rice, soy or oat milk, but avoid canned coconut milk.

- Replace the dairy yogurt or sour cream with an equal weight or volume of unsweetened plain or Greek-style vegan yogurt.

- Replace the dairy buttermilk with an equal weight or volume of homemade vegan buttermilk (see page 25).

- Replace the dairy butter with an equal weight or volume of a firm vegan butter block (not a soft spread). Or, replace the dairy butter with 80% of a neutral oil and 15% of dairy-free milk. Multiply the weight of butter by 0.8 to get the weight of oil and 0.15 to get the weight of dairy-free milk. For volume, use 7 tablespoons of oil and 1 tablespoon of dairy-free milk for every stick of butter.

- **For each egg or egg white removed:**

  » Add 20g (2½ tablespoons) of gluten-free flour blend.

  » Add 30g (2 tablespoons) of dairy-free milk or unsweetened plain or Greek-style vegan yogurt.

**For all the science**

↓

**Case Study 2: Chocolate Cake (p.107)**

# Rules for Adapting Swiss Rolls & Sponge Cakes

**To make gluten-free**

- Use a gluten-free flour blend and reduce the amount of flour by 10% by multiplying the weight of the flour by 0.9, or by reducing its volume by 1½ tablespoons per cup of flour in the recipe.

- Add ¾ teaspoon of xanthan gum per 120g (1 cup) of gluten-free flour blend (or ½ teaspoon if your blend already contains binders).

- Ideally, use the rolling method detailed on page 113.

*If you're starting with a vegan bake without any ground nuts or cocoa powder in the batter: add 20g (3½ tablespoons) of almond flour per 120g (1 cup) of gluten-free flour blend (if you have a nut allergy, use an equal weight of finely ground sunflower seeds).*

**To make dairy-free**

- Replace the dairy milk with an equal weight or volume of a dairy-free milk, such as almond, rice, soy or oat milk, but avoid canned coconut milk.

- Replace the dairy yogurt or sour cream with an equal weight or volume of unsweetened plain or Greek-style vegan yogurt.

- Replace the dairy buttermilk with an equal weight or volume of homemade vegan buttermilk (see page 25).

- Replace the dairy butter with an equal weight or volume of a firm vegan butter block (not a soft spread). Or, you can replace the dairy butter with 80% of a neutral-tasting oil like sunflower or vegetable oil by multiplying the weight of the butter by 0.8. In terms of volume, use 7 tablespoons of oil for each stick of butter.

**To make egg-free**

- Add ½ teaspoon of xanthan gum per 120g (1 cup) of flour.

- For the best texture (and minimal cracking in a Swiss roll), use oil not butter: replace the butter with 80% of oil by multiplying the weight of the butter by 0.8. In terms of volume, use 7 tablespoons of oil for every stick of butter replaced.

→

## APPLY TO

- **Swiss rolls and roulades**

- **foam or sponge cakes that rely on whipped eggs (or whipped egg whites) for their texture**

## DON'T APPLY TO

- **layer cakes, traybakes (sheet cakes), loaf cakes and pound cakes prepared with a creaming method (for those, see page 52)**

- **cupcakes or muffins (for those, see page 52)**

NOTE

The rules for making eggless Swiss rolls are quite complex because you need to change a large number of different things. So, it might be easier (and less time consuming) to start with the already optimized free-from recipes in the case-studies chapter (Chapter 4; pages 120–22) and then tweak them by adding whatever flavourings and add-ins you fancy.

## To make egg-free (continued)

- **For each egg or egg white removed:**
  - » Add 10g (1½ tablespoons) of flour (true for wheat flour and gluten-free flour blend).
  - » Add 40g (2½ tablespoons) of milk (true for dairy and dairy-free ingredients).
  - » Add 15g (2½ teaspoons) of condensed milk (true for dairy and dairy-free ingredients). Reduce the amount of sugar by half of the total weight of condensed milk to account for the extra sweetness.
  - » Add ⅛ teaspoon of baking powder and ¼ teaspoon of apple cider vinegar.
- Ideally, bake at 160°C (325°F) and use the rolling method detailed on page 113.

*If you're starting with a gluten-free Swiss roll or sponge cake: use ¾ teaspoon of xanthan gum per 120g (1 cup) of gluten-free flour blend (or ½ teaspoon if your blend contains binders).*

## To make vegan

- Replace the dairy milk with an equal weight or volume of a dairy-free milk, such as almond, rice, soy or oat milk, but avoid canned coconut milk.
- Replace the dairy yogurt or sour cream with an equal weight or volume of unsweetened plain or Greek-style vegan yogurt.
- Replace the dairy buttermilk with an equal weight or volume of homemade vegan buttermilk (see page 25).
- For the best texture (and minimal cracking in a Swiss roll), use oil not butter: replace the butter with 80% of oil by multiplying the weight of the butter by 0.8. In terms of volume, use 7 tablespoons of oil for every stick of butter replaced.
- Add ½ teaspoon of xanthan gum per 120g (1 cup) of flour.
- **For each egg or egg white removed:**
  - » Add 10g (1½ tablespoons) of flour (for wheat flour and gluten-free flour blend).
  - » Add 40g (2½ tablespoons) of dairy-free milk.
  - » Add 15g (2½ teaspoons) of vegan condensed milk (see pages 26 and 27). Reduce the sugar by half the total weight of condensed milk (to adjust the sweetness).
  - » Add ⅛ teaspoon of baking powder and ¼ teaspoon of apple cider vinegar.
- Ideally, bake at 160°C (325°F) and use the rolling method detailed on page 113.

*If you're starting with a gluten-free Swiss roll or sponge: use ¾ teaspoon of xanthan gum per 120g (1 cup) of gluten-free flour blend (or ½ teaspoon if the blend already contains binders). If you're starting with a gluten-free bake without ground nuts or cocoa powder in the batter: add 20g (3½ tablespoons) of almond flour per 120g (1 cup) of gluten-free flour blend (if you have a nut allergy, use an equal weight of finely ground sunflower seeds).*

Continued overleaf →

- Use a gluten-free flour blend and reduce the amount of flour by 10% by multiplying the weight of the flour by 0.9, or by reducing its volume by 1½ tablespoons per cup of flour in the recipe.

- Add ¾ teaspoon of xanthan gum per 120g (1 cup) of gluten-free flour blend (or ½ teaspoon if your blend already contains binders).

- Replace the dairy milk with an equal weight or volume of a dairy-free milk, such as almond, rice, soy or oat milk, but avoid canned coconut milk.

- Replace the dairy yogurt or sour cream with an equal weight or volume of unsweetened plain or Greek-style vegan yogurt.

- Replace the dairy buttermilk with an equal weight or volume of homemade vegan buttermilk (see page 25).

- For the best texture (and minimal cracking in a Swiss roll), use oil not butter: replace the butter with 80% of oil by multiplying the weight of the butter by 0.8. In terms of volume, use 7 tablespoons of oil for each stick of butter.

- **For each egg or egg white removed:**

  » Add 10g (1½ tablespoons) of gluten-free flour blend.

  » Add 40g (2½ tablespoons) of dairy-free milk.

  » Add 15g (2½ teaspoons) of vegan condensed milk (see pages 26 and 27). Reduce the sugar by half the total weight of condensed milk (to adjust the sweetness).

  » Add ⅛ teaspoon of baking powder and ¼ teaspoon of apple cider vinegar.

- Ideally, bake at 160°C (325°F) and use the rolling method detailed on page 113.

- **If the starting, regular recipe has no ground nuts or cocoa powder:** add 20g (3½ tablespoons) of almond flour per 120g (1 cup) of gluten-free flour blend (if you have a nut allergy, use an equal weight of finely ground sunflower seeds).

For all the science
↓
Case Study 3:
Vanilla Swiss Roll
(p.113)

# Rules for Adapting Brownies

**To make gluten-free**

- Replace the plain (all-purpose) wheat flour with an equal weight or volume of the gluten-free flour blend.

- Add ¼ teaspoon of xanthan gum per 120g (1 cup) of gluten-free flour blend (omit if your blend already contains binders).

*If you're starting with egg-free or vegan brownies: add ½ teaspoon of xanthan gum per 120g (1 cup) of gluten-free flour blend instead (or ¼ teaspoon if your blend already contains binders) and reduce the amount of fat by 30% by multiplying the weight of the butter by 0.7, or by reducing its volume by 2½ tablespoons for each stick of butter.*

**To make dairy-free**

- Replace the dairy butter with an equal weight or volume of a firm vegan butter block (not a soft spread).

- Replace the dairy milk with an equal weight or volume of a dairy-free milk, such as almond, rice, soy or oat milk, but avoid canned coconut milk.

**To make egg-free**

- **For chocolate brownies (with melted chocolate in the batter) and for blondies:** Add 20g (3 tablespoons) of cornflour (cornstarch) or cocoa powder per 120g (1 cup) of flour (true for wheat flour and gluten-free flour blend).

- **For each egg or egg removed:**

  » Add 30g (4 tablespoons) of flour (true for wheat flour and gluten-free flour blend).

  » Add 40g (2½ tablespoons) of water or milk (true for whole dairy milk and dairy-free milk).

  » Add ⅛ teaspoon of baking powder. (You can omit this if you prefer denser, extra fudgy brownies.)

*If you're starting with gluten-free brownies: use ½ teaspoon of xanthan gum per 120g (1 cup) of gluten-free flour blend (or ¼ teaspoon if your blend already contains binders) and reduce the amount of fat by 30% by multiplying the weight of the butter by 0.7, or by reducing its volume by 2½ tablespoons for each stick of butter.*

- **chocolate brownies with melted chocolate in the batter**

- **cocoa brownies with only cocoa powder and no melted chocolate in the batter**

- **brownie cookies**

- **blondies (note the extra rules for egg-free, vegan and gluten-free vegan)**

- Replace the dairy butter with an equal weight or volume of a firm vegan butter block (not a soft spread).

- Replace the dairy milk with an equal weight or volume of a dairy-free milk, such as almond, rice, soy or oat milk, but avoid canned coconut milk.

- **For chocolate brownies (that contain melted chocolate in the batter) and for blondies:** Add 20g (3 tablespoons) of cornflour (cornstarch) or cocoa powder per 120g (1 cup) of flour (true for wheat flour and gluten-free flour blend).

- **For each egg removed:**

  » Add 30g (4 tablespoons) of flour (true for wheat flour and gluten-free flour blend).

  » Add 40g (2½ tablespoons) of water or dairy-free milk, such as almond, soy, rice or oat milk (but avoid canned coconut milk).

  » Add ⅛ teaspoon of baking powder. (You can omit this if you prefer denser, extra-fudgy brownies.)

*If you're starting with gluten-free brownies: use ½ teaspoon of xanthan gum per 120g (1 cup) of gluten-free flour blend (or ¼ teaspoon if your blend already contains binders) and reduce the amount of fat by 30% by multiplying the weight of the butter by 0.7, or by reducing its volume by 2½ tablespoons for each stick of butter.*

- Replace the flour with an equal weight or volume of the gluten-free flour blend.

- Add ½ teaspoon of xanthan gum per 120g (1 cup) of gluten-free flour blend (or ¼ teaspoon if your blend already contains binders).

- Replace the dairy milk with an equal weight or volume of a dairy-free milk, such as almond, rice, soy or oat milk, but avoid canned coconut milk.

- Use a firm vegan butter block (not a soft spread), and reduce the amount of fat by 30% by multiplying the weight of butter by 0.7, or by reducing the volume of butter by 2½ tablespoons for each stick of butter.

- **For chocolate brownies (with melted chocolate in the batter) and for blondies:** Add 20g (3 tablespoons) of cornflour (cornstarch) or cocoa powder per 120g (1 cup) of gluten-free flour blend.

- **For each egg or egg removed:**

  » Add 30g (4 tablespoons) of gluten-free flour blend.

  » Add 40g (2½ tablespoons) of water or dairy-free milk, such as almond, soy, rice or oat milk (but avoid canned coconut milk).

  » Add ⅛ teaspoon of baking powder. (You can omit this if you prefer denser, extra fudgy brownies.)

**For all the science**
↓
**Case Study 4: Cocoa Brownies (p.135)**

# Rules for Adapting Cookies that Hold Their Shape During Baking

**To make gluten-free**

- Replace the plain (all-purpose) wheat flour with an equal weight or volume of a gluten-free flour blend.
- Add ¼ teaspoon xanthan gum per 120g (1 cup) of gluten-free flour blend (omit if your blend already contains binders).
- Reduce the amount of fat by 20%, by multiplying the weight of butter by 0.8, or by reducing its volume by 1½ tablespoons for each stick of butter.

*If you're starting with egg-free or vegan cut-out cookies and you want them to maintain their shape to within a few millimetres: use ½ teaspoon of xanthan gum per 120g (1 cup) of gluten-free flour blend instead (or ¼ teaspoon if your blend already contains binders).*

**To make dairy-free**

- Replace the dairy milk with an equal weight or volume of a dairy-free milk, such as almond, rice, soy or oat milk, but avoid canned coconut milk.
- Replace the dairy butter with an equal weight or volume of a firm vegan butter block (not a soft spread).

**To make egg-free**

- Add 40g (2½ tablespoons) of milk for each egg removed (true for whole dairy milk and dairy-free milk).
- **For cut-out cookies:** Add 10g (1½ tablespoons) of cornflour (cornstarch) per 120g (1 cup) of flour. Or, you can use an equal weight of another starch, such as arrowroot, potato or tapioca starch instead.

*If you're starting with gluten-free cut-out cookies and you want them to maintain their shape to within a few millimetres: use ½ teaspoon of xanthan gum per 120g (1 cup) of gluten-free flour blend (or ¼ teaspoon if your blend already contains binders).*

## APPLY TO

- cookies that hold their shape in the oven and cut-out cookies that maintain the shape of the cookie cutter (such as shortbread biscuits, cut-out sugar cookies, gingerbread, Linzer cookies, slice-and-bake cookies, thumbprint cookies and similar)
- cookie bars and similar bakes that are based on the above cookie recipes (such as apple pie bars, crumble bars, fruit bars, jam bars, crisps, and crumbles with a shortbread-like dough)

## DON'T APPLY TO

- cookies that spread out in the oven, such as chocolate chip cookies (for those, see page 66)
- cakey cookies, such as crinkle cookies or whoopie pies (for those, see page 68)

- Replace the dairy milk with an equal weight or volume of a dairy-free milk, such as almond, rice, soy or oat milk, but avoid canned coconut milk.

- Replace the dairy butter with an equal weight or volume of a firm vegan butter block (not a soft spread).

- Add 40g (2½ tablespoons) of dairy-free milk for each egg removed.

- **For cut-out cookies:** Add 10g (1½ tablespoons) of cornflour (cornstarch) per 120g (1 cup) of flour. Or, you can use an equal weight of another starch, such as arrowroot, potato or tapioca starch instead.

*If you're starting with gluten-free cut-out cookies and you want them to maintain their shape to within a few millimetres: use ½ teaspoon of xanthan gum per 120g (1 cup) of gluten-free flour blend (or ¼ teaspoon if your blend already contains binders).*

- Replace the plain (all-purpose) wheat flour with an equal weight or volume of a gluten-free flour blend.

- Add ¼ teaspoon of xanthan gum per 120g (1 cup) of gluten-free flour blend (omit if your blend already contains binders).

- Replace the dairy milk with an equal weight or volume of a dairy-free milk, such as almond, rice, soy or oat milk, but avoid canned coconut milk.

- Use a firm vegan butter block (not a soft spread) and reduce the amount of butter by 20%, by multiplying the weight of butter by 0.8, or by reducing its volume by 1½ tablespoons for each stick of butter.

- Add 40g (2½ tablespoons) of dairy-free milk for each egg removed.

- **For cut-out cookies that need to maintain their shape to within a few millimetres:** Use ½ teaspoon of xanthan gum per 120g (1 cup) of gluten-free flour blend instead (or ¼ teaspoon if your blend already contains binders), and add 10g (1½ tablespoons) of cornflour (cornstarch) per 120g (1 cup) of flour. Or, you can use an equal weight of another starch, such as arrowroot, potato or tapioca starch instead.

**For all the science**
↓
**Case Study 5: Cut-out Sugar Cookies (p.147)**

# Rules for Adapting Cookies that Spread During Baking

**To make gluten-free**

- Replace the plain (all-purpose) wheat flour with an equal weight or volume of a gluten-free flour blend.

- Reduce the amount of butter by 30%, by multiplying its weight by 0.7, or by reducing its volume by 2½ tablespoons for each stick of butter. Ideally, use softened rather than melted butter.

- Add ¼ teaspoon of xanthan gum per 120g (1 cup) of gluten-free flour blend (omit if your blend already contains binders).

*If you're starting with dairy-free or vegan cookies: use softened butter instead of melted.*

**To make dairy-free**

- Replace the dairy butter with an equal weight or volume of a firm vegan butter block (not a soft spread).

*If you're starting with gluten-free cookies: use softened butter instead of melted.*

**To make egg-free**

- Substitute the eggs, egg yolks and/or egg whites with an equal weight of milk or unsweetened plain or Greek-style yogurt (true for whole dairy and dairy-free versions). Specifically, add 50g (3½ tablespoons) of milk or yogurt for each egg removed, 35g (2½ tablespoons) for each egg white removed and 15g (1 tablespoon) for each egg yolk removed.

**To make vegan**

- Replace the dairy butter with an equal weight or volume of a firm vegan butter block (not a soft spread).

- Substitute the eggs, egg yolks and/or egg whites with an equal weight of dairy-free milk or vegan yogurt. Specifically, add 50g (3½ tablespoons) of milk or yogurt for each egg removed, 35g (2½ tablespoons) for each egg white removed and 15g (1 tablespoon) for each egg yolk removed.

*If you're starting with gluten-free cookies: use softened vegan butter instead of melted.*

## APPLY TO

- cookies that spread out in the oven (such as chocolate chip cookies, snickerdoodles, gingersnaps, molasses cookies, peanut butter blossom cookies, soft oatmeal cookies and drop cookies)

- cookie bars and similar bakes based on the above cookie recipes (such as chocolate chip cookie bars and skillet cookies)

## DON'T APPLY TO

- cookies that hold their shape in the oven, such as shortbread biscuits, cut-out sugar cookies, gingerbread, Linzer cookies, thumbprint cookies or slice-and-bake cookies (for those, see page 64)

- cakey cookies, such as crinkle cookies or whoopie pies (for those, see page 68)

**To make gluten-free vegan**

- Replace the plain (all-purpose) wheat flour with an equal weight or volume of a gluten-free flour blend.

- Use a firm vegan butter block (not a soft spread) and reduce the amount of butter by 30% by multiplying its weight by 0.7, or by reducing its volume by 2½ tablespoons for each stick of butter. Use softened butter rather than melted butter. (For best results, use a vegan butter block with a fat content of at least 75% and a high saturated fat content, of 40% or higher.)

- Add ¼ teaspoon of xanthan gum per 120g (1 cup) of gluten-free flour blend (omit if your blend already contains binders).

- Substitute the eggs, egg yolks and/or egg whites with an equal weight of dairy-free milk or vegan yogurt. Specifically, add 50g (3½ tablespoons) of milk or yogurt for each egg removed, 35g (2½ tablespoons) for each egg white removed and 15g (1 tablespoon) for each egg yolk removed.

**For all the science**
↓
**Case Study 6: Chocolate Chip Cookies (p.159)**

# Rules for Adapting Cakey Cookies

**To make gluten-free**

- Use a gluten-free flour blend and reduce the amount of flour by 10% by multiplying the weight of the flour by 0.9, or by reducing its volume by 1½ tablespoons per cup of flour.

- Add ¼ teaspoon of xanthan gum per 120g (1 cup) of gluten-free flour blend (omit if your blend already contains binders).

*If you're starting with egg-free or vegan cookies: use ½ teaspoon of xanthan gum per 120g (1 cup) of gluten-free flour blend instead (or ¼ teaspoon if your blend already contains binders).*

**To make dairy-free**

- Replace the dairy butter with an equal weight or volume of a firm vegan butter block (not a soft spread).

- Replace the dairy milk with an equal weight or volume of a dairy-free milk, such as almond, rice, soy or oat milk, but avoid canned coconut milk.

- Replace the dairy yogurt or sour cream with an equal weight or volume of unsweetened plain or Greek-style vegan yogurt.

- Replace regular dairy buttermilk with an equal weight or volume of homemade vegan buttermilk (see page 25).

**To make egg-free**

- Add 40g (2½ tablespoons) of milk for each egg removed (true for whole dairy milk and dairy-free milk).

*If you're starting with gluten-free cookies: use ½ teaspoon of xanthan gum per 120g (1 cup) of gluten-free flour blend (or ¼ teaspoon if your blend already contains binders).*

## APPLY TO

- cakey cookies, such as crinkle cookies, whoopie pies, black and white cookies or biscotti (the latter are just dried-out cakey cookies) – with the exception of biscotti, these all have a tender, moist and cakey crumb

## DON'T APPLY TO

- cookies that hold their shape in the oven, such as shortbread biscuits, cut-out sugar cookies, gingerbread, Linzer cookies, thumbprint cookies or slice-and-bake cookies (for those, see page 64)

- cookies that spread out in the oven, such as chocolate chip cookies, snickerdoodles, gingersnaps, molasses cookies, peanut butter blossom cookies, soft oatmeal cookies and drop cookies (for those, see page 66)

**To make vegan**

- Replace the dairy butter with an equal weight or volume of a firm vegan butter block (not a soft spread).

- Replace the dairy milk with an equal weight or volume of a dairy-free milk, such as almond, rice, soy or oat milk, but avoid canned coconut milk.

- Replace the dairy yogurt or sour cream with an equal weight or volume of unsweetened plain or Greek-style vegan yogurt.

- Replace the dairy buttermilk with an equal weight or volume of homemade vegan buttermilk (see page 25).

- Add 40g (2½ tablespoons) of dairy-free milk for each egg removed.

*If you're starting with gluten-free cookies: use ½ teaspoon of xanthan gum per 120g (1 cup) of gluten-free flour blend (or ¼ teaspoon if your blend already contains binders).*

**To make gluten-free vegan**

- Use a gluten-free flour blend and reduce the amount of flour by 10%, which is equivalent to multiplying the weight of the flour by 0.9, or to reducing its volume by 1½ tablespoons per cup of flour in the recipe.

- Add ½ teaspoon of xanthan gum per 120g (1 cup) of gluten-free flour blend (or ¼ teaspoon if your blend already contains binders).

- Replace the dairy butter with an equal weight or volume of a firm vegan butter block (not a soft spread).

- Replace the dairy milk with an equal weight or volume of a dairy-free milk, such as almond, rice, soy or oat milk, but avoid canned coconut milk.

- Replace the dairy yogurt or sour cream with an equal weight or volume of unsweetened plain or Greek-style vegan yogurt.

- Replace dairy buttermilk with an equal weight or volume of homemade vegan buttermilk (see page 25).

- Add 40g (2½ tablespoons) of dairy-free milk for each egg removed.

**For all the science**

↓

**Case Study 7: Lemon Crinkle Cookies (p.169)**

# Rules for Adapting Shortcrust Pastry

**To make gluten-free**

- Replace the plain (all-purpose) wheat flour with an equal weight or volume of a gluten-free flour blend.

- Add ½ teaspoon of xanthan gum per 120g (1 cup) of gluten-free flour blend (or ¼ teaspoon if your blend already contains binders).

- Reduce the amount of butter by 20% by multiplying the weight of butter by 0.8, or by reducing its volume by 1½ tablespoons for each stick of butter.

*If you're starting with a vegan shortcrust pastry: add ¼ teaspoon of baking powder and 20g (3½ tablespoons) of almond flour per 120g (1 cup) of gluten-free flour blend (if you're allergic to nuts, use an equal weight of finely ground sunflower seeds). Add the dairy-free milk (an egg replacement) slowly, until the pastry comes together – you'll need about 40% less milk than in the vegan version made with plain (all-purpose) wheat flour.*

**To make dairy-free**

- Replace the dairy butter with an equal weight or volume of a firm vegan butter block (not a soft spread).

- Substitute 20% of flour with an equal weight of a starch, such as cornflour (cornstarch), potato starch, tapioca starch or arrowroot starch.

**To make egg-free**

- Substitute the eggs and/or egg yolks with an equal weight of milk (true for whole dairy milk and dairy-free milk). Specifically, add 50g (3½ tablespoons) of milk for each egg removed and 15g (1 tablespoon) for each egg yolk removed.

- Substitute 20% of flour with an equal weight of a starch, such as cornflour (cornstarch), potato starch, tapioca starch or arrowroot starch.

**APPLY TO**

- **shortcrust pastry, pâte sucrée, pâte sablée**

**DON'T APPLY TO**

- **flaky pastry, including American-style flaky pie crust and rough puff pastry (for those, see page 72)**

- Replace the dairy butter with an equal weight or volume of a firm vegan butter block (not a soft spread).

- Substitute the eggs and/or egg yolks with an equal weight of a dairy-free milk alternative, such as almond, soy, rice or oat milk (but avoid canned coconut milk). Specifically, add 50g (3½ tablespoons) of milk for each egg removed and 15g (1 tablespoon) for each egg yolk removed.

- Substitute 20% of flour with an equal weight of a starch, such as cornflour (cornstarch), potato starch, tapioca starch or arrowroot starch.

*If you're starting with a gluten-free shortcrust pastry: add ¼ teaspoon of baking powder and 20g (3½ tablespoons) of almond flour per 120g (1 cup) of gluten-free flour blend (if you're allergic to nuts, use an equal weight of finely ground sunflower seeds). Use 30g (2 tablespoons) of dairy-free milk for each egg removed to bring the pastry together.*

- Replace the plain (all-purpose) wheat flour with an equal weight or volume of a gluten-free flour blend.

- Add ½ teaspoon of xanthan gum per 120g (1 cup) of gluten-free flour blend (or ¼ teaspoon if your blend already contains binders).

- Add ¼ teaspoon of baking powder per 120g (1 cup) of gluten-free flour blend.

- Add 20g (3½ tablespoons) of almond flour per 120g (1 cup) of gluten-free flour blend (if you're allergic to nuts, use an equal weight of finely ground sunflower seeds).

- Use a firm vegan butter block (not a soft spread) and reduce the amount of butter by 20% by multiplying the weight of butter by 0.8, or by reducing its volume by 1½ tablespoons for each stick of butter in the recipe.

- Add 30g (2 tablespoons) of vegan milk for each egg removed. You can use dairy-free milks such as almond, soy, rice or oat milk, but avoid canned coconut milk. If you're replacing egg yolks rather than whole eggs, add the dairy-free milk slowly until the pastry comes together in a ball.

**For all the science**
↓
**Case Study 8: Shortcrust Pastry (p.179)**

# Rules for Adapting Flaky Pastry

**To make gluten-free**

- Replace the plain (all-purpose) wheat flour with an equal weight or volume of a gluten-free flour blend.

- Add ½ teaspoon of xanthan gum per 120g (1 cup) of gluten-free flour blend (or ¼ teaspoon if your blend already contains binders).

- Increase the amount of water by 20% by multiplying the weight of the water by 1.2, or by increasing its volume by about 3 tablespoons per cup of water.

*If you're starting with a vegan pie crust: use a 50:50 mixture of vegetable shortening and a firm vegan butter block (not a soft spread). Ideally, the vegan butter should have a high fat content, of 75% or higher, and a high saturated fat content, of 40% or higher. Work the vegan butter into the dry ingredients to a greater extent (until you get approximately pea-sized pieces) and use just enough water to bring the dough together – you'll need about 10% less water than in the vegan version made with plain (all-purpose) wheat flour.*

**To make vegan**

- Replace the dairy butter with an equal weight or volume of a firm vegan butter block (not a soft spread), vegetable shortening, or a 50:50 mixture of both (see pages 192–3 for how the choice of fat will affect the pie-crust texture).

*If you're starting with a gluten-free pie crust: use a 50:50 mixture of vegetable shortening and a firm vegan butter block (not a soft spread). Ideally, the vegan butter should have a high fat content, of 75% or higher, and a high saturated fat content, of 40% or higher. Work the vegan butter into the dry ingredients to a greater extent (until you get approximately pea-sized pieces) and use just enough water to bring the dough together – you'll need about 25% less water than in the gluten-free version made with dairy butter.*

**APPLY TO**

- flaky pastry, including American-style flaky pie crust and rough puff pastry

**DON'T APPLY TO**

- shortcrust pastry, pâte sucrée, pâte sablée (for those, see page 70)

**For all the science**

↓

**Case Study 9:
Flaky Pie Crust
(p.187)**

**To make gluten-free vegan**

- Replace the plain (all-purpose) wheat flour with an equal weight or volume of a gluten-free flour blend.

- Add ½ teaspoon of xanthan gum per 120g (1 cup) of gluten-free flour blend (or ¼ teaspoon if your blend already contains binders).

- Replace the dairy butter with a 50:50 mixture of a firm vegan butter block (not a soft spread) and vegetable shortening. That means that you need to replace 115g (1 stick) of dairy butter with 55g (½ stick) of vegan butter and 55g (¼ cup + ½ tablespoon) of vegetable shortening. Ideally, the vegan butter should have a fat content of at least 75% and a high saturated fat content, of 40% or higher. (However, if you find a firm vegan butter block that has a high saturated fat content and that's perfect for making flaky pastry, then you can use vegan butter only, without any vegetable shortening at all. In that case, replace the dairy butter with an equal weight or volume of the vegan butter.)

- Work the vegan fat into the dry ingredients until you get approximately pea-sized pieces (not any larger than that).

- Use just enough water to fully hydrate all the flour and to bring the dough together – you'll need about 10% less water, which is equivalent to multiplying the weight of water by 0.9, or to reducing the volume of water by 1½ tablespoons per cup.

**NOTE: A RULE ABOUT ADDING WATER**

Whenever you're making any type of flaky pastry, you should use the amounts of water listed (or calculated) only as a rough guideline. Always add the water gradually, 1–2 tablespoons at a time, and mix well after each addition until the ingredients come together into a shaggy dough and all the flour (wheat flour or gluten-free) has been hydrated. This may require more or less water than that listed in the recipe.

# Rules for Adapting British Scones

**To make gluten-free**

- Replace the plain (all-purpose) wheat flour with an equal weight or volume of a gluten-free flour blend.

- Add 40g (2½ tablespoons) of milk per 120g (1 cup) of gluten-free flour blend (true for whole dairy milk and dairy-free milk).

- Add 1g (½ teaspoon) of xanthan gum per 120g (1 cup) of gluten-free flour blend (or ¼ teaspoon if your blend already contains binders).

- Add 3g (2 teaspoons) of psyllium husk per 120g (1 cup) of gluten-free flour blend. Mix it into the milk and allow to stand for 5–10 minutes until a loose gel forms, then add it to the rest of the ingredients.

**APPLY TO**

- **British scones**

**DON'T APPLY TO**

- **American buttermilk biscuits or American scones (for those, see page 76)**

**To make dairy-free**

- Replace the dairy butter with an equal weight or volume of a firm vegan butter block (not a soft spread).

- Replace the dairy milk with an equal weight or volume of a dairy-free milk, such as almond, rice, soy or oat milk, but avoid canned coconut milk.

- Replace the dairy yogurt or sour cream with an equal weight or volume of unsweetened plain or Greek-style vegan yogurt.

- Replace the dairy buttermilk with an equal weight or volume of homemade vegan buttermilk (see page 25).

- Replace the dairy double (heavy) cream with an equal weight or volume of vegan double (heavy) cream.

**To make egg-free**

- Add 40g (2½ tablespoons) of milk for each egg removed (true for whole dairy milk or dairy-free milk).

**To make vegan**

- Replace the dairy butter with an equal weight or volume of a firm vegan butter block (not a soft spread).

- Replace the dairy milk with an equal weight or volume of a dairy-free milk, such as almond, rice, soy or oat milk, but avoid canned coconut milk.

- Replace the dairy yogurt or sour cream with an equal weight or volume of unsweetened plain or Greek-style vegan yogurt.

- Replace the dairy buttermilk with an equal weight or volume of homemade vegan buttermilk (see page 25).

- Replace the dairy double (heavy) cream with an equal weight or volume of vegan double (heavy) cream.

- Add 40g (2½ tablespoons) of dairy-free milk for each egg removed.

**To make gluten-free vegan**

- Replace the plain (all-purpose) wheat flour with an equal weight or volume of a gluten-free flour blend.

- Replace the dairy butter with an equal weight or volume of a firm vegan butter block (not a soft spread). Ideally, use a vegan butter with a fat content of at least 75% and a high saturated fat content, of 40% or higher.

- Replace the dairy milk with an equal weight or volume of a dairy-free milk, such as almond, rice, soy or oat milk, but avoid canned coconut milk.

- Replace the dairy yogurt or sour cream with an equal weight or volume of unsweetened plain or Greek-style vegan yogurt.

- Replace the dairy buttermilk with an equal weight or volume of homemade vegan buttermilk (see page 25).

- Replace the dairy double (heavy) cream with an equal weight or volume of vegan double (heavy) cream.

- Add 40g (2½ tablespoons) of dairy-free milk per 120g (1 cup) of gluten-free flour blend.

- Add 40g (2½ tablespoons) of dairy-free milk for each egg removed.

- Add 1g (½ teaspoon) of xanthan gum per 120g (1 cup) of gluten-free flour blend (or ¼ teaspoon if your blend already contains binders).

- Add 3g (2 teaspoons) of psyllium husk per 120g (1 cup) of gluten-free flour blend. Mix it into the dairy-free milk and allow to stand for 5–10 minutes until a loose gel forms, then add it to the rest of the ingredients.

For all the science
↓
Case Study 10:
British Scones
(p.205)

# Rules for Adapting American Buttermilk Biscuits

**To make gluten-free**

- Replace the plain (all-purpose) wheat flour with an equal weight or volume of a gluten-free flour blend.
- Add ½ teaspoon of baking powder per 120g (1 cup) of gluten-free flour blend.
- Add 1g (½ teaspoon) of xanthan gum per 120g (1 cup) of gluten-free flour blend (or ¼ teaspoon if your blend already contains binders).
- Add 1.5g (1 teaspoon) of psyllium husk and 15g (1 tablespoon) of water per 120g (1 cup ) of gluten-free flour blend. Reduce the amount of buttermilk by the total weight or volume of the water added. Mix the psyllium husk with the water to make the psyllium gel, then mix the gel into the buttermilk and add the mixture to the rest of the ingredients.

**To make vegan**

- Replace the dairy butter with an equal weight or volume of a firm vegan butter block (not a soft spread).
- Replace the dairy buttermilk with an equal weight or volume of a dairy-free alternative (see the homemade vegan buttermilk recipe on page 25).

**To make gluten-free vegan**

- Replace the plain (all-purpose) wheat flour with an equal weight or volume of a gluten-free flour blend.
- Add ½ teaspoon of baking powder per 120g (1 cup) of gluten-free flour blend.
- Replace the dairy butter with an equal weight or volume of a firm vegan butter block (not a soft spread). Ideally, use a vegan butter with a fat content of at least 75% and a high saturated fat content, of 40% or higher.
- Replace the dairy buttermilk with an equal weight or volume of a dairy-free alternative (see the homemade vegan buttermilk recipe on page 25).
- Add 1g (½ teaspoon) of xanthan gum per 120g (1 cup) of gluten-free flour blend (or ¼ teaspoon if your blend already contains binders).
- Add 1.5g (1 teaspoon) of psyllium husk and 15g (1 tablespoon) of water per 120g (1 cup ) of gluten-free flour blend. Reduce the amount of buttermilk by the total weight or volume of the water added. Mix the psyllium husk with the water to make the psyllium gel, then mix the gel into the buttermilk and add the mixture to the rest of the ingredients.

**APPLY TO**

- **American buttermilk biscuits**
- **American scones**

**DON'T APPLY TO**

- **British scones (for those, see page 74)**

**For all the science**
↓
**Case Study 11: American Buttermilk Biscuits (p.215)**

# Rules for Adapting Thin Pancakes & Crêpes

## To make gluten-free

- Use a gluten-free flour blend and reduce the amount of flour by 10%, by multiplying the weight of the flour by 0.9 or by reducing its volume by 1½ tablespoons per cup of flour.

- Add ¼ teaspoon of xanthan gum per 120g (1 cup) of gluten-free flour blend (omit if your blend already contains xanthan gum or other binders).

*If you're starting with vegan pancakes: replace 25% of the dairy-free milk with an equal weight of vegan condensed milk, and halve the amount of sugar in the recipe. In volume measurements, this is equivalent to using 3 tablespoons of condensed milk for every 4 tablespoons of milk that you're replacing. You can use a shop-bought vegan condensed milk or make your own using either of the recipes on pages 26 and 27.*

**APPLY TO**

- thin French-style crêpes and other similar thin pancakes

**DON'T APPLY TO**

- fluffy American-style pancakes, fluffy buttermilk pancakes, waffles (for those, see page 79)

## To make dairy-free

- Replace the dairy butter with an equal weight or volume of a firm vegan butter block (not a soft spread). Or, you can replace the dairy butter with 80% of a neutral-tasting oil like sunflower or vegetable oil. Multiply the weight of the butter by 0.8 to get the weight of the oil. In terms of volume, use 7 tablespoons of oil for each stick of butter.

- Replace the dairy milk with an equal weight or volume of a dairy-free milk, such as almond, rice, soy or oat milk, but avoid using canned coconut milk.

- Increase the amount of sugar by about 5–10g (½–1 tablespoon) per 240g (1 cup) of dairy-free milk.

## To make egg-free

- **For each egg removed:**
  » Add 10g (1½ tablespoons) of flour (true for wheat flour and for gluten-free flour blend).
  » Add 30g (2 tablespoons) of milk (true for whole dairy and dairy-free milk).

## To make vegan

- Replace the dairy butter with an equal weight or volume of a firm vegan butter block (not a soft spread). I don't recommend using oil (see page 231).

- Replace the dairy milk with an equal weight or volume of a dairy-free milk, such as almond, rice, soy or oat milk, but avoid using canned coconut milk.

- Increase the amount of sugar by about 5–10g (½–1 tablespoon) per 240g (1 cup) of dairy-free milk.

Continued overleaf →

- **For each egg removed:**

  » Add 10g (1½ tablespoons) of flour (true for wheat flour and gluten-free flour blend).

  » Add 30g (2 tablespoons) of dairy-free milk.

*If you're starting with gluten-free pancakes: replace one quarter (25%) of the dairy-free milk with an equal weight of vegan condensed milk, and halve the amount of sugar in the recipe. In volume measurements, this is equivalent to using 3 tablespoons of condensed milk for every 4 tablespoons of milk that you're replacing. You can use a shop-bought vegan condensed milk or make your own using either of the recipes on pages 26 and 27.*

- Use a gluten-free flour blend and reduce the amount of flour by 10% by multiplying the weight of the flour by 0.9, or by reducing its volume by 1½ tablespoons per cup of flour in the recipe.

- Add ¼ teaspoon of xanthan gum per 120g (1 cup) of gluten-free flour blend (omit if your blend already contains binders).

- Increase the amount of sugar by about 5–10g (½–1 tablespoon) per 240g (1 cup) of milk in the recipe.

- Replace the dairy butter with an equal weight or volume of a firm vegan butter block (not a soft spread). I don't recommend using oil (see page 231).

- Replace 75% of the total dairy-milk content with an equal weight or volume of a dairy-free milk, such as almond, soy, rice or oat milk, but avoid canned coconut milk.

- Replace the remaining 25% of the dairy milk with an equal weight of vegan condensed milk (or, if using volume measurements, use 3 tablespoons of condensed milk for every 4 tablespoons of milk that you're replacing) and halve the amount of sugar in the recipe. You can use a shop-bought vegan condensed milk or make your own (see pages 26 and 27).

- **For each egg removed:**

  » Add 10g (1½ tablespoons) of gluten-free flour blend.

  » Add 30g (2 tablespoons) of dairy-free milk.

**For all the science**

↓

**Case Study 12: Thin French-style Crêpes (p.229)**

# Rules for Adapting Fluffy Pancakes

**To make gluten-free**

- Use a gluten-free flour blend and reduce the amount of flour by 10% by multiplying the weight of the flour by 0.9, or by reducing its volume by 1½ tablespoons per cup of flour in the recipe.

- Add ½ teaspoon of xanthan gum per 120g (1 cup) of gluten-free flour blend (or ¼ teaspoon if your blend already contains binders). If you're using a thicker liquid to make the pancakes (such as buttermilk), use only ¼ teaspoon of xanthan gum per 120g (1 cup) of gluten-free flour blend (omit if your blend already contains binders).

*If you're starting with egg-free or vegan pancakes: add 20g (3½ tablespoons) of almond flour (or finely ground sunflower seeds) per 120g (1 cup) of gluten-free flour blend.*

**To make dairy-free**

- Replace the dairy butter with an equal weight or volume of a firm vegan butter block (not a soft spread). Or, you can replace the dairy butter with 80% of a neutral-tasting oil like sunflower or vegetable oil. Multiply the weight of the butter by 0.8 to get the weight of the oil. In terms of volume, use 7 tablespoons of oil for each stick of butter.

- Replace the dairy milk with an equal weight or volume of a dairy-free milk, such as almond, rice, soy or oat milk, but avoid canned coconut milk.

- Replace the dairy buttermilk with an equal weight or volume of a dairy-free alternative (see page 25).

- Increase the amount of sugar by about 10g (1 tablespoon) per 240g (1 cup) of dairy-free milk in the recipe.

**To make egg-free**

- **For each egg or egg white removed:**
  » Add 10g (1½ tablespoons) of flour (true for wheat flour and gluten-free flour blend).
  » Add 30g (2 tablespoons) of milk (true for dairy and dairy-free milk).
  » Add ¼ teaspoon of baking powder and ½ teaspoon of apple cider vinegar.

*If you're starting with gluten-free pancakes: add 20g (3½ tablespoons) of almond flour (or finely ground sunflower seeds) per 120g (1 cup) of gluten-free flour blend.*

## APPLY TO

- **Fluffy American-style pancakes**
- **Fluffy buttermilk pancakes**
- **Waffles**

## DON'T APPLY TO

- **Thin French-style crêpes and other similar thin pancakes (for those, see page 77)**

Continued overleaf →

- Replace the dairy butter with an equal weight or volume of a firm vegan butter block (not a soft spread). Or, replace the dairy butter with 80% of a neutral-tasting oil like sunflower or vegetable oil. Multiply the weight of the butter by 0.8 to get the weight of the oil. In terms of volume, use 7 tablespoons of oil for each stick of butter.

- Replace the dairy milk with an equal weight or volume of a dairy-free milk, such as almond, rice, soy or oat milk, but avoid canned coconut milk.

- Replace the dairy buttermilk with an equal weight or volume of a dairy-free alternative (see page 25).

- Increase the amount of sugar by about 10g (1 tablespoon) per 240g (1 cup) of dairy-free milk in the recipe.

- **For each egg or egg white removed:**

  » Add 10g (1½ tablespoons) of flour (true for wheat flour and gluten-free flour blend).

  » Add 30g (2 tablespoons) of dairy-free milk.

  » Add ¼ teaspoon of baking powder and ½ teaspoon of apple cider vinegar.

*If you're starting with gluten-free pancakes: add 20g (3½ tablespoons) of almond flour (or finely ground sunflower seeds) per 120g (1 cup) of gluten-free flour blend.*

- Use a gluten-free flour blend and reduce the amount of flour by 10% by multiplying the weight of the flour by 0.9, or by reducing its volume by 1½ tablespoons per cup of flour in the recipe.

- Add 20g (3½ tablespoons) of almond flour (or finely ground sunflower seeds) per 120g (1 cup) of gluten-free flour blend.

- Add ½ teaspoon of xanthan gum per 120g (1 cup) of gluten-free flour blend (or ¼ teaspoon if your blend already contains binders). If you're using a thicker liquid to make the pancakes (such as buttermilk), use only ¼ teaspoon of xanthan gum per 120g (1 cup) of gluten-free flour blend (omit if your blend already contains binders).

- Replace the dairy butter with an equal weight or volume of a firm vegan butter block (not a soft spread). Or, you can replace the dairy butter with 80% of a neutral-tasting oil like sunflower or vegetable oil. Multiply the weight of the butter by 0.8 to get the weight of the oil. In terms of volume, use 7 tablespoons of oil for each stick of butter.

- Replace the dairy milk with an equal weight or volume of a dairy-free milk, such as almond, rice, soy or oat milk, but avoid canned coconut milk.

- Replace the dairy buttermilk with an equal weight or volume of a dairy-free alternative (see page 25).

- Increase the amount of sugar by about 10g (1 tablespoon) per 240g (1 cup) of dairy-free milk in the recipe.

- **For each egg or egg white removed:**

  » Add 10g (1½ tablespoons) of gluten-free flour blend.

  » Add 30g (2 tablespoons) of dairy-free milk.

  » Add ¼ teaspoon of baking powder and ½ teaspoon of apple cider vinegar.

**For all the science**

↓

**Case Study 13: Fluffy American-style Pancakes (p.237)**

# Rules for Adapting a Baked Cheesecake

**To make gluten-free**

- Use an equal amount of gluten-free digestive biscuits (graham crackers) in the cheesecake crust.

**APPLY TO**

- **Baked cheesecakes**
- **Baked cheesecake bars**

**DON'T APPLY TO**

- **No-bake cheesecakes or cheesecake bars**
- **Raw vegan cheesecakes or cheesecake bars**

**To make dairy-free**

- Replace the dairy butter in the cheesecake crust with an equal weight or volume of a firm vegan butter block (not a soft spread).

- Replace the dairy cream cheese with an equal weight or volume of a vegan cream cheese. Use a vegan cream cheese that has a similar texture to dairy cream cheese and one that has a relatively low water content.

- If your vegan cream cheese is too soft and watery, strain it using a cheesecloth (see page 316).

- Replace the dairy yogurt with an equal weight or volume of unsweetened Greek-style vegan yogurt.

- Replace the dairy double (heavy) cream with an equal weight or volume of a vegan double (heavy) cream.

- Add 5g (2 teaspoons) of cornflour (cornstarch) per 225g (1 cup) of vegan cream cheese in the recipe.

- If your cheesecake also contains double (heavy) cream, add 10g (1½ tablespoons) of cornflour (cornstarch) per 230g (1 cup) of vegan double (heavy) cream in the recipe.

**To make egg-free**

- **For each egg removed:**
  - » Add 20g (1½ tablespoons) of milk and 20g (1½ tablespoons) of unsweetened plain or Greek-style yogurt.
  - » Add 5g (2 teaspoons) of cornflour (cornstarch).

- Replace the dairy butter in the cheesecake crust with an equal weight or volume of a firm vegan butter block (not a soft spread).

- Replace the dairy cream cheese with an equal weight or volume of a vegan alternative. Use a vegan cream cheese that has a similar texture to dairy cream cheese and one that has a relatively low water content.

- If your vegan cream cheese is too watery, strain it through a cheesecloth (see page 316).

- Replace the vegan yogurt with an equal weight or volume of unsweetened Greek-style vegan yogurt.

- Replace the dairy double (heavy) cream with an equal weight or volume of vegan double (heavy) cream.

- Add 5g (2 teaspoons) of cornflour (cornstarch) per 225g (1 cup) of vegan cream cheese in the recipe.

- If your cheesecake also contains double (heavy) cream, add 10g (1½ tablespoons) of cornflour (cornstarch) per 230g (1 cup) of vegan double (heavy) cream in the recipe.

- **For each egg removed:**

  » Add 40g (3 tablespoons) of unsweetened Greek-style vegan yogurt.

  » Add 5g (2 teaspoons) of cornflour (cornstarch).

**For all the science**

**Case Study 14: Baked New York-style Cheesecake (p.247)**

# Rules for Adapting Bread & Yeasted Bakes

This section is slightly unusual because, as you'll soon see, there are no rules for making bread recipes gluten-free and gluten-free vegan. The science behind gluten-free bread is incredibly different from that behind regular bread made with wheat flour. And it's pretty much impossible to summarize all these differences in a simple set of rules.

However, when it comes to replacing dairy and eggs in bread recipes, that's much easier. With dairy, you can directly swap the dairy ingredients (milk or butter) with an equal weight or volume of their dairy-free equivalents. Eggs are primarily used in brioche and enriched bread recipes to provide extra richness and to add moisture – knowing that, they're also very easy to substitute.

**To make gluten-free**

Converting a regular bread recipe to gluten-free involves so many different variables – such as the higher moisture absorption of gluten-free flours, the presence of binders such as psyllium husk and xanthan gum that themselves absorb a lot of moisture, the varying proportion of starches in your gluten-free flour blend depending on what kind of bread you're making, and so on. This large number of variables means that we can't establish a simple set of rules for converting a regular bread recipe to gluten-free – instead, refer to the "Gluten-free Bread 101" section in Chapter 5 (see pages 272–7), which includes two fundamental gluten-free bread recipes (for a simple non-enriched bread and for brioche dough). Use these as the starting point for numerous other bakes.

**To make dairy-free**

- Replace the dairy butter with an equal weight or volume of a firm vegan butter block (not a soft spread). Or, you can replace the dairy butter with 80% of a neutral-tasting oil like sunflower or vegetable oil. Multiply the weight of the butter by 0.8 to get the weight of the oil. In terms of volume, use 7 tablespoons of oil for each stick of butter.

- Replace the dairy milk with an equal weight or volume of a dairy-free milk, such as almond, rice, soy or oat milk, but avoid canned coconut milk.

**To make egg-free**

- **For regular bread made with wheat flour:** add 20g (1½ tablespoons) of milk and 15g (1 tablespoon) of butter (or 12g/1 tablespoon of oil) for each egg removed (true for dairy and dairy-free ingredients).

- **For gluten-free bread:** add 30–40g (2–2½ tablespoons) of milk and 15g (1 tablespoon) of butter (or 12g/1 tablespoon of oil) for each egg removed (true for dairy and dairy-free ingredients).

- Replace the dairy butter with an equal weight or volume of a firm vegan butter block (not a soft spread). Or, you can replace the dairy butter with 80% of a neutral-tasting oil, like sunflower or vegetable oil, by multiplying the weight of the butter by 0.8. In terms of volume, use 7 tablespoons of oil for each stick of butter.

- Replace the dairy milk with an equal weight or volume of a dairy-free milk, such as almond, rice, soy or oat milk, but avoid canned coconut milk.

- **For regular bread made with wheat flour:** add 20g (1½ tablespoons) of dairy-free milk and 15g (1 tablespoon) of vegan butter (or 12g/1 tablespoon of oil) for each egg removed.

- **For gluten-free bread:** add 30–40g (2–2½ tablespoons) of dairy-free milk and 15g (1 tablespoon) of vegan butter (or 12g/1 tablespoon of oil) for each egg removed.

Use the two fundamental gluten-free bread recipes on pages 276 and 277 in Chapter 5 together with the "To make vegan" rules above, and use the resulting gluten-free vegan basic recipes as the starting point for whatever bake you want to make.

# Chapter
# 4

# Cs
## Case Studies

Are you overwhelmed yet? I know from experience that entering the world of free-from baking and recipe modification can be rather bamboozling. There are so many ingredients and ingredient properties to keep track of, ratios to consider, and things to tweak. But I want to make all of this information as accessible, interesting and fun as possible – because it is all of that, while also being a total game-changer.

While the rules for adapting recipes into their various free-from versions in the previous chapter are probably the most important part of this book, I'm a big believer in giving you not just the information, but also the insight into and understanding of how it works.

I wish I could just pop into your kitchen and take you through the whole process in person, step by step, and explain why eggs, for example, can be a pain to substitute in baking (but it definitely can be done, I promise!) while we snack on chocolate chip cookies, still warm and gooey from the oven. That is, unfortunately, impossible. So, here's the next best thing: what I like to call "case studies" – or "worked examples", if I may borrow the term from high-school maths and science textbooks. Don't worry, though, these worked examples are much more fun and you get to enjoy incredibly delicious results in the end.

The case studies take you through the whole process of adapting a recipe from beginning to end, explaining each change in the recipe as I take it from the "regular" original to the gluten-, dairy- and egg-free versions, and then also to the vegan and gluten-free vegan variations. Through them, you'll be able to see how and why the rules work, in the context of actual real-life recipe examples. And that, in turn, will hopefully help the rules make more sense as you go on to use them in your own baking.

# How the Case Studies Work

For each case study, I begin by introducing the original regular recipe and any particularly important ingredients or methods that make it work. I've made sure to start with the best possible recipe each time (remember my top tips for adapting recipes on page 45).

Then, I'll take you through each of the free-from variations in turn, explaining which properties of the eliminated ingredient(s) are crucial to consider and how we can substitute them in this free-from version to get the best possible result.

Importantly, the purpose of these case studies and all the variations isn't just to show you how to get from point A (the regular version) to the best possible point B (the free-from variations), but also how to get there in the fewest possible steps. I'm not just showing you how to adapt each recipe to be gluten-, dairy- or egg-free or vegan – I've also simplified the whole process, so that it's straightforward to apply in your own kitchen.

Along the way, you'll encounter photos that compare the free-from versions to their regular counterpart, so you can actually see the difference between them for yourself. I want you to be able to observe the texture and appearance of the bakes, and how they (do or don't) change as we remove and substitute the various ingredients.

Then, there's the actual recipes. For each case study, I've condensed all the different variations into a single recipe with a table instead of the usual ingredients list and one (or two, if necessary) set of instructions. The ingredients table has several purposes: for one, it makes my inner spreadsheet-loving nerd very happy – but, more importantly, it allows you to compare the ingredients and their quantities for all the different variations in one place, as a nice overview of all the changes. And it also prevents repetition: there's little point in repeating almost identical recipes over and over with a few minor variations here and there.

The findings and the rules that I've derived based on all these case studies are compiled in the previous chapter (see pages 48–85), and I've made sure to reference them at the relevant points in each case study.

## Why these specific case-study recipes?

The selection of the case-study recipes isn't random. I've chosen the fundamental recipes from which many other recipes follow and which also allow me to explain the basic rules of recipe modification – those rules that crop up again and again, so you really need to know and understand them.

Let's look at the example of the buttery vanilla cake (page 95). You can take that simple vanilla cake recipe (and any dietary variation of it) and transform it into hundreds of other recipes – both in terms of the flavour profile and in terms of the type of cake you make. You can use it as the basis to make everything from a raspberry and lemon traybake (by adding lemon zest and fresh raspberries to the batter, and baking it in a 23x33cm/9x13in baking tin) to a hazelnut and milk chocolate layer cake (by adding ground toasted hazelnuts to the batter, baking it in several round cake tins, and sandwiching everything together with some milk-chocolate frosting).

At the same time, because the vanilla cake is such a fundamental recipe that numerous other recipes are based on, the rules for adapting it to become, for example, gluten- and egg-free also apply to all those other bakes. So, that one simple vanilla cake, along with all the rules for adapting it to be free-from, really opens the door to an endless number of other bakes.

## But where's the bread?

If you look through this chapter, you'll notice that there's no case study focusing on bread. While there are rules for adapting bread recipes to be dairy-free, egg-free and vegan in the previous chapter, there are no rules for making them gluten-free or gluten-free vegan (see page 84).

That doesn't mean that there are no bread recipes in this book – quite the opposite! You can find gluten-free bread recipes on pages 297–306, an egg-free brioche recipe on page 387, a vegan brioche recipe on page 422 and gluten-free vegan bread recipes on pages 457–462.

In addition, there is a detailed section all about gluten-free bread in the gluten-free chapter that begins on page 272, where I've also given you two fundamental gluten-free bread recipes: for a simple non-enriched loaf and for (sweet or savoury) brioche dough. You can use these basic recipes to make all sorts of different variations, by playing around with the flavours and shaping. I've done precisely that in the gluten-free chapter to make a honey and sesame artisan loaf (page 297), chocolate-stuffed braided brioche muffins (page 301) and cheesy garlic pull-apart bread (page 305).

# Cakes

Let me start with a potentially controversial statement: the best cakes I've ever made or eaten were all gluten-free. And, importantly, they were also the easiest to make. Now, that's not just me saying it because I got used to gluten-free baking over the years – even my non-gluten-free taste testers preferred them over their wheat-based equivalents.

With gluten-free cakes, it's much easier to achieve a tender, delicate texture that simply melts in your mouth. You also don't have to worry about over-mixing the batter, as there's no gluten to develop that would make your cake rubbery or dense or result in "tunnelling" – those rather unsightly holes running through your cake that you can discover only when you cut into your wheat-flour-containing creation.

Truthfully, I've often found making cakes with wheat flour rather stressful, with the threat of over-mixing constantly looming over me. But then, I decided to take a page out of the gluten-free baking book and replaced some of the plain (all-purpose) wheat flour in my non-gluten-free cakes with cornflour – or cornstarch, as it's better known in the US (other starches, such as potato starch or tapioca starch, work as well). This effectively reduces the total protein (gluten) content in the flour – in a way mimicking what those in the US call "cake flour", although that has a few additional characteristics – and thus reduces the chances of over-mixing while also giving the final, baked cakes a more tender, plush crumb.

You can replace up to about 10% of the weight of the plain (all-purpose) wheat flour in a cake recipe with an equal weight of cornflour (cornstarch) for a more tender, plush crumb and a reduced chance of over-mixing the batter.

Before we get to the science of the different cake case studies, let's first define the types of cake we'll be considering. Very broadly speaking, you can divide cakes into four different types: pound cakes, butter cakes, foam cakes and sponge cakes (see opposite).

Of course, most cake recipes don't fall strictly within the limits of these groups. For example, many layer and loaf cakes have characteristics of a butter cake, but with extra moisture sources added, such as milk, yogurt, sour cream, coffee or citrus juice – either to add flavour or to make them extra moist and tender.

Now, this might all seem like a lot of unnecessary additional information (who cares about what exact type of cake we're making, as long as it tastes amazing?) but, as you'll soon see, different types of cake require different adjustments to make them free-from. For example, to make an egg-free butter cake requires very different tweaks to making an egg-free sponge cake – after all, in the latter case, we're talking about a cake that relies on whipped eggs for its texture.

# Four cake types

## 1.
### Pound cakes

These have a high proportion of butter and they get their name from the fact that, traditionally, they contain a pound each of butter, sugar, eggs and flour. There are typically no raising agents in the batter and all the lift comes from creaming together the butter and sugar. These types of cake are typically moist, rich, buttery and fairly dense.

## 2.
### Butter cakes

These are similar to pound cakes in that they contain a high proportion of butter and there's no source of moisture in the batter other than eggs, but they do contain some raising agents. They are moist, soft and on the denser side, although they're typically not as dense as pound cakes.

## 3.
### Foam cakes

These have a high proportion of eggs and they contain no raising agents. Instead, they rely on whipped eggs for their rise and fluffy texture. They typically contain no fat other than that coming from the egg yolks.

## 4.
### Sponge cakes

These are similar to foam cakes in that they rely on whipped eggs for their rise and structure, but they might contain some raising agents and extra fat.

Regular

Gluten-free

Dairy-free

Egg-free

Vegan

Gluten-free vegan

**Rules for adapting buttery cakes**

**p.52**

# Case Study 1:
# Buttery Vanilla Cake

The starting point of this first case study is a regular buttery vanilla cake that uses plain all-purpose wheat flour, cornflour (cornstarch), baking powder, sugar, salt, dairy butter, eggs, dairy milk and vanilla. The cake is light golden in colour, with a beautifully caramelized exterior. The texture is soft, moist and spongy, with an even aeration (that is, the holes in the crumb are even both in size and in distribution), and very slight doming.

The buttery vanilla cake we're considering here is closest in type to a butter cake, but it contains milk as an additional source of moisture. In terms of texture, it's softer, fluffier and has a more open crumb compared to a typical butter cake. This is the classic cake you'd use to make a layer cake, like a birthday cake.

**NOTE: BUTTER VS OIL**

If you want to make an even softer and fluffier cake with a greater rise, and one that stays softer for longer, you can substitute half of the butter for a neutral-tasting oil, such as sunflower, vegetable or rapeseed (canola) oil. That's mainly because oil is a liquid fat and butter is a solid fat at and around room temperature. In my experiments, a cake made with a mixture of butter and oil was about 4–5mm (⅛–¼in) taller than the cake made with only butter.

Regular dairy butter is composed of about 80% fat, 15% water and 5% milk solids – so, when you're swapping butter for oil, it's not a 1:1 substitution. Instead, you need to replace the butter with 80% of oil and 15% of milk. In terms of weight, that means that you need to multiply the weight of the butter by 0.8 to get the weight of the oil and 0.15 to get the weight of the milk. In terms of volume, you need to use 7 tablespoons (100ml) of oil and 1 tablespoon (15ml) of milk for every stick (115g) of butter you're replacing.

Finally, before we get to the actual recipe-adapting part, there's one more thing to consider: the way in which we prepare the cake batter. There are three main creaming methods by which to prepare buttery cakes: the standard, the reverse and the all-in-one creaming method.

**The standard creaming method** involves creaming the butter and sugar together until pale and fluffy, adding the eggs one at a time (mixing well after each addition) and then adding the dry and the wet ingredients in alternating batches, starting and ending with the dry. This method is all about preserving the butter emulsion and it incorporates a lot of additional air into the batter by mechanical means. The result is a very fluffy cake with an open crumb. However, this method often results in an uneven aeration and significant doming, which can be a problem with layer cakes (although you can, of course, always trim off any doming).

**The reverse creaming method** was pioneered by US baker and author Rose Levy Beranbaum. It involves working the butter (and other fats) into the dry ingredients and sugar until you get a texture resembling breadcrumbs. Then, you add the wet ingredients in several batches, mix well until you get a smooth batter, and bake. This method incorporates little to no air into the batter, so the cake relies almost exclusively on the raising agents for its rise.

The result is a more even aeration and less doming. Cakes prepared using this method typically have a very delicate, tender, melt-in-the-mouth crumb. An additional benefit when making cakes with regular wheat flour is that the fat particles coat the flour particles, which inhibits gluten formation.

**The all-in-one creaming method** is what you might use to prepare a Victoria sponge, where you put all the cake ingredients into a bowl, mix them all together into a smooth batter and bake. I don't use this method a lot as it doesn't give you precise control over the way in which the ingredients are combined. However, a similar method using melted rather than softened butter becomes important when you make egg-free, vegan and gluten-free vegan cakes.

To make this regular buttery vanilla cake, I recommend using the reverse creaming method. It gives a wonderfully soft and tender cake with a fairly flat top, which is perfect for assembling layer cakes.

Now that the scene is set, let's look at how you can make this simple vanilla cake X-free, where X = gluten, dairy, eggs or a combination of these.

## Gluten-free

To make the gluten-free variation, there are two main things to consider:

1. **The greater moisture absorption capacity of gluten-free flours and blends (the fat response is less important here so we can ignore it; see page 42).**

2. **The need for a binder, which mimics the effects of gluten and prevents the cake from being too crumbly.**

You can solve **1** by reducing the amount of flour by 10% – in practical terms, multiply the weight of the flour by 0.9 or reduce the volume of flour by about 1½ tablespoons per cup of flour used in the recipe, and **2** by adding xanthan gum, which acts as a binder or gluten substitute. (If you were to use the same amount of flour as in a wheat-based cake, your gluten-free cake would turn out too dry.)

In general, for cakes and similar bakes, I recommend using ¼ teaspoon of xanthan gum per 120g (1 cup) of gluten-free flour blend. If you're using a store-bought gluten-free flour blend that already contains xanthan gum or other binders, you don't need to add any extra when making a buttery vanilla cake or other similar cakes, so just omit it from the recipe.

Once you make these two changes, all other things stay the same. (If you're starting from a vegan cake and you want to make it gluten-free, you might need to add some almond flour to achieve the best possible crumb – see pages 101 and 102.) The resulting gluten-free sponge is almost indistinguishable from the original, regular version. In fact, I'd go as far as to say that it's slightly better.

**NOTE**
Because the gluten-free batter contains 10% less flour compared to the wheat-based equivalent, it will be slightly runnier and it's more likely to appear curdled or split. When using the reverse creaming method, and especially if you're working in a warm kitchen, it can happen that your flour-butter mixture will be somewhat clumpy and paste-like, rather than looking like breadcrumbs. Don't worry if any of this happens – your cake will still be perfectly delicious.

To make the dairy-free cake, we need to substitute both the butter and the milk with their dairy-free equivalents. Although vegan butter often has a lower fat content and therefore contains a higher proportion of water compared to dairy butter, we can disregard this difference as long as we use a firm vegan butter block with a fat content of around 75–80%.

Similarly, although whole dairy milk and dairy-free milks have slightly different fat contents, this amounts to a very small difference of only about 3–3.5g of fat per 100g of milk. So, we can safely assume that we can substitute the dairy butter and milk with an equal weight or volume of their dairy-free equivalents.

As far as choosing a dairy-free milk is concerned, you can use the majority of dairy-free alternatives such as almond, soy, rice or oat milk – most of these are predominantly composed of water, so they are interchangeable. I don't recommend using canned coconut milk owing to its high fat content, which can make the cake greasy, dense or oily.

You also have the option of replacing the dairy butter with a neutral-tasting oil, such as sunflower, vegetable or rapeseed (canola) oil. As I've mentioned before, this isn't a 1:1 substitution, because while oil is essentially 100% fat, butter comprises about 80% fat, 15% water and 5% milk solids (if we round off all the numbers to the nearest 5%).

This means that for this dairy-free cake, you need to replace the butter with 80% of oil and 15% of dairy-free milk. In terms of weight, that means that you need to multiply the weight of the butter by 0.8 to get the weight of the oil and 0.15 to get the weight of the milk (for example, you can replace 100g of butter with 80g of oil and 15g of dairy-free milk). In terms of volume, you need to use 7 tablespoons (100ml) of oil and 1 tablespoon (15ml) of milk for every stick (115g) of butter you're replacing.

The resulting dairy-free cake is incredibly similar to the regular version. In fact, the dairy-free cake stays moister and softer for longer compared to the regular one. That's because, regardless of whether you're using vegan butter or oil, the fat you're using is largely composed of fats that are naturally liquid at room temperature (for example, major components of vegan butter are often rapeseed/canola or sunflower oil) as compared to the dairy butter, which is solid at room temperature.

The only notable differences between the regular and the dairy-free cake are the lack of that typical buttery flavour and the reduced browning of the dairy-free version.

**NOTE: THE MAILLARD REACTION**

**Dairy milk solids are largely composed of casein protein and whey protein, and it's these protein particles that are responsible for the browning through a process known as the Maillard reaction. This is a chemical reaction where amino acids (the building blocks of proteins) react with sugars in the presence of heat. Because dairy-free milk, vegan butter, and oil don't contain these milk solids, and therefore the proteins and amino acids necessary for this reaction, the dairy-free cake doesn't brown as easily as one made using dairy.**

# Egg-free

Out of all the free-from modifications, replacing eggs is definitely the trickiest. Eggs play a multitude of important roles in the recipe for vanilla cake. On the whole, egg whites are the more important part of the egg for creating the typical spongy, fluffy texture of cakes. If you think back to Chapter 2, you'll remember that I categorized egg whites as structure-providing and aerating ingredients that also act as a moisture source (see page 38).

So, in order to create the perfect egg-free buttery vanilla cake, you need to increase the amount of the only other structure-providing ingredient (the flour), add an alternative moisture source, and increase the amount of raising agent to provide the additional lift that would otherwise have come from the egg whites.

Increasing the amount of flour is very important here. Without the extra flour, the cake would lack the necessary structure to hold up to the tenderizing (structure-destroying) effects of the butter, which would result in a pudding-y, stodgy texture of the final, baked cake.

To replace some of the moisture that would have been added by eggs, you can either increase the amount of milk that's already in the recipe or add some unsweetened plain or Greek-style yogurt. Either works great as an alternative moisture source.

It may seem rather counterintuitive to be adding both flour and milk or yogurt to the cake batter when replacing eggs – after all, in a way, they almost cancel each other out as far as removing and adding moisture goes. However, as well as mimicking the texture of the regular cake, the aim is to keep the height or thickness of the egg-free cake as similar to the original as possible. And that's why we're adding both a dry and a wet ingredient as part of the process for replacing the eggs.

In addition to increasing the amount of raising agent in the recipe, it's helpful to add a small amount of an acidic ingredient: in this case, apple cider vinegar. The vinegar reacts with the basic component of baking powder and gives it an extra activity boost, making the cake even softer and fluffier – and thus closer to its regular starting point. And don't worry, you can't taste the vinegar in the final, baked cake.

For each egg or egg white removed, you therefore need to:

- **Increase the amount of flour by 20g (2½ tablespoons) – true for regular wheat flour and for gluten-free flour blends.**

- **Add 30g (2 tablespoons) of whole milk or unsweetened plain or Greek-style yogurt (true for both dairy and dairy-free ingredients).**

- **Add ¼ teaspoon of baking powder and ½ teaspoon of apple cider vinegar.**

As an aside, all that tells you why the popular "egg replacements" are usually a gross oversimplification. While you might find all kinds of advice online that instructs you to replace an egg with a ¼ cup of mashed banana or apple sauce or a "chia (flax) egg" or whatever else the latest claim is, "egg substitutes" just don't work. They usually focus on just one aspect of what eggs actually bring to a bake (usually the moisture and binding elements) and neglect all else – frequently to the detriment of the texture of your bake.

### The preparation method

Even after you've correctly adjusted all the ingredient quantities, egg-free cakes made with softened butter and either the standard or the reverse creaming method (page 95) still tend to turn out rather dense, doughy and/or greasy, and they also often collapse as they come out of the oven. This is primarily a concern for the standard creaming method, but neither method will give good results. It turns out that the answer is using melted butter and a variation on the all-in-one mixing method, where you mix together all the wet and all the dry ingredients separately, and then briefly and gently whisk them together to get a smooth, runny cake batter with no flour clumps. There are two reasons why changing the state of the butter and using the simple wet+dry mixing method are effective:

1. **It achieves the correct batter fluidity** For egg-free cakes (and also for vegan and gluten-free vegan ones), you want the batter to be fairly loose and runny, so that it rises easily in the oven. The simplest way to achieve this texture is to use either melted butter, or oil. (By comparison, batter made with softened butter tends to be much thicker and it doesn't rise as efficiently during baking.)

2. **It minimizes the gluten development** Using melted butter and the simple wet+dry mixing method means that you have to mix the batter as little as possible, which keeps the gluten development in check. Cakes that use softened butter typically require more mixing, which negatively affects their baked texture.

The issue of gluten development is a more pressing one in egg-free (and vegan) cakes. While milk and yogurt are the perfect alternative moisture sources, they're also much better at promoting gluten development than eggs are. The standard creaming method requires a lot of mixing owing to the gradual addition of ingredients. This means that by the time the standard-creamed cake batter is ready to be baked, too much gluten development has taken place – and that's responsible for the rather unfortunate final cake texture.

This effect isn't as prominent with the reverse creaming method, where the fat particles coat the flour particles, thus reducing the gluten development. Nonetheless, even the reverse creaming method requires more mixing than the simple wet+dry mixing method.

Using melted butter and the simple method of just whisking the wet ingredients with the dry gives a much looser and runnier batter with minimal gluten development. Consequently, the cake rises beautifully in the oven to form a slightly domed top that it retains even after cooling, and it has a beautiful open, tender, even crumb that's pretty much indistinguishable from that of the regular version. There's no doughiness and there are no dense areas, and the texture is perfectly springy and spongy, just like any good cake should be.

# Vegan

With the dairy-free and egg-free variations perfected, making the vegan version of the buttery vanilla cake is as easy as combining all the changes (and rules) required for the two. That's really all there is to it!

In practice, that means that you need to make all the same changes to make up for the absence of the structure-, lift- and moisture-providing egg whites and swap the dairy ingredients for the dairy-free equivalents. When it comes to replacing butter, you can use either a vegan butter block or a neutral-tasting oil such as sunflower, vegetable or rapeseed (canola) oil; just remember that the latter isn't a 1:1 butter substitute as butter is only 80% fat – for more details, see the dairy-free section on page 97.

Just like with the egg-free cake, it's best to use melted (not softened) vegan butter, or oil, and the simple wet+dry mixing method where you whisk the wet ingredients with the dry until only just combined to get a fairly runny cake batter with minimal gluten development (see page 99).

The resulting vegan vanilla cake is deliciously soft, fluffy and moist, with a tender crumb but also enough sturdiness that you can easily trim and handle it if making a layer cake. It's very pale golden on top and around the edges – the lack of browning is because of the lack of milk solids, just as with the dairy-free version (see page 97). It has a slightly domed top and it's only minimally shorter than the regular equivalent.

If we compare vegan cakes made with either melted vegan butter or oil, the former has a slightly richer and more well-rounded flavour. So, if you're making a simple vanilla cake with no other intense flavourings, I recommend using a good-quality vegan butter block whose flavour you really like instead of oil – you will definitely be able to taste it in the final, baked cake. Furthermore, be generous with the vanilla and you could also add a drop or two of almond extract – not so much as to be overpowering, but just to give a buttery undertone.

## Gluten-free vegan

The gluten-free vegan version combines all the gluten-, dairy- and egg-free adjustments we've looked at so far, with a few extra tweaks. You need to account for the greater moisture absorption capacity of gluten-free flours, the lack of gluten, the absence of structure-, lift- and moisture-providing egg whites, and the fact that you need to swap dairy ingredients for their dairy-free equivalents.

Note that for the gluten-free adjustment, you need to decrease the amount of flour by 10% (equivalent to reducing the volume of flour by about 1½ tablespoons for each cup of flour in the recipe) because gluten-free flours absorb more moisture than regular wheat flour. However, to account for the absence of eggs, you need to add 20g (2½ tablespoons) of flour for each egg or egg white removed. The order in which you do the calculation doesn't really matter, as long as you're substituting a maximum of 2–3 eggs (or egg whites) per cake sponge.

If you hate maths, I'm really sorry for this part, but I think it's a good way to clarify. This is honestly as difficult as the maths will ever get in this book. Here's a worked example based on the buttery vanilla cake recipe (note that I'm rounding off all the values to the nearest 5g):

If we start with a regular cake that contains 160g of flour and 2 eggs, we need to reduce the amount of flour by 10%, that is:

**160g x 0.9 = 144g (145g to the nearest 5g)**

And then we need to add 20g of flour for each egg removed:

**145g + 20g + 20g = 185g**

So, you need a total of 185g of flour in the gluten-free vegan version. See? Not that tricky at all!

In addition to all the changes mentioned so far, there's something else we need to consider. You see, if you were to make just the changes listed above for this gluten-free vegan buttery vanilla cake, it would come out of the oven slightly gummy – which is definitely not something you'd expect for a gluten-free vegan bake! And that's not because of the xanthan gum. Instead, it's a result of the interactions that happen in the oven between the gluten-free flours and the oil or oil-based vegan butter.

This gumminess is very specific to gluten-free vegan vanilla buttery cakes and similar bakes, like vanilla cupcakes or muffins. It's absent in cakes that contain ground nuts, cocoa powder or melted chocolate in the batter, and it also doesn't apply to banana or pumpkin bread. (It's also not relevant if you're making a gluten- and egg-free cake that contains dairy!)

To avoid this strangely gummy texture in these specific instances, you need to add some almond flour to the cake batter: specifically, you need to add 20g (3½ tablespoons) of almond flour per 120g (1 cup) of gluten-free flour blend used in the recipe. This will give you a wonderfully tender and delicate texture that's just crumbly enough (no gumminess in sight). The almond flour also adds some extra richness and it helps with the browning, which would otherwise be greatly reduced because of the absence of the dairy milk solids and eggs. If you have a nut allergy, you can use an equal weight of finely ground sunflower seeds instead –

they're a great alternative as they're fairly neutral in flavour – they will just make your vanilla cake a tiny bit darker in colour.

This small extra tweak allows you to make the most perfect gluten-free vegan vanilla cake. It has a texture that's incredibly similar to its regular counterpart: it's soft, spongy and tender, with a well-defined open crumb – no stodgy, gummy, doughy or pudding-y texture here! It has a good rise, with a slightly rounded top and, importantly, no collapsed or sunken centre. It's slightly shorter than the regular version but the height difference is actually surprisingly small considering that we've removed all of the usual structural ingredients: gluten-containing wheat flour and eggs.

*With almond flour*   *No almond flour*

Just like with the egg-free and vegan versions, it's best to use melted rather than softened vegan butter and the wet+dry mixing method when making the gluten-free vegan buttery vanilla cake. While there's no gluten to develop in this case (and therefore over-mixing isn't an issue), the batter fluidity still matters. With melted butter, you get a highly fluid, runny batter that rises easily in the oven, to give a very tender, open, light crumb. In comparison, the cake made with softened butter has a slightly denser crumb and it's also more likely to collapse in the centre during cooling.

## OPTIMIZING FLAVOUR

**To make your gluten-free vegan cakes as delicious as possible, there are three main things to consider.**

1. The flavour of the gluten-free flour blend stands out in a gluten-free vegan cake. If you don't like the flavour you get with your shop-bought blend, consider making your own homemade version (see page 24). I use a blend of tapioca starch, millet flour and sorghum flour, as that comes closest to the flavour of regular wheat flour.

2. You can really taste the butter alternative – so, for the best flavour, I recommend using a good-quality vegan butter block whose flavour you really like.

3. In a regular cake recipe, you get lots of flavour and richness from the butter and the eggs. In a gluten-free vegan cake, you need to play around with other flavourings. Be generous with the vanilla extract or paste, and try adding a few drops of almond extract: not so much as to be overpowering or to make it an almond cake, but just to give it a subtle rich, buttery undertone.

Regular

Gluten-free

Dairy-free

Egg-free

Vegan

Gluten-free
vegan

# Buttery vanilla cake: recipe

This recipe makes one 20cm (8in) sponge or two 15cm (6in) sponges for the vanilla cake. Double the recipe to make a two-layer 20cm (8in) cake. You can pair the sponges with any of the frostings on pages 469–79 or with your own favourite frosting recipe. The baking times refer to one 20cm (8in) cake sponge.

| | DIET | | | | | |
|---|---|---|---|---|---|---|
| | **Regular** | **Gluten-free** | **Dairy-free** | **Egg-free** | **Vegan** | **GF Vegan** |
| plain flour [1] | 160g*<br>1⅓ cups* | 145g<br>1 cup + 3½ tbsp | 160g*<br>1⅓ cups* | 200g*<br>1⅔ cups* | 200g*<br>1⅔ cups* | 185g<br>1½ cups + 1 tbsp |
| almond flour [2] | / | / | / | / | / | 30g<br>5 tbsp |
| caster or granulated sugar | 125g<br>½ cup + 2 tbsp | 125g<br>½ cup + 2 tbsp | 125g<br>½ cup + 2 tbsp | 125g<br>½ cup + 2 tbsp | 125g<br>½ cup + 2 tbsp | 125g<br>½ cup + 2 tbsp |
| baking powder | 1½ tsp | 1½ tsp | 1½ tsp | 2 tsp | 2 tsp | 2 tsp |
| xanthan gum | / | ¼ tsp** | / | / | / | ¼ tsp ** |
| salt | ¼ tsp | ¼ tsp | ¼ tsp | ¼ tsp | ¼ tsp | ¼ tsp |
| unsalted butter [3] | 115g (softened)<br>1 stick | 115g (softened)<br>1 stick | 115g (softened)<br>1 stick | 115g (melted)<br>1 stick | 115g (melted)<br>1 stick | 115g (melted)<br>1 stick |
| eggs, room temp [4] | 2 | 2 | 2 | / | / | / |
| milk, room temp [5] | 90g<br>⅓ cup + 2 tsp | 90g<br>⅓ cup + 2 tsp | 90g<br>⅓ cup + 2 tsp | 150g<br>½ cup + 2 tbsp | 150g<br>½ cup + 2 tbsp | 150g<br>½ cup + 2 tbsp |
| vanilla paste [6] | ½ tsp | ½ tsp | ½ tsp | ½ tsp | ½ tsp | ½ tsp |
| apple cider vinegar | / | / | / | 1 tsp | 1 tsp | 1 tsp |
| **Preparation method** | Method 1:<br>reverse creaming | Method 1:<br>reverse creaming | Method 1:<br>reverse creaming | Method 2:<br>wet+dry | Method 2:<br>wet+dry | Method 2:<br>wet+dry |

## METHOD 1: Reverse creaming method (egg-containing cakes)

1. Adjust the oven rack to the middle position and pre-heat the oven to 180°C/350°F. Lightly butter a 20cm (8in) round baking tin and line the bottom with baking paper.

2. In a large bowl (or the bowl of a stand mixer, if using), sift together the flour, sugar, baking powder, xanthan gum (if using) and salt.

3. Add the softened butter and, by hand using your fingertips, with a hand-held mixer fitted with the double beaters or with a stand mixer fitted with the paddle, work it into the dry ingredients until you get a mixture resembling breadcrumbs.

4. In a separate bowl or jug, whisk together the eggs, milk and vanilla. Add them to the flour-butter mixture in 2–3 batches, mixing well after each addition, until you get a smooth cake batter with no flour clumps. Scrape along the bottom and inside of the bowl occasionally to prevent any unmixed patches.

5. Transfer the batter into the prepared baking tin and smooth out the top. Tap it a few times on the work surface to get rid of any trapped air pockets.

6. Bake for about 20–25 minutes or until the cake is well risen, a toothpick or cake tester inserted into the centre comes out clean, and the cake starts pulling away from the sides of the tin.

7. Allow the cake to cool in the tin for about 10 minutes, then turn it out of the tin on to a wire rack to cool completely.

## METHOD 2: Wet+dry mixing method (eggless cakes)

1. Adjust the oven rack to the middle position and pre-heat the oven to 180°C/350°F. Lightly butter a 20cm (8in) round baking tin and line the bottom with baking paper.

2. In a large bowl, whisk together the dry ingredients: flour, almond flour (if using), sugar, baking powder, xanthan gum (if using) and salt.

3. In a separate large bowl, whisk together the wet ingredients: melted butter, milk, vanilla and apple cider vinegar.

4. Add the wet ingredients to the dry, and whisk well until you get a smooth, fairly runny batter with no flour clumps. Be careful not to over-mix the batter.

5. Transfer the batter into the prepared baking tin and smooth out the top. Tap it a few times on the work surface to get rid of any trapped air pockets.

6. Bake for about 20–25 minutes or until the cake is well risen, a toothpick or cake tester inserted into the centre comes out clean and the cake starts pulling away from the sides of the tin.

7. Allow the cake to cool in the tin for about 10 minutes, then turn it out of the tin on to a wire rack to cool completely.

[1] Either plain (all-purpose) wheat flour or plain gluten-free flour blend. For the latter, use shop-bought or make your own (see page 24).

[2] If you have a nut allergy, use an equal weight of finely ground sunflower seeds.

[3] Either dairy or vegan butter. For the latter, use a firm vegan butter block. For the dairy-free, vegan and GF vegan versions, you can replace the butter with 90g (7 tablespoons) of oil and an extra 15g (1 tablespoon) of dairy-free milk.

[4] UK medium eggs (US large eggs).

[5] Either whole dairy milk or a dairy-free milk, excluding canned coconut milk.

[6] Double the quantity if using vanilla extract.

* For a more tender, plush crumb and a reduced risk of over-mixing, replace up to 10% of the flour with an equal weight of a starch, such as cornflour (cornstarch), potato starch or tapioca starch.

** Omit if your gluten-free flour blend already contains binders.

Regular

Gluten-free

Egg-free

Vegan

Gluten-free vegan

**Rules for adapting chocolate cakes**

↓

**p.55**

# Case Study 2:
# Chocolate Cake with Melted Chocolate in the Batter

**NOTE**

If you're making a chocolate cake that doesn't contain any melted chocolate in the cake batter but instead relies only on cocoa powder for its flavour, it will follow the same rules as the buttery vanilla cake (see Case Study 1, page 95).

I'm a big believer in adding actual melted chocolate into the batter of a chocolate cake instead of relying on only cocoa powder for the flavour. I've made my fair share of all sorts of chocolate cakes, and those with melted chocolate in the sponges were consistently richer in flavour and, for want of a better word, more chocolatey. However, the addition of melted chocolate into chocolate cakes makes adapting them simultaneously easier and also more difficult.

The process is easier because chocolate has a naturally tenderizing effect on cakes (largely because of its acidic pH that boosts the activity of the raising agents), which results in a delicate, tender crumb.

However, the process is also more difficult… and also because chocolate has a naturally tenderizing effect on cakes. If you start out with a recipe that itself isn't optimized in terms of ingredient quantities and ratios, you'll be left with a chocolate cake that crumbles into tiny little pieces the moment you so much as touch it.

To get a perfectly moist, rich, soft and fluffy chocolate cake that melts in your mouth but is also sturdy enough so you can handle, trim and stack it without any issues, your chocolate-cake batter needs to contain a high enough proportion of liquid, or wet ingredients. The liquid can come in the form of milk (regular or dairy-free), water or even coffee.

I usually use water – specifically, boiling water – to "bloom" the cocoa powder. Blooming is simply combining the powder with hot liquid, to bring out its richness and complex flavours.

The large quantity of wet ingredients means that your chocolate cake batter will be rather runny – almost like a thick hot chocolate, which might look a bit odd or feel wrong, but don't worry, that's exactly as it should be.

The choice of fat (butter or oil) is also important. While butter will give you a slightly richer flavour, I recommend using oil as it gives a much better texture – one that's less crumbly and that stays moister for longer. And because the cake contains plenty of other intense flavours (chocolate and cocoa powder), the flavour difference is pretty negligible.

Finally, chocolate cakes with melted chocolate in the cake batter are best baked at 160°C/325°F, a slightly lower-than-usual oven temperature. This is true across the board, from the regular version to all other free-from (gluten-, dairy-, egg-free and so on) variations. Chocolate cakes baked at 160°C/325°F have a more even crumb, less doming and are, crucially, less crumbly than cakes baked at 180°C/350°F.

## Gluten-free

To make a gluten-free chocolate cake, the changes you need to make are similar to those for a buttery vanilla cake (page 96): use a gluten-free flour blend (either shop-bought or homemade, see page 24), reduce the amount of flour by 10% because gluten-free flours absorb more moisture than wheat flour (in practical terms, multiply the weight of the flour by 0.9 or reduce the volume of flour by about 1½ tablespoons per cup of flour), and use xanthan gum.

However, you need to use a larger amount of xanthan gum for a chocolate cake with melted chocolate in the cake batter (compared with that for a vanilla cake). Specifically, you need to use ½ teaspoon of xanthan gum per 120g (1 cup) of gluten-free flour blend (or ¼ teaspoon if your gluten-free flour blend already contains xanthan gum or other binders).

You need this greater quantity of xanthan gum in order to balance out the tenderizing properties of the melted chocolate and to ensure that your gluten-free chocolate cake isn't too delicate and crumbly. Instead, with this larger amount of xanthan gum, the gluten-free version is virtually indistinguishable from the regular equivalent.

Finally, like I've mentioned above, if you're making a gluten-free chocolate cake that doesn't contain any melted chocolate in the batter, then it will follow the same rules and use the same amount of xanthan gum as the buttery vanilla cake: ¼ teaspoon per 120g (1 cup) of gluten-free flour blend (omit if your blend already contains binders).

**NOTE**

If you're starting out with an egg-free or a vegan chocolate cake and you want to make it gluten-free as well, use 1 teaspoon of xanthan gum (rather than ½ teaspoon, see left) – I explain why in the gluten-free vegan section, opposite.

## Dairy-free

The regular chocolate cake that we're considering in this case study is accidentally dairy-free already, as it uses water and oil with no milk, butter or other dairy ingredients in the batter.

However, if you were to start out with a chocolate cake recipe that contains dairy ingredients, the substitutions would be straightforward: simply replace the dairy butter, milk or yogurt with an equal weight or volume of the dairy-free/vegan alternatives. In the case of butter, you could either replace it with a vegan butter block or with a neutral-tasting oil, such as sunflower, vegetable or rapeseed (canola) oil, keeping in mind that while butter has a fat content of only about 80% (with a 15% water content), oil is essentially 100% fat.

This means that you'd need to replace the butter with 80% of oil and 15% of dairy-free milk. In terms of weight, you need to multiply the weight of the butter by 0.8 to get the weight of the oil and 0.15 to get the weight of the milk (for example, you can replace 100g of butter with 80g of oil and 15g of dairy-free milk). In terms of volume, you need to use 7 tablespoons (100ml) of oil and 1 tablespoon (15ml) of milk for every stick (115g) of butter you're replacing.

## Egg-free

As long as you're starting out with a reliable recipe, the changes necessary to make the egg-free version of a chocolate cake are less extensive than those required for a vanilla cake.

Namely, you don't have to alter the amounts of the raising agents in any way. That's because chocolate is acidic, which means that it will react with the raising agents in the cake batter, thus boosting their activity. This adds enough aeration to the egg-free chocolate cake to make up for the absence of the lift-providing eggs – in a way, the melted chocolate carries out a similar role to the apple cider vinegar in the egg-free buttery vanilla cake (see page 98).

So, the only changes you need to make are:

- **Increase the amount of flour by 20g (2½ tablespoons) for each egg removed (as it's the main structure-providing ingredient in the absence of eggs) – true for regular wheat flour and for gluten-free flour.**
- **Add 30g (2 tablespoons) of milk or unsweetened plain or Greek-style yogurt for each egg removed – either works great as an alternative moisture source (true for regular dairy and dairy-free ingredients).**

All other things, including the preparation method, stay the same. And the result is a wonderfully rich, soft chocolate cake that's almost impossible to tell apart from the regular one.

## Vegan

For the vegan chocolate cake, you just need to combine all the dairy-free and egg-free adjustments. It's really as simple as that. The resulting vegan chocolate cake has essentially the same texture, flavour and appearance as the regular equivalent.

## Gluten-free vegan

As you might anticipate, to make the gluten-free vegan version you just have to combine all the changes necessary to make the gluten-, dairy- and egg-free versions – but there is also a small tweak to the amount of xanthan gum.

Whereas you need to use ½ teaspoon of xanthan gum per 120g (1 cup) of gluten-free flour blend when making the gluten-free cake, you need to increase this to 1 teaspoon when making a gluten-free vegan (or gluten- and egg-free) version. That's because you need to add a bit more structure to the cake, considering that it lacks all the usual structure-providing ingredients (gluten and eggs) that would otherwise balance out the tenderizing properties of the melted chocolate in the batter. (Note that if your gluten-free flour blend already contains xanthan gum or other binders, you need to add only ¾ teaspoon.)

Unlike with the buttery vanilla cake, you don't have to add any almond flour to achieve the perfect texture – and that's all thanks to the presence of the melted chocolate in the cake batter.

Once you've made these changes, the gluten-free vegan chocolate cake is incredibly similar to the regular version. It is slightly shorter and a tiny bit more delicate because of the absence of the usual structure-providing ingredients, but it has the same wonderfully moist crumb and rich chocolate flavour, and it's still sturdy enough that you can easily trim and stack it if you're making a layered cake.

# Chocolate cake: recipe

This recipe makes one 20cm (8in) sponge or two 15cm (6in) sponges. Double the recipe to make a two-layer 20cm (8in) cake. You can pair the sponges with any of the frostings on pages 469–79; or use your own favourite frosting recipe. The baking times refer to one 20cm (8in) cake sponge.

| | DIET | | | | | |
|---|---|---|---|---|---|---|
| | **Regular** | **Gluten-free** | **Dairy-free** [1] | **Egg-free** | **Vegan** | **GF Vegan** |
| Dutch processed cocoa powder | 25g<br>¼ cup | 25g<br>¼ cup | 25g<br>¼ cup | 25g<br>¼ cup | 25g<br>¼ cup | 25g<br>¼ cup |
| boiling hot water | 220g<br>¾ cup + 2½ tbsp | 220g<br>¾ cup + 2½ tbsp | 220g<br>¾ cup + 2½ tbsp | 220g<br>¾ cup + 2½ tbsp | 220g<br>¾ cup + 2½ tbsp | 220g<br>¾ cup + 2½ tbsp |
| dark chocolate [2] | 70g<br>2½oz | 70g<br>2½oz | 70g<br>2½oz | 70g<br>2½oz | 70g<br>2½oz | 70g<br>2½oz |
| sunflower oil [3] | 55g<br>¼ cup | 55g<br>¼ cup | 55g<br>¼ cup | 55g<br>¼ cup | 55g<br>¼ cup | 55g<br>¼ cup |
| caster or granulated sugar | 150g<br>¾ cup | 150g<br>¾ cup | 150g<br>¾ cup | 150g<br>¾ cup | 150g<br>¾ cup | 150g<br>¾ cup |
| eggs, room temp [4] | 1 | 1 | 1 | / | / | / |
| milk or yogurt, room temp [5] | / | / | / | 30g<br>2 tbsp | 30g<br>2 tbsp | 30g<br>2 tbsp |
| vanilla paste [6] | ½ tsp | ½ tsp | ½ tsp | ½ tsp | ½ tsp | ½ tsp |
| plain flour [7] | 130g<br>1 cup + 1½ tbsp | 120g<br>1 cup | 130g<br>1 cup + 1½ tbsp | 150g<br>1¼ cup | 150g<br>1¼ cup | 135g<br>1 cup + 2 tbsp |
| baking powder | 1 tsp | 1 tsp | 1 tsp | 1 tsp | 1 tsp | 1 tsp |
| bicarbonate of soda (baking soda) | ½ tsp | ½ tsp | ½ tsp | ½ tsp | ½ tsp | ½ tsp |
| salt | ¼ tsp | ¼ tsp | ¼ tsp | ¼ tsp | ¼ tsp | ¼ tsp |
| xanthan gum | / | ½ tsp* | / | / | / | 1 tsp** |

1. Adjust the oven rack to the middle position and pre-heat the oven to 160°C/325°F. Lightly butter a 20cm (8in) round cake tin and line its bottom with a round of baking paper.

2. In a large bowl, combine the cocoa powder and boiling-hot water, and whisk until combined. Add the chocolate and mix well until it's completely melted. Set aside to cool until lukewarm.

3. Once the mixture has cooled, add the oil, sugar, eggs (if using), milk or yogurt (if using) and vanilla, and whisk well to combine.

4. In a separate bowl, whisk together the flour, baking powder, bicarbonate of soda (baking soda), salt, and xanthan gum (if using).

5. Add the dry ingredients to the wet, and whisk everything together until you get a smooth, runny batter with no flour clumps.

6. Transfer the batter into the prepared baking tin, and lightly tap it on the work surface to level out the batter and remove any large air bubbles.

7. Bake for about 30–35 minutes, or until the cake is well risen and a toothpick or cake tester inserted into the centre comes out clean or with a few moist crumbs attached.

8. Allow the cake to cool in the tin for about 10–15 minutes, then turn it out of the tin on to a wire rack to cool completely.

[1] These are the same quantities as for the regular version, as there is no dairy in the batter.

[2] Use a high-quality chocolate with 60–70% cocoa solids, chopped.

[3] Or use any neutral-tasting oil, such as vegetable or rapeseed (canola) oil. Or, use olive oil for an olive-oil chocolate cake.

[4] UK medium eggs (US large).

[5] Whole dairy milk or a dairy-free milk, excluding canned coconut milk; or unsweetened plain or Greek-style dairy or vegan yogurt.

[6] Double the quantity if using vanilla extract.

[7] Either plain (all-purpose) wheat flour or plain gluten-free flour blend. For the latter, use shop-bought or make your own (see page 24).

* If your gluten-free flour blend already contains binders, use only ¼ teaspoon.

** If your gluten-free flour blend already contains binders, use only ¾ teaspoon.

Regular

Gluten-free

Dairy-free

Egg-free

Vegan

Gluten-free vegan

**Rules for adapting Swiss rolls & sponge cakes**

p.58

# Case Study 3:
# Vanilla Swiss Roll

**NOTE**

There aren't many bakes with particularly complicated adaptation rules. Swiss rolls (especially egg-free, vegan and gluten-free vegan ones) are the exception – you need to adjust a large number of ingredients *and* their quantities. It might be easier to use the optimized free-from Swiss roll recipes on page 120 and adapt them with other flavourings, fillings and glazes, rather than try to achieve the same result by modifying an existing, regular recipe.

Swiss rolls – that is, roulades that comprise a soft and fluffy sponge rolled up with a sweet filling – can be tricky. Many people are hesitant to attempt making even regular ones, made with wheat flour, eggs and dairy, because they're afraid that the delicate sponge will crack on rolling and the whole thing will end in a messy disaster.

Truth be told, I was the same. I didn't make a single Swiss roll for years. But that all changed when I came across the truly brilliant method of assembling Swiss rolls by Stella Parks from Serious Eats – because, as it turns out, the downfall of many Swiss roll recipes isn't the ingredients or the sponge itself, but rather the way in which you roll it up.

The traditional way to assemble Swiss rolls has you roll up the hot sponge in a tea towel, then unroll it once it's cooled and finally roll it up again after you've filled it. That's a lot of rolling and unrolling, and therefore a lot of unnecessary stress placed on what's already a fairly delicate sponge. It's really no wonder that it often ends up cracking!

The method pioneered by Stella Parks is genius in its simplicity: it makes use of the steam generated by the hot sponge to keep it flexible and supple, so that you can roll it up smoothly and effortlessly with no cracking whatsoever. In Stella's method, you cover the hot sponge, straight out of the oven, with a sheet of foil and then leave it to cool to room temperature. This traps the steam released by the sponge within the sponge itself, which preserves its flexibility even after it's cooled down. Then, once the sponge is fully cooled, you can fill it with whatever deliciousness you fancy and roll it up with no problems and no cracking in sight.

My method of assembling Swiss rolls is essentially the same, but I dust the hot sponge with some icing (powdered) sugar and cover it first with a clean tea towel and then cover it with the foil. This minimizes the amount of condensation on the bottom of the foil, which prevents it from sticking to the sponge.

In terms of its composition, the regular vanilla Swiss roll that is the starting point of this case study belongs to the sponge cake category (see page 93): it relies on whipped eggs for its rise and structure, but it also contains some raising agents (baking powder and bicarbonate of soda/baking soda) to ensure that it's perfectly fluffy. It also has some extra fat (melted butter) for richness and flavour, and to keep it more supple.

The method of making the regular sponge relies on whipping the eggs and sugar until the mixture is pale, very fluffy, about tripled in volume and you reach the ribbon stage – which means that when you lift the whisk out of the mixture, the batter should fall in thick trails, and leave a "ribbon" on top of the mixture for a second or two before it disappears into the bulk. Then, add the melted butter and vanilla, followed by the dry ingredients. This is a really quick and easy way to prepare the sponge and, as long as you make sure that you've whipped the eggs and sugar for long enough, it produces consistently soft, fluffy and delicious results.

Combined with the failsafe rolling method, this way to prepare Swiss rolls produces outstanding results: a soft, fluffy, delicate texture and a perfect swirl with no cracking – and it truly couldn't be easier.

Choosing your filling can be just as important as the way in which you prepare and roll the sponge. The filling is, of course, largely determined by what kind of flavour you want your Swiss roll to be. But if you're a beginner when it comes to making Swiss rolls, if your previous attempts had mixed results and, as you'll soon see, especially if you're making egg-free, vegan or gluten-free vegan Swiss rolls, then the texture of the filling is also very important. I recommend using quite stable, sturdy fillings, such as buttercream, ganache or (stabilized) whipped cream – these will give your Swiss roll much more structure than a looser, "slippery" filling like jam. Essentially, these sturdier fillings hold the rolled-up sponge in place and thus even further prevent cracking. Jam, on the other hand, will often allow the sponge to slide all over the place, which can increase the likelihood of cracking, especially if you're making a Swiss roll that doesn't have the benefit of the structure- (and flexibility-) providing eggs.

## Gluten-free

The main problem commonly encountered with gluten-free Swiss rolls is that the absence of gluten makes them more fragile than their wheat-containing counterpart and they're therefore more prone to cracking. However, if you use the rolling method outlined on page 113 along with a slightly larger amount of xanthan gum, the gluten-free Swiss roll is just as easy to make and roll up as the regular version – and with no cracking!

While many gluten-free cakes, like the gluten-free buttery vanilla cake (page 96), require only ¼ teaspoon of xanthan gum per 120g (1 cup) of gluten-free flour blend to achieve the perfect texture, you need to use ¾ teaspoon when making a gluten-free Swiss roll. This larger quantity of xanthan gum gives the sponge just enough extra flexibility that you can roll it up smoothly without cracking (with the help of the optimized rolling method, of course). If your gluten-free flour blend already contains xanthan gum or other binders, then you need to add only ½ teaspoon per 120g (1 cup) of gluten-free flour blend.

This larger quantity of xanthan gum doesn't make the sponge gummy or tough in any way – it's still perfectly soft, fluffy and tender, and almost indistinguishable from its regular equivalent. The sponge thickness is also pretty much the same.

Just like with the buttery vanilla cake, you need to take into account the fact that gluten-free flours and blends absorb more moisture than wheat flour (as the moisture response is more important than the fat response here; see page 42). So, to prevent your gluten-free sponge from being too dry and therefore possibly also too crumbly, you need to reduce the amount of flour by 10%. In practice, this is equivalent to multiplying the weight of the flour by 0.9 or, if you're using cups (volume measurement), to reducing the volume of flour by about 1½ tablespoons per cup of flour in the recipe.

These three simple things (the rolling method, the increased amount of xanthan gum and the reduced amount of flour) allow you to achieve a truly perfect swirl and a fluffy, melt-in-the-mouth crumb on your gluten-free Swiss roll. (If you're starting from a vegan Swiss roll and you want to make it gluten-free as well, you might need to add some almond flour to achieve the best possible crumb – you can read more about this on page 119.)

# Dairy-free

The dairy-free adjustments are undoubtedly the easiest: just replace the regular dairy butter with an equal weight or volume of a vegan butter block – that's all there is to it!

For an even fluffier sponge, you can instead swap the dairy butter for oil. In that case, use only 80% of the weight of the butter, as butter is only about 80% fat whereas oil is 100% fat (note that the quantity of butter that you're replacing is fairly small in most Swiss-roll recipes, so you don't have to account for the difference in the moisture content between butter and oil).

The end result is a gorgeous dairy-free Swiss roll with a perfect swirl, a soft and fluffy texture, and amazing flavour. The only minor difference between the dairy-free and the regular version is that there's slightly less browning on the sponge in the former case because of the absence of the dairy milk solids (just like with the buttery vanilla cake on page 97). But that's only a tiny difference, and in all other aspects, the regular and the dairy-free Swiss rolls are pretty much indistinguishable.

When it comes to filling your dairy-free Swiss roll, I recommend having a look at the dairy-free frosting recipes on pages 469–79, there are plenty of options to choose from.

# Egg-free

The egg-free Swiss roll has been, without a doubt, the trickiest thing to figure out and perfect in the process of writing this book – it's given me many a headache. That's because regular Swiss rolls rely significantly on the eggs for their texture and flexibility, and without them the likelihood of a cracked roll is greatly increased (even with the typically failsafe rolling method).

With that in mind, let's just get one thing out of the way: you will get a crack here or there when you make an egg-free (or a vegan or a gluten-free vegan) Swiss roll. Without the eggs, you simply can't achieve the same amount of flexibility and elasticity, especially if you want to keep the sponge beautifully soft, fluffy and tender at the same time.

It's a balance – you need to accept the presence of a few small cracks to achieve the perfect texture... or you need to accept a gummier, denser texture if you want the egg-free Swiss roll to be 100% crack-free. Personally, I find the texture more important – I want the egg-free Swiss roll to be a complete and total joy to eat, so I'm willing to accept a small crack or two. But don't worry: you'll still get a gorgeous swirl, it just won't be quite as perfect as the regular version. And with a generous dusting of icing (powdered) sugar, a drizzle of ganache or a bit of frosting, you won't even notice those tiny imperfections.

That's also why I recommend using quite stable, sturdy fillings when making egg-free (or vegan or gluten-free vegan) Swiss rolls: fillings such as whipped cream, buttercream or ganache will give your Swiss roll much more structure than a "slippery", loose filling like jam. Those sturdier fillings will stabilize your rolled-up sponge to hold it in place, and thus prevent any further cracking. Jam, on the other hand, will allow the sponge to slide.

With these caveats out of the way, let's focus on how you can actually achieve an egg-free Swiss roll that's as close as possible to the original, regular version – because it is possible, and it can be done. A few changes that you need to make should actually be familiar from the egg-free section of the buttery vanilla cake case study on page 98.

**The ingredients**

Spoiler alert: you don't need to use aquafaba (the liquid from a tin of chickpeas that's indispensable for making egg-free or vegan meringue; see page 358). In fact, you *shouldn't* use aquafaba – it won't help the texture or the flexibility of your egg-free sponge in any way. At first glance, aquafaba might seem like the obvious choice because egg-containing Swiss rolls start by whipping eggs and sugar together until fluffy and you can do something similar with aquafaba. But in practice, that's very much not the case: in the presence of fat, aquafaba quickly deflates, especially once it hits the heat of the oven – so it doesn't contribute anything in terms of aeration, and it also doesn't add any flexibility to the sponge.

Instead, you can account for the aerating (lift-providing) properties of eggs by adding ⅛ teaspoon of baking powder and ¼ teaspoon of apple cider vinegar for each egg removed. This adjustment is similar to that for the egg-free buttery vanilla cake (page 98), just with slightly smaller quantities.

Because the eggs also act as a structure-providing ingredient and as a moisture source, we need to increase the quantity of flour and wet ingredients, respectively – however, this is where things get a bit more complex.

With the egg-free buttery vanilla cake, we just had to add some extra flour and milk (or yogurt), and that was it. But here, that simply wouldn't provide enough flexibility, and an egg-free sponge made that way would crack to the point of crumbling apart.

Instead, we need to add some extra ingredients that will achieve a level of flexibility that at least approaches that of the regular Swiss roll. Enter two, perhaps unexpected, ingredients: **xanthan gum and condensed milk**.

Rarely seen outside of the realm of gluten-free baking and cooking, xanthan gum is a binder that acts as a glue to hold (gluten-free) bakes together and lend them some extra elasticity and flexibility – and that's exactly why it's so useful here. We definitely need the extra flexibility when it comes to egg-free Swiss rolls, even though we're using regular, gluten-containing wheat flour. (You can read more about xanthan gum on page 263.)

When it comes to the wet ingredients, you need to use a mixture of whole milk and condensed milk. The whole milk acts simply as a source of moisture, whereas the condensed milk acts both as a wet ingredient and, importantly, as an extra source of structure and flexibility. Condensed milk is, in many ways, the unexpected hero of the egg-free Swiss roll. Along with the xanthan gum, it transforms the overly delicate sponge that's prone to breaking into a wonderfully flexible (but still fluffy and tender!) sponge that rolls up like a dream.

Because condensed milk is sweet, though, you need to reduce the amount of sugar slightly – otherwise, your Swiss roll can end up too sugary. Specifically, reduce the amount of sugar by half of the weight of the condensed milk.

*In summary*

I know all this may seem a rather overwhelming number of changes, so here they are again, summarized and with actual numbers to make things simpler:

For each egg removed, you need to:

- **Add ⅛ teaspoon of baking powder and ¼ teaspoon of apple cider vinegar.**
- **Add 10g (1½ tablespoons) of flour (true for wheat flour and gluten-free flour blends).**
- **Add 40g (2½ tablespoons) of milk (true for dairy and dairy-free ingredients).**

- **Add 15g (2½ teaspoons) of condensed milk (true for dairy and dairy-free ingredients). Reduce the amount of sugar by half of the total weight of condensed milk to account for the extra sweetness.**
- **Add ½ teaspoon of xanthan gum per 120g (1 cup) of flour (this increases to ¾ teaspoon if you're using a gluten-free flour blend – more about that in the gluten-free vegan section on pages 118–19).**

I also recommend using oil rather than butter in egg-free Swiss rolls. This will give you a sponge that's slightly more flexible – and, honestly, when it comes to making the perfect egg-free Swiss roll, every little bit of extra flexibility helps. It's best to use an oil that's neutral in flavour, like sunflower, vegetable or rapeseed (canola) oil.

### The preparation method

Because there are no eggs (and no aquafaba) to whip up, making the batter is as easy as whisking together all the wet and all the dry ingredients separately, and then combining them until smooth. Just be careful not to over-mix, as that can make the sponge slightly dense and tough – whisk only until all the ingredients have been combined and there are no clumps – but no more than that.

Because you haven't incorporated any air (either via whipped eggs or whipped aquafaba), the volume of the batter will be noticeably smaller than that for egg-containing Swiss-roll sponges. That means that the layer of batter in the baking sheet will be much thinner, but that's okay: it will puff up and rise beautifully in the oven; just make sure to spread it into a very even layer (an offset spatula really helps with this). And don't grease your baking paper, as that can cause problems with spreading.

To ensure a very even bake and to maximize flexibility, it's best to bake the sponge at a slightly lower oven temperature of 160°C/325°F rather than the 180°C/350°F used for egg-containing Swiss rolls. The lower oven temperature ensures that the edges don't dry out, which further reduces the chances of cracking.

Egg-free sponges have a greater tendency to be almost too moist – that's why I don't recommend covering the hot sponge with foil, as you would with the regular, gluten-free and dairy-free versions. Instead, you need to allow some (but not all!) of the steam to escape. So, after dusting the hot egg-free sponge with some icing (powdered) sugar, cover it with a clean tea towel (or two tea towels on top of each other if they're on the thinner side). This traps just enough steam to make the sponge nicely flexible, but it also allows enough steam to escape so that the sponge doesn't end up sticky or doughy from the excessive moisture.

Finally, it's important that you tightly wrap the filled and rolled-up egg-free Swiss roll in baking paper and chill it in the fridge for at least 1 hour before you finish decorating it. This chilling step helps to achieve a more stable Swiss roll that holds its shape – even if it stands at room temperature afterwards – after you've finished decorating.

The combination of all of these changes and steps results in a truly gorgeous egg-free Swiss roll, with a lovely swirl, a soft and fluffy crumb with no gumminess or doughiness, and a sponge thickness very similar to the regular version.

Don't stress too much if you get the occasional crack – those are particularly likely at the beginning of the roll, when you first start to fold the sponge over itself. And keep in mind that you're making an egg-free Swiss roll! If you get a nice swirl, even if it's not 100% perfect, pat yourself on the back because you should absolutely be proud.

# Vegan

Once you have the egg-free version figured out, making a vegan Swiss roll is straightforward. All you have to do is take all the adjustments necessary to make the egg-free version and replace all the dairy ingredients with dairy-free alternatives. In this case, this means using a dairy-free milk such as almond, soy, rice or oat milk instead of dairy milk, and using a dairy-free condensed milk instead of dairy condensed milk.

Avoid using canned coconut milk, as it can make the sponge too heavy and oily owing to its high fat content. When it comes to the vegan *condensed* milk, you can use either a shop-bought one (condensed coconut and oat milk both work great) or make your own using either of the recipes on pages 26 and 27, depending on whether you want it to be coconut-free or not.

Just like with the egg-free Swiss roll, oil will give you a better result than melted vegan butter – you'll get a fluffier sponge that's slightly more flexible. Similarly, a lower oven temperature of 160°C/325°F will give you a more supple sponge that will roll up smoothly with less cracking.

The resulting vegan Swiss roll is a real beauty, with a soft, fluffy sponge with an open, delicate crumb that rolls with only minimal cracking. Also, the sponge thickness is very similar to the regular version. As I've mentioned before, though, remember that some cracking is to be expected – it's basically inevitable in the absence of eggs. However, the xanthan gum and the dairy-free condensed milk along with the lower baking temperature and the optimized rolling method ensure that you'll get a degree of flexibility in your vegan sponge that's as close as you can possibly get to the initial, regular recipe.

# Gluten-free vegan

Before we get to the science behind making a gluten-free vegan Swiss roll, let's just take a moment to appreciate what we're actually discussing here: a soft and fluffy sponge that needs to be flexible enough so that we can roll it up with only minor cracking – with no gluten and no eggs to help us. It's absolutely insane and, honestly, I still can't quite believe that it's actually possible. Because that's probably the most insane part of all: you *can* make a gluten-free vegan Swiss roll that doesn't crumble into a thousand little pieces but rather gives you a surprisingly lovely swirl.

The gluten-free vegan version is, for the most part, a simple combination of all the gluten-, dairy- and egg-free adjustments, with one extra tweak.

You need to reduce the amount of flour by 10% to account for the greater moisture-absorption capacity of the gluten-free flour blend and also add ¾ teaspoon of xanthan gum per 120g (1 cup) of gluten-free flour blend. This is the same quantity of xanthan gum as for the gluten-free version on page 114. While you might expect that you'd need even more xanthan gum for this gluten-free vegan version (as it's missing both the gluten and the eggs), too much xanthan gum can make the sponge quite gummy and unpleasant to eat. Instead, ¾ teaspoon is perfect for both a lovely texture and a good amount of flexibility. Note that if your gluten-free flour blend already contains xanthan gum or other binders, add only ½ teaspoon per 120g (1 cup) of gluten-free flour blend.

The adjustments needed to account for the absence of eggs are quite numerous, as you've seen in the egg-free section (pages 115–17). Specifically, for each egg removed, you need to:

- **Add ⅛ teaspoon of baking powder and ¼ teaspoon of apple cider vinegar.**

- **Increase the amount of gluten-free flour blend by 10g (1½ tablespoons).**

- **Add 40g (2½ tablespoons) of dairy-free milk, such as almond, rice soy or oat milk. Avoid using canned coconut milk, as it can make the sponge too heavy and greasy because of its high fat content.**

- **Add 15g (2½ teaspoons) of dairy-free condensed milk (either shop-bought or a homemade version; see pages 26 and 27). Reduce the amount of sugar by half of the total weight of the condensed milk to account for the extra sweetness.**

Just like with the egg-free and vegan versions, oil will give you a better sponge texture and more flexibility than using melted vegan butter block.

In addition to all of this, there's one more change we need to make: in order to ensure that you get a sponge texture that's perfectly soft, fluffy and just delicate enough, you need to add some almond flour – just like with the gluten-free vegan buttery vanilla cake on pages 101–102. Specifically, you need to add 20g (3½ tablespoons) of almond flour per 120g (1 cup) of gluten-free flour blend. Without it, the sponge can quickly become a bit doughy, but just that small amount of almond flour will greatly improve the crumb. If you're allergic to almonds, an equal weight of finely ground sunflower seeds is a great alternative, although it will give your sponge a slightly darker colour.

Once again, as with the egg-free and vegan variations, you'll get better results if you bake the sponge at the slightly lower oven temperature of 160°C/325°F. The gentler rolling method (see page 113) is also absolutely crucial. If you were to follow the traditional rolling method, you'd be left with your cake in pieces.

The kind of filling you choose is also very important – even more so than it was with the egg-free and vegan versions. Avoid loose, "slippery" fillings like jam that don't add any structure or stability. Instead, go for sturdier fillings, such as vegan buttercream or ganache or stabilized whipped vegan cream (where you add some vegan cream cheese to the whipped cream) – these will give your Swiss roll some extra structure and that'll support your sponge and hold it in place, thus further helping to prevent any excessive cracking.

The resulting gluten-free vegan Swiss roll has a lovely swirl, a soft and fluffy texture with no doughiness or gumminess, and although the sponge is slightly thinner than the regular one, it is shockingly good considering that it lacks everything (namely gluten and eggs) that typically makes a Swiss roll possible.

# Vanilla Swiss roll: recipe

This recipe makes one 25cm-long (10in) Swiss roll. You can fill the roll with any of the frostings on pages 469–79, with a simple vanilla whipped cream, or with your own favourite frosting or filling recipe.

| | DIET | | | | | |
|---|---|---|---|---|---|---|
| | **Regular** | **Gluten-free** | **Dairy-free** | **Egg-free** | **Vegan** | **GF Vegan** |
| eggs, room temp [1] | 4 | 4 | 4 | / | / | / |
| caster or granulated sugar | 150g<br>¾ cup | 150g<br>¾ cup | 150g<br>¾ cup | 120g<br>½ cup + 1½ tbsp | 120g<br>½ cup + 1½ tbsp | 120g<br>½ cup + 1½ tbsp |
| vanilla paste [2] | ½ tsp | ½ tsp | ½ tsp | ½ tsp | ½ tsp | ½ tsp |
| unsalted butter, melted [3] | 55g<br>½ stick | 55g<br>½ stick | 55g<br>½ stick | / | / | / |
| sunflower oil or vegetable oil | / | / | / | 45g<br>3½ tbsp | 45g<br>3½ tbsp | 45g<br>3½ tbsp |
| milk, room temp [4] | / | / | / | 160g<br>⅔ cup | 160g<br>⅔ cup | 160g<br>⅔ cup |
| condensed milk [5] | / | / | / | 60g<br>3 tbsp | 60g<br>3 tbsp | 60g<br>3 tbsp |
| apple cider vinegar | / | / | / | 1 tsp | 1 tsp | 1 tsp |
| plain flour [6] | 120g<br>1 cup | 110g<br>¾ cup + 2½ tbsp | 120g<br>1 cup | 160g<br>1⅓ cups | 160g<br>1⅓ cups | 150g<br>1¼ cups |
| almond flour [7] | / | / | / | / | / | 25g<br>¼ cup |
| baking powder | ¾ tsp | ¾ tsp | ¾ tsp | 1¼ tsp | 1¼ tsp | 1¼ tsp |
| bicarbonate of soda (baking soda) | ¼ tsp | ¼ tsp | ¼ tsp | ¼ tsp | ¼ tsp | ¼ tsp |
| salt | ¼ tsp | ¼ tsp | ¼ tsp | ¼ tsp | ¼ tsp | ¼ tsp |
| xanthan gum | / | ¾ tsp* | / | ½ tsp | ½ tsp | ¾ tsp* |
| **Preparation method** | Method 1: whipping eggs + sugar | Method 1: whipping eggs + sugar | Method 1: whipping eggs + sugar | Method 2: wet+dry | Method 2: wet+dry | Method 2: wet+dry |

## METHOD 1: Whipping eggs + sugar (egg-containing cakes)

1. Adjust the oven rack to the middle position, pre-heat the oven to 180°C/350°F and line a 25x38cm (10x15in) rimmed baking sheet with baking paper. Lightly grease the baking paper and the sides of the baking sheet with oil (or spray it with non-stick baking spray).

2. Using a stand mixer fitted with the whisk attachment or a hand-held mixer fitted with the double beaters, whisk the eggs and sugar together until pale, thick, fluffy and about tripled in volume (the ribbon stage). This should take about 5–7 minutes on a high speed setting.

3. Add the vanilla and melted butter, and whisk briefly until combined.

4. In a separate bowl, sift together the flour, baking powder, bicarbonate of soda (baking soda), salt and xanthan gum (if using).

5. Add the dry ingredients to the egg mixture and whisk well for about 15–30 seconds until no flour clumps remain. Scrape down the bottom and inside of the bowl to prevent any unmixed patches.

6. Transfer the batter to the lined baking sheet and smooth it out into an even layer. Tap it a few times on the counter to make it level and to get rid of any large trapped air pockets.

7. Bake for about 10–12 minutes, or until the sponge is light golden brown on top, well risen, soft and spongy to the touch, and an inserted toothpick or cake tester comes out clean.

8. Immediately out of the oven, dust the top of the sponge with icing (powdered) sugar and cover the baking sheet first with a clean tea towel and then with a large sheet of foil. Leave to cool to room temperature or lukewarm – ideally, the temperature of the sponge shouldn't drop below 22°C/72°F.

9. Once the sponge is sufficiently cooled, loosen it from the edges of the baking sheet with an offset spatula or a thin knife.

10. Turn it out on to a large sheet of baking paper, so that the caramelized "skin" side is facing down (so that it's on the outside of the Swiss roll when you roll it up). Peel away the baking paper that you used to line the baking sheet.

11. Spoon dollops of your chosen filling evenly over the sponge and use a small offset spatula to spread it out into an even layer all the way to the edges.

12. Turn the sponge so that a short edge is closest to you. Using the baking paper underneath to help you, roll up the sponge until you get a 25cm-long (10in) log. Make sure to keep the roll fairly tight from the very beginning, otherwise you'll be left with an empty hole in the centre of your Swiss roll.

13. Wrap the Swiss roll in baking paper and chill it in the fridge for at least 1 hour before dusting it with icing (powdered) sugar and serving.

[1] UK medium eggs (US large).

[2] Double the quantity if using vanilla extract.

[3] Either dairy or vegan butter. For the latter, use a firm vegan butter block.

[4] Either whole dairy or a dairy-free milk, excluding canned coconut milk.

[5] Either dairy or a vegan condensed milk, such as condensed coconut or oat milk. For vegan, use shop-bought or make your own (see pages 26 and 27).

[6] Either plain (all-purpose) wheat flour or plain gluten-free flour blend. For the latter, use shop-bought or make your own (see page 24).

[7] If you have a nut allergy, use an equal weight of finely ground sunflower seeds.

* If your gluten-free flour blend already contains xanthan gum or other binders, use only ½ teaspoon.

→

**METHOD 2: Wet+dry (eggless cakes)**

1. Adjust the oven rack to the middle position, pre-heat the oven to 160°C/325°F and line a 25x38cm (10x15in) rimmed baking sheet with baking paper (don't grease the baking paper).

2. In a large bowl, whisk together the sugar, vanilla, oil, milk, condensed milk and vinegar.

3. In a separate bowl, sift together the flour, almond flour (if using), baking powder, bicarbonate of soda (baking soda), salt and xanthan gum.

4. Add the dry ingredients to the wet and whisk until you get a smooth cake batter with no flour clumps. Be careful not to over-mix, especially when you're using regular flour – whisk until all the ingredients are combined and there are no clumps, but no more.

5. Transfer the batter to the lined baking sheet and smooth it out to an even, fairly thin layer. Tap it a few times on the counter to level it and to get rid of any large trapped air pockets.

6. Bake for about 12–14 minutes, or until the sponge is light golden brown on top, well risen, soft and spongy to the touch, and an inserted toothpick or cake tester comes out clean.

7. Immediately out of the oven, dust the top of the sponge with icing (powdered) sugar and cover the baking sheet with a clean tea towel (if your tea towel is fairly thin, use two tea towels on top of each other). Leave to cool to room temperature or lukewarm – ideally, the temperature of the sponge shouldn't drop below 22°C/72°F.

8. Once the sponge is sufficiently cooled, loosen it from the edges of the baking sheet with an offset spatula or a thin knife.

9. Turn it out on to a large sheet of baking paper, so that the caramelized "skin" side is facing down (so that it's on the outside of the Swiss roll when you roll it up). Peel away the baking paper that you used to line the baking sheet.

10. Spoon dollops of your chosen filling evenly over the sponge and use a small offset spatula to spread it out into an even layer all the way to the edges.

11. Turn the sponge so that a short edge is closest to you. Using the baking paper underneath to help you, roll up the sponge until you get a 25cm-long (10in) log. Make sure to keep the roll fairly tight from the very beginning, otherwise you'll be left with an empty hole in the centre of your Swiss roll.

12. Wrap the Swiss roll in baking paper and chill it in the fridge for at least 1 hour before dusting it with icing (powdered) sugar and serving.

*Regular*

*Gluten-free*

*Dairy-free*

*Egg-free*

*Vegan*

*Gluten-free vegan*

Regular

Gluten-free

Dairy-free

Egg-free

Vegan

Gluten-free vegan

# Cupcakes & Muffins

Cupcakes and muffins follow the same science and therefore the same rules as the buttery vanilla cake or chocolate cake, depending on whether or not they contain melted chocolate in the batter. So, there's no need for detailed case studies here – but, for completeness, over the following pages I've included my go-to recipes for vanilla cupcakes and chocolate chip muffins in all the free-from variations.

This way, you can use the rules beginning either on page 52 or on page 55 to adapt your favourite cupcake and muffin recipes to whatever free-from version you need, or you can use the following two recipes and tweak them with whatever flavourings and add-ins you fancy.

**NOTE: ONE SMALL EXCEPTION**

For gluten-free and gluten-free vegan muffins you need to add ½ teaspoon of xanthan gum per 120g (1 cup) of gluten-free flour blend – whereas with a buttery vanilla cake or vanilla cupcakes, you need to add just ¼ teaspoon. This isn't to prevent the muffins from being too crumbly (just ¼ teaspoon is enough for that) but rather to achieve the correct batter consistency, which will give you beautifully tall muffin tops that don't spread too much horizontally during baking.

You can compare this to the adjustments needed to make gluten-free fluffy American-style pancakes (see page 239). There, you also need a slightly larger amount of xanthan gum to achieve the correct pancake-batter consistency, so that the pancakes don't spread too much but instead cook up nicely thick and squishy.

# Vanilla cupcakes: recipe

This recipe makes 12 vanilla cupcakes with a fluffy, plush crumb and a flat, only gently rounded top that is perfect for a piped frosting. A slightly lower oven temperature of 160°C/325°F ensures that the cupcakes are light golden in colour with no doming. You can pair them with any of the frostings on pages 469–475 or your own favourite frosting recipe.

| | DIET | | | | | |
| --- | --- | --- | --- | --- | --- | --- |
| | **Regular** | **Gluten-free** | **Dairy-free** | **Egg-free** | **Vegan** | **GF Vegan** |
| plain flour [1] | 210g<br>1¾ cups | 190g<br>1½ cups + 1½ tbsp | 210g<br>1¾ cups | 250g<br>2 cups + 1 tbsp | 250g<br>2 cups + 1 tbsp | 230g<br>1¾ cups +<br>2½ tbsp |
| almond flour [2] | / | / | / | / | / | 40g<br>⅓ cup + 1 tbsp |
| caster or granulated sugar | 200g<br>1 cup | 200g<br>1 cup | 200g<br>1 cup | 200g<br>1 cup | 200g<br>1 cup | 200g<br>1 cup |
| baking powder | 2½ tsp | 2½ tsp | 2½ tsp | 3 tsp | 3 tsp | 3 tsp |
| xanthan gum | / | ½ tsp* | / | / | / | ½ tsp* |
| salt | ¼ tsp | ¼ tsp | ¼ tsp | ¼ tsp | ¼ tsp | ¼ tsp |
| unsalted butter [3] | 55g (softened)<br>½ stick | 55g (softened)<br>½ stick | 55g (softened)<br>½ stick | 55g (melted)<br>½ stick | 55g (melted)<br>½ stick | 55g (melted)<br>½ stick |
| sunflower or vegetable oil | 55g<br>¼ cup | 55g<br>¼ cup | 55g<br>¼ cup | 55g<br>¼ cup | 55g<br>¼ cup | 55g<br>¼ cup |
| milk, room temp [4] | 150g<br>½ cup +<br>2 tbsp | 150g<br>½ cup +<br>2 tbsp | 150g<br>½ cup +<br>2 tbsp | 210g<br>¾ cup +<br>2 tbsp | 210g<br>¾ cup +<br>2 tbsp | 210g<br>¾ cup +<br>2 tbsp |
| eggs, room temp [5] | 2 | 2 | 2 | / | / | / |
| vanilla paste [6] | ½ tsp | ½ tsp | ½ tsp | ½ tsp | ½ tsp | ½ tsp |
| apple cider vinegar | / | / | / | 1 tsp | 1 tsp | 1 tsp |
| **Preparation method** | Method 1:<br>reverse creaming | Method 1:<br>reverse creaming | Method 1:<br>reverse creaming | Method 2:<br>wet+dry | Method 2:<br>wet+dry | Method 2:<br>wet+dry |

## METHOD 1: Reverse creaming method (egg-containing cupcakes)

1. Adjust the oven rack to the middle position and pre-heat the oven to 160°C/325°F. Line a 12-hole muffin tin with paper liners.

2. In a large bowl (or the bowl of a stand mixer), whisk together the flour, sugar, baking powder, xanthan gum (if using) and salt.

3. Add the softened butter and, by hand using your fingertips, with a hand-held mixer fitted with the double beaters or with a stand mixer fitted with the paddle, work it into the dry ingredients until you get a mixture resembling breadcrumbs.

4. In a separate bowl or jug, whisk together the oil, milk, eggs and vanilla. Add them to the flour-butter mixture in 2–3 batches, mixing well after each addition, until you get a smooth batter with no flour clumps. Scrape along the bottom and inside of the bowl occasionally to prevent any unmixed patches.

5. Divide the batter evenly between the paper liners, filling each about ⅔–¾ full.

6. Bake for about 22–24 minutes, or until well risen with a gently rounded top and an inserted toothpick or cake tester comes out clean.

7. Leave the cupcakes to cool in the tin for 5 minutes before transferring them to a wire rack to cool completely.

## METHOD 2: Wet+dry (eggless cupcakes)

1. Adjust the oven rack to the middle position and pre-heat the oven to 160°C/325°F. Line a 12-hole muffin tin with paper liners.

2. In a large bowl, whisk together the dry ingredients: flour, almond flour (if using), sugar, baking powder, xanthan gum (if using) and salt.

3. In a separate large bowl, whisk together the wet ingredients: melted butter, oil, milk, vanilla and apple cider vinegar.

4. Add the wet ingredients to the dry, and whisk well until you get a smooth, fairly runny batter with no flour clumps. Be careful not to over-mix the batter.

5. Divide the batter evenly between the paper liners, filling each about ⅔–¾ full.

6. Bake for about 22–24 minutes, or until well risen with a gently rounded top and an inserted toothpick or cake tester comes out clean.

7. Leave the cupcakes to cool in the tin for 5 minutes before transferring them to a wire rack to cool completely.

[1] Either plain (all-purpose) wheat flour or plain gluten-free flour blend. For the latter, use shop-bought or make your own (see page 24).

[2] If you have a nut allergy, use an equal weight of finely ground sunflower seeds.

[3] Either dairy or vegan butter. For the latter, use a firm vegan butter block.

[4] Either whole dairy or a dairy-free milk, excluding canned coconut milk.

[5] UK medium eggs (US large).

[6] Double the quantity if using vanilla extract.

* Omit if your gluten-free flour blend already contains binders.

# Chocolate chip muffins: recipe

This recipe makes 12 perfectly soft and fluffy bakery-style muffins with tall, beautifully caramelized domed tops. You can easily replace the chocolate chips with fresh or frozen blueberries or raspberries or nuts of your choice (chopped walnuts, pecans or hazelnuts, for example, all work great).

| | DIET | | | | | |
|---|---|---|---|---|---|---|
| | Regular | Gluten-free | Dairy-free | Egg-free | Vegan | GF Vegan |
| plain flour [1] | 320g<br>2⅔ cups | 290g<br>2⅓ cups + 1 tbsp | 320g<br>2⅔ cups | 360g<br>3 cups | 360g<br>3 cups | 330g<br>2¾ cups |
| almond flour [2] | / | / | / | / | / | 50g<br>½ cup |
| caster or granulated sugar | 200g<br>1 cup | 200g<br>1 cup | 200g<br>1 cup | 200g<br>1 cup | 200g<br>1 cup | 200g<br>1 cup |
| baking powder | 2 tsp | 2 tsp | 2 tsp | 2½ tsp | 2½ tsp | 2½ tsp |
| bicarbonate of soda (baking soda) | 1 tsp | 1 tsp | 1 tsp | 1 tsp | 1 tsp | 1 tsp |
| xanthan gum | / | 1 tsp* | / | / | / | 1 tsp* |
| salt | ¼ tsp | ¼ tsp | ¼ tsp | ¼ tsp | ¼ tsp | ¼ tsp |
| unsalted butter, melted [3] | 55g<br>½ stick | 55g<br>½ stick | 55g<br>½ stick | 55g<br>½ stick | 55g<br>½ stick | 55g<br>½ stick |
| sunflower or vegetable oil | 55g<br>¼ cup | 55g<br>¼ cup | 55g<br>¼ cup | 55g<br>¼ cup | 55g<br>¼ cup | 55g<br>¼ cup |
| milk, room temp [4] | 160g<br>⅔ cup | 160g<br>⅔ cup | 160g<br>⅔ cup | 220g<br>¾ cup + 2½ tbsp | 220g<br>¾ cup + 2½ tbsp | 220g<br>¾ cup + 2½ tbsp |
| yogurt, room temp [5] | 150g<br>⅔ cup | 150g<br>⅔ cup | 150g<br>⅔ cup | 150g<br>⅔ cup | 150g<br>⅔ cup | 150g<br>⅔ cup |
| eggs, room temp [6] | 2 | 2 | 2 | / | / | / |
| vanilla paste [7] | ½ tsp | ½ tsp | ½ tsp | ½ tsp | ½ tsp | ½ tsp |
| apple cider vinegar | / | / | / | 1 tsp | 1 tsp | 1 tsp |
| dark chocolate chips | 180g<br>1 cup | 180g<br>1 cup | 180g<br>1 cup | 180g<br>1 cup | 180g<br>1 cup | 180g<br>1 cup |

1. Adjust the oven rack to the middle position and pre-heat the oven to 190°C/375°F. Line a 12-hole muffin tin with paper liners (or lightly butter the muffin tin holes to prevent the muffins from sticking if you're not using liners).

2. In a large bowl, whisk together the flour, almond flour (if using), sugar, baking powder, bicarbonate of soda (baking soda), xanthan gum (if using) and salt.

3. In a separate large bowl or jug, whisk together the melted butter, oil, milk, yogurt, eggs (if using), vanilla and apple cider vinegar (if using).

4. Add the wet ingredients to the dry, and use a rubber spatula or a wooden spoon to fold them together into a smooth batter with no flour clumps. Take care not to over-mix the batter.

5. Add the chocolate chips, reserving some for scattering over the muffins before baking, and mix briefly until they're evenly distributed throughout the batter.

6. Use an ice-cream scoop or a spoon to divide the batter equally between the 12 liners, filling each to the brim. Scatter the reserved chocolate chips on top of the muffins.

7. Bake for about 20–22 minutes, or until the muffins are well risen, golden brown on top with slightly darker edges, and an inserted toothpick or cake tester comes out clean or with a few moist crumbs attached.

8. Leave to cool in the muffin tin for about 5–10 minutes, then transfer them to a wire rack to cool further. Serve warm or at room temperature.

[1] Either plain (all-purpose) wheat flour or plain gluten-free flour blend. For the latter, use shop-bought or make your own (see page 24).

[2] If you have a nut allergy, use an equal weight of finely ground sunflower seeds.

[3] Either dairy or vegan butter. For the latter, use a firm vegan butter block not a soft spread.

[4] Either whole dairy or a dairy-free milk, excluding canned coconut milk.

[5] Unsweetened plain or Greek-style either full-fat dairy or vegan yogurt.

[6] UK medium eggs (US large).

[7] Double the quantity if using vanilla extract.

* If your gluten-free flour blend already contains binders, use only ½ teaspoon.

Regular

Gluten-free

Dairy-free

Egg-free

Vegan

Gf vegan

# Brownies

Broadly speaking, there are two types of brownie. Interestingly, both types actually follow the same set of rules when it comes to converting them into the various free-from versions (gluten-, dairy-, egg-free and so on), and you can find the rules summarized on page 62.

## Two brownie types

### 1.
**Chocolate brownies**

**Chocolate brownies have actual melted chocolate in the batter, and sometimes also some cocoa powder for extra depth of flavour, although it's not a necessity.**

### 2.
**Cocoa brownies**

**As the name suggests, cocoa brownies contain no melted chocolate in the batter and instead rely exclusively on cocoa powder for their flavour (although they can contain chopped chocolate pieces or chocolate chips, as add-ins).**

In the following case study, we'll focus on cocoa brownies. That's because when it comes to actually figuring out the science of modifying brownie recipes, cocoa brownies are a bit more challenging. They're far more sensitive to changes in ingredient ratios, and the moment you do something wrong, you'll know it – because you'll end up with either a gloopy, gluey soup or a dry, crumbly mess. In comparison, chocolate brownies are far less demanding. The melted chocolate in the batter acts as a failsafe by adding structure and ensuring that the brownies set into a fudgy texture even if the amounts of all the other ingredients aren't 100% spot on.

So, once you've understood why and mastered how you can adapt cocoa brownies to be free-from, you can apply the same rules to chocolate brownies – with one tweak, which is specific to eggless (egg-free, vegan and gluten-free vegan) chocolate brownies. For those, you need to add some extra cornflour (cornstarch) to the batter, to deal with the extra fat you'll introduce when you add the melted chocolate. Adding 20g (3 tablespoons) of cornflour (cornstarch) per 120g (1 cup) of flour or gluten-free flour blend ensures that the chocolate brownies come out of the oven perfectly fudgy with no greasiness or oiliness.

Now, I take brownies very seriously – and I've spent many hours and numerous experiments trying to determine what my perfect brownie looks and tastes like. My ideal brownies (be they chocolate or cocoa brownies) are perfectly fudgy, with a hint of chewiness and a gorgeous paper-thin, shiny, crinkly crust. Importantly, we're not making cakey brownies here. Let's just say that I have very strong opinions about cakey brownies... and they're all negative.

In all of the free-from variations, the aim is to maintain both the fudgy texture and the paper-thin, crinkly, shiny top. So, all of the changes to the ingredient quantities and ratios and to the preparation method will be made with that in mind. Before we can dive into the science of modifying brownie recipes, though, there are a few more brownie fundamentals that we need to cover, including the origins of the paper-thin, glossy crust, the various preparation methods, and why a lower oven temperature is the way to go when baking brownies.

**The paper-thin, shiny, crinkly top**

This thin, glossy crust is often mistakenly attributed to the formation of a meringue-like layer on top of the brownies. That wrongly implies that the presence of eggs is crucial for its existence – which isn't the case. Instead, it's all about crystalline sugar dissolving in a limited amount of liquid or a wet ingredient (which can be eggs, milk or even water). Then, during baking, part of the sugar migrates to the surface of the brownies to form the crinkly, glossy top. This works best with white caster (superfine) or granulated sugar, but it also works well with light brown sugar and coconut sugar. Therefore, it's very important that the quantity of liquid or wet ingredients in the brownies isn't too large – it should be sufficient for the sugar to dissolve fully but not much more than that, otherwise the glossy top will disappear.

So, for example, if you want to add coffee to your brownies (assuming they already contain eggs), make sure to use either a small amount of highly concentrated brewed coffee or instant coffee dissolved in hot water. Even better, add the coffee in the form of espresso powder or crushed instant coffee granules, which doesn't add any extra moisture. Reducing the amount of sugar can also make the shiny top disappear, and it can negatively impact the texture of the brownies.

### Preparation and baking

While brownies are definitely an everyday, minimal-fuss kind of bake, the method by which you prepare them is very important. There are several preparation methods you could use, but we'll focus on just two of them. These are the methods that I swear by because they give the most consistent, reliable and delicious results.

**The whipping method**

Here, you need to whip the eggs and sugar together until pale, fluffy and about tripled in volume and you reach the ribbon stage. Then, you add the rest of the ingredients – melted chocolate (if you're making chocolate brownies), melted butter and the dry ingredients. With this method, you're relying on room-temperature eggs and prolonged beating to make the sugar dissolve in the eggs – which then results in the shiny, crinkly top. This is my go-to method for making regular chocolate brownies.

**The heating method**

In this method, gently heat the eggs and sugar together over a pot of simmering water until the sugar has fully dissolved. Stir the mixture with a rubber spatula – no whisking or whipping, so you introduce only a negligible amount of air. The heat encourages the sugar to dissolve faster, but doesn't scramble the eggs – you need to heat the mixture to about 28–32°C/82–90°F, and no higher. Then, add the rest of the ingredients. This method is efficient at producing shiny-top brownies and it's my go-to for making regular cocoa brownies. As you'll see, the heating method is also very important when making egg-free and vegan variations of both cocoa and chocolate brownies.

Finally, if you want to ensure that your brownies have a perfect shiny, crinkly top and a gloriously fudgy texture, it's best to bake them at a slightly lower oven temperature of 160°C/325°F. This is true for chocolate and cocoa brownies, and for all the different variations – both the regular one and all the free-from ones. The lower oven temperature results in a slower, longer bake, which gives the shiny top time to form fully across the whole brownie and it also gives you better control over the exact brownie texture.

Regular

Gluten-free

Dairy-free

Egg-free

Vegan

Gluten-free vegan

**Rules for
adapting brownies**

↓

**p.62**

# Case Study 4:
# Cocoa Brownies

The starting point for this case study is my ideal, regular cocoa brownies, made with caster (superfine) sugar, light brown soft sugar, eggs, unsalted dairy butter, plain (all-purpose) wheat flour, Dutch-processed cocoa powder, a generous pinch of salt and a dash of vanilla.

The combination of the two types of sugar ensures that you get both a gorgeous paper-thin, glossy, crinkly top (thanks to the white caster/superfine sugar) and the rich, fudgy texture (thanks to the light brown sugar). The light brown sugar also gives the cocoa brownies the depth of flavour that they might have lacked in the absence of actual melted chocolate in the batter. While I prefer to use caster (superfine) sugar because of its smaller granules which dissolve very quickly in any wet ingredients, you can instead use granulated sugar.

It's very important that you use a high-quality Dutch-processed cocoa powder here. As there's no melted chocolate in the batter, the cocoa powder is the main flavour-imparting ingredient. If the cocoa is mediocre in flavour, so your brownies will be. What's more, the quality of the cocoa powder doesn't affect just the flavour of the brownies – it also affects their texture (and that's even more true with egg-free and vegan cocoa brownies). So, make sure to use high-quality ingredients. Your brownies (and your taste buds) will thank you.

The best preparation method for making cocoa brownies is the heating method (see page 133). Whipping the eggs and sugar together usually results in cocoa brownies that are rather cakey in texture. The heating method, on the other hand, ensures that the sugar fully dissolves in the eggs (giving the baked brownies a gorgeous paper-thin, crinkly, shiny top) without introducing too much air into the mixture. Thus, by using the heating method, you'll get cocoa brownies that are beautifully fudgy and just as good as (or, some might say, even better than) chocolate brownies.

When it comes to knowing when the brownies are baked to perfection, it's best to use the baking times listed in the recipe as loose guidelines and instead rely mostly on the "toothpick test". For this, you need to insert a toothpick, skewer or cake tester into the centre of the brownies and observe how it comes out. For gooey brownies, look for a toothpick covered in half-baked batter. For fudgy brownies, look for a toothpick covered in a mixture of half-baked batter and many moist crumbs. Remember that it's better to under-bake rather than over-bake your brownies, especially because of carryover baking, where the brownies will continue to bake for a few minutes longer even after you've taken them out of the oven (owing to the high heat of the baking tin and also the outermost layer of the brownies themselves).

In general, regardless of whether you're considering the regular version or any of the free-from variations, cocoa brownies will always be better the day after baking. That's because the moisture in the brownies needs time to redistribute – it will "migrate", so to speak, from the moist, fudgy centre to the edges of the brownie. The flavour will also be better the next day.

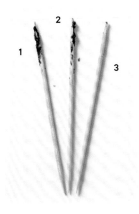

**The toothpick test**

1. Gooey brownies

2. Fudgy brownies

3. Dry, overbaked brownies

## Gluten-free

The crucial consideration when it comes to converting the cocoa brownie recipe to gluten-free is the difference between the moisture and the fat responses of the gluten-free flour blend in comparison to regular wheat flour (see page 42). While the gluten-free flour blend absorbs more moisture than wheat flour, it actually has a lower fat tolerance – that is, it can take on a smaller amount of fat.

In the case of egg-containing cocoa brownies, the different moisture and fat responses actually cancel each other out, so you can simply just substitute the wheat all-purpose flour with an equal weight or volume of the gluten-free flour blend. (This is different to, for example, the buttery vanilla cake, where the moisture response is the more important one and you therefore have to reduce the amount of flour to prevent the cake from being too dry and crumbly).

To make up for the lack of gluten, you need to add ¼ teaspoon of xanthan gum (a structure-providing binder) per 120g (1 cup) of gluten-free flour blend. If your gluten-free flour blend already contains xanthan gum or other binders, you don't need to add any extra.

The preparation method (the heating method) and everything else stays the same. The results are gluten-free cocoa brownies that are pretty much indistinguishable from the original, regular version. They're fabulously fudgy and they boast that gorgeous, crinkly, glossy top.

You've probably noticed that I specified "egg-containing" cocoa brownies when I was talking about the changes necessary to make them gluten-free. This basically assumes that you're starting from a regular brownie recipe, as laid out in this case study.

However, if you start out with an egg-free or a vegan cocoa brownie recipe, the situation is very different because of the absence of the structure-providing eggs. I've covered the additional changes that are necessary in that case in the gluten-free vegan section of this case study (see page 138).

## Dairy-free

The change from regular to dairy-free cocoa brownies is definitely the easiest one to make. You just need to substitute the dairy butter with an equal weight or volume of a vegan butter – that's all there is to it. You don't have to change anything about the preparation or the baking method and you will still get fudgy brownies with a paper-thin, glossy top. Just like with the majority of other dairy-free recipes in this book, I recommend using a firm vegan butter block instead of a soft spread.

## Egg-free

In cocoa brownies, eggs are primarily a structure-providing ingredient and a source of moisture used to dissolve the sugar. They're crucial to give the regular brownies their fudgy texture and the beautiful shiny, crinkly top. But although we're interested in fudgy rather than cakey brownies, eggs still provide a tiny amount of aeration (even if you use the heating rather than the whipping method) – so they also act as aerating or lift-providing ingredients here, even if that effect is only minimal.

Let's first focus on alternative moisture sources. The best ones to use in brownies are either water or milk – you need to add 40g (2½ tablespoons) of either of them for each egg removed. I usually use milk, as it gives slightly richer, more decadent brownies, but water will work, too.

It's important that you control the amount of moisture (milk or water) in the recipe. Too much and your brownies will lose the shiny top and may end up like either strange brown soup or a disappointing chocolate cake, depending on the recipe you're starting with and on the baking time. If you don't add enough, though, there will be insufficient moisture present to fully dissolve the sugar, and your brownies may be too dry or crumbly. Using 40g (2½ tablespoons) for each egg removed is the best amount to get consistently brilliant results.

In the absence of the structure-providing eggs, you need to increase the amount of the only other structure-providing ingredient present: the flour. Specifically, you need to add 30g (4 tablespoons) of flour for each egg removed. This gives enough structure to the brownies so that they're not too soft or too gooey – and, at the same time, the extra amount of flour (a dry ingredient) isn't so large that it would result in dry brownies.

Because the eggs provide a small amount of aeration, you need to add ⅛ teaspoon of baking powder per each egg removed. This small amount of baking powder won't make the brownies cakey. Instead, it prevents the egg-free brownies from being too dense and it gives them a wonderful melt-in-the-mouth texture.

**NOTE**

If you're adapting a gluten-free brownie to be also egg-free, you'll need to make all of the changes outlined so far – but you'll also need to reduce the amount of fat by 30% and increase the amount of xanthan gum to ½ teaspoon of xanthan gum per 120g (1 cup) of gluten-free flour blend (or ¼ teaspoon if your blend already contains binders). See page 138 for details.

The best preparation method for making the perfect egg-free cocoa brownies is just a slightly tweaked version of the heating method (see page 133). You need to combine the sugar and milk in a saucepan, and heat the mixture with frequent stirring until the sugar is fully dissolved. You don't want the mixture to come to a boil or the milk to start evaporating; you just want the sugar to fully dissolve – you can check this by rubbing a small amount of the (slightly cooled) mixture between your fingertips (you shouldn't feel any graininess).

Then, add the cubed cold butter and mix well until it's fully melted – this also helps to cool down the mixture, as it needs to be lukewarm, or around 35–36°C/95–97°F, before you add the dry ingredients. After stirring everything together with a rubber spatula (no need to use a whisk), you'll get a glossy, runny, luscious batter that will bake to give fudgy brownies with a glossy top. This method – essentially making a sugar syrup before you add the dry ingredients – might sound a bit odd, but it works brilliantly and it gives consistent, reliable results.

Finally, note that egg-free brownies tend to get a bit chewier over time, while egg-containing versions have a slightly more delicate texture. The egg-free brownies are, of course, incredibly delicious and they'll still melt in your mouth, it's just that the texture is a tiny bit different.

# Vegan

**NOTE**

If you're starting out with gluten-free brownies and you want to make them vegan, reduce the amount of fat and increase the amount of xanthan gum in addition to all the other changes. See page 138 for details.

As is often the case with vegan recipes, the vegan variation of the cocoa brownie recipe is just a simple sum of the dairy- and egg-free modifications.

So, you need to replace the dairy butter with an equal weight or volume of a dairy-free/vegan butter block and then, for each egg removed:

- **Add 40g (2½ tablespoons) of water or a dairy-free milk alternative, such as almond, rice, oat or soy milk. I don't recommend using canned coconut milk due to its high fat content, which can make the brownies too greasy.**

- **Add 30g (4 tablespoons) of flour (true for wheat flour and gluten-free flour blends).**

- **Add ⅛ teaspoon of baking powder.**

The preparation method is the same as for the egg-free brownies: heat the mixture of sugar and dairy-free milk until the sugar is fully dissolved, stir in the butter until it's melted, and cool the mixture until it's lukewarm or around 35–36°C/95–97°F. Then, add in the dry ingredients, mix everything together into a smooth, glossy brownie batter, and, finally, bake to rich and perfectly fudgy brownies, with a gorgeous glossy top – just like the original, regular version.

## Gluten-free vegan

Making gluten-free vegan cocoa brownies isn't quite as straightforward as simply just combining all the relevant rules we've established so far.

While you do have to make all the necessary changes for the gluten-, dairy- and egg-free variations (using a gluten-free flour blend, adding xanthan gum, replacing dairy butter with a dairy-free equivalent, and adding 40g/2½ tablespoons of dairy-free milk or water, 30g/4 tablespoons of gluten-free flour blend and ⅛ teaspoon of baking powder for each egg removed), there are two further tweaks. (Note that these additional changes apply to both the gluten-free vegan and the gluten- and egg-free versions.)

**1. Reduce the amount of vegan butter by 30%.**

This is because, when it comes to determining how to substitute the regular flour with a gluten-free flour blend, it's all about looking at the different and opposing moisture and fat responses of the gluten-free flour blend in comparison to wheat flour (see page 42), and then determining which is the more important in that specific recipe.

For eggless cocoa brownies (both egg-free and vegan ones), the fat response is the dominant factor. That's because fat has a tenderizing (structure-destroying) effect and in the absence of eggs, that's very strongly felt by the gluten-free flour blend, which has a "weaker" structure- or framework-providing effect than regular wheat flour.

To account for that, you need to reduce the fat-to-flour ratio. Adding 30g (4 tablespoons) of extra flour for each egg removed still doesn't reduce the fat-to-flour ratio sufficiently – the gluten-free vegan brownies would end up far too soft and gloopy.

To reduce the fat-to-flour ratio further, you need to reduce the amount of fat by 30%. If doing this by weight, you simply need to multiply the weight of the vegan butter by 0.7. If you're using volume measurements, reduce the amount of butter by 2½ tablespoons per stick (115g) of butter.

**2. Increase the amount of xanthan gum compared with an egg-containing gluten-free brownie recipe.**

This accounts for the fact that you're missing two important structural ingredients: gluten and eggs. You need to use ½ teaspoon of xanthan gum per 120g (1 cup) of gluten-free flour blend (or ¼ teaspoon if your blend already contains xanthan gum or other binders).

Finally, the gluten-free vegan cocoa brownies also need longer in the oven to achieve a fudgy texture that isn't too soft or too gooey. Add 5–10 minutes to the baking time and look for a toothpick that's mostly covered in moist crumbs, with only minor patches of half-baked batter.

The resulting gluten-free vegan cocoa brownies are a complete revelation – deeply chocolatey (even without any actual melted chocolate in the batter), rich and fudgy and with the crowning glory of a glossy, paper-thin crust on top. They are a tiny bit softer than the regular version, but that's only really obvious if you compare them side by side.

Regular

Gluten-free

Dairy-free

Egg-free

Vegan

Gluten-free vegan

# Cocoa brownies: recipe

**This recipe makes 16 brownies, baked in a 23cm (9in) square baking tin. You can include any add-ins you fancy (chocolate chips and/or chopped nuts work great).**

| | DIET | | | | | |
|---|---|---|---|---|---|---|
| | **Regular** | **Gluten-free** | **Dairy-free** | **Egg-free** | **Vegan** | **GF Vegan** |
| caster or granulated sugar | 200g<br>1 cup | 200g<br>1 cup | 200g<br>1 cup | 200g<br>1 cup | 200g<br>1 cup | 200g<br>1 cup |
| light brown soft sugar | 100g<br>½ cup | 100g<br>½ cup | 100g<br>½ cup | 100g<br>½ cup | 100g<br>½ cup | 100g<br>½ cup |
| eggs, room temp [1] | 3 | 3 | 3 | / | / | / |
| milk [2] | / | / | / | 120g<br>½ cup | 120g<br>½ cup | 120g<br>½ cup |
| unsalted butter [3] | 210g (melted)<br>1¾ sticks + 1 tbsp | 210g (melted)<br>1¾ sticks + 1 tbsp | 210g (melted)<br>1¾ sticks + 1 tbsp | 210g (chilled)<br>1¾ sticks + 1 tbsp | 210g (chilled)<br>1¾ sticks + 1 tbsp | 150g (chilled)<br>1 stick + 2½ tbsp |
| vanilla paste [4] | ½ tsp | ½ tsp | ½ tsp | ½ tsp | ½ tsp | ½ tsp |
| plain flour [5] | 120g<br>1 cup | 120g<br>1 cup | 120g<br>1 cup | 210g<br>1¾ cup | 210g<br>1¾ cup | 210g<br>1¾ cup |
| Dutch processed cocoa powder | 75g<br>¾ cup | 75g<br>¾ cup | 75g<br>¾ cup | 75g<br>¾ cup | 75g<br>¾ cup | 75g<br>¾ cup |
| salt | ½ tsp | ½ tsp | ½ tsp | ½ tsp | ½ tsp | ½ tsp |
| xanthan gum | / | ¼ tsp* | / | / | / | ¾ tsp** |
| baking powder | / | / | / | ¼ tsp | ¼ tsp | ¼ tsp |
| **Preparation method** | Method 1:<br>egg-containing | Method 1:<br>egg-containing | Method 1:<br>egg-containing | Method 2:<br>eggless | Method 2:<br>eggless | Method 2:<br>eggless |

[1] UK medium eggs (US large).

[2] Either whole dairy or dairy-free milk, excluding canned coconut milk.

[3] Either dairy or vegan butter. If the latter, use a firm vegan butter block.

[4] Double the quantity if using vanilla extract.

[5] Either plain (all-purpose) wheat flour or plain gluten-free flour blend. For the latter, use shop-bought or make your own (see page 24).

* Omit if your gluten-free flour blend already contains binders.

** If your gluten-free flour blend already contains binders, use only ¼ teaspoon.

**METHOD 1: Egg-containing brownies**

1. Adjust the oven rack to the middle position, pre-heat the oven to 160°C/325°F, and line a 23cm (9in) square baking tin with baking paper. Leave some paper overhanging, which will help with removing the baked brownie later on.

2. In a large heatproof bowl, mix together the caster (superfine) or granulated sugar, light brown sugar and eggs with a wooden spoon or a rubber spatula until combined. Don't aerate the mixture with a whisk.

3. Place the egg-sugar mixture over a pot of simmering water and heat it, with constant stirring, until it reaches 28–32°C/82–90°F and the sugar has fully dissolved (when you rub the mixture between your fingertips, it should be completely smooth with no graininess).

4. Remove the bowl from the heat and stir in the melted butter and vanilla.

5. Sift in the flour, cocoa powder, salt and xanthan gum (if using), and mix well until you get a smooth, glossy batter with no flour clumps.

6. Transfer the batter to the lined baking tin, smooth out the top and bake for about 24–26 minutes, or until an inserted toothpick or cake tester comes out covered in a mixture of half-baked batter and moist crumbs.

7. Allow the brownies to cool completely to room temperature before you remove them from the tin. Use a sharp knife to slice them into individual portions – make sure to wipe the knife clean between cuts for neat slices. (Note that cocoa brownies will always be better the following day.)

**METHOD 2: Eggless brownies**

1. Adjust the oven rack to the middle position, pre-heat the oven to 160°C/325°F, and line a 23cm (9in) square baking tin with baking paper. Leave some paper overhanging, which will help with removing the baked brownie later on.

2. In a saucepan, mix together the caster (superfine) or granulated sugar, light brown sugar, milk and vanilla, and heat the mixture over medium heat until the sugar has fully dissolved (when you rub the mixture between your fingertips, it should be completely smooth with no graininess). Don't allow the mixture to come to a boil or the milk to start evaporating.

3. Remove the mixture from the heat and mix in the cold cubed butter until it's fully melted. Allow the mixture to cool until it's lukewarm or around 35–36°C/95–97°F (you can speed up this process by using a cold water bath).

4. Sift in the flour, cocoa powder, salt, xanthan gum (if using) and baking powder, and mix well until you get a smooth, glossy batter with no flour clumps.

5. Transfer the batter into the lined baking tin, smooth out the top and bake for about 26–28 minutes (for egg-free and vegan brownies) or 30–32 minutes (for gluten-free vegan brownies) or until an inserted toothpick or cake tester comes out covered in a mixture of half-baked batter and moist crumbs.

6. Allow the brownies to cool completely to room temperature before you remove them from the tin. Use a sharp knife to slice them into individual portions – make sure to wipe the knife clean between cuts for neat slices. (Note that cocoa brownies will always be better the following day.)

# Chocolate brownies: recipe

This recipe makes 16 brownies, baked in a 23cm (9in) square baking tin. You can include any add-ins you fancy (chocolate chips and/or chopped nuts work great). Egg-containing chocolate brownies are best prepared using the whipping method (see page 133), whereas eggless chocolate brownies use a variation of the heating method, similar to eggless cocoa brownies.

| | DIET | | | | | |
|---|---|---|---|---|---|---|
| | **Regular** | **Gluten-free** | **Dairy-free** | **Egg-free** | **Vegan** | **GF Vegan** |
| dark chocolate, chopped [1] | 200g 7oz | 200g 7oz | 200g 7oz | 200g 7oz | 200g 7oz | 200g 7oz |
| unsalted butter [2] | 170g 1½ sticks | 170g 1½ sticks | 170g 1½ sticks | 170g 1½ sticks | 170g 1½ sticks | 115g 1 stick |
| eggs, room temp [3] | 3 | 3 | 3 | / | / | / |
| milk [4] | / | / | / | 120g ½ cup | 120g ½ cup | 120g ½ cup |
| caster or granulated sugar | 150g ¾ cup | 150g ¾ cup | 150g ¾ cup | 150g ¾ cup | 150g ¾ cup | 150g ¾ cup |
| light brown soft sugar | 100g ½ cup | 100g ½ cup | 100g ½ cup | 100g ½ cup | 100g ½ cup | 100g ½ cup |
| vanilla paste [5] | ½ tsp | ½ tsp | ½ tsp | ½ tsp | ½ tsp | ½ tsp |
| plain flour [6] | 90g ¾ cup | 90g ¾ cup | 90g ¾ cup | 180g 1½ cups | 180g 1½ cups | 180g 1½ cups |
| Dutch processed cocoa powder | 30g ⅓ cup | 30g ⅓ cup | 30g ⅓ cup | 30g ⅓ cup | 30g ⅓ cup | 30g ⅓ cup |
| salt | ½ tsp | ½ tsp | ½ tsp | ½ tsp | ½ tsp | ½ tsp |
| xanthan gum | / | ¼ tsp* | / | / | / | ¾ tsp** |
| cornflour (cornstarch) | / | / | / | 30g 4 tbsp | 30g 4 tbsp | 30g 4 tbsp |
| baking powder | / | / | / | ¼ tsp | ¼ tsp | ¼ tsp |
| **Preparation method** | Method 1: whipping method | Method 1: whipping method | Method 1: whipping method | Method 2: heating method | Method 2: heating method | Method 2: heating method |

### METHOD 1: Whipping method (egg-containing brownies)

1. Adjust the oven rack to the middle position, pre-heat the oven to 160°C/325°F, and line a 23cm (9in) square baking tin with baking paper. Leave some paper overhanging, which will help with removing the baked brownie later on.

2. In a large heatproof bowl, either in the microwave or over a pot of simmering water, melt the chocolate and butter together. Set aside to cool until warm.

3. Using a hand-held mixer with the double beaters or a stand mixer fitted with the whisk, whisk the eggs, caster (superfine) or granulated sugar and light brown sugar together on high speed for 5–7 minutes until the mixture is pale, fluffy, about tripled in volume and it reaches the ribbon stage (where the mixture briefly piles up on itself when it falls off the whisk).

4. Fold in the melted chocolate and vanilla until mostly incorporated.

5. Sift in the flour, cocoa powder, salt and xanthan gum (if using), and fold them in until you get a smooth, glossy batter with no flour clumps.

6. Transfer the batter into the lined baking tin, smooth out the top and bake for about 24–26 minutes, or until an inserted toothpick or cake tester comes out covered in a mixture of half-baked batter and moist crumbs.

7. Leave the brownies to cool completely to room temperature before you remove them from the tin. Use a sharp knife to slice them into individual portions – make sure to wipe the knife clean between cuts for neat slices.

### METHOD 2: Heating method (eggless brownies)

1. Adjust the oven rack to the middle position, pre-heat the oven to 160°C/325°F, and line a 23cm (9in) square baking tin with baking paper. Leave some paper overhanging, which will help with removing the baked brownie later on.

2. In a large heatproof bowl, either in the microwave or over a pot of simmering water, melt the chocolate and butter together. Set aside to cool until warm.

3. In a saucepan, mix together the caster (superfine) or granulated sugar, light brown sugar, milk and vanilla, and then heat the mixture over medium heat until the sugar has fully dissolved (when you rub the mixture between your fingertips, it should be completely smooth with no graininess). Don't allow the mixture to come to a boil or the milk to start evaporating. Remove the mixture from the heat and allow to cool until warm.

4. Whisk together the warm melted chocolate mixture and the warm sugar syrup, then set aside and allow the mixture to cool until it's lukewarm or around 35–36°C/95–97°F (you can speed up this process by using a cold water bath).

5. Sift in the flour, cocoa powder, salt, xanthan gum (if using), cornflour (cornstarch) and baking powder, and mix well until you get a smooth, glossy batter with no flour clumps.

6. Transfer the batter into the lined baking tin, smooth out the top and bake for about 28–30 minutes (for egg-free and vegan brownies) or 30–32 minutes (for gluten-free vegan brownies), or until an inserted toothpick or cake tester comes out covered in a mixture of half-baked batter and moist crumbs.

7. Leave the brownies to cool completely to room temperature before you remove them from the tin. Use a sharp knife to slice them into individual portions – make sure to wipe the knife clean between cuts for neat slices.

[1] I recommend using dark chocolate with 60–70% cocoa solids.

[2] Either dairy or vegan butter. For the latter, use a firm vegan butter block not a soft spread.

[3] UK medium eggs (US large).

[4] Either whole dairy milk or a dairy-free milk, excluding canned coconut milk.

[5] Double the quantity if using vanilla extract.

[6] Either plain (all-purpose) wheat flour or plain gluten-free flour blend. For the latter, use shop-bought or make your own (see page 24).

* Omit if your gluten-free flour blend already contains binders.

** If your gluten-free flour blend already contains binders, use only ¼ teaspoon.

# Cookies

There's no one-size-fits-all when it comes to converting cookie recipes into the different free-from variations. Adapting chocolate chip cookies, for example, requires different tweaks to modifying a shortbread biscuit or a cut-out sugar cookie recipe.

Very broadly speaking, you can divide most cookie recipes into three categories, based on their behaviour during baking and their texture: cookies that hold their shape during baking, cookies that spread during baking and cakey cookies.

Before you can modify a cookie recipe to be free-from (gluten-, dairy-, egg-free and so on), you need to determine what type of cookie you're working with. Doing that is quite straightforward: you just need to consider whether or not the cookies are meant to spread out during baking, and what type of texture they have (crisp and buttery, chewy and fudgy, or cakey and tender). And then, proceed from there. To help you along, I've included a quick overview of the most popular types of cookie and which category they belong to on the opposite page.

We'll look at an example from each of these categories in the next three case studies. Cut-out sugar cookies will act as representatives for the first category (cookies that hold their shape), chocolate chip cookies will cover the second one (cookies that spread) and lemon crinkle cookies will give you some insight into the third (cakey cookies).

For completeness, I've also included my go-to shortbread recipe in all its variations – both the regular one and all the free-from ones (see page 156). As a type of cookie that holds its shape during baking, it follows the same rules as the cut-out sugar cookies.

# Three cookie types

### 1.
### Cookies that hold their shape during baking

These are cookies that spread only very minimally in the oven and they maintain their initial shape well throughout baking, which makes them ideal for cutting out with cookie cutters and for decorating. They will often have a crisp, tender and slightly crumbly texture, although they can be chewy as well, as is the case with gingerbread.

- shortbread biscuits
- cut-out sugar cookies
- Linzer cookies
- gingerbread cookies
- slice-and-bake cookies
- digestive biscuits
- thumbprint cookies
- snowball cookies
- spritz cookies (butter cookies)

### 2.
### Cookies that spread during baking

Typically starting out as balls or scoops of cookie dough, these cookies then spread during baking to achieve their characteristic shape and appearance. They tend to be fudgier and chewier in texture.

- chocolate chip cookies
- snickerdoodles
- gingersnaps
- molasses cookies
- peanut butter blossom cookies
- oatmeal cookies
- chocolate chip cookie bars
- skillet cookies

### 3.
### Cakey cookies

As the name suggests, these are cookies that have a soft, tender, cakey crumb. Somewhat counterintuitively, biscotti also belong to this category – they're simply cakey cookies that have been dried out very thoroughly, which results in their dry, crunchy texture. Cakey cookies have a high proportion of moisture in their cookie dough (from eggs or other wet ingredients), which results in a different chemistry and behaviour compared to the other two categories.

- chocolate crinkle cookies
- lemon crinkle cookies
- whoopie pies
- black and white cookies
- biscotti
- soft pumpkin cookies

Regular

Gluten-free

Dairy-free

Egg-free

Vegan

Gluten-free vegan

**Rules for adapting cookies that hold their shape during baking**

↓

**p.64**

# Case Study 5:
# Cut-out Sugar Cookies
## (cookies that hold their shape during baking)

**NOTE**

Both for the regular sugar cookies and for all the free-from versions, I rolled out the cookie dough to about 6mm (¼in) thick and cut out the individual cookies with a 6.5cm (2½in) round cookie cutter. This makes it very easy to keep track of just how much the various free-from versions spread during baking and how well they keep their neat edges. The original, regular version spreads only negligibly to a final diameter of about 6.6–6.7cm (2½–2⅝in).

The starting point for this case study is regular cut-out sugar cookies, made with just six ingredients: plain (all-purpose) wheat flour, caster (superfine) or granulated sugar, salt, softened unsalted dairy butter, an egg and a good dash of vanilla. These sugar cookies have just the right balance between crisp and soft, with the slightest hint of chewiness. Because they're typically decorated (with royal icing, for example), it's important that they hold their shape well throughout baking – ideally, you don't want them to spread by more than a few millimetres and they need to keep their neat, straight edges and a smooth top surface.

I've tested numerous cut-out sugar cookie recipes in the process of developing this optimized "regular" version, and there are two main things that help to minimize the spread of the cookies during baking:

- **No raising agents** (no baking powder or bicarbonate of soda/baking soda) in the cookie dough.

- **The reverse creaming method** for preparing the cookie dough. Just like with the buttery vanilla cake, the aim of using the reverse creaming method here is to minimize the amount of air that's mechanically incorporated into the dough. That's because any trapped air pockets will expand in the oven, resulting in the cookies spreading and losing their shape and neat edges. So, instead of creaming the butter and sugar together, you work the softened butter into the dry ingredients until you get a mixture resembling breadcrumbs, then add the egg, to bring the mixture together into a workable dough.

**NOTE: THE NEED FOR CHILLING**

You'll see that I don't mention chilling the cookie dough as an important factor for preventing the cookies spreading in the oven. While chilling can reduce the spread by a millimetre or two, it's by no means a failsafe that could transform melted cookie puddles into neat cookies with straight edges and no spread. So, while I do recommend chilling the cut-out cookies in the fridge for about 15–30 minutes before baking, this is not the most important aspect of the recipe. Rather, the key to well-shaped cut-out cookies is using the right ingredients in the right proportions and combining them in the right way. The reverse creaming method will give a cookie dough that's firm enough to roll out and cut out without any chilling (unless you're working in a very warm kitchen). And that's true for regular cookies and all free-from versions!

I like to bake the cookies for a relatively short time, so that they stay nicely soft and not too crisp – at this point, they'll be only very light golden around the edges. If you prefer crisper cookies with more of a "snap" to them as you break them in half, you can bake them for a few minutes longer.

## Gluten-free

When it comes to gluten-free cut-out sugar cookies, the fat response of the gluten-free flour blend is more important than its moisture response – remember, gluten-free flours and blends can take on less fat than plain (all-purpose) wheat flour (you can read more about this on page 42). If you were to use the full amount of butter in this recipe, your gluten-free cookies would spread quite dramatically, by as much as 1cm (½in), and they'd also be slightly too delicate and too crumbly. So, to account for this, you need to reduce the amount of butter by 20%, which is equivalent to multiplying its weight by 0.8, or to reducing its volume by 1½ tablespoons per stick (115g) of butter.

20% less butter    Full amount of butter

In addition to reducing the amount of butter, you'll also need to add ¼ teaspoon of xanthan gum per 120g (1 cup) of gluten-free flour blend. If your blend already contains xanthan gum or other binders, you don't need to add any extra.

These two simple changes will give you gluten-free cut-out sugar cookies that hold their shape beautifully – they spread to a final diameter of about 6.6–6.8cm (2⅔in), just like the regular version. They also maintain their neat edges and they have the perfect texture with a soft centre and crisp rim. The gluten-free version is slightly more delicate than the regular one, but I'd go so far as to say that it's actually better: it's not too crumbly but instead has that delicious melt-in-the-mouth quality that I really love in cookies.

The great thing about making gluten-free cut-out cookies is also that you don't have to worry about over-working or over-kneading the dough. Here, you can knead the gluten-free cookie dough as much as you wish and re-use the scraps numerous times, and every single batch will be perfectly delicious with no risk of becoming tough.

**NOTE**

When you start out with either egg-free or vegan cookies, you might have to increase the amount of xanthan gum to ½ teaspoon per 120g (1 cup) of gluten-free flour blend, or ¼ teaspoon if your blend already contains binders. This is generally true for cut-out cookies that you want to maintain their shape to within a few millimetres of the cookie cutter, but it's not essential for other types of cookie. (See also pages 151–2.)

You need just one simple swap here: replace the regular dairy butter with an equal weight or volume of a firm vegan butter block (not a soft spread). I recommend using a vegan butter block with a high fat content of at least 75% for best results.

In addition, it's important to choose a butter alternative whose flavour you like (or, at least, don't mind). As there are no intense flavours present in the recipe other than vanilla, the flavour of butter really shines through, which means you can definitely taste a slight difference in flavour between dairy-free and regular cookies. You might have to try out a few different brands to find your favourite, but it's definitely worth it.

Different brands of vegan butter can, to a smaller extent, also affect the texture of your cookies. However, I've tested this simple 1:1 substitution with numerous brands and while there were some textural differences (some cookies were slightly softer, others slightly crisper), they all resulted in really delicious cut-out sugar cookies that held their shape well during baking and that maintained their neat, straight edges. In all cases, the cookies spread only minimally to a diameter of about 6.6–6.8cm (2⅔in).

## Egg-free

In the dough for cut-out sugar cookies, eggs have two main functions: first, they act as a moisture source that helps to bring all the ingredients together into a workable cookie dough and, second, they act as an additional structure-providing ingredient that helps the cookies to hold their shape. They don't contribute any lift or aeration, so we don't need to add any raising agents to the egg-free cookie dough.

The moisture source is easy to replicate: simply replace the eggs with 40g (2½ tablespoons) of milk for each egg removed.

You could stop at this stage without making any further changes – and the cookies you'd get would be quite tasty. They also don't spread out significantly: their final diameter is around 6.6–6.9cm (2⅔in), so fairly similar to the regular version. However, they do look strangely misshapen, with an uneven, bumpy top surface and a bottom that appears to have "melted" where they came into contact with the hot baking sheet. Chilling the cookie dough for several hours or even overnight doesn't help. Instead, you need to make one more adjustment: add some cornflour (cornstarch).

Cornflour (cornstarch) is brilliant at helping cookies to maintain their shape during baking: adding just 10g (1½ tablespoons) per 120g (1 cup) of flour is enough to transform the cookies from oddly misshapen to perfectly neat and even, with straight edges and minimal spread. The final diameter of these cookies is around 6.5–6.7cm (2½–2⅔in) and they're nearly indistinguishable from the regular version, both in terms of appearance and in terms of their final texture.

*With cornflour*     *Without cornflour*

If you're sensitive to corn, you can replace the cornflour (cornstarch) with an equal weight of another starch, such as arrowroot, potato or tapioca starch. Note also that the addition of a starch is mostly just a necessity when you're making egg-free cut-out cookies, where you want to maintain very neat edges. With other recipes that still fall into the category of cookies that hold their shape during baking, but where perfect edges aren't a concern, such as biscotti, slice-and-bake cookies and thumbprint cookies, you don't need to add this extra cornflour (cornstarch). Nor is the adjustment necessary when it comes to making shortbread, as that's a naturally egg-free recipe – although I often add some cornflour (cornstarch) to my shortbread recipes anyway, as it gives them a neater shape and a slightly more delicate, melt-in-the-mouth texture.

## Vegan

The vegan version is, unsurprisingly enough, just a simple combination of all the changes necessary to make the dairy- and egg-free variations.

So, you need to:

- **Replace the regular dairy butter with an equal weight or volume of a firm vegan butter block (making sure to use one whose flavour you like).**

- **Add 40g (2½ tablespoons) of dairy-free milk for each egg removed to account for the absence of the moisture-providing eggs.**

- **Add 10g (1½ tablespoons) of a starch, such as cornflour (cornstarch), arrowroot starch, tapioca starch or potato starch, per 120g (1 cup) of flour to ensure that your cookies maintain their shape with neat edges and a smooth, even top surface perfect for decorating.**

The resulting vegan cut-out sugar cookies spread only negligibly in the oven to give a final diameter of about 6.5–6.7cm (2½–2⅗in), just like the regular version. They have a lovely flavour and a gorgeous melt-in-the-mouth texture with slightly crisp edges and a soft centre.

## Gluten-free vegan

The gluten-free vegan version is a combination of all the changes necessary to arrive at the gluten-free and the vegan versions, with one extra tweak: a slightly increased amount of xanthan gum.

That means that to get from the regular to the gluten-free vegan cut-out sugar cookies, you need to:

- **Replace the regular wheat flour with an equal weight or volume of a gluten-free flour blend.**

- **Add ½ teaspoon of xanthan gum per 120g (1 cup) of gluten-free flour blend (if your blend already contains xanthan gum or other binders, add only ¼ teaspoon).**

- **Replace the regular dairy butter with a firm vegan butter block (not a soft spread), and reduce the amount of butter by 20% because the fat response of the gluten-free flour blend outweighs its moisture response. This is equivalent to multiplying the weight of the butter by 0.8 or to reducing its volume by 1½ tablespoons per stick (115g) of butter in the recipe. Also, make sure to use a vegan butter whose flavour you like.**

- **Add 40g (2½ tablespoons) of dairy-free milk for each egg removed to account for the absence of the moisture-providing eggs.**

- **Add 10g (1½ tablespoons) of starch, such as cornflour (cornstarch), arrowroot starch, tapioca starch or potato starch per 120g (1 cup) of flour to ensure that your cookies maintain their shape with neat edges and a smooth, even top surface that is perfect for decorating.**

You'll note that for the gluten-free vegan version (and the same goes for the gluten- and egg-free version as well), you need to use ½ teaspoon of xanthan gum per 120g (1 cup) of gluten-free flour blend, which is double that necessary for the gluten-free version. That's because in the absence of eggs, the gluten-free flour blend doesn't provide enough structure to prevent the cookies from spreading out too much.

If you used just ¼ teaspoon of xanthan gum (as in the gluten-free version), the gluten-free vegan cookies would spread to a final diameter of about 7cm (2¾in), although they do keep their neat, straight edges. The larger quantity of xanthan gum, on the other hand, provides enough extra structure to better control the spread, and the final gluten-free vegan sugar cookies are much closer to the original, regular version, with a diameter of 6.6–6.8cm (about 2⅔in), straight edges and a perfectly smooth top surface. They also have a lovely flavour and a texture that's just the right balance of soft, crisp and crumbly.

Note that this larger amount of xanthan gum is optional and relevant only for cut-out cookies, such as sugar cookies, Linzer cookies and gingerbread cookies, where you want them to maintain their shape to within a few millimetres. If you're making another type of cookie that holds its shape during baking, such as shortbread biscuits, thumbprint cookies or slice-and-bake cookies, where maintaining an exact shape isn't that important, you can use the smaller quantity of ¼ teaspoon per 120g (1 cup) of gluten-free flour blend. Similarly, if you're not too worried about your cut-out cookies spreading a bit more, you can use the smaller amount of xanthan gum.

Regular

Gluten-free

Dairy-free

Egg-free

Vegan

Gluten-free vegan

# Cut-out sugar cookies: recipe

**This recipe makes 32–36 sugar cookies, about 6mm (¼in) thick and cut out with a 6.5cm (2½in) cookie cutter.**

| | DIET | | | | | |
|---|---|---|---|---|---|---|
| | **Regular** | **Gluten-free** | **Dairy-free** | **Egg-free** | **Vegan** | **GF Vegan** |
| plain flour [1] | 360g<br>3 cups | 360g<br>3 cups | 360g<br>3 cups | 360g<br>3 cups | 360g<br>3 cups | 360g<br>3 cups |
| cornflour (cornstarch) [2] | / | / | / | 30g<br>4 tbsp | 30g<br>4 tbsp | 30g<br>4 tbsp |
| caster or granulated sugar | 200g<br>1 cup | 200g<br>1 cup | 200g<br>1 cup | 200g<br>1 cup | 200g<br>1 cup | 200g<br>1 cup |
| xanthan gum | / | ¾ tsp* | / | / | / | 1½ tsp** |
| salt | ¼ tsp | ¼ tsp | ¼ tsp | ¼ tsp | ¼ tsp | ¼ tsp |
| unsalted butter, softened [3] | 225g<br>2 sticks | 180g<br>1½ sticks + 1 tbsp | 225g<br>2 sticks | 225g<br>2 sticks | 225g<br>2 sticks | 180g<br>1½ sticks + 1 tbsp |
| eggs, room temp [4] | 1 | 1 | 1 | / | / | / |
| milk [5] | / | / | / | 40g<br>2½ tbsp | 40g<br>2½ tbsp | 40g<br>2½ tbsp |
| vanilla paste [6] | 1 tsp | 1 tsp | 1 tsp | 1 tsp | 1 tsp | 1 tsp |

[1] Either plain (all-purpose) wheat flour or plain gluten-free flour blend. For the latter, use shop-bought or make your own (see page 24).

[2] Or use an equal weight of arrowroot starch, potato starch or tapioca starch instead.

[3] Either dairy or vegan butter. For the latter, use a firm vegan butter block not a soft spread.

[4] UK medium eggs (US large).

[5] Either whole dairy or a dairy-free milk, excluding canned coconut milk.

[6] Double the quantity if using vanilla extract.

* Omit if your gluten-free flour blend already contains binders.

** If your gluten-free flour blend already contains binders, use only ¾ teaspoon.

1. Line two large baking sheets with baking paper and set them aside until needed.

2. In a large bowl (or the bowl of a stand mixer), whisk together the flour, cornflour (cornstarch; if using), sugar, xanthan gum (if using) and salt.

3. Add the softened butter and, by hand using your fingertips or with a stand mixer fitted with the paddle, work it into the dry ingredients until you get a mixture resembling breadcrumbs.

4. Add the egg or milk (depending on which version you're making) and vanilla, and mix well, either by hand with a wooden spoon or a rubber spatula or with the stand mixer, until the cookie dough comes together in a smooth ball with no patches of dry, unmixed flour. (If you're working in a very warm kitchen and your cookie dough feels too soft to easily handle, chill it in the fridge for about 15 minutes before proceeding to the next step.)

5. Roll out the cookie dough on a lightly floured surface until it's about 6mm (¼in) thick.

6. Cut out individual sugar cookies with a 6.5cm (2½in) round cookie cutter (or other cookie cutter of choice) and transfer them on to the lined baking sheets. Re-use any scraps by gently kneading them together and re-rolling.

7. Chill the cookies in the fridge for 15–30 minutes. While the cookies are chilling, adjust the oven rack to the middle position and pre-heat the oven to 180°C/350°F.

8. One baking sheet at a time, bake the cookies for about 8–10 minutes, or until they are light golden around the edges. (You can bake them a few minutes longer if you want them to be crisper.)

9. Allow the cookies to cool on the baking sheet for about 10 minutes, then transfer them to a wire rack to cool completely.

# Shortbread biscuits: recipe

This recipe makes 16 perfectly buttery, melt-in-the-mouth shortbread biscuits, cut into about 8x2.5cm (3x1in) sticks about 1cm (½in) thick. When making the shortbread cookie dough, it's important that you don't cream the butter and sugar together, as that can make the shortbread spread too much during baking (see page 147) and it can also make it slightly too crumbly. While the shortbread biscuits follow the same modification rules as the cut-out sugar cookies, note that you don't need to add any cornflour (cornstarch) and that you can use just ¼ teaspoon of xanthan gum per 120g (1 cup) of gluten-free flour blend for both the gluten-free and the gluten-free vegan version.

| | DIET | | | |
|---|---|---|---|---|
| | **Regular** | **Gluten-free** | **Dairy-free/ vegan** | **GF Vegan** |
| unsalted butter, softened [1] | 130g<br>1 stick + 1 tbsp | 105g<br>¾ stick + 1½ tbsp | 130g<br>1 stick + 1 tbsp | 105g<br>¾ stick + 1½ tbsp |
| caster or granulated sugar | 50g<br>¼ cup | 50g<br>¼ cup | 50g<br>¼ cup | 50g<br>¼ cup |
| vanilla paste [2] | ½ tsp | ½ tsp | ½ tsp | ½ tsp |
| plain flour [3] | 200g<br>1⅔ cups | 200g<br>1⅔ cups | 200g<br>1⅔ cups | 200g<br>1⅔ cups |
| salt | ¼ tsp | ¼ tsp | ¼ tsp | ¼ tsp |
| xanthan gum | / | ½ tsp* | / | ½ tsp* |

[1] Either dairy or vegan butter. For the latter, use a firm vegan butter block.

[2] Double the quantity if using vanilla extract.

[3] Either plain (all-purpose) wheat flour or plain gluten-free flour blend. For the latter, use shop-bought or make your own (see page 24).

* Omit if your gluten-free flour blend already contains binders.

1. Adjust the oven rack to the middle position, pre-heat the oven to 160°C/325°F and line two large baking sheets with baking paper.

2. In a large bowl, using a wooden spoon or a rubber spatula, mix together the softened butter, sugar and vanilla until combined. Don't cream or aerate the mixture.

3. In a separate bowl, whisk together the flour, salt and xanthan gum (if using).

4. Add the dry ingredients to the butter-sugar mixture, and mix together until you get a slightly crumbly cookie dough. The mixture might look a bit dry at this stage, but that's okay. Gently knead the cookie dough by pressing it against the inside of the bowl, until it comes together in a smooth ball. (Don't overwork the dough if you're using wheat flour.)

5. Roll out the cookie dough between two sheets of baking paper into a 15x20cm (6x8in) rectangle about 1cm (½in) thick. (If you're working in a very warm kitchen, and especially if you're using vegan butter, use the baking paper to slide the rolled-out dough on to a baking sheet, and chill in the fridge for 15–30 minutes before cutting.)

6. Use a sharp knife or a bench scraper to cut the rectangle into sixteen 2.5x8cm (1x3in) sticks and transfer them to the lined baking sheets.

7. Bake the cookies for about 18–22 minutes, or until they are light golden around the edges. Cool on the baking sheets for 10 minutes, then transfer to a wire rack to cool completely.

Regular

Gluten-free

Vegan

Gluten-free vegan

Regular

Gluten-free

Dairy-free

Egg-free

Vegan

Gluten-free vegan

**Rules for adapting cookies that spread during baking**

↓

**p.66**

# Case Study 6:
# Chocolate Chip Cookies
(Cookies that spread during baking)

There are numerous variations of chocolate chip cookies out there. Aside from changing up the type of chocolate and other add-ins you incorporate into the dough, you can play around with the texture. From tall and gooey "Levain-bakery-style" cookies to thin and crisp cookies, there's something for everyone.

Personally, I'm a big believer in the superiority of fudgy chocolate chip cookies. The kind that aren't too soft and cakey, but are wonderfully gooey straight from the oven and fudgy when they cool down, and that get progressively chewier with time. They should have crisp edges and shouldn't be too thick.

To get that perfect gooey-fudgy texture, it's important to underbake your chocolate chip cookies. Aim for cookies that are golden all over, with slightly darker golden-brown edges. The centre of the cookies should be noticeably underbaked when you take them out of the oven – remember that as the cookies stand on the hot baking sheet, they will continue baking and setting for a bit longer, so avoid baking them all the way through (unless you're aiming for a crispy texture).

Before we get to the individual free-from variations, here are a few general tips that you should keep in mind as you progress through this case study:

- **With chocolate chip cookies, it's all about balancing how much and in what way the cookies spread. If they spread too much, you'll end up with thin, crisp puddles. If they spread too little, you'll get balls of baked cookie dough that look nothing like proper chocolate chip cookies. You need to find that middle ground that gives the best texture and appearance.**

- **If a recipe calls for chilling the cookie dough, do not (under any circumstances) skip that step… even if you're an impatient baker like me. Chilling the chocolate chip cookie dough is an incredibly important step that ensures your cookies won't end up as sad little puddles in the oven, and it allows the flavours to mingle and develop.**

- **In general, the texture of your butter (melted or softened) plays a very important role in determining how much your cookies will spread during baking. Using melted butter will typically give cookies that desired spread more than those made with softened butter. Therefore, correctly deciding whether to use melted or softened butter is just as important as chilling the cookie dough.**

- **When using melted butter in a chocolate chip cookie recipe, make sure it's not too warm. Use it when it's lukewarm or at around room temperature.**

**NOTE**

For all of the chocolate chip cookie variations in this case study, I portioned out the cookie dough with a 3-tablespoon ice-cream/ cookie scoop. I prefer larger cookies, but you can easily make smaller ones using a 2-tablespoon scoop, they will just need slightly less time in the oven. This original, regular version, spreads to a final diameter of about 10cm (4in) with a thickness of about 1cm (½in).

With these general guidelines out of the way, let's first look at our starting point: the regular chocolate chip cookie recipe. The ingredients list includes regular dairy butter, light brown soft sugar, caster (superfine) or granulated sugar, room-temperature eggs, a bit of vanilla, plain (all-purpose) wheat flour, baking powder, bicarbonate of soda (baking soda), salt and, of course, a very generous amount of chocolate (either chopped chocolate or chocolate chips).

We'll use melted rather than softened butter to get a fudgier, chewier texture and cookies that spread out quite a bit in the oven, giving a final diameter of about 10cm (4in). Using both white (caster/superfine or granulated) sugar and light brown sugar controls the spread of the cookies, and the brown sugar adds a wonderful depth of flavour that imparts almost caramel-like notes.

The final cookie dough will be quite soft (because of the melted butter) but shouldn't be too sticky or tacky to the touch. This softness can feel a bit counterintuitive – but resist the temptation to add more flour, as that will give you much cakier, doughier cookies that won't spread properly in the oven.

The next step is to chill the cookie dough in the fridge for an hour or two, which cools down the butter and makes it much easier to scoop the individual cookies or shape them into balls with your hands. It also prevents the cookies from turning into sad, flat puddles in the oven – instead, the chilled cookie dough will spread in a controlled manner, resulting in cookies with the perfect thickness, texture and appearance. You can prepare the dough in advance and chill it in the fridge overnight, which will allow the flavours to develop even further.

The final cookies are golden, with a rippled, crinkly surface and crisp, caramelized edges. They're deliciously gooey straight from the oven, and then they get fudgier and chewier as they cool down.

**NOTE**

**To get perfectly round cookies, use the cookie-cutter trick: immediately out of the oven, when the cookies are still hot, soft and malleable, use a round cookie cutter slightly larger than the cookie diameter to nudge the baked cookies into a more evenly rounded shape.**

## Gluten-free

The most common issue you might encounter when making gluten-free chocolate chip cookies is them spreading far too much – almost comically so – during baking.

Compared to regular cookies made with wheat flour, they're much more likely to melt into thin puddles that will eventually make thin, crisp cookies – nothing like the fudgy deliciousness we're aiming for.

There are two main reasons for this: **(1)** the absence of gluten and **(2)** the lower fat tolerance of the gluten-free flour blend compared to regular wheat flour. We can solve **(1)** by adding a binder: you need to add ¼ teaspoon of xanthan gum per 120g (1 cup) of gluten-free flour blend (but no need to add extra if your blend already contains xanthan gum or other binders).

Just like with the cut-out sugar cookies (see page 148), the fat response of the gluten-free flour blend is much more important than the moisture response when making chocolate chip cookies. You can read more about the different moisture and fat responses of gluten-free flours and blends on page 42. In the case of these gluten-free chocolate chip cookies, this means that using the same amount of butter as in the regular version would result in cookies that spread out far too much during baking, essentially melting into puddles.

*30% less butter*          *Full amount of butter*

So, to solve **(2)**, you need to reduce the amount of butter by 30%. This might seem like a lot but rest assured that you'll still get all of that wonderful rich, buttery flavour – it's just that you'll also get cookies that are far more similar in appearance and spread to their regular counterpart. In practice, this means that you need to multiply the weight of the butter by 0.7. If you're working with volume measurements, you'll need to reduce the amount of butter by 2½ tablespoons per stick (115g) of butter in the recipe.

I also recommend using softened rather than melted butter. This is more a suggestion than a strict rule when you're making gluten-free chocolate chip cookies with dairy butter. I've made numerous batches of incredibly delicious cookies with melted butter without any issues – but if you're finding that your cookies still spread too much even after you've reduced the amount of butter, then I definitely recommend switching to softened butter. However, if you're making gluten-free chocolate chip cookies with vegan butter, then using softened butter becomes a necessity (see page 164).

It's very important that you allow the gluten-free cookie dough to chill in the fridge for at least 1–2 hours. This not only cools down and firms up the butter, it also gives the gluten-free flour blend time to properly hydrate, which results in a much nicer appearance and texture for the final baked cookies.

With all these adjustments, the final gluten-free chocolate chip cookies are almost indistinguishable from their regular, gluten-containing equivalent. They have an amazing flavour, the perfect fudgy-chewy texture and they look absolutely mouth-watering.

# Dairy-free

Overall, making the dairy-free variation of these chocolate chip cookies is incredibly straightforward. All you need is a simple 1:1 substitution, where you replace the dairy butter with an equal weight or volume of a vegan butter. I recommend using a firm vegan butter block rather than a soft spread.

The dairy-free dough will be noticeably softer than the regular cookie dough made with dairy butter, even after having been chilled in the fridge for a few hours. That's because vegan butter will always be softer than regular butter at the same temperature, even straight from the fridge.

However, regardless of the different chilled cookie-dough textures, the baked dairy-free chocolate chip cookies (made with wheat flour) actually have a very similar appearance and texture to their regular equivalent. They have an almost identical diameter and thickness, and they're also just as delicious.

**NOTE**

**If you start out with gluten-free chocolate chip cookies and want to substitute dairy butter with a vegan equivalent, you need to use softened rather than melted butter (even if the original recipe calls for melted). (See page 164 for more.)**

# Egg-free

The egg-free replacements are surprisingly simple. I say "surprisingly" because while eggs usually play a number of different, and all incredibly important roles in a recipe (from acting as a binding agent to providing structure and lift) – here, we're interested in them only as a source of moisture. That's because the raising agents and the creaming method are far more impactful than eggs when it comes to the texture of these cookies, and the plain (all-purpose) wheat flour provides more structure than the eggs, so we can ignore their aerating and structure-providing properties.

So, for these cookies, eggs are very easy to substitute with an equal weight of unsweetened plain or Greek-style yogurt, or whole milk. Specifically, you need to add 50g (3½ tablespoons) of milk or yogurt for each egg removed, 35g (2½ tablespoons) for each egg white removed, and 15g (1 tablespoon) for each egg yolk removed.

Yogurt tends to give slightly better results in terms of spread and appearance, especially with a shorter chilling time of only 1–2 hours. Cookies made with milk tend to spread a bit more in the oven, so they'll end up thinner and with a larger diameter compared to the regular version. This difference is easy to understand when you consider the difference in consistency and water content between yogurt and milk. Yogurt is closer in consistency to eggs – and therefore, unsurprisingly, gives more similar results.

However, the difference between the yogurt and the milk versions decreases with an overnight chill in the fridge. Chilling the cookie dough made with milk overnight gives the flour more time to thoroughly absorb the moisture. And, when you bake the cookies the next day, the result is incredibly similar to regular egg-containing cookies – in terms of both their appearance and their texture.

Yogurt

Milk

2-hour chill

24-hour chill

## Vegan

The vegan variation is a straightforward combination of the dairy-free and egg-free adjustments, and you'll need vegan yogurt or dairy-free milk as the egg substitutes. You can use most vegan yogurts, and almond, soy, rice or oat milk – but don't use canned coconut milk, as it can make the cookies too greasy or oily because of its higher fat content.

The only other thing we really need to consider is the difference between the vegan chocolate chip cookies made with either vegan yogurt or dairy-free milk as the egg substitute.

Yogurt

Milk

2-hour chill

Using vegan yogurt as the egg replacement gives gorgeous cookies that spread out slightly less than regular cookies (and are slightly thicker as a consequence) but it's not a huge difference. The cookie dough is of a similar texture and consistency as the regular equivalent.

In comparison, the cookie dough made with dairy-free milk as the egg replacement is noticeably softer than that of the yogurt version: it's almost batter-like, although it does firm up after some time in the fridge. Just like with the egg-free version (see page 162), the milk version spreads out more than the yogurt version after a chill of between 1 and 2 hours in the fridge, but the difference gets progressively smaller, the longer you chill both cookie doughs.

All that said, both egg replacements work great, and you can use either to get truly amazing vegan cookies that taste just as delicious as the original, regular version. If you want slightly thinner cookies that spread out more, use milk. If you want thicker cookies (or if you're impatient and don't want to chill the cookie dough overnight), go with yogurt.

## Gluten-free vegan

The gluten-free vegan variation is just a straightforward combination of all the adjustments we've discussed so far.

So, to make the cookies gluten-free, you need to swap the regular wheat flour for an equal weight or volume of a gluten-free flour blend, add ¼ teaspoon of xanthan gum per 120g (1 cup) of gluten-free flour blend to make up for the lack of gluten (no need to add extra if your blend already contains binders) and reduce the amount of butter by 30% to account for the lower fat tolerance of the gluten-free flour blend.

Then, to make the cookies vegan, you need to substitute the dairy butter with a firm vegan butter block (not a soft spread), and replace the eggs with an equal weight of an unsweetened plain or Greek-style vegan yogurt, or dairy-free milk – about 50g (3½ tablespoons) for each egg removed.

However, unlike all the previous free-from versions, this gluten-free vegan recipe is by far the most sensitive to small changes in ingredients – specifically, to the kind of vegan butter you use. First, it's very important that you use softened rather than melted vegan butter – melted butter would result in sad-looking flat puddles rather than cookies, whereas softened butter helps to control the spread so that the cookies end up with a similar diameter and thickness to the initial, regular version.

Softened butter   Melted butter

Interestingly, the composition (and therefore the brand) of the vegan butter is also very important. Specifically, I've found that firm vegan butters with a fat content of 75% or higher and a high saturated fat content, of 40% or higher, give the best results. That is, they give gluten-free vegan cookies that are closest in appearance and texture to the regular version. In comparison, vegan butters with a similar fat content but a lower saturated fat content (below 30%) result in cookies that are still tasty, but which appear slightly oilier and tend to "melt" around the edges to give a much crisper, crunchier final texture.

*High saturated fat*  *Low saturated fat*

This trend makes sense when you consider that you're trying to replace regular dairy butter, which has a fat content of 80–82% and a saturated fat content of around 50–52%. Using a vegan butter with a composition that's as close as possible to regular dairy butter will naturally give the best results. Note that the effect of different vegan butter compositions is much less prominent with the dairy-free and vegan versions (pages 162 and 163–4, respectively) because those contain gluten and/or eggs, which effectively act as failsafes that ensure that the cookies will spread and bake in a controlled manner. With this gluten-free vegan version, we've removed all these failsafes, so choosing the best possible vegan butter is much more important. (And don't worry – finding out the composition of the vegan butter doesn't require any maths on your part; it's all included in the nutritional information on the packaging or the relevant brand's website!) So, if you're not very happy with how your gluten-free vegan chocolate chip cookies are turning out, try swapping to a different brand of vegan butter, it just might be the answer to all your troubles.

For gluten-free vegan chocolate chip cookies, I also recommend a slightly longer chilling time (even if you want to bake them on the same day). While all other variations work well with a 2-hour chill time, you'll get the best result if you chill your gluten-free vegan cookies for at least 3–4 hours (or ideally overnight).

Finally, once you've made all these changes, the gluten-free vegan chocolate chip cookies are shockingly similar to the regular version. And I don't use the word "shockingly" lightly – they have an amazing, rich flavour and a wonderful chewy-fudgy texture with pleasantly crisp edges. And they look simply gorgeous.

# Chocolate chip cookies: recipe

This recipe makes 12 large chocolate chip cookies (about 10cm/4in diameter), portioned out using a 3-tablespoon ice-cream or cookie scoop.

| | DIET | | | | | |
|---|---|---|---|---|---|---|
| | **Regular** | **Gluten-free** | **Dairy-free** | **Egg-free** | **Vegan** | **GF Vegan** |
| unsalted butter [1] | 150g (melted) 1 stick + 2½ tbsp | 100g (softened) ¾ stick + 1 tbsp | 150g (melted) 1 stick + 2½ tbsp | 150g (melted) 1 stick + 2½ tbsp | 150g (melted) 1 stick + 2½ tbsp | 100g (softened)* ¾ stick + 1 tbsp |
| light brown soft sugar | 120g ½ cup + 1½ tbsp | 120g ½ cup + 1½ tbsp | 120g ½ cup + 1½ tbsp | 120g ½ cup + 1½ tbsp | 120g ½ cup + 1½ tbsp | 120g ½ cup + 1½ tbsp |
| caster or granulated sugar | 70g ¼ cup + 1½ tbsp | 70g ¼ cup + 1½ tbsp | 70g ¼ cup + 1½ tbsp | 70g ¼ cup + 1½ tbsp | 70g ¼ cup + 1½ tbsp | 70g ¼ cup + 1½ tbsp |
| vanilla paste [2] | ½ tsp | ½ tsp | ½ tsp | ½ tsp | ½ tsp | ½ tsp |
| eggs, room temp [3] | 1 | 1 | 1 | / | / | / |
| milk or yogurt, room temp [4] | / | / | / | 50g 3½ tbsp | 50g 3½ tbsp | 50g 3½ tbsp |
| plain flour [5] | 200g 1⅔ cups | 200g 1⅔ cups | 200g 1⅔ cups | 200g 1⅔ cups | 200g 1⅔ cups | 200g 1⅔ cups |
| baking powder | 1 tsp | 1 tsp | 1 tsp | 1 tsp | 1 tsp | 1 tsp |
| bicarbonate of soda (baking soda) | ½ tsp | ½ tsp | ½ tsp | ½ tsp | ½ tsp | ½ tsp |
| salt | ½ tsp | ½ tsp | ½ tsp | ½ tsp | ½ tsp | ½ tsp |
| xanthan gum | / | ½ tsp** | / | / | / | ½ tsp** |
| dark chocolate, chopped or chips | 120g ⅔ cup | 120g ⅔ cup | 120g ⅔ cup | 120g ⅔ cup | 120g ⅔ cup | 120g ⅔ cup |

[1] Either dairy or vegan butter. For the latter, use a firm vegan butter block not a soft spread.

[2] Double the quantity if using vanilla extract.

[3] UK medium eggs (US large).

[4] Either unsweetened dairy or dairy-free plain or Greek-style yogurt; or, either whole dairy or dairy-free milk, excluding canned coconut milk.

[5] Either plain (all-purpose) wheat flour or plain gluten-free flour blend. For the latter, use shop-bought or make your own (see page 24).

* For best results, use a firm vegan butter block with a fat content of at least 75% and a high saturated fat content, of 40% or higher (see page 165).

** Omit if your gluten-free flour blend already contains xanthan gum or other binders.

1. By hand using a large balloon whisk or using a stand mixer fitted with the paddle or a hand-held mixer with the double beaters, mix together the butter, both sugars and the vanilla until well combined. You don't need to cream the mixture or incorporate any air into it at this stage.

2. Add the egg, milk or yogurt (depending on which version you're making) and whisk for a few minutes until the mixture has lightened in colour and is slightly fluffy.

3. In a separate bowl, whisk together the flour, baking powder, bicarbonate of soda (baking soda), salt and xanthan gum (if using).

4. Add the dry ingredients to the wet and mix well until you get a smooth and soft cookie dough with no patches of unmixed flour (if you're making the cookie dough by hand, use a wooden spoon or a rubber spatula).

5. Add in most of the chopped chocolate, reserving some for adding on top of the cookies just before baking. Mix well until evenly distributed.

6. Chill the cookie dough in the fridge for at least 2 hours (or at least 3–4 hours for the gluten-free vegan version) until firm enough to scoop. You can chill it overnight if you wish.

7. While the cookie dough is chilling, adjust the oven rack to the middle position, pre-heat the oven to 180°C/350°F and line two large baking sheets with baking paper.

8. Use a 3-tablespoon ice-cream or cookie scoop to portion out individual balls of cookie dough. You should get 12 cookies in total.

9. Place the cookies on the lined baking sheets, with 6 cookies per baking sheet. Make sure to leave plenty of space between them (at least 5cm/2in), as they will spread out quite a lot during baking.

10. Before they go into the oven, add a few extra pieces of chopped chocolate to the top of each cookie dough ball. This will give you gorgeous puddles of melted chocolate on top of the baked cookies.

11. One baking sheet at a time, bake the cookies for 12–14 minutes, or until they're golden around the edges but the centres still look slightly underbaked. While one baking sheet is in the oven, place the other one in the fridge so that the cookies aren't out at room temperature while they're waiting.

12. Immediately out of the oven, you can correct the shape of the cookies into a more evenly round one. To do this, use a round cookie cutter slightly larger than the cookie diameter to nudge the cookies into shape (see note, page 160).

13. Allow the cookies to cool on the baking sheet for about 5–10 minutes, then transfer them to a wire rack to cool completely.

Regular

Gluten-free

Dairy-free

Egg-free

Vegan

Gluten-free vegan

**Rules for adapting cakey cookies**

**p.68**

# Case Study 7:
# Lemon Crinkle Cookies
**(Cakey cookies)**

Cakey cookies are a somewhat niche cookie category. For the most part, they have a more delicate, tender, moist and – as the name suggests – cakey crumb. They're not crisp and buttery like shortbread, or fudgy and chewy like chocolate chip cookies. These are cookies like chocolate or lemon crinkle cookies, whoopie pies and black-and-white cookies.

I say "for the most part" because this category also includes, rather counterintuitively, the crisp, crunchy and dry biscotti. At first glance, these are the odd cookie out – but actually, they are simply cakey cookies that have gone through a drying process. Their name means "twice baked", and the second bake is at a low oven temperature, which dries them out and gives them their characteristic dry, crunchy texture that makes them perfect for dipping into tea, coffee or hot chocolate.

When it comes to cakey cookies, the thing that gives them their soft, cakey texture and that really defines their chemistry is the relatively high proportion of moisture in the cookie dough compared to the fat content. You can add the moisture through eggs or other ingredients such as milk, yogurt and lemon (or other citrus) juice. For example, take the lemon crinkle cookies that we'll be considering in this case study. They contain 70g (½ stick + 1 tablespoon) of melted butter and a total of about 130g of moisture from the 2 eggs (about 50g for each egg) and 30g (2 tablespoons) of lemon juice.

The high moisture content of cakey cookies often means that their cookie dough is on the softer side (in fact, it can even be almost batter-like) and needs to be chilled in the fridge before you shape and bake it.

Cakey cookies do expand and spread slightly during baking, but that's mostly down to the raising agents. It's not the same spreading action as with chocolate chip cookies, for example, which is largely owing to their high fat and sugar contents. Cakey cookies also don't end up as thin, fudgy and chewy as chocolate chip cookies usually do.

The starting point for this case study is moist, buttery, melt-in-the-mouth-tender lemon crinkle cookies. They're the zesty, lemony version of the perhaps more familiar chocolate crinkle cookies, and they're incredibly delicious.

Initially, the cookie dough will be very soft and sticky, almost batter-like – as is common for cakey cookies with their high moisture content. You need to chill the dough in the fridge for about 2 hours to set the butter within the dough and give the flour time to hydrate (absorb some of the moisture). After this, you can easily scoop and shape the cookies and they won't spread out too much in the oven as they bake.

To achieve their characteristic crinkly appearance, you roll the cookie dough balls in icing (powdered) sugar before baking – this gives them a lovely white, fluffy coat that cracks as the cookies expand. Sometimes, icing sugar can melt into the dough (this can vary depending on numerous factors, including the brand and the exact composition of your icing sugar). As an insurance policy against this, roll the cookie dough balls in granulated sugar before you roll them in the icing sugar.

**NOTE**

**Lemon crinkle cookies get their gorgeous yellow colour mostly from the egg yolks and, to a lesser extent, from the melted butter and the abundance of lemon zest. In the egg-containing versions, you shouldn't need to add any food colouring, but if your egg yolks are on the paler side, you can add a drop or two of yellow colouring if you wish.**

As they bake, the regular lemon crinkle cookies do expand and spread a bit, which results in their characteristic cracking, but they still retain their nicely rounded shape. They definitely don't spread out as much as chocolate chip cookies, for example!

To get an even more tender, melt-in-the-mouth crumb, you can replace up to 10% of the flour with an equal weight of a starch, such as cornflour (cornstarch), potato starch, tapioca starch or arrowroot starch. This follows the same logic as the buttery vanilla cake on page 92: by replacing some of the wheat flour with a starch, you get less gluten development and that, in turn, results in a more delicate texture.

## Gluten-free

With the previous two cookie case studies, the main gluten-free consideration has been the lower fat tolerance of gluten-free flours and blends compared to regular wheat flour. Because those types of cookie contain more fat than moisture, the fat response of the gluten-free flour blend was naturally more important than the moisture response (see page 42).

With cakey cookies, and specifically with these lemon crinkle cookies, the situation is different because they contain a greater amount of moisture from the eggs and lemon juice. Here, the moisture response (that is, the fact that gluten-free flours and blends absorb more moisture than regular wheat flour) is more important.

So, rather than reducing the amount of butter like we did with the gluten-free cut-out sugar cookies and chocolate chip cookies, we need to reduce the amount of flour by 10%, which is equivalent to multiplying the weight of flour by 0.9, or to reducing its volume by 1½ tablespoons per cup of flour in the recipe (just like with the buttery vanilla cake).

You also need to add a binder that mimics the effects of gluten and prevents the cookies from being too delicate and crumbly. Specifically, you need to add ¼ teaspoon of xanthan gum per 120g (1 cup) of gluten-free flour blend (if your blend already contains xanthan gum or other binders, you don't need to add any extra).

The resulting gluten-free lemon crinkle cookies are delightfully buttery, moist and tender, with a delicious lemony flavour and they simply melt in your mouth. You'd certainly never know that they're gluten-free!

**NOTE**

If you're starting out with an egg-free or a vegan cakey cookie recipe and want to make it gluten-free as well, you'll need to add ½ teaspoon of xanthan gum per 120g (1 cup) of gluten-free flour blend instead (or ¼ teaspoon if your blend already contains binders) to account for both the absence of gluten and the structure-providing eggs (see page 172).

## Dairy-free

To make these cakey cookies dairy-free, the changes are straightforward: just swap the dairy butter with an equal weight or volume of a firm vegan butter block – that's it!

Because vegan butter has a slightly lower melting point, the cookie dough will be softer than the regular equivalent even after it's been chilled. However, the 2-hour chilling time will still be sufficient to make the cookie dough firm enough to scoop and then roll in the sugar.

A common difference between dairy-containing and dairy-free bakes is the reduced browning in the latter because of the absence of the milk solids that typically participate in the Maillard reaction (see page 97). However, these lemon crinkle cookies have a relatively short baking time and even the regular ones don't get much (or any) browning in the 8–10 minutes they're in the oven. Plus, they're covered in icing (powdered) sugar anyway, so the dairy-free version is pretty much indistinguishable from the regular one – not just in terms of the flavour and texture, but also visually.

## Egg-free

**NOTE**

Just as with the regular version (and all versions that use wheat flour), you can replace up to 10% of the flour with a starch such as cornflour (cornstarch), potato starch, tapioca starch or arrowroot starch for a more tender, melt-in-the-mouth cookie texture.

Much like with the other two cookie categories we've considered so far, in cakey cookies the eggs mainly play the role of a moisture source.

While they are also a binder and they do provide some lift, this is negligible compared to the structure-providing effects of the flour and the aerating function of the raising agents (baking powder), respectively. So, the only thing that we need to adjust in order to make an egg-free version of these lemon crinkle cookies is to add an alternative moisture source. Here, milk is the best choice – specifically, you need to add 40g (2½ tablespoons) of milk for each egg removed.

The resulting cookie dough will be soft and batter-like (just like with the regular version), but the 2-hour chilling time will firm up the butter in the dough and also give the flour time to absorb some of the moisture. This results in a much firmer dough that you can easily scoop and shape into the individual balls, ready for rolling in icing (powdered) sugar and baking.

As mentioned in the note on page 169, regular egg-containing lemon crinkle cookies get their gorgeous yellow colour from the egg yolks. To make up for their absence in this egg-free version, add a drop or two of yellow food colouring or a pinch of turmeric to achieve a similar effect. Just make sure to add it slowly, as you can always add more but you can't take it away – and you most certainly don't want these to turn out neon yellow! This colour consideration is fairly specific to these lemon crinkles and it isn't relevant with most other cakey cookies. For example, you don't have to worry about it when making chocolate crinkle cookies, biscotti or whoopie pies.

The final egg-free lemon crinkle cookies are incredibly delicious with a delicate, moist, buttery mouthfeel and they look pretty much indistinguishable from the original, regular version.

# Vegan

The vegan version is just a straightforward combination of the dairy-free and the egg-free adjustments: replace the butter with an equal weight or volume of a firm vegan butter block (not a soft spread) and add 40g (2½ tablespoons) of dairy-free milk for each egg removed. Almond, soy, rice and oat milk will all work great, but avoid using canned coconut milk, as it can make the cookies too dense and greasy or oily owing to its high fat content.

Just like with the egg-free version, you can add a drop of yellow food colouring or a pinch of turmeric to achieve that gorgeous yellow colour typical of lemon crinkles. And as before, you can replace up to 10% of the regular wheat plain (all-purpose) flour with an equal weight of a starch (such as cornflour/cornstarch, potato starch, tapioca starch or arrowroot starch) to give the cookies a more tender, delicate crumb by reducing the gluten development.

# Gluten-free vegan

Rather unsurprisingly, the gluten-free vegan version is, for the most part, just the sum of all the changes necessary to make the gluten-free, dairy-free and egg-free variations:

- **Use a gluten-free flour blend and reduce the amount of flour by 10%, which is equivalent to multiplying the weight of the flour by 0.9, or to reducing its volume by 1½ tablespoons per cup (120g) of flour in the recipe. This is necessary because the moisture response of the gluten-free flour blend is more important than the fat response when it comes to cakey cookies (see page 42).**

- **Add xanthan gum to act as a gluten substitute (binder).**

- **Replace the regular dairy butter with an equal weight or volume of a firm vegan butter block (not a soft spread).**

- **Add 40g (2½ tablespoons) of dairy-free milk for each egg replaced.**

However, you need to use slightly more xanthan gum with this gluten-free vegan version than was necessary with the egg-containing gluten-free cookies. Instead of adding ¼ teaspoon per 120g (1 cup) of gluten-free flour blend, you need to add ½ teaspoon instead (or ¼ teaspoon if your gluten-free flour blend already contains xanthan gum or other binders). The same is true if you're making gluten- and egg-free cookies.

This greater quantity of xanthan gum is necessary to account for the absence of both the gluten and the structure-providing eggs. If we were to use only ¼ teaspoon, the cookies would spread too much in the oven and they'd turn out far too crumbly. The slightly larger amount of xanthan gum ensures that they keep their shape and that they have the correct texture: sturdy enough so you can pick them up and have a bite, while also being tender enough so that they simply melt in your mouth.

And just like with all the other eggless versions so far, I recommend adding a drop or two of yellow food colouring or a pinch of turmeric to achieve that lovely yellow colour that lemon crinkle cookies are known for.

Despite the larger quantity of xanthan gum, the gluten-free vegan cookie dough will be noticeably softer and stickier than that of all the other variations, even after a 2-hour chill in the fridge, and it will also spread out more in the oven to give larger and thinner cookies.

So, while you can easily shape the cookie dough into balls with your hands for all the other versions, I recommend dropping it straight into the granulated sugar (see method on page 175) with this gluten-free vegan version to make it less sticky and therefore easier to handle.

Alternatively, you can chill the gluten-free vegan cookie dough in the freezer for 1 hour before shaping and baking the cookies. This has two benefits: first, it makes the cookie dough much easier to handle; and second, the cookies will spread less in the oven, resulting in a taller, more rounded shape much more similar to the original, regular version.

2-hour chill          1-hour freeze

# Lemon crinkle cookies: recipe

This recipe makes 30 small (1-tablespoon) lemon crinkle cookies or 15 large (2-tablespoon) ones. To make the cookies even richer, increase the amount of butter to 85g (¾ stick), but they will spread more during baking.

|  | DIET | | | | | |
|---|---|---|---|---|---|---|
|  | **Regular** | **Gluten-free** | **Dairy-free** | **Egg-free** | **Vegan** | **GF Vegan** |
| caster or granulated sugar | 150g<br>¾ cup | 150g<br>¾ cup | 150g<br>¾ cup | 150g<br>¾ cup | 150g<br>¾ cup | 150g<br>¾ cup |
| lemon zest | 2 lemons | 2 lemons | 2 lemons | 2 lemons | 2 lemons | 2 lemons |
| unsalted butter, melted [1] | 70g<br>½ stick + 1 tbsp | 70g<br>½ stick + 1 tbsp | 70g<br>½ stick + 1 tbsp | 70g<br>½ stick + 1 tbsp | 70g<br>½ stick + 1 tbsp | 70g<br>½ stick + 1 tbsp |
| vanilla paste [2] | ½ tsp | ½ tsp | ½ tsp | ½ tsp | ½ tsp | ½ tsp |
| eggs, room temp [3] | 2 | 2 | 2 | / | / | / |
| lemon juice | 30g<br>2 tbsp | 30g<br>2 tbsp | 30g<br>2 tbsp | 30g<br>2 tbsp | 30g<br>2 tbsp | 30g<br>2 tbsp |
| milk, room temp [4] | / | / | / | 80g<br>⅓ cup | 80g<br>⅓ cup | 80g<br>⅓ cup |
| plain flour [5] | 270g*<br>2¼ cups | 240g<br>2 cups | 270g*<br>2¼ cups | 270g*<br>2¼ cups | 270g*<br>2¼ cups | 240g<br>2 cups |
| baking powder | 1 tsp | 1 tsp | 1 tsp | 1 tsp | 1 tsp | 1 tsp |
| salt | ¼ tsp | ¼ tsp | ¼ tsp | ¼ tsp | ¼ tsp | ¼ tsp |
| xanthan gum | / | ½ tsp** | / | / | / | 1 tsp*** |
| yellow food colouring | / | / | / | optional | optional | optional |
| granulated sugar | 100g<br>½ cup | 100g<br>½ cup | 100g<br>½ cup | 100g<br>½ cup | 100g<br>½ cup | 100g<br>½ cup |
| icing (powdered) sugar | 90g<br>¾ cup | 90g<br>¾ cup | 90g<br>¾ cup | 90g<br>¾ cup | 90g<br>¾ cup | 90g<br>¾ cup |

1. Add the caster or granulated sugar and lemon zest to a large bowl and use your fingertips to rub the zest into the sugar. This helps to release more essential oils from the zest, and it will make your cookies even more lemony and aromatic.

2. Add the melted butter, vanilla, the eggs or milk (depending on which version you're making) and lemon juice, and whisk well until combined.

3. **Optional for egg-free, vegan and gluten-free vegan versions:** add a drop of yellow food colouring or a pinch of turmeric for more vibrant yellow cookies. (Egg-containing cookies get their colour from the egg yolks.)

4. In a separate bowl, whisk together the flour, baking powder, salt and xanthan gum (if using), and add the mixture to the wet ingredients.

5. Mix with a wooden spoon or a rubber spatula until you get a smooth, batter-like cookie dough. At this stage, the cookie dough will really be more like a batter – very loose, soft and sticky, bordering on runny. That's how it should be. Don't add more flour!

6. Chill the cookie dough in the fridge for at least 2 hours, or overnight if you want to bake the cookies the next day. If you're making gluten-free vegan cookies, I recommend freezing them for 1 hour before you start shaping them (see page 173).

7. Adjust the oven rack to the middle position, pre-heat the oven to 180°C/350°F and line two large baking sheets with baking paper.

8. Scoop out the cookie dough into either 1-tablespoon (about 17g) or 2-tablespoon (about 35g) portions. You should get 30–32 of the smaller cookies or 15–16 of the larger cookies in total.

9. Drop each portion of cookie dough directly into a bowl of granulated sugar and roll it around until it's evenly coated. The sugar coating will allow you to handle the cookie dough without it sticking.

10. Once it's covered in granulated sugar, roll each cookie dough ball in icing (powdered) sugar until it's thoroughly coated.

11. Place the sugar-coated cookie dough balls on the lined baking sheets, at least 4–5cm (1½–2in) apart. The cookies will spread and expand slightly during baking.

12. One baking sheet at a time, bake the cookies for 8–10 minutes for the smaller cookies or 9–12 minutes for the larger cookies, or until the cookies have risen and expanded into little rounded mounds with cracks in their sugar coating. The cookies are done when the cracks no longer look wet or shiny. (While the first baking sheet of cookies is in the oven, place the other one in the fridge until needed.)

13. The cookies will be very soft and delicate immediately out of the oven. Leave them to cool on the baking sheet, for at least 10 minutes before transferring them to a wire rack to cool completely.

[1] Either dairy or vegan butter. For the latter, use a firm vegan butter block not a soft spread.

[2] Double the quantity if using vanilla extract.

[3] UK medium eggs (US large).

[4] Either whole dairy or a dairy-free milk, excluding canned coconut.

[5] Either plain (all-purpose) wheat flour or plain gluten-free flour blend. For the latter, use shop-bought or make your own (see page 24).

* For a more tender crumb, replace up to 10% of flour with an equal weight of starch, such as cornflour (cornstarch), potato starch or tapioca starch.

** Omit if your gluten-free flour blend already contains binders.

*** If your gluten-free flour blend already contains binders, use only ½ teaspoon.

# Pastry

While the term "pastry" encompasses a wide range of different (and all incredibly scrumptious) bakes, we'll be focusing specifically on the types of pastry you use when making pies, tarts, galettes and similar.

The crucial aspect of this kind of pastry, and the one that determines its chemistry and how you can adapt it to be free-from (gluten-, dairy-, egg-free, and so on), is how the butter has been incorporated into the dough. On the one hand, it can be fully, intimately incorporated with the rest of the ingredients into a fairly homogeneous dough – as is the case with shortcrust pastry. On the other hand, the butter (or other solid fat) can be left in discrete pieces in the dough, resulting in a flaky texture – this is the case for flaky pie crust.

In the following two case studies, we'll look at both of these examples. The science behind them and the rules for modifying them into their free-from variations are very different, and that's purely because of how we incorporate the butter.

**Rules for adapting shortcrust pastry**

↓

**page 70**

# Case Study 8:
# Shortcrust Pastry

When it comes to shortcrust pastry (or pâte sucrée) and all the free-from variations of it, there are two main things to consider. First, how to achieve a manageable dough that you can roll out and transfer into a tart tin without it being either too soft to handle or so delicate that it cracks and crumbles. And, second, how to get the best possible texture of the baked pastry – one that has just the right balance between crisp and tender.

You want a pastry that's crumbly enough so that it's a joy to eat and easy to cut with a fork – but also sturdy enough that it can hold any fillings. There's little more disappointing than a tart shell that falls apart because it's too delicate... well, except for a tart shell that's so rock-hard you could break your teeth on it.

So, as we look at all the different free-from versions of the shortcrust pastry and how to arrive at them, these are the things we should keep in mind: a manageable dough and a pleasant (but still sturdy enough) baked-pastry texture.

The starting point for this case study is a regular, sweet shortcrust pastry recipe that includes just five ingredients: plain (all-purpose) wheat flour, icing (powdered) sugar, a pinch of salt, chilled dairy butter and an egg. To make it, you combine the flour, sugar and salt, then rub in the chilled butter with your fingertips until you get a mixture resembling breadcrumbs, add the egg and knead everything together into a smooth dough (being careful not to overwork it). Alternatively, you can make the pastry with the help of a food processor, or a stand mixer fitted with the paddle attachment.

It's best to chill the dough in the fridge before you roll it out, just to make it easier to handle. While some recipes require you to bake the pastry with the filling already added (for example, when making a Bakewell tart), we'll be looking at fully blind-baked pastry here, as that gives the best insight into the properties (texture, appearance and flavour) of the shortcrust pastry.

# Gluten-free

Gluten-free shortcrust pastry poses two problems: **(1)** gluten-free pastry dough can be difficult to handle, as it has a greater tendency to crack and tear, and **(2)** the baked pastry can be too delicate and too crumbly. These issues arise because of the lack of gluten.

To solve them, first, you need to add a binder or a gluten substitute. For pastry, use xanthan gum – it enables you to make a dough that handles well and contributes toward the sturdiness of the final bake. For the best results, use ½ teaspoon of xanthan gum per 120g (1 cup) of gluten-free flour blend (or ¼ teaspoon if your blend already contains binders).

For shortcrust pastry, the fat response of the gluten-free flour blend is more important than its moisture response (see page 42). If you were to use the same amount of butter as in the regular version, the gluten-free pastry would be too crumbly, even with the addition of xanthan gum. So, in order to make a gluten-free pastry that's sturdier and less crumbly, you need to reduce the amount of butter by 20%. This might seem like quite a lot, but don't worry, your finished pastry will still have a deliciously rich, buttery flavour – while also having the perfect texture. In practice, this means that you need to multiply the weight of butter by 0.8, or reduce its volume by 1½ tablespoons per stick (115g) of butter in the recipe.

Finally, always chill the gluten-free pastry for at least 30 minutes before rolling it out. Gluten-free dough tends to be a bit softer owing to the absence of gluten, and the chilling step firms up the butter in the dough and gives the gluten-free flour blend some time to hydrate and better absorb the moisture. The result is a chilled pastry that's far easier to roll out and handle.

**NOTE**

**You'll notice that you're using a slightly greater amount of xanthan gum in gluten-free pastry than you'd use, for example, in a typical cake recipe. That's because pastry needs slightly more elasticity and flexibility than your average layer-cake sponge.**

# Dairy-free

Converting a shortcrust pastry recipe to be dairy-free starts by replacing the regular dairy butter with an equal weight or volume of a dairy-free alternative. I recommend using a firm vegan butter block – something that's fairly solid straight from the fridge instead of a soft spread. This ensures that your pastry won't be too soft or too sticky to handle. Additionally, it's best to use a vegan butter block with a fat content of at least 75%.

You might think that just 1:1 substituting dairy butter for its dairy-free equivalent would be the end of the story... but it's not. The resulting pastry would be far too hard and crunchy, and not at all pleasant to eat. The reason for that is not clear – it could be that the greater amount of water in the vegan butter reacts differently with the wheat flour, resulting in greater gluten formation. Or, it could be that vegan butter is really composed of oils, which differ greatly from dairy butter and therefore result in a completely different pastry texture. Regardless of the reason, though, something else must change to get the very best dairy-free shortcrust pastry.

The easiest solution is to reduce the amount of the main structure-providing ingredient: gluten. Substituting 20% of the flour with an equal weight of a starch, such as cornflour (cornstarch), transforms the pastry – it has the ideal texture (crumbly enough to be delicious, sturdy enough to stand up to any fillings) and the dough handles beautifully as well.

In fact, this is great general advice for any shortcrust pastry made with wheat flour: if your baked pastry is too hard and crunchy, substitute about 20% of the flour with an equal weight of a starch to make it more delicate and tender. Or, you could substitute part of the flour with ground nuts, such as hazelnuts or almonds – also a great way to add flavour to your pastry. If you're allergic to nuts, you can use finely ground sunflower seeds instead.

**NOTE**

**The dairy-free pastry dough will never firm up during chilling as much as the regular version. This is because vegan butter will always be softer than regular dairy butter, even when cold from the fridge, and this textural difference carries through to the chilled pastry. However, provided that you chill the pastry for at least 30 minutes, it should become firm enough to roll out and handle without any issues.**

# Egg-free

While eggs play many important roles in baking in general, their primary function in the regular, sweet shortcrust pastry recipe is that of a moisture source. They're what brings all the other ingredients together into a workable dough. They do play a minor structure-providing role as well, but that's negligible when compared to the amount of structure provided by the regular wheat flour. The eggs also don't provide any lift or aeration to the pastry, so we don't need to add any raising agents to this egg-free version.

You have two main options when it comes to choosing an egg substitute: yogurt and milk. I've tested this recipe with both a plain full-fat yogurt and with whole milk. While both give a nice egg-free pastry, the one made with milk is much better: it has a slightly crumblier, more delicate texture.

So, in order to modify the regular shortcrust pastry to be egg-free, you need to substitute the eggs, egg whites and/or egg yolks with an equal weight of milk. Specifically, add 50g (3½ tablespoons) of milk for each egg removed, 35g (2½ tablespoons) for each egg white removed and 15g (1 tablespoon) for each egg yolk removed.

However, only substituting the egg with milk produces a pastry that's still slightly too hard and crunchy to be absolutely perfect – and we are, after all, aiming for perfection here... or as close to it as possible.

So, we'll do the same thing as with the dairy-free version opposite: substitute 20% of the flour with an equal weight of a starch, such as cornflour (cornstarch), tapioca starch, arrowroot starch or potato starch. This reduces the amount of the structure-providing wheat flour (and the amount of gluten) in the pastry, giving a much more delicate, tender texture.

The final, blind-baked egg-free shortcrust pastry has a delicious just-crumbly-enough texture and a gorgeous golden colour. When you first prepare the egg-free dough, it might be slightly stickier to the touch than the regular version, but it'll be wonderful to handle after chilling.

# Vegan

The vegan version of the shortcrust pastry recipe is a straightforward combination of the dairy- and egg-free adjustments, with no extra tweaks necessary.

So, in order to modify a regular shortcrust pastry recipe to be vegan, you need to:

- **Substitute the dairy butter with an equal weight or volume of a firm vegan butter block (not a soft spread).**

- **Substitute the eggs, egg whites and/or egg yolks with an equal weight of dairy-free milk. Specifically, add 50g (3½ tablespoons) of milk for each egg removed, 35g (2½ tablespoons) for each egg white removed and 15g (1 tablespoon) for each egg yolk removed. Dairy-free milks, such as almond, rice, soy or oat milk, will all work great, but avoid using canned coconut milk.**

- **Replace 20% of the regular wheat flour with an equal weight of starch, such as cornflour (cornstarch), potato starch, tapioca starch or arrowroot starch.**

The resulting pastry dough handles beautifully, especially after you've chilled it in the fridge for at least 30 minutes. The blind-baked pastry is beautifully golden and it has the perfect texture that has just the right balance between crumbly and sturdy. So, it's both delicious to eat and stable enough to be filled and sliced.

# Gluten-free vegan

Rather unsurprisingly, the gluten-free vegan variation of shortcrust pastry is the trickiest to get just right – and it's caused me many a headache.

You might expect a gluten-, egg- and dairy-free version to be extremely delicate and crumbly, because of the absence of both main structure-providing ingredients (gluten and eggs). However, the opposite is true. When I initially combined the rules for the gluten-free and for the vegan shortcrust pastry (with no extra tweaks), the baked pastry turned out rock-hard. It was impossible to cut into or break apart... I didn't even want to consider biting into it.

So, in order to get a gluten-free vegan shortcrust pastry that's actually pleasant to eat, we need to increase it crumbliness. You can achieve this in two ways: either introduce some aeration (air pockets) into it; or "disturb" its crumb structure by adding some almond flour (other ground nuts or ground sunflower seeds work as well).

You'll get the best result, though, if you combine the two. So, in order to go from a tooth-breaking, rock-hard pastry to one that has just the right balance between crumbly and sturdy, you need to add ¼ teaspoon of baking powder and 20g (3½ tablespoons) of almond flour per 120g (1 cup) of gluten-free flour blend. If you're allergic to nuts, you can use an equal weight of finely ground sunflower seeds instead – they're a great alternative as they won't add much flavour to your pastry, but they will give it a slightly darker colour. These two simple changes (in addition to all the other gluten-, dairy- and egg-free adjustments) produce a gluten-free vegan shortcrust pastry that's wonderfully crisp, just tender enough, really pleasant to eat and not too hard or too crunchy at all.

Because you're using a gluten-free flour blend that provides less structure than regular wheat flour, plus dairy-free milk instead of eggs, and the softer vegan butter, the pastry would be far too soft and sticky if you were to use the full 50g (3½ tablespoons) of milk for each egg removed, as in the egg-free and vegan variations. Instead, you need to use just enough liquid to bring the ingredients together into a workable dough – about 30g (2 tablespoons) of dairy-free milk is usually the perfect amount for each egg removed. (Note that you can use the full 50g/3½ tablespoons of milk in the gluten- and egg-free versions, as the regular dairy butter isn't as soft.)

This'll give you a gluten-free vegan pastry that's very easy to handle after about 30 minutes chilling in the fridge. While it is slightly more delicate and prone to cracking than the regular version, the difference is minor. I do, though, recommend rolling it out on a sheet of cling film – this will allow you to transfer it into the tart tin without having to worry about it cracking or tearing.

Regular

Gluten-free

Dairy-free

Egg-free

Vegan

Gf vegan

# Shortcrust pastry: recipe

**This recipe makes enough shortcrust pastry for one 23cm (9in) tart.**

| | DIET | | | | | |
|---|---|---|---|---|---|---|
| | **Regular** | **Gluten-free** | **Dairy-free** | **Egg-free** | **Vegan** | **GF Vegan** |
| plain flour [1] | 180g<br>1½ cups | 180g<br>1½ cups | 150g<br>1¼ cups | 150g<br>1¼ cups | 150g<br>1¼ cups | 180g<br>1½ cups |
| cornflour (cornstarch) [2] | / | / | 30g<br>¼ cup | 30g<br>¼ cup | 30g<br>¼ cup | / |
| almond flour [3] | / | / | / | / | / | 30g<br>5 tbsp |
| icing (powdered) sugar | 40g<br>⅓ cup | 40g<br>⅓ cup | 40g<br>⅓ cup | 40g<br>⅓ cup | 40g<br>⅓ cup | 40g<br>⅓ cup |
| salt | ¼ tsp | ¼ tsp | ¼ tsp | ¼ tsp | ¼ tsp | ¼ tsp |
| xanthan gum | / | ¾ tsp* | / | / | / | ¾ tsp* |
| baking powder | / | / | / | / | / | ½ tsp |
| unsalted butter, cubed, chilled [4] | 85g<br>¾ stick | 70g<br>½ stick + 1 tbsp | 85g<br>¾ stick | 85g<br>¾ stick | 85g<br>¾ stick | 70g<br>½ stick +1 tbsp |
| eggs [5] | 1 | 1 | 1 | / | / | / |
| milk [6] | / | / | / | 50g<br>3½ tbsp | 50g<br>3½ tbsp | 30g<br>2 tbsp |

[1] Either plain (all-purpose) wheat flour or plain gluten-free flour blend. For the latter, use shop-bought or make your own (see page 24).

[2] Or use an equal weight of tapioca, potato or arrowroot starch.

[3] If you have a nut allergy, use an equal weight of finely ground sunflower seeds.

[4] Either dairy or vegan butter. For the latter, use a firm vegan butter block not a soft spread.

[5] UK medium eggs (US large).

[6] Either whole dairy or a dairy-free milk, excluding canned coconut milk.

* If your gluten-free flour blend already contains binders, use only ½ teaspoon.

### By hand

1. In a large bowl, whisk together the flour, cornflour (cornstarch; if using), almond flour (if using), icing (powdered) sugar, salt, xanthan gum (if using) and baking powder (if using).

2. Add the butter and use your fingertips or a pastry cutter to work it into the dry ingredients until you get a mixture resembling breadcrumbs.

3. Add the egg or milk (depending of which free-from version you're making) and mix well until the dough starts coming together, then give it a gentle knead until the dough forms a smooth ball. Wrap it tightly in cling film and chill it in the fridge for at least 30 minutes before you use it in a recipe.

### With a stand mixer

1. In the bowl of a stand mixer fitted with the paddle, whisk together the flour, cornflour (cornstarch; if using), , almond flour (if using), icing (powdered) sugar, salt, xanthan gum (if using) and baking powder (if using).

2. Add the butter and mix with the stand mixer on medium–low speed until you get a mixture resembling breadcrumbs.

3. Add the egg or milk (depending of which free-from version you're making) and mix well until the dough comes together in a ball. Wrap it tightly in cling film and chill it in the fridge for at least 30 minutes before you use it in a recipe.

### With a food processor

1. Add the flour, cornflour (cornstarch; if using), almond flour (if using), icing (powdered) sugar, salt, xanthan gum (if using) and baking powder (if using) to the bowl of a food processor. Pulse a couple of times to combine.

2. Add the butter and pulse until you get a mixture resembling breadcrumbs.

3. Add the egg or milk (depending of which free-from version you're making) and pulse until the dough comes together in a ball. Wrap it tightly in cling film and chill it in the fridge for at least 30 minutes before you use it in a recipe.

### Blind baking

1. Roll out the chilled pastry until it's about 3–4mm (⅛in) thick and use it to line a 23cm (9in) loose-bottom tart tin (about 3.5cm/1½in deep). Cut away any excess pastry.

2. Chill the pastry in the fridge for at least 30 minutes. In the meantime, pre-heat the oven to 180°C/350°F with a large baking sheet on the middle oven rack.

3. Dock the bottom of the chilled pastry with a fork, line it with a sheet of baking paper and fill it to the brim with baking beans (rice or dried beans work too). Place the tart tin directly on the hot baking sheet and blind bake for 18–20 minutes, or until the edges are light golden.

4. Remove the baking beans and baking paper, and bake for a further 8–10 minutes, or until the pastry is evenly golden (with slightly darker edges), fully baked through, and crisp.

5. Allow the pastry to cool completely in the tart tin before you add any fillings or use it according to your chosen recipe.

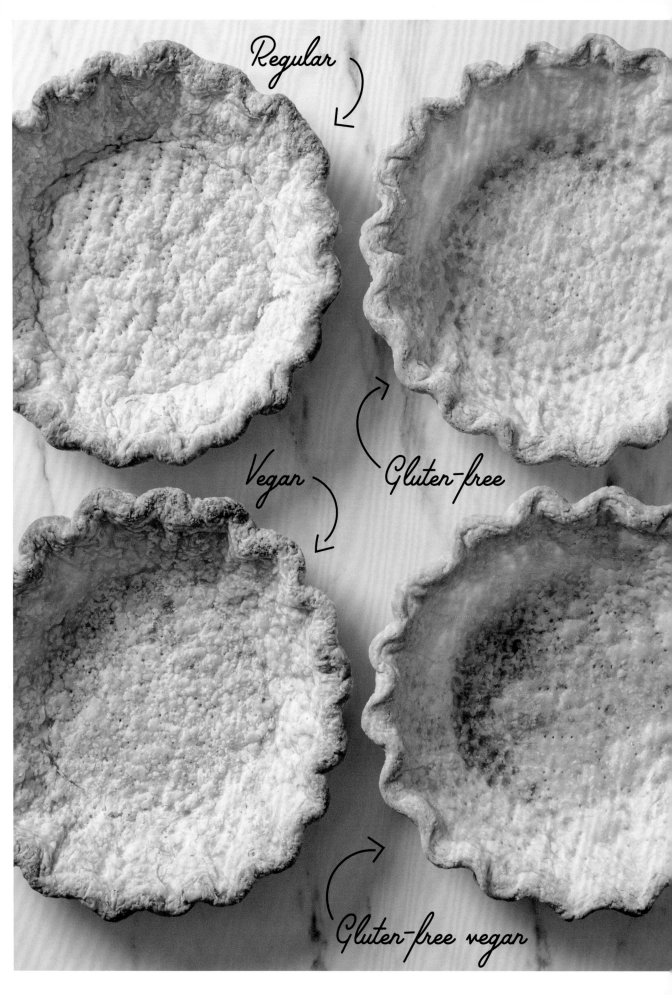

Regular

Gluten-free

Vegan

Gluten-free vegan

**Rules for adapting flaky pastry**

↓

**p.72**

# Case Study 9:
# Flaky Pie Crust

While there are numerous pie-crust variations out there, here we're talking about the classic ultra-flaky pie crust you'd use to make an apple pie, for example, complete with a pretty lattice on top and a decorative crimp around the edges. We want to achieve the maximum flakiness and a pastry that puffs up and gets all golden and gorgeous during baking. It should also be beautifully tender, so that it shatters when you cut or bite into it.

With any flaky pastry (be that flaky pie crust, puff pastry, rough puff pastry or even croissant dough), it's really all about the butter existing in discrete pieces or layers in a dough "matrix", rather than being completely incorporated into the dough as it is with shortcrust pastry (see page 179). What you really want to achieve with a flaky pie crust are a multitude of butter-dough layers. When such a pastry enters a hot oven, the butter melts and the water content in the butter turns into steam, which forces the dough layers apart, resulting in that characteristic, deliciously flaky texture.

The most common method of achieving these butter-dough layers in a pie crust (and the one we'll use in this case study) is to toss regular dairy butter – chilled, straight from the fridge and cut into 1cm (½in) cubes – in the flour and then squish each piece between your fingertips until your butter pieces are approximately the size of walnut halves. Leaving the butter pieces fairly large is crucial here, as it ensures maximum flakiness.

In addition to the butter being responsible for the flaky texture and the puffing action during baking, it also plays a tenderizing role in the pie crust. That's because some of it gets more thoroughly incorporated into the dry ingredients as you're squishing all the butter pieces – and this ensures that the baked pastry is beautifully shatter-y and delicate rather than tough or hard. Ideally, it should be tender enough that you can easily cut through it with a fork.

Once you've worked the butter into the dry ingredients, you need to add just enough very cold water so that all the flour is properly hydrated and the dough starts coming together. It's very important that you don't add too much water, as that can result in too much gluten development and therefore a tough baked pastry. Your final pie dough should be "shaggy" in appearance and somewhat stick together, but it shouldn't feel wet or sticky to the touch. Note that any water amounts listed in pie-crust recipes are merely rough guidelines – always add water gradually (1–2 tablespoons at a time) and make sure to toss the mixture properly to get the moisture as evenly distributed as possible before adding the next portion of water.

In order to get all those lovely butter-dough layers, it's crucial that the butter pieces don't soften too much and melt into the surrounding dough. So, make sure to chill the pastry at regular intervals – and never let it get so soft or warm that the butter pieces start melting. And if you happen to have warm hands, I recommend tossing the mixture with a fork or spatula rather than your hands or fingertips as you add the water.

The final step in achieving the flakiest pie crust possible is lamination – that is, folding the pastry over itself (many times) to multiply the number of butter-dough layers. This is the same process you'd use when making croissant dough or puff pastry. Here, I've found that two letter folds are just enough to get perfectly flaky pie crust. To do a letter fold, roll out the pastry into a long rectangle and then fold it as you would a letter: one third down toward the middle and then the other third up over that. For this flaky pie crust, you need to do this twice, rotating the dough by 90 degrees after the first fold.

In addition to making the final pie crust flakier, the laminating step makes it smoother and easier to handle when you roll it out and assemble the pie.

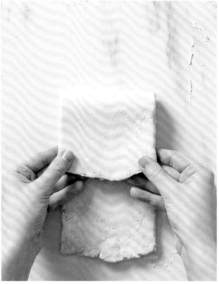

**NOTE**

For all the pie crusts in this case study, I rolled out the dough to about 2–3mm (⅛in) thick. Then, I baked it in two forms: as small "free form" sheets that were allowed to puff up without docking them or weighing them down; and as a fully blind-baked 23cm (9in) pie crust – at 200°C/400°F covered with a sheet of baking paper and filled with baking beans for 18–20 minutes, then uncovered for a further 10 minutes, or until evenly golden brown.

The result is a ridiculously tender, flaky, shatter-y pie crust that puffs up beautifully in the oven if left to its own devices (that is, if you don't weigh it down with baking beans or rice, as you would when blind baking). It's so flaky and puffy that you can, in fact, use it as you would (rough) puff pastry – so it is a 2-for-1 recipe! (To make rough puff pastry, I recommend doing a total of four letter folds.)

This pie dough is a real joy to work with. It's very easy to roll out and handle, and you can easily crimp the edges or use it to create a lattice top for a double-crust pie. Just make sure to chill the pastry again before you bake it – this cools down and sets the butter in the pie crust and prevents it from leaking out during baking.

A final piece of advice: if you've ever struggled with transferring the rolled-out pie crust into the pie dish, I recommend rolling it out on a sheet of cling film or baking paper. This makes transfer much easier, and it reduces the chances of the pie crust tearing as you're handling it, which is even more important when you're making the more fragile gluten-free and gluten-free vegan pie crust variations (pages 191 and 194, respectively).

Before we get to the free-from versions, we first need to define a couple of terms you'll find me using to describe the properties of the various pie crusts: flakiness, puffiness and tenderness. Many recipe books use the terms interchangeably, but they actually describe slightly different aspects of the pastry. And, as we'll be analyzing all the different versions in quite a bit of detail, we want to be precise about what exactly each of these terms is referring to.

**TENDERNESS**

**How tender the pastry is – how easy it is to break apart, to bite into or to cut.** There is some correlation between flakiness and tenderness in that the flakier the pastry is, the more tender it will be – after all, several paper-thin "sheets" of pastry stacked together are far more delicate than one thick pastry layer, all other things staying the same. However, while flakiness is one of the factors that determines the tenderness of the pastry, there are others too.

**PUFFINESS**

**How much the flaky pastry puffs up during baking if it's left to its own devices (when it's not, say, docked with a fork or weighed down with a baking sheet or baking beans).** Puffiness and flakiness are often conflated simply because flakier pastries are often also puffier – but, as we'll soon see, that's by no means a firm rule. If we want to be more quantitative, puffiness measures how much the individual pastry layers are pushed apart by the steam generated from the moisture content of butter (or an alternative fat source) during baking.

**FLAKINESS**

**The presence of individual pastry layers that become visible as you break the pastry or cut it in half.** The flakier the pastry, the more well-defined the layers, the greater their number, and, usually, the thinner they are, although that also depends on how thinly you've rolled the pastry out.

# Gluten-free

There are two things that we need to consider for a gluten-free flaky pie crust: **(1)** the absence of gluten and therefore the lack of the elasticity and extensibility that it adds to the pastry, and **(2)** the greater water-absorption capacity of gluten-free flours and blends. Because butter is predominantly present in discrete pieces in the pie dough, the fat response is less important here and we can ignore it.

The tweaks, then, for a gluten-free flaky pie crust are straightforward: add xanthan gum to act as a gluten substitute and increase the amount of water slightly to account for the fact that the gluten-free flour blend absorbs more moisture than regular wheat flour.

In comparison to cake or cookie recipes, you need to use a slightly larger amount of xanthan gum (½ teaspoon per 120g/1 cup of gluten-free flour blend, or ¼ teaspoon if your blend already contains binders) because the pie crust needs a greater amount of flexibility than, for example, a chocolate chip cookie or a vanilla layer cake. After all, you want to be able to handle it easily through two rounds of lamination and then through assembling an actual pie, including crimping the edges and possibly also creating a lattice top – all without the pastry cracking, crumbling or tearing.

You need to increase the amount of water by about 20% compared to the regular version, which is usually sufficient to hydrate all the gluten-free flour blend and give a shaggy pie dough that comes together in a ball. As with the regular version, it's very important that all the flour is properly hydrated and that there are no patches of dry flour – otherwise, they'll give you trouble down the line. An increase of 20% corresponds to multiplying the weight of the water listed in the recipe by 1.2, or to increasing its volume by about 3 tablespoons per cup of water used.

However, as with the regular version, it's best to add the water slowly (1–2 tablespoons at a time) and use the amount given in the recipe (or calculated from the rules) only as a rough guideline. This is especially important with this gluten-free version because different gluten-free flour blends can vary widely in terms of how much water they absorb – you might need to add either less or more water than is listed in the recipe on page 200 (and also in comparison to the recipe you might be modifying using the rules on page 72).

With these two simple adjustments, you'll get a gluten-free flaky pie dough that handles really well. Although it is slightly more delicate than the regular flaky pie dough, there's not an enormous difference (and the two rounds of letter folds make it smoother and more flexible). If your gluten-free pie crust has been in the fridge for a few hours or overnight, leave it out on the counter at room temperature until it's more malleable – a pie crust that's too cold and hard is more likely to crack. It shouldn't be so warm and soft that the butter starts melting or that it sticks to the work surface, but it should be pliable enough that you can roll out, bend and fold the pastry without it cracking.

Again, I recommend rolling out the pie crust on a sheet of cling film or baking paper. This will help you to transfer it into the pie dish without having to worry about it tearing as you lift it up, especially given that it will always be slightly more fragile than a flaky pie dough made with regular wheat flour. Any small tricks that help you to get it into the pie dish in one pristine piece, I think are always very useful to know.

The final baked gluten-free pastry is wonderfully flaky and tender, and it's incredibly similar to the original, regular version. The most notable difference is that it puffs up slightly less in the oven when it's baked without being weighed down, but that's only a minor difference and it's not hugely important when making a pie crust.

As the flaky pie crust doesn't contain any eggs, the dairy-free and the vegan versions of it are the same. With this vegan flaky pie crust, we have two vegan butter alternatives to choose from: vegan butter block and vegetable shortening. My go-to butter alternative for most of dairy-free and vegan baking is a firm vegan butter block, as it fairly accurately mimics the composition of dairy butter in terms of the fat and water content. There are, of course, some differences: vegan butter contains slightly less fat – usually in the 75–80% range compared to 80–82% for dairy butter – and therefore slightly more water.

Also, not all vegan butter blocks are created equal. The composition in one brand can differ significantly compared with another. Most notably this is true of the saturated fat, the content of which can vary from about 25% to 50%. That's not hugely important when it comes to vegan pie crust, where the wheat flour acts as a failsafe to ensure the pie crust will work out perfectly almost regardless of what kind of vegan butter you use – as long as it's a firm vegan butter block, not a soft spread. However, the composition is far more important when you're making a gluten-free vegan pie crust – more on that on pages 194–5.

Compared to vegan butter, vegetable shortening is 100% fat with zero water content. And when it comes to flaky pie crust, vegetable shortening is a very handy extra trick to have up your sleeve. Because of the different fat and water contents of the vegan butter block and vegetable shortening, they result in very different pie-crust textures in terms of their flakiness, puffiness and tenderness.

To explore these differences in a bit more detail, let's have a look at three different versions of the vegan flaky pie crust: one made only with vegan butter, one made only with vegetable shortening and one made with a 50:50 ratio of the two. The total combined weight of the vegan butter alternatives is the same as that of dairy butter in the regular pie crust, so it's a 1:1 substitution. In all cases, I used cubed, chilled fat from the fridge (not frozen). I tossed it in the dry ingredients and then worked it in until it was approximately the size of walnut halves. Then, I followed the same method as with the regular pastry: add cold water, bring the pastry together, chill, and laminate with two letter folds.

**Flakiness**

All three versions are fundamentally the same in terms of flakiness: they all comprise a multitude of very thin, well-defined pastry layers that are clearly visible when you break the pastry apart or cut into it.

*Vegan butter block*   *50:50*   *Vegetable shortening*

### Puffiness

There are much more pronounced differences in puffiness. The vegan butter version is puffiest by far, the shortening version is the least puffy, and the 50:50 version falls in between. This makes sense when you think about the origins of puffiness.

Any regular flaky, laminated pastry made with dairy butter (be that a flaky pie crust, puff pastry or a quick rough puff pastry) comprises a multitude of butter-dough layers. It puffs up during baking because of the moisture content in those layers. As the pastry enters the hot oven, that moisture turns into steam, forcing the dough layers apart. *Et voilà!* The pastry puffs up.

As vegan butter, like dairy butter, has a significant water content, pie crust made with vegan butter will also puff up during baking. However, vegetable shortening is 100% fat with no moisture content to speak of, so it puffs only very slightly. The 50:50 version falls between the two, as it has a moisture content that's 50% smaller than that of vegan butter (and 50% greater than that of shortening).

Even though the vegan pie crust made with vegan butter does puff up, it does so noticeably less than the regular version. When you bake the two pie crusts in the form of small sheets without weighing them down, the regular version reaches about 2cm (¾in) high, whereas the vegan butter version puffs only to about 1.2cm (½in) – about 50% less.

However, that's not a crucial consideration when it comes to making pie crust. Here, we're far more interested in the flakiness and tenderness. After all, much of the pie crust ends up weighed down anyway, either with a pie filling or baking beans.

### Tenderness

Just like with the puffiness, there are notable differences in the tenderness of the three versions of the dairy-free/vegan flaky pie crust. Shortening produces a flaky pie crust that's very tender, whereas that made with only vegan butter is noticeably crisper. That's not to say that it's hard or tough in any way (it's still very delicious), there's just a slight textural difference. The 50:50 version is closer to the all-shortening version, with a very tender texture.

This difference in tenderness is especially obvious on the day of baking – over time, as the pastry absorbs some of the ambient moisture and also the moisture from any fillings, the tenderness of the three versions becomes far more comparable.

All three versions give a pie dough that's easy to roll and handle, including when you crimp the edges and assemble a pie lattice. However, the softer consistency of vegan butter carries over to the dough, so it is slightly softer compared to the regular version, even if it's been in the fridge for a few hours. The vegan butter and vegetable shortening both melt faster than dairy butter, so do chill your flaky pie crust if it's getting too soft and too warm during making.

**NOTE: A WORD ON COCONUT OIL**

You might be wondering why I haven't mentioned coconut oil as a suitable butter alternative for a vegan pie crust. While coconut oil is a solid fat at and around room temperature and so a seemingly suitable substitute, it actually solidifies too much when you chill the pastry in the fridge – it turns into rock-hard shards that cut into the pastry as you try to roll it out and laminate it. And while the final, baked pie crust does show a surprising amount of flakiness, its texture and thickness tend to be rather inconsistent and patchy (even if you roll it out very evenly to the same thickness throughout). That's why I don't recommend using coconut oil as a dairy butter substitute in flaky pastry – a firm vegan butter block or vegetable shortening will give you far better (and more consistent) results.

# Gluten-free vegan

The gluten-free vegan pie crust is by far the trickiest one to perfect, simply because minor changes in the ingredients, ingredient quantities and preparation method can drastically change its texture from pleasantly crisp to tooth-breakingly crunchy.

Just as with the gluten-free flaky pie crust, you need to add ½ teaspoon of xanthan gum per 120g (1 cup) of gluten-free flour blend (or ¼ teaspoon if your blend already contains binders). This acts as a gluten substitute and it will give the pie dough some flexibility and elasticity so that it's easier to handle and less likely to crumble apart. However, there are four other very important factors that affect the texture of the gluten-free vegan pie crust.

1. **The size of the fat pieces** How large you keep the fat pieces when you rub the vegan butter and/or vegetable shortening into the dry ingredients determines how much butter leakage you'll get. The larger the fat pieces, the more likely it is that they'll leak out during baking, resulting in a greasy and very hard, crunchy pie crust. I recommend working the vegan butter into the dry ingredients until you get smaller, pea-sized pieces.

2. **The amount of water** Choosing the right amount of water to add to the gluten-free vegan pie dough is a balancing act. More water will give you a flaky pie dough that's more pliable and less likely to crack – but it's also more likely to leak fat during baking, resulting in a hard, crunchy pastry. Less water will give you a more tender, delicate baked pastry – but the dough is more likely to crack and tear as you roll it out and handle it.

3. **The composition of the vegan butter block** Choosing the correct vegan butter block is absolutely essential if you want your gluten-free vegan pie crust to be perfectly flaky and tender. For best results, use a firm vegan butter block (not a soft spread) with a high fat content (75% or higher) and a high saturated fat content (40% or higher).

4. **The ratio of vegan butter to vegetable shortening** Just like with the vegan pie crust (see pages 192–3), adjusting the ratio of the vegan butter block to vegetable shortening allows you to tailor the tenderness and crispness of the pie crust. With this gluten-free vegan version, this effect is much more pronounced.

**Preparation method and amount of water**

Vegan butters have a greater tendency to leak out of the pastry during baking because of their lower melting point compared to dairy butter. With the vegan version, this isn't as noticeable because the regular wheat flour creates a stronger, more flexible "framework" that better envelopes the fat particles and therefore reduces the fat leakage. With the gluten-free vegan version, however, this tendency toward melting and fat leakage is very much of significance, and definitely a potential headache.

You can reduce the chances of fat leakage by working the chosen vegan butter alternative into the dry ingredients until you get smaller, pea-sized pieces (instead of walnut-sized pieces as was the case with all the other pie-crust versions so far). Although the fat pieces are smaller, they'll still provide a good degree of flakiness, while also ensuring that you don't end up with a greasy, oily mess and a smoke-filled oven.

*Pea-sized butter pieces*      *Walnut-sized butter pieces*

Working the vegan fat into the dry ingredients to a greater extent has another important effect on the pastry: it means that you'll need less water to bring the pastry together into a workable dough. After all, there are essentially two things that bring a pie dough together: fat that's finely, intimately mixed with the flour, and water. So, the greater the amount of that kind of fat, the less water you'll need.

This brings us to the second point: it's VERY important (yes, so important that it calls for all caps) that you don't use too much water in the gluten-free vegan pie crust. Compared to the regular and vegan versions, you need to reduce the amount of water by about 10%, and compared to the gluten-free variation made with dairy butter, you need to reduce it by about 25%. The reason for this lies in the all-important fat and moisture responses of gluten-free flours and blends (see page 42).

Simply put, when the gluten-free vegan flaky pie crust enters the oven and the vegan butter melts, the water and the melted fat have to fight each other for which one will get preferentially absorbed by the gluten-free flour blend in the pastry. Water will always get absorbed first (and some of it will, of course, evaporate) and if you use too much of it, there won't be enough gluten-free flour blend around to absorb the fat. So, the fat will instead leak out, resulting in an oily mess and a rock-hard, unpleasantly crunchy pie crust. Using a smaller amount of water will prevent of all that.

That said, keep in mind that as with all the pie-crust versions so far, the amount of water listed in any recipe is just a rough guideline, and you might need to use more or less water depending on several factors, including the exact gluten-free flour blend you're using.

Even with the smaller amount of water, the gluten-free vegan flaky pie dough can feel a bit sticky or tacky initially, before the first chill in the fridge. But don't worry – much of that apparent stickiness comes from the vegan butter and shortening becoming a bit softer as they warm up at room temperature. If you lightly touch a part of the pie dough that doesn't have any fat on its surface, you'll see that it's not sticky. Furthermore, lots of moisture will get absorbed by the gluten-free flour blend during the first chill in the fridge. So, while you do have to reduce the amount of water slightly, don't go overboard, otherwise you'll be left with a very dry and crumbly pie dough. Reducing it by 10% compared to the regular pie crust (and by 25% compared to the gluten-free one) is more than enough.

### Vegan butters

Choosing the correct vegan butter block is absolutely crucial – it's far more important than it was with the vegan-only version on page 192. I've found that you'll get the best result if you use a firm vegan butter block (not a soft spread) with a high fat content in the 75–80% range and, most importantly, with a high saturated fat content, of 40% or higher. (Don't worry – finding out the composition of the vegan butter block doesn't require any maths; it's all included in the nutritional information on the packaging or the relevant brand's website.)

Gluten-free vegan pie crust made with a vegan butter block with a high saturated fat content is pleasantly tender and crisp, so that you can easily bite or cut into it. In comparison, pie crust made with vegan butter with a lower saturated fat content, below 30%, can be horrendously hard and crunchy, so much so that it's almost inedible. This makes sense when you consider that you're trying to replace dairy butter, which has a saturated fat content of around 50–52%. And the closer you can get to that value with your vegan butter, the better the end result. Therefore, it's definitely worth experimenting with different brands of vegan butter until you find the one that's best suited to making flaky pastry – it truly makes an enormous difference.

### Tailor the tenderness with vegetable shortening

You can further tweak the texture of your gluten-free vegan pie crust by adding vegetable shortening into the mixture. In fact, this allows you to get away with using a vegan butter block with a lower saturated fat content, just in case you can't find an alternative.

To analyze the effect of vegetable shortening, we'll once again look at the versions made only with a firm vegan butter block, only with vegetable shortening, and with a 50:50 ratio of the two. In all cases, the total combined weight of the vegan butters is the same as that of dairy butter in the regular flaky pie crust, so it's a 1:1 substitution.

*Vegan butter block*    *50:50*    *Vegetable shortening*

Overall, the trends of the vegan variations (see pages 192–3) continue here, but they're much more exaggerated, especially when it comes to the tenderness of the pie crust. All three versions give comparable levels of flakiness, and the puffiness follows the same outcomes as before, with vegan butter giving the puffiest pastry, vegetable shortening resulting in a pastry that puffs up only negligibly in the oven, and the 50:50 version falling somewhere in between.

But when it comes to tenderness, the differences are enormous – and hugely important: using only vegan butter gives the crispest pastry, whereas the vegetable shortening version is the complete opposite in that it is so tender that it's almost too crumbly. In fact, it's almost shortbread-like in its delicate texture.

The 50:50 mixture of vegan butter and vegetable shortening gives just the right balance of the sturdiness of the all-vegan-butter version and the tenderness of the all-shortening version. If we extrapolate this, you could tailor the tenderness of your gluten-free vegan pie crust by adjusting the ratio of vegan butter to vegetable shortening. For example, if the only option available to you is to use a vegan butter with a low saturated fat content, then I definitely recommend using a 50:50 mixture of the vegan butter and shortening; or, if you want the pastry to be even more tender, you could increase the proportion of vegetable shortening further, to a shortening-to-vegan butter ratio as high as 2:1.

However, if you find a firm vegan butter block that has a high saturated fat content and that's perfect for making flaky pastry, then you can get away with not using any vegetable shortening at all.

### Handling the pie dough

Vegan butter actually gives a pie dough that's the easiest to work with, whereas the all-shortening version is almost impossible to fold and crimp, as it cracks and crumbles very easily. The 50:50 mixture is far more manageable and, while not as flexible and pliable as the all-vegan-butter version, it still gives a fairly polished pie crust with a nice crimp.

Unfortunately, you will have to accept that the gluten-free vegan pie crust will always be more prone to cracking and tearing than the regular and vegan versions made with wheat flour – and also the gluten-free one, as dairy butter lends it some malleability and flexibility. But when you consider that we've removed gluten and dairy from a pie-crust recipe whose main components are gluten-containing wheat flour and dairy butter... well, the finished pie crust is actually shockingly delicious! It has a good degree of flakiness, a delicate and tender texture, and there's just enough puff to it.

Because the gluten-free vegan flaky pie dough is more fragile, I recommend rolling it out on a sheet of cling film or baking paper. This will help you to transfer it into the pie dish without having to worry about it tearing as you lift it up.

### Blind baking

Blind baking a gluten-free vegan flaky pie crust will always result in some degree of fat leakage. It's inevitable. Even if you do all the right things and follow my advice and the recipe to the letter, and your pie crust ends up perfectly flaky and tender, it will probably still leak a bit of fat during baking. For this reason, I recommend placing the pie dish on a large baking sheet in the oven. This way, any leaks won't end up on the bottom of the oven, and you'll avoid both smoking out your kitchen and having to clean up your oven afterwards. And don't worry if you see a bit of oil on top of your gluten-free vegan flaky pie crust after you've removed the baking beans and baking paper – it will get reabsorbed during the rest of baking and subsequent cooling.

**NOTE**

As with the dairy-free flaky pie crust, a warning about coconut oil. Using coconut oil in this dough would turn it rock solid when you chill it in the fridge. This makes rolling it out very challenging, even if you allow the pastry to stand at room temperature beforehand. It will crack and crumble and therefore be impossible to handle.

Regular

Gluten-free

Dairy-free / Vegan

Gluten-free vegan

# Flaky pie crust: recipe

This recipe makes enough pie dough for one single-crust 23cm (9in) pie. To make a double-crust pie (with a base and lid), double the recipe.

| | DIET | | | |
|---|---|---|---|---|
| | **Regular** | **Gluten-free** | **Dairy-free/ Vegan** | **GF Vegan** |
| plain flour [1] | 160g<br>1⅓ cups | 160g<br>1⅓ cups | 160g<br>1⅓ cups | 160g<br>1⅓ cups |
| caster or granulated sugar | 5g<br>1 tsp | 5g<br>1 tsp | 5g<br>1 tsp | 5g<br>1 tsp |
| salt | ¼ tsp | ¼ tsp | ¼ tsp | ¼ tsp |
| xanthan gum | / | ½ tsp* | / | ½ tsp* |
| unsalted butter, cubed, chilled [2] | 115g<br>1 stick | 115g<br>1 stick | 115g**<br>1 stick | 55g***<br>½ stick |
| vegetable shortening | / | / | / | 55g<br>¼ cup + ½ tbsp |
| cold water | 60g<br>¼ cup | 75g<br>¼ cup + 1 tbsp | 60g<br>¼ cup | 55g<br>3½ tbsp |
| **Size of fat pieces in pie dough** | size of walnut halves | size of walnut halves | size of walnut halves | pea-size |
| **First chilling time** | 30 mins | 30 mins | 1 hour | 1 hour |

[1] Either plain (all-purpose) wheat flour or plain gluten-free flour blend. For the latter, use shop-bought or make your own (see page 24).

[2] Either dairy or vegan butter. For the latter, use a firm vegan butter block, not a soft spread.

* If your gluten-free flour blend already contains binders, use only ¼ teaspoon.

** For the vegan pie crust, use vegan butter block only (115g/1 stick), vegetable shortening only (115g/½ cup + 1 tablespoon), or a 50:50 mixture of both (55g/½ stick butter and 55g/¼ cup + ½ tablespoon shortening). (See page 192.)

*** For best results, use a firm vegan butter block with a fat content of at least 75% and a high saturated fat content, of 40% or higher (see page 196).

**Making the flaky pie dough**

1. In a large bowl, whisk together the flour, sugar, salt and xanthan gum (if using).

2. Cut the chilled butter and/or vegetable shortening into cubes and toss them in the dry ingredients. Work the fat into the dry ingredients until you get fat pieces the size of walnut halves (for regular, gluten-free and vegan pie crust) or peas (for gluten-free vegan pie crust).

3. Gradually add the cold water, 1 tablespoon at a time. After each addition of water, use your fingertips, a fork or a rubber spatula to toss the mixture around so that the flour gets evenly hydrated. (For the vegan and gluten-free vegan pie crusts, it's best to use a fork or spatula to prevent the vegan butter and shortening melting in the heat of your hands.)

4. Continue adding the water and tossing the mixture until all the flour has been hydrated and the mixture starts clumping together in places. It might still look crumbly at this point. You might need slightly more or less water than is listed in the recipe. If there are any patches of dry flour, sprinkle them with some extra cold water.

5. Bring the pie dough together into a ball by giving it a gentle knead and pressing it against the inside of the bowl. Your dough won't look perfectly smooth at this stage – it will look slightly "shaggy" and uneven, with a few cracks here or there. Be careful not to overwork it, as that can cause the butter to start melting thanks to the heat from your hands, which can reduce the flakiness of the final pastry.

6. Wrap the pie dough in cling film, and chill it for at least 30 minutes (if using dairy butter) or for 1 hour (if using a vegan butter).

**Laminating the dough – two letter folds**

1. On a lightly floured work surface, roll out the chilled flaky pie dough into a long rectangle about 5–6mm (¼in) thick. The exact dimensions of the rectangle aren't important, just aim for a length that's about three times the width.

2. Make the first letter fold. Fold one third of the rectangle down toward the centre of the rectangle and then fold the other third up and over it (as you would a letter).

3. Rotate the folded pastry by 90 degrees, so that the open ends are closest to and farthest from you, and roll it out the again into a long rectangle.

4. Make the second letter fold. Fold one third of the rectangle down toward the centre and then fold the other third up over it (as you would a letter).

5. Wrap the finished pie dough tightly in cling film and chill it in the fridge until needed. It's best to chill the pastry for 30–45 minutes before you roll it out, if you want to use it straight away (although you can chill it for longer).

6. Use the dough as instructed in your chosen recipe. (If your pie crust has been in the fridge for several hours or overnight, leave it out on the counter at room temperature for about 5 minutes until it's more pliable – that will make it easier to roll out without cracking.)

# British Scones & American Buttermilk Biscuits

Scones and buttermilk biscuits are quite different from all the other bakes we've discussed so far in this chapter, so they deserve a separate section all on their own. First of all, though, a quick terminology 101: American biscuits are not what British people call "biscuits" (that is, cookies) – they are not at all cookie-like in any way, shape or form. Both British scones and American buttermilk biscuits are so-called "quick breads" – bread-like pastries that are leavened with chemical raising agents (baking powder or bicarbonate of soda, for example) rather than yeast.

There are two main differences between British scones and American buttermilk biscuits: their texture and the ingredients used to make them. Scones are lightly crisp on the outside, with a fluffy, soft and slightly crumbly interior. Buttermilk biscuits are much flakier and not as crumbly in texture, and they're more buttery and richer in flavour.

British scone ↓    American buttermilk biscuit ↓

While both are made from the usual dry ingredients (flour, raising agents, salt and sugar) and butter, the way in which the butter is incorporated is quite different. With scones, the butter is worked into the dry ingredients until you get a mixture resembling breadcrumbs. This gives the scones that characteristic tender, slightly crumbly texture. With buttermilk biscuits, the butter is left in larger pieces, which results in a much flakier texture.

The wet ingredients used to bring the dough together are also not the same. Scones typically use milk and often also eggs. Buttermilk biscuits, on the other hand, typically contain buttermilk (as the name suggests), and usually don't contain any eggs. Because buttermilk is acidic, buttermilk biscuits can use both baking powder and bicarbonate of soda (baking soda) as the raising agents (although many recipes, including the one in this book, use only baking powder). The scone dough, on the other hand, doesn't contain any acidic ingredients for the bicarbonate of soda (baking soda) to react with, so you can only use baking powder.

**NOTE: THE SCONE – UK VS USA**

While we're discussing terminology, I should probably clear up the difference between British scones and American scones. British scones are typically round or, more rarely, square. They're usually plain or studded with dried fruit, such as raisins, sultanas or currants. American scones are usually wedges or triangles, and they're much denser and flakier, and nowhere near as tall as British ones. Their texture and preparation method are, in fact, closer to those of American buttermilk biscuits. They also come in myriad different flavours (some examples include blueberry, strawberry, chocolate chip and pumpkin) and they're often glazed with a simple vanilla or lemon icing, depending on the main scone flavour.

In the following two case studies, we'll focus first on British scones and then on American buttermilk biscuits. We won't discuss American scones, although their chemistry and the rules for adapting them are largely the same as those for American buttermilk biscuits.

The important thing to keep in mind as we move through the following two case studies is that both scones and buttermilk biscuits are much more bread-like (hence, "quick breads") than the bakes we've looked at so far. And while it's true for both of these bakes that you shouldn't handle the dough too much, as that could lead to too much gluten development and consequently a tough, dense final result, you do need *some* gluten development.

Moderate gluten development creates just enough of a structural framework within the scone and biscuit dough to allow them to achieve their lofty heights during baking and also to maintain that height after they've come out of the oven. This will become especially important when we consider the gluten-free and gluten-free vegan versions. In those cases, we can no longer rely just on xanthan gum as the only binder to replace that gluten framework. Instead, we also need to introduce psyllium husk – the binder that's at the very centre of gluten-free bread (see pages 264–6).

Regular

Gluten-free

Dairy-free

Egg-free

Vegan

Gluten-free vegan

**Rules for adapting British scones**

↓

**p.74**

# Case Study 10:
# British Scones

The starting point for this case study is the beautifully tall, golden, tender regular British scone, made with plain (all-purpose) wheat flour, sugar, baking powder, salt, cold unsalted dairy butter, dairy milk and an egg.

I don't use self-raising flour in my scone recipe. While it is a popular choice for others, I like to control the amount of raising agent in my bakes quite exactly – and that's easiest when you use plain (all-purpose) flour and add the raising agents yourself.

To achieve the scone's characteristic tender, slightly crumbly texture, you need to work the cold butter into the dry ingredients until you get a mixture resembling breadcrumbs, with a few pea-sized butter pieces here and there. Then, you need to whisk together the milk and the egg, add them to the dry ingredients, and mix everything together into a fairly soft and sticky dough. So soft, in fact, that you might think that something went wrong. But it's absolutely correct, you just need to give it a gentle knead on a generously floured surface until the dough is smoother and easier to handle.

In many scone recipes, you'll read that you should handle the dough as little as possible, otherwise too much gluten might develop, and your scones could become tough and dense. While that is true to some extent – you definitely don't want to knead the dough until it's so elastic that it passes the windowpane test – it's also not the case that you can't knead the dough at all. Instead, a small amount of kneading is absolutely crucial if you want to get a dough that you can handle and if you want your scones to rise properly in the oven.

Instead of the typical kneading motions you might use when making a loaf of bread, I recommend the following: turn out the dough on to a generously floured surface and flatten it into a rectangle. Fold that rectangle in half and rotate it by 90 degrees. Then, repeat the flatten-fold-rotate process a few more times until you get a smooth dough that's still on the softer side but much easier to handle (see the photographs on the following page). It shouldn't be too elastic, so don't over-knead it – I usually do the flatten-fold-rotate process about four to six times in total. This kneading also gives the dough a bit more strength and structure, which translates into scones that rise taller and more evenly during baking – without making them tough or too chewy.

When cutting out the scones, always push the cookie cutter straight down, without any twisting motion (which could prevent the scones rising properly in the oven). I like to gently bush the tops of the scones with some extra milk just before baking. That's sufficient to give them gorgeous golden brown tops, although you can of course use an egg wash, if you prefer.

The final scones are beautifully tall and golden brown on the top and bottom. They have a slightly crisp exterior, which tends to soften with time, as the scones cool down. Their interior is deliciously soft and fluffy, with just the right amount of crumbliness.

These scones are definitely at their very best warm, fresh from the oven. There will be a natural split around the middle, which makes it very easy to tear them horizontally in half before piling on the jam and cream (in whichever order you prefer – I know that that can be a controversial issue).

**NOTE**

For all the scones in this case study, I rolled the dough to a thickness of 2.5cm (1in) and cut out the scones with a 6.5cm (2½in) round cookie cutter (smooth or fluted edges work well). The regular scones made with wheat flour, dairy and eggs rise in the oven to a final average height of about 4cm (1½in).

# Gluten-free

Technically, you could get away with using just xanthan gum as the only binder (gluten replacement) in a gluten-free scone – you'd get a final bake that's good enough.

Using xanthan gum only (½ teaspoon per 120g/1 cup of gluten-free flour blend) gives a very soft and sticky dough, with none of the slight elasticity of the regular version. However, it is still a workable dough, largely thanks to the binding power of eggs (as you'll see on page 210, their absence makes the xanthan-only version of the gluten-free vegan scones a giant sticky mess).

Once baked, the xanthan-only version of the scones is okay. It's not quite as tall as the regular version and the outside is slightly craggier but you still get a good rise, nice browning and a lovely texture. The scones are very slightly crumblier than the regular ones (although it's not a huge difference) and they also dry out faster. Like I say, the results are "good enough".

**NOTE**

To read more about the importance of psyllium husk in gluten-free bread-baking, see pages 264–6.

However, *we're not interested in good enough*. We're interested in the best possible free-from versions that are as close to the regular original as possible. And for that, we need to add psyllium husk, too. In short: psyllium husk is a binder (gluten substitute) that's absolutely pivotal when it comes to successful gluten-free bread, because it gives you a dough that you can knead and shape. It also gives it enough flexibility and extensibility that the dough can prove properly; and it gives the final gluten-free bread a chewy texture reminiscent of regular bread. As scones are a "quick bread", it makes sense that psyllium husk is necessary if we want the gluten-free version to be as similar as possible to the regular one.

Adding psyllium husk serves two purposes. First, it makes the dough much easier to handle. It's no longer as soft and sticky – instead, it has more elasticity to it, so that it's closer to the regular version made with wheat flour. Second, it gives the gluten-free scones a stronger structural framework that allows them to rise taller in the oven, and to maintain that rise and height even after they've cooled down. The gluten-free scones made with both xanthan gum and psyllium husk have the same final height as the regular version, about 4cm (1½in).

So, to get truly outstanding gluten-free scones that are nearly indistinguishable from their regular equivalent, you need to use both psyllium husk and xanthan gum, in an approximately 3:1 ratio by weight. Specifically, you need to use 1g (½ teaspoon) of xanthan gum and 3g (2 teaspoons) of psyllium husk per 120g (1 cup) of gluten-free flour blend (if your blend already contains binders, add only ¼ teaspoon of xanthan gum).

Xanthan gum only ↓          Xanthan & psyllium ↓

You also need to increase the amount of liquid (milk) to account not just for the greater moisture-absorption capacity of the gluten-free flour blend, but also for the fact that both binders (and especially psyllium husk) absorb a lot of moisture as well. You need to add about 40g (2½ tablespoons) of extra milk per 120g (1 cup) of gluten-free flour blend.

Finally, it's best to incorporate the psyllium husk into the dough in the form of a gel, where you mix it with the milk and allow it to stand for 5–10 minutes before adding it to the rest of the ingredients. Note that you need to wait longer for the psyllium gel to form when you use milk – with water, the gel forms in under a minute. That's because the two liquids interact quite differently with psyllium husk, and milk will give a much softer, looser gel.

The benefit of adding the psyllium husk in gel form is that it will give you a manageable dough straight away. Otherwise, you'd have to wait for the dry psyllium husk that's been mixed into all the other dry ingredients to hydrate – and if you're an impatient baker like me, that's a step you definitely like to skip.

The final gluten-free scones are beautifully tall and tender, with a plush interior and a pleasantly crisp crust – and you'd really never know that they're gluten-free.

## Dairy-free

Making dairy-free scones is incredibly straightforward: you simply need to replace the dairy butter with an equal weight or volume of a firm vegan butter block (not a soft spread) and the dairy milk with an equal weight or volume of a dairy-free milk, such as almond, rice, oat or soy milk. Avoid using canned coconut milk, as it can make the scones too dense and heavy because of its high fat content.

All other things – the quantities of the other ingredients, the preparation method, and so on – stay the same. The resulting dairy-free scones are incredibly delicious. There is a bit less browning because of the absence of the milk solids (see page 97), but you could egg wash the tops if you want them to get a deeper golden brown during baking.

Otherwise, the dairy-free version is very similar to the regular one, both in terms of the initial dough texture and in terms of the final, baked scones. They are in fact slightly taller than the regular ones, standing at a final height of about 4.3–4.5cm (1⅔–1¾in), and they're also a bit softer and fluffier (and they stay that way for longer). That's all down to the fact that the vegan butter is oil-based and, much like with cakes, oil will always give a taller, fluffier final bake than butter.

## Egg-free

While eggs are often a rather complex ingredient to replace in baking, here their substitution is surprisingly straightforward. You just need to add 40g (2½ tablespoons) of extra milk for each egg you remove. That's it.

The reason for this simplicity is that in a scone recipe made with wheat flour, the eggs have one primary function: they're mostly just a moisture source that helps to bring all the other ingredients together into a workable dough. In a way, their function in the scone dough is the same as that of the milk – so, we can account for their absence by adding more milk instead.

In comparison to the eggs' role as a moisture source, their functions as structure-providing and aerating ingredients are far less important. That's because the structure that they provide is negligible compared to that provided by the main structural ingredient: wheat flour. Meanwhile, baking powder acts as the main aerating ingredient, and the lift it provides is far, far greater than any lift provided by the eggs.

The simple adjustment of adding more milk gives an egg-free dough that handles very similarly to the regular one. It is slightly stickier initially, but it quickly becomes easily manageable after a quick, gentle knead on a generously floured surface (see the kneading method described on page 205 and shown on 206).

The final, baked egg-free scones are very similar to the regular starting point. They reach a final height of about 4cm (1½in), and they have a closely comparable texture: they're just as soft and fluffy, and the absence of the eggs doesn't make them crumblier or too delicate.

## Vegan

As with most case studies so far, the vegan version is a straightforward combination of all the dairy- and egg-free adjustments. So, to make the vegan scones, you need to:

- **Replace the dairy butter with an equal weight or volume of a firm vegan butter block (not a soft spread).**

- **Replace the regular dairy milk with an equal weight or volume of a dairy-free milk alternative, such as almond, rice, oat or soy milk. Avoid using canned coconut milk, as it can make the scones too dense and heavy because of its high fat content.**

- **Add 40g (2½ tablespoons) of dairy-free milk for each egg removed.**

The resulting vegan dough is very slightly stickier than the regular one, but just like with the egg-free version, it becomes much easier to handle after a few repeats of the flatten-fold-rotate kneading process (see pages 205–6) on a generously floured surface.

The final baked vegan scones stand at a height of about 4cm (1½in), just like the regular ones. They also have the same texture – they're wonderfully soft and fluffy, with just the right amount of crumbliness. Visually, they too have a natural split around the centre, but you should expect them to be paler in colour. This lack of browning is easy to understand – after all, the vegan scones don't contain any eggs or dairy, and both of these ingredients are central to promoting browning in the regular version.

# Gluten-free vegan

The gluten-free vegan variation is a combination of all the gluten-free and vegan adjustments. And just like with the gluten-free scones, adding psyllium husk is incredibly important. In fact, it's absolutely crucial here. You could get away with using only xanthan gum with the gluten-free scones, but that's pretty much impossible when you want to make them vegan too, because of the absence of the structure-providing eggs, which otherwise act as a failsafe.

Using xanthan gum as the only binder gives a ridiculously soft and sticky dough that's impossible to handle without incorporating a small mountain of extra flour into it. And even with the extra flour, the scones don't rise as much in the oven – the maximum final scone height you can get with the xanthan-only gluten-free vegan dough is around 3.5cm (1⅜in). The scones are also not quite as soft and fluffy as they should be, and they dry out and get crumblier much too quickly once they've cooled down.

Therefore, adding psyllium husk is crucial. As with the gluten-free version, it's best to use both psyllium husk and xanthan gum: you need to add 1g (½ teaspoon) of xanthan gum and 3g (2 teaspoons) of psyllium husk per 120g (1 cup) of gluten-free flour blend (if your blend already contains xanthan gum or other binders, add only ¼ teaspoon of xanthan gum).

And to account for the large amount of moisture absorbed not just by the gluten-free flour blend but also by the two binders, you need to increase the amount of dairy-free milk by 40g (2½ tablespoons) per 120g (1 cup) of gluten-free flour blend. (Note that this is in addition to the 40g/2½ tablespoons of dairy-free milk that you need to add for each egg removed.)

Although you add the xanthan gum to the dry ingredients, it's best to add the psyllium husk in gel form, by first mixing it with the dairy-free milk and letting it stand for 5–10 minutes before you add it to the rest of the ingredients. This will give you a manageable dough straight away.

The addition of psyllium husk results in an almost magical transformation: you go from a sloppy, sticky mess to a dough that's more elastic and as easy to handle as the regular one made with wheat flour, dairy and eggs.

The psyllium husk also gives the gluten-free vegan scones the structural framework that they need in order to rise during baking and to maintain that height even after they've come out of the oven. Thus, they reach a height of about 3.8–4cm (1½in), only negligibly shorter than the regular version. However, they are quite pale in appearance owing to the absence of both eggs and dairy.

In terms of texture, they're very similar to regular scones: crisp on the outside (especially while still warm) with a soft and fluffy interior. And while you might expect scones made without any gluten, eggs or dairy to be unbearably crumbly, that's not the case at all. Instead, they're just crumbly enough to be tender, but not so much that they would collapse as you eat them.

Interestingly, just as with the gluten-free vegan pie crust (see page 196), the type of vegan butter that you use to make gluten-free vegan scones matters. In addition to using a firm vegan butter block rather than a soft spread, it's best to use a vegan butter with a fat content of at least 75% and a high saturated fat content, of 40% or higher. This will give you the best possible results in terms of both texture and appearance. In comparison, vegan butters with a lower saturated fat content will give you scones that are a bit shorter and denser, and not quite as soft and fluffy.

**NOTE**

As you combine all the ingredients in the gluten-free vegan scones, the baking powder will react and release gases as it comes into contact with the dairy-free milk. In turn, that will make the dough much softer, making kneading (see page 205) even more important. Kneading helps to knock out the forming gases, making the dough firmer and easier to handle.

**NOTE**

The flavour of the gluten-free flour blend really comes through in final, baked scones. So, consider mixing your own blend to your own tastes (see page 24), using the gluten-free flours you like.

Regular

Gluten-free

Dairy-free

Egg-free

Vegan

Gluten-free vegan

# British scones: recipe

This recipe makes 7–8 larger scones (cut out with a 6.5cm/2½in round cookie cutter) or 8–10 smaller scones (cut out with a 5cm/2in cookie cutter).

| | DIET | | | | | |
|---|---|---|---|---|---|---|
| | **Regular** | **Gluten-free** | **Dairy-free** | **Egg-free** | **Vegan** | **GF Vegan** |
| plain flour [1] | 240g<br>2 cups | 240g<br>2 cups | 240g<br>2 cups | 240g<br>2 cups | 240g<br>2 cups | 240g<br>2 cups |
| caster or granulated sugar | 50g<br>¼ cup | 50g<br>¼ cup | 50g<br>¼ cup | 50g<br>¼ cup | 50g<br>¼ cup | 50g<br>¼ cup |
| baking powder | 4 tsp | 4 tsp | 4 tsp | 4 tsp | 4 tsp | 4 tsp |
| salt | ½ tsp | ½ tsp | ½ tsp | ½ tsp | ½ tsp | ½ tsp |
| xanthan gum | / | 2g*<br>1 tsp | / | / | / | 2g*<br>1 tsp |
| unsalted butter, cubed, chilled [2] | 75g<br>½ stick + 1½ tbsp | 75g<br>½ stick + 1½ tbsp | 75g<br>½ stick + 1½ tbsp | 75g<br>½ stick + 1½ tbsp | 75g<br>½ stick + 1½ tbsp | 75g**<br>½ stick + 1½ tbsp |
| milk, chilled [3] | 110g<br>⅓ cup + 2 tbsp | 150g<br>½ cup + 2 tbsp | 110g<br>⅓ cup + 2 tbsp | 150g<br>½ cup + 2 tbsp | 150g<br>½ cup + 2 tbsp | 190g<br>¾ cup + ½ tbsp |
| whole psyllium husk [4] | / | 6g<br>4 tsp | / | / | / | 6g<br>4 tsp |
| egg, chilled [5] | 1 | 1 | 1 | / | / | / |

[1] Either plain (all-purpose) wheat flour or plain gluten-free flour blend. For the latter, use shop-bought or make your own (see page 24).

[2] Either dairy or vegan butter. For the latter, use a firm vegan butter block, not a soft spread.

[3] Either whole dairy or dairy-free milk, excluding canned coconut milk.

[4] If using psyllium husk powder (which has a greater density than the whole husk), use only 85% of the amount listed, so 5g (2 tsp).

[5] UK medium eggs (US large eggs).

* If your gluten-free flour blend already contains binders, use only 1g (½ teaspoon).

** For best results, use a firm vegan butter block with a fat content of at least 75% and a high saturated fat content, of 40% or higher (see page 210).

1. **For gluten-free and gluten-free vegan versions:** In a bowl or jug, mix together the milk and psyllium husk. Set aside until needed, mixing occasionally. A very loose gel will form after 5–10 minutes.

2. Adjust the oven rack to the middle position, pre-heat the oven to 220°C/425°F and line a large baking sheet with baking paper.

3. In a large bowl, whisk together the flour, sugar, baking powder, salt and xanthan gum (if using).

4. Add the cold butter and work it into the dry ingredients until you get a mixture resembling breadcrumbs, with a few pea-sized butter pieces.

5. Whisk together the milk (or the milk-psyllium mixture, for gluten-free and gluten-free vegan versions) and the egg (if using), and then add them to the dry ingredients. With a wooden spoon, a fork or a rubber spatula, mix everything together until you get a smooth, soft and fairly sticky dough.

6. Turn out the dough on to a generously floured surface, and give it a gentle knead by patting it down into a rectangle, folding it in half, rotating by 90 degrees, and then repeating the process about 4–6 times until you get a smooth dough that's easier to handle – but be careful not to overwork the dough. (See page 206 for photographs.)

7. Roll out or pat down the dough until it's about 2.5cm (1in) thick. Dip a 6.5cm (2½in) or 5cm (2in) round cookie cutter into flour and use it to cut out the individual scones. Make sure to push the cookie cutter straight down, without any twisting motion, as that can prevent the scones from rising properly. Transfer the scones on to the lined baking sheet.

8. Re-use any scraps by gently re-kneading and re-rolling them. Cut out more scones – you should get 7–8 larger or 8–10 smaller scones in total.

9. Gently brush the top of each scone with some extra milk.

10. Bake for 10–14 minutes, or until well risen and golden brown on top.

11. To serve, split open the warm scones horizontally through the middle and fill them with jam and a dollop of (regular or vegan) clotted or whipped double (heavy) cream.

Regular

Gluten-free

Vegan

Gluten-free vegan

# Case Study 11:
# American Buttermilk Biscuits

While British scones and American buttermilk biscuits may at first appear to be very similar bakes, they're actually fairly different and they follow slightly different rules when it comes to free-from modification. That's mostly because, compared to British scones, buttermilk biscuits have a slightly firmer dough and some degree of lamination that gives them their characteristic flaky texture.

Furthermore, as the name suggests, buttermilk biscuits use buttermilk as the main (and usually only) source of moisture – and buttermilk behaves fairly differently from milk in that it's acidic and it tends to lose less moisture during baking. As you'll see later on, this becomes very important when we consider the gluten-free and gluten-free vegan variations (pages 218–19 and 221, respectively).

The starting point for this case study is tall, buttery, beautifully flaky buttermilk biscuits made with wheat flour, baking powder, sugar, salt, cold unsalted dairy butter and cold regular dairy buttermilk. The small amount of sugar in the dough helps with the browning but it doesn't make the final bake actually sweet.

In order to maximize flakiness, you need to keep the biscuit dough as cold as possible at all stages in the process – that's why we're using chilled butter and chilled buttermilk. I like to use chilled cubed butter, straight from the fridge. In comparison, many other recipes use coarsely grated frozen butter, which works great – but if you're a somewhat absent-minded baker like I am, and you forget to freeze your butter in time to make your biscuits, well, chilled butter from the fridge is the way to go. And you'll still get gloriously flaky results.

When working the chilled butter into the dry ingredients, it's best to stop at the stage when your butter pieces are approximately pea-sized. This will give you just the right amount of flakiness. Any smaller (if you were, for example, to work the butter in until you get a mixture resembling breadcrumbs) and your biscuits will be crumbly rather than flaky. Any larger (for example, if you leave them the size of walnut halves) and your biscuits can end up too flaky – so much so that they can puff up rather comically in the oven, and they'll end up lopsided, like small, buttery leaning towers of Pisa.

The next step is adding the buttermilk. The amount of buttermilk listed in a recipe is more of a guideline than a rule. Different brands of buttermilk can vary in consistency from fairly thick to very runny – so, you might not need all of it, or you might need more. Aim for a shaggy dough that's fully hydrated with no patches of dry flour, but it shouldn't be too sticky to the touch. (Be careful not to overwork the dough – just mix all the ingredients together and then give it a gentle knead until it comes together in a ball, and no more.)

To achieve the perfect flaky texture, there's an extra laminating step that multiplies the number of butter-dough layers. For this, roll out or pat the dough into a square about 2cm (¾in) thick (see the photographs, opposite), cut it into quarters and stack them on top of each other. Then, repeat this process once more.

**NOTE**

For all the buttermilk biscuits in this case study, I rolled the dough to a thickness of 2cm (¾in) and cut out square biscuits, about 6.5cm (2½in) in size. The regular biscuits made with wheat flour and dairy rise in the oven to a final average height of about 3.8–4.2cm (1½–1⅝in).

When it comes to cutting out the biscuits, you could use a 6.5–7.5cm (2½–3in) round cookie cutter, but in order to minimize the amount of scraps, I prefer to cut them into squares. To ensure that they rise tall and as evenly as possible, it's best to trim the very edges of the dough rectangle before dividing it into the individual biscuits.

If you want your buttermilk biscuits to be extra flaky, you can chill them in the fridge for about 20 minutes or in the freezer for about 10 minutes before baking – this sets and cools down the butter, resulting in very well-defined butter-dough layers and reduced butter leakage.

Then, you need to bake them at a fairly high oven temperature of 220°C/425°F. This helps to quickly transform the water content in the butter layers into steam, which forces the dough layers apart and creates both flakiness and rise – it's the same process that you'd see with flaky pie crust and puff pastry.

Once you've optimized all these factors, the final results are beautifully flaky, tall, golden buttermilk biscuits with a deliciously rich, buttery flavour. They're so flaky, in fact, that you can see some of the lamination along their sides and edges.

# Gluten-free

There are two sources of rise with buttermilk biscuits: lamination and raising agents (baking powder and/or bicarbonate of soda, depending on the recipe).

Unfortunately, the rise owing to the lamination (that is, steam generated from the butter layers forcing the dough layers apart) will always be smaller with any gluten-free bake compared to a gluten-containing equivalent (see also the flaky pie crust on page 191). Wheat flour is simply better at creating very well-defined butter-dough layers than gluten-free flour, and so ultimately wheat flour gives more puffing action. Furthermore, the developed gluten also lends regular dough more elasticity, so it expands more effortlessly as it puffs up. Even with the help of binders (xanthan gum and/or psyllium husk), we cannot completely replicate that strong gluten framework.

To make up for the fact that the lamination in gluten-free buttermilk biscuits will always result in a smaller rise than that in wheat-based biscuits, we can increase the amount of rise we get from the other source: raising agents. In practical terms, we need to increase the amount of baking powder by ½ teaspoon per 120g (1 cup) of gluten-free flour blend. This will bring the final height of the gluten-free buttermilk biscuits closer to that of the regular original.

When it comes to choosing which binders to use, you'll get better results if you use both xanthan gum and psyllium husk in your gluten-free buttermilk biscuits, just like with the gluten-free British scones (see page 207).

Without the psyllium husk (using just ½ teaspoon of xanthan gum per 120g/1 cup of gluten-free flour blend), the buttermilk biscuits rise to a final height of only about 3cm (1⅛in), which is significantly shorter than the regular version – even with the extra baking powder. The dough is also noticeably softer and more delicate. However, the final baked biscuits do have a lovely, buttery flavour.

So, it's clear that it's pretty much impossible to get the same amount of flakiness and rise without the help of psyllium husk. However, the amount of psyllium husk that you need and the way in which you add it are different compared to the method for the gluten-free British scone recipe on page 207.

If you were to use the same amount of psyllium husk as you did with scones, you'd end up with buttermilk biscuits that are fairly gummy. That's largely because buttermilk holds on to more moisture during baking than the milk you use when making scones. And it's the moisture evaporation from wet ingredients (including the psyllium gel) during baking that helps to achieve a light, soft, fluffy crumb.

To make perfectly risen gluten-free American buttermilk biscuits, you therefore need to make the following two adjustments:

- **Use 1.5g (1 teaspoon) of psyllium husk per 120g (1 cup) of gluten-free flour blend (in addition to the 1g or ½ teaspoon of xanthan gum). This is only half the amount you need to make gluten-free British scones.**

- **Add a small amount of water to the recipe and use that to make your psyllium gel (rather than mixing psyllium husk with buttermilk). This will ensure that more moisture is lost during baking, avoiding that gummy texture. And to make sure that your biscuit dough won't be too soft and sticky because of the added water, you need to reduce the amount of buttermilk by the same amount.**

In practical terms, for each 120g (1 cup) of gluten-free flour blend, mix together 1.5g (1 teaspoon) of psyllium husk and 15g (1 tablespoon) of water to make the psyllium gel. And, to account for the extra moisture, reduce the amount of buttermilk by the total weight or volume of the water added. To ensure that the gel gets evenly incorporated and distributed throughout the dough, mix it with the buttermilk before you add it to the dry ingredients.

These small tweaks (using more baking powder, using both xanthan gum and psyllium husk, and using water to make the psyllium gel) all come together to completely transform the gluten-free buttermilk biscuits. The final biscuits are perfectly flaky and tender, with no unpleasant gumminess at all. They also rise beautifully in the oven to a final height of about 3.5cm (1⅓in), only slightly less than the regular version. And if you want them to be even taller, you can roll the dough to a greater thickness of 2.5cm (1in) instead.

The psyllium husk also makes the dough easier to handle and, as it holds on to more moisture than xanthan gum, it prevents the biscuits from drying out too quickly and from becoming too crumbly after they've cooled.

**NOTE: KNOCKING OUT THE AIR**

As you're making the gluten-free buttermilk biscuits, your dough will be noticeably softer initially, immediately after you've combined all the ingredients. That's largely because the baking powder starts to react with the acidic buttermilk, which releases gas (carbon dioxide), and this makes the dough softer. To make it easier to handle, just give it a quick, gentle knead on a lightly floured surface, which will knock out most of the released gases to firm up the dough. Then, you can move on to the laminating step without any issues. (This softness is less noticeable with the regular buttermilk biscuits because of the stronger structural framework and the greater dough elasticity provided by the gluten in the wheat flour.)

## Dairy-free/vegan

As there are no eggs in the buttermilk biscuit recipe we're considering, the dairy-free and the vegan versions are one and the same. There are two substitutions we need to make to transform the regular version into its dairy-free equivalent.

- **Substitute the dairy butter with an equal weight or volume of a firm vegan butter block (not a soft spread).**

- **Replace the dairy buttermilk with an equal weight or volume of a dairy-free alternative. You can use the homemade vegan buttermilk on page 25, which comprises plain, unsweetened vegan yogurt and dairy-free milk in a 2:1 ratio, with a small amount of apple cider vinegar (or lemon juice) to achieve a similar degree of acidity. Using both vegan yogurt and milk ensures that this homemade version has a similar consistency to shop-bought dairy buttermilk.**

After these two simple swaps, all other things (ingredient quantities, preparation method, chilling time, oven temperature, and so on) stay the same. The biscuit dough is slightly softer than the regular version but it's not a huge difference, and the laminating process makes the dough much easier to handle.

While the chilling step is optional with the regular buttermilk biscuits, it's very much recommended with this dairy-free version. That's because vegan butter, with its lower melting point, is more prone to leaking compared to dairy butter. Making sure that the biscuits are thoroughly chilled before you pop them into the oven minimizes the chances of butter leakage and ensures that you'll get beautifully flaky, tender vegan buttermilk biscuits.

Once baked, the buttermilk biscuits reach a final height of about 3.5cm (1⅜in), so they're only slightly shorter than the regular version. That's largely because vegan butter doesn't result in quite as much puffing action in laminated bakes, as we've seen before with the dairy-free/vegan flaky pie crust on page 192. The vegan buttermilk biscuits are also slightly paler in colour. This reduced browning is because of the absence of the dairy milk solids, which are typically responsible for browning in dairy-containing bakes through a process known as the Maillard reaction (see page 97).

To get gluten-free vegan buttermilk biscuits, you just need to take the gluten-free version and substitute in an equal weight or volume of the dairy-free alternatives (the firm vegan butter block and the vegan buttermilk alternative; see page 25) instead of their dairy equivalents. That's really all there is to it.

Choosing the best possible vegan butter, though, is absolutely crucial. You'll get the best result if you use a firm vegan butter block (not a soft spread) with a high fat content of at least 75% and, most importantly, a high saturated fat content, of 40% or higher. (Don't worry – finding out the composition of the vegan butter block doesn't require any maths – it's all included in the nutritional information on the packaging or the relevant brand's website.)

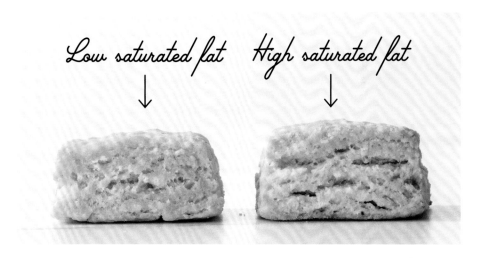

This kind of vegan butter will give you wonderfully flaky buttermilk biscuits that rise beautifully in the oven. In comparison, using a vegan butter block with a low saturated fat content (especially if it's below 30%) results in shorter, fairly squat buttermilk biscuits with a final height of only about 2.5cm (1in) that also aren't as flaky. This makes sense when you consider that you're trying to replace dairy butter, which has a saturated fat content of around 50–52%. The closer you can get to that value with your vegan butter, the better the end result.

Using psyllium husk, in addition to xanthan gum, is incredibly important, too – even more so than it was with the gluten-free variation on pages 218–19. It ensures that you get a manageable dough that you can easily handle, and it also ensures that the buttermilk biscuits rise properly in the oven. In comparison, xanthan-only gluten-free vegan buttermilk biscuits have a much poorer rise, and they dry out and become crumblier much quicker once they've cooled down.

Even with the addition of the psyllium husk, the gluten-free vegan dough will be noticeably softer initially, immediately after you've combined all the ingredients. The reason is the same as with the gluten-free buttermilk biscuits: once the acidic buttermilk comes into contact with the baking powder, the two start reacting and releasing gas – carbon dioxide – which makes the dough appear softer than it actually is. Just give it a quick, gentle knead on a lightly floured surface to knock out most of these developed gases from the dough. The knocking back will make the dough firmer and so easier to handle. Then, you can move on to the laminating step.

The fact that part of the baking powder reacts with the buttermilk before the buttermilk biscuits enter the oven shouldn't concern you. There's plenty of active baking powder still left in the dough to ensure that your biscuits will rise beautifully in the oven.

Just as with the vegan version, I firmly recommend chilling the cut-out buttermilk biscuits in the fridge for about 20 minutes or in the freezer for about 10 minutes before you bake them. The chilling step minimizes the chances of vegan butter leakage.

The optimized gluten-free vegan buttermilk biscuits reach a final height of about 3.3cm (1¼in). They're slightly shorter than both the gluten-free and the dairy-free/vegan versions but they still have a decent rise and a beautifully flaky texture. It's important that you use a gluten-free flour blend and a vegan butter whose flavour you actually like, as you can definitely taste them in the final bake. So, if you don't like how they taste when you make them with your usual shop-bought gluten-free flour blend, it's worth mixing it up yourself (based on the recipe on page 24). My go-to flour combination is tapioca starch, millet flour and sorghum flour, as I've found that it comes closest to the flavour of regular wheat flour.

The gluten-free vegan version also shows the least amount of browning because of the absence of the dairy milk solids and the fact that gluten-free flours (especially those high in starches, as is the case with most shop-bought blends) tend to brown slightly less during baking than regular wheat flour.

Regular

Gluten-free

Vegan

Gluten-free vegan

# American buttermilk biscuits: recipe

**This recipe makes 8 flaky buttermilk biscuits.**

| | DIET | | | |
|---|---|---|---|---|
| | **Regular** | **Gluten-free** | **Dairy-free/ Vegan** | **GF Vegan** |
| plain flour [1] | 240g<br>2 cups | 240g<br>2 cups | 240g<br>2 cups | 240g<br>2 cups |
| baking powder | 3 tsp | 4 tsp | 3 tsp | 4 tsp |
| caster or granulated sugar | 10g<br>2 tsp | 10g<br>2 tsp | 10g<br>2 tsp | 10g<br>2 tsp |
| salt | 1 tsp | 1 tsp | 1 tsp | 1 tsp |
| xanthan gum | / | 2g*<br>1 tsp | / | 2g*<br>1 tsp |
| unsalted butter, cubed, chilled [2] | 85g<br>¾ stick | 85g<br>¾ stick | 85g<br>¾ stick | 85g**<br>¾ stick |
| buttermilk, chilled [3] | 180g<br>¾ cup + 1 tbsp | 150g<br>⅔ cup | 180g<br>¾ cup + 1 tbsp | 150g<br>⅔ cup |
| whole psyllium husk [4] | / | 3g<br>2 tsp | / | 3g<br>2 tsp |
| cold water | / | 30g<br>2 tbsp | / | 30g<br>2 tbsp |

[1] Either plain (all-purpose) wheat flour or plain gluten-free flour blend. For the latter, use shop-bought or make your own (see page 24).

[2] Either dairy or vegan butter. For the latter, use a firm vegan butter block, not a soft spread.

[3] Either dairy buttermilk or the vegan buttermilk alternative on page 25.

[4] If using psyllium husk powder (which has a greater density than the whole husk), use only 85% of the amount listed, so 2.5g (1 teaspoon).

* If your gluten-free flour blend already contains binders, use only 1g (½ teaspoon).

** For best results, use a firm vegan butter block with a fat content of at least 75% and a high saturated fat content, of 40% or higher (see page 221).

1. Adjust the oven rack to the middle position, pre-heat the oven to 220°C/425°F and line a large baking sheet with baking paper.

2. **For gluten-free and gluten-free vegan American buttermilk biscuits:** In a bowl or jug, mix together the psyllium husk and cold water. After about 10–15 seconds, a gel will form. Add the buttermilk to the psyllium gel and mix well. Keep it chilled in the fridge until needed.

3. In a large bowl, whisk together the flour, baking powder, sugar, salt and xanthan gum (if using).

4. Add the cold butter and work it into the dry ingredients until it's approximately pea-sized.

5. Add the buttermilk (or the buttermilk-psyllium mixture for the gluten-free and gluten-free vegan versions) and use a wooden spoon, a fork or a rubber spatula to mix everything together into a shaggy dough. Depending on the consistency of your buttermilk, you might not need all of it, or you might need a tablespoon or two extra. Aim for a shaggy dough that holds together well and doesn't have any patches of dry flour, but it shouldn't be too sticky.

6. Turn out the dough on to a lightly floured surface and give it a gentle knead (this will knock out any gases that start forming from the reaction between the acidic buttermilk and baking powder, making the dough firmer and easier to handle).

7. Roll out or pat the dough into an approximately square shape, until it's about 2cm (¾in) thick.

8. Use a sharp knife or a bench scraper to divide the dough into quarters. Stack the pieces on top of each other, and roll out or pat them down into a square about 2cm (¾in) thick again.

9. Cut the dough into quarters again. Stack the pieces on top of each other, and then roll out or pat them down into an approximately 10x20cm (4x8in) rectangle, about 2cm (¾in) thick. (If you want your biscuits to be even taller, you can roll out or pat down the dough until it's about 2.5cm/1in thick instead.)

10. Use a sharp knife or a bench scraper to cut the rectangle into eight equal 5cm (2in) square buttermilk biscuits and transfer them to the lined baking sheet.

11. **Optional (recommended if using vegan butter):** cover the biscuits with cling film and chill them in the fridge for about 20 minutes or in the freezer for about 10 minutes.

12. Gently brush the top of each biscuit with melted butter or milk (dairy or dairy-free, depending on what version you're making) and bake them for 12–15 minutes, or until they're well risen and golden brown on top. Serve warm.

# Pancakes

While pancakes don't strictly belong in the baking category (after all, they're usually cooked on the stovetop), I wanted to include them because they're such a popular and delicious breakfast staple, and I definitely think that you should know how to adapt them into whatever X-free (gluten-, dairy-, egg-free, and so on) version you fancy.

We'll focus on two different types of pancake recipe: first, the thin and delicate French-style crêpes, and then the much fluffier, thicker American-style pancakes. While both belong to the pancake family, their very different textures and batter consistencies mean that they follow slightly different modification rules.

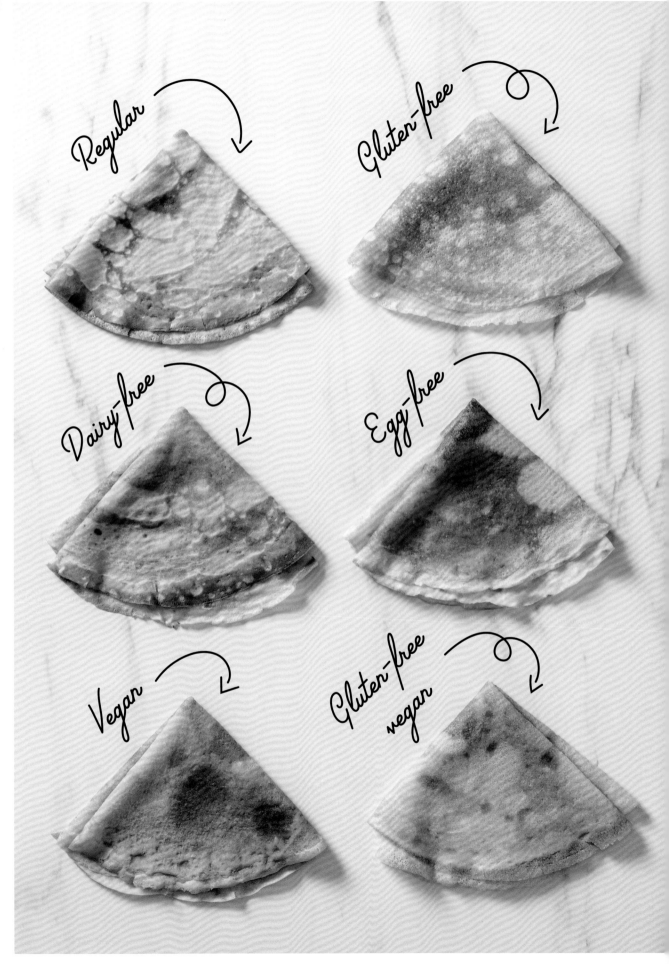

Regular

Gluten-free

Dairy-free

Egg-free

Vegan

Gluten-free
vegan

# Case Study 12:
# Thin French-style Crêpes

The starting point for this case study is regular French crêpes: very thin and delicate, with a slightly crisp, lacy edge, and a nice, even golden brown colour. There's a subtle sweetness to them that goes so well with a multitude of different toppings and fillings. They have a very, very slightly chewy texture, and a delicate elasticity to them when you tear them apart – but pleasantly so!

The basic crêpe batter contains just six simple ingredients: plain (all-purpose) wheat flour, sugar, salt, eggs, regular dairy milk and some melted unsalted dairy butter for extra richness. The batter consistency is crucial: you want it to be runny enough that it thinly coats the bottom of the pan – this will ensure that your crêpes are beautifully thin.

## Gluten-free

When it comes to making crêpes, just like with cakes, the moisture response of the gluten-free flour blend outweighs its fat response. So, you need to account for the greater moisture absorption capacity of gluten-free flours by reducing the amount of flour by 10%. In practice, this means that you need to multiply the weight of flour by 0.9, or reduce its volume by 1½ tablespoons per cup of flour in the recipe.

To make up for the absence of gluten, you need to add ¼ teaspoon of xanthan gum per 120g (1 cup) of gluten-free flour blend. If your blend already contains xanthan gum or other binders, there's no need to add extra.

The resulting gluten-free-batter consistency is very similar to the regular one: it coats the pan thinly to give delicate, thin crêpes that are almost indistinguishable (in texture and appearance) from their regular equivalent made with wheat flour.

The only difference is that gluten-free crêpes are marginally more delicate and not as chewy as regular ones – they lack some of the elasticity that's otherwise contributed by the gluten in wheat flour. But you notice really only when you compare the two side by side.

Gluten-free crêpes can also dry out a tiny bit faster if they're allowed to stand uncovered at room temperature for a long time. So, it's important that you either eat or serve them straight away, or keep them covered (in a closed container or wrapped with cling film, foil or even a clean tea towel) if you want to store them for longer.

## Dairy-free

For the most part, adapting the crêpe recipe to be dairy-free is a simple case of 1:1 substitution of the dairy ingredients (milk and melted unsalted butter) with their dairy-free equivalents. You can replace the dairy milk with an equal weight or volume of a dairy-free milk, such as almond, rice, oat or soy milk. I don't recommend using canned coconut milk, as it can make the crêpes too greasy or oily because of its higher fat content.

Similarly, you can replace the melted dairy butter with an equal weight or volume of a melted vegan butter. Or, you can use a neutral-tasting oil – but use only 80% of the weight of the butter, as butter is only about 80% fat whereas oil is 100% fat (note that the quantity of butter that you're replacing is fairly small in most crêpe recipes, so you don't have to account for the difference in the moisture content between butter and oil). Furthermore, while oil is a suitable butter substitute in dairy-free crêpes, you'll see that it's best avoided in the vegan variation.

However, there's one more change you need to make to get the dairy-free crêpes as close as possible to their regular equivalent, especially in terms of appearance and flavour. Despite containing the same amount of sugar as the regular version, the dairy-free crêpes prepared with just this simple 1:1 substitution actually taste less sweet – and they also brown less during cooking, so that they're noticeably paler in appearance.

That's because the dairy milk used in regular crêpes contains natural sugars, which contribute to the sweet taste of regular (and other dairy-containing) crêpes. These naturally occurring sugars, along with the milk solids present in dairy milk and dairy butter, also promote browning and caramelization.

So, to make up for the lack of these sugars and milk solids, you need to increase the amount of sugar by about 5–10g (½–1 tablespoon) per 240g (1 cup) of milk in the recipe.

The final dairy-free crêpes are almost indistinguishable from the original, regular version. Thanks to the extra sugar, they brown beautifully during cooking so that they're evenly golden brown, and they're a real joy to eat – even without any fillings or toppings!

## Egg-free

To successfully and reliably adapt the regular crêpe recipe to be egg-free, we first need to analyze the role that eggs play in the recipe. They mostly act as a moisture source and a structure-providing ingredient. Their aerating or lift-providing capabilities are not important here (unlike with the fluffy American-style pancakes on pages 237–43), so you don't need to add any raising agents to the egg-free batter.

In practice, this means that, for each egg removed, you need to:

- **Add 30g (2 tablespoons) of milk as an alternative moisture source.**

- **Increase the amount of flour (the only other structure-providing ingredient present) by 10g (1½ tablespoons).**

With these two simple changes, the egg-free crêpes are easy to make and surprisingly similar to the regular starting point. It may seem counterintuitive to add both milk (a wet ingredient) and flour (a dry ingredient) to the recipe as they do, effectively, cancel each other out to some extent. However, adding both helps to maintain a similar volume of the crêpe batter so that you keep the recipe yield (the number of crêpes) the same. It also preserves the batter consistency really well, so that it coats the frying pan or skillet evenly and thinly.

Of course, if your egg-free batter is slightly too runny or too thick (which can depend on the recipe you've started with), you can always correct it by adding a bit more flour or milk, respectively. Just make sure that you add the extra ingredients gradually (a teaspoon at a time for flour; a tablespoon at a time for milk) and whisk well after each addition.

The resulting egg-free crêpes are incredibly similar to the regular ones: thin and delicate, with a gorgeous, even caramelization and a wonderful flavour. The egg-free version is slightly softer or "floppier", so to speak, than regular crêpes because of the absence of the structure-providing eggs. But the difference is very subtle and noticeable only really when you compare the two batches of crêpes side by side.

There is a small difference in terms of flavour too, but the addition of the melted butter ensures that the egg-free version is pleasantly rich with a delicious flavour.

## Vegan

The vegan version is just the combination of all the changes necessary to make the dairy-free and the egg-free versions – that's really all there is to it.

So, you need to make a 1:1 substitution of the dairy ingredients with their dairy-free equivalents, increase the amount of sugar to make up for the absence of the sugars and milk solids naturally present in dairy milk and butter, and account for the absence of the moisture- and structure-providing eggs by adding some extra (dairy-free) milk and flour. All of these changes are summarized and quantified in the rules on pages 77–8.

While oil was a suitable butter substitute in the dairy-free crêpes, I don't recommend using it in this vegan variation. That's because oil will give you vegan crêpes that are gummier in texture, as well as slightly greasy and oily, and they show only minimal browning. In comparison, melted vegan butter gives a much better result: a nicer texture and just the right amount of browning.

The vegan crêpes might appear slightly too dry and crisp initially, immediately after cooking, but don't let that fool you: as you stack them together, the steam released by the hot crêpes will soften them to the optimal delicate, tender texture that we all know and love.

The resulting vegan version looks and tastes incredibly similar to the regular one. The slightly greater amount of sugar ensures that the vegan crêpes have just the right amount of browning and caramelization, and they have a lovely soft texture with slightly crisp edges.

They are a tiny bit more elastic and slightly chewier than the regular equivalent, and they're also not quite as rich – after all, we've removed the eggs and all the regular dairy ingredients. But just as with all the free-from variations so far, the differences are not really noticeable unless you're comparing the vegan and the regular batches side by side.

The exact ratio of milk to flour and therefore the consistency of your vegan crêpe batter will, of course, somewhat depend on which regular recipe you choose as your starting point. It's very important that your batter isn't too runny, otherwise you'll be left with very gummy crêpes that will always appear undercooked (no matter how long you cook them for) and that are almost impossible to flip. The liquid-to-flour ratio should ideally be below 2.5:1 by weight. When in doubt, use the optimized, 100% reliable vegan crêpe recipe on pages 234–5.

# Gluten-free vegan

The gluten-free vegan crêpes are, for the most part, a straightforward sum of all the gluten-free, dairy-free and egg-free adjustments so far – with one small, but very important, difference. You need to replace one quarter (25%) of all the dairy-free milk in the recipe with an equal weight of vegan condensed milk, while also halving the amount of sugar in the recipe to make up for the extra sweetness. If you're working with volume measurements, this means using 3 tablespoons of condensed milk for every 4 tablespoons of milk that you're replacing.

You can use a shop-bought vegan condensed milk or you can make your own using either the condensed coconut milk recipe on page 26 or the coconut-free vegan condensed milk recipe on page 27.

Admittedly, condensed milk is a rather unusual addition to a crêpe batter – but it makes an enormously positive difference to how well the gluten-free vegan crêpes brown and cook through, and it also greatly improves their texture.

Without the vegan condensed milk, the crêpes tend to be strangely gummy and they'll often appear undercooked no matter how long you cook them for. They also have little to no structure, so they end up oddly floppy – and overall rather unappetizing. The process of cooking them is highly sensitive to the heat and the thickness of the crêpe batter, which makes it fairly unreliable and inconsistent. And, importantly, they also brown only minimally, so they lack that gorgeous golden colour typical of a good crêpe.

Adding the vegan condensed milk completely transforms the crêpes. They cook through beautifully, so that there's no more gumminess – instead, the texture is absolutely perfect: soft and tender, with deliciously crisp edges. They also brown beautifully, which is greatly helped along by the vegan condensed milk that promotes the caramelization process.

When you're cooking gluten-free vegan crêpes, it's very important that you don't rush and attempt to flip them too early. You need to cook them until the underside is golden brown, which takes a bit longer than with the regular version – even up to 2–3 minutes on medium heat. Only then can you flip them and cook them on the other side for about 1 minute more, until you see brown spots appearing on the underside.

The final gluten-free vegan crêpes made with the trick of adding vegan condensed milk are incredibly similar to the regular starting point. They're just as delicious – and I guarantee that they'll be a hit with absolutely everyone, no matter their dietary requirements.

**NOTE**

Adding condensed milk is not necessary if you're making gluten- and egg-free crêpes that contain dairy milk and butter. In those cases, the presence of dairy is sufficient to ensure a lovely texture with no gumminess.

Regular

Gluten-free

Dairy-free

Egg-free

Vegan

Gf vegan

# Thin French-style crêpes: recipe

**This recipe makes 6–7 crêpes, about 23–25cm (9–10in) in diameter.**

| | DIET | | | | | |
|---|---|---|---|---|---|---|
| | **Regular** | **Gluten-free** | **Dairy-free** | **Egg-free** | **Vegan** | **GF Vegan** |
| plain flour [1] | 120g<br>1 cup | 110g<br>¾ cup + 3 tbsp | 120g<br>1 cup | 140g<br>1 cup + 3 tbsp | 140g<br>1 cup + 3 tbsp | 130g<br>1 cup + 1½ tbsp |
| caster or granulated sugar | 15g<br>1 tbsp | 15g<br>1 tbsp | 25g<br>2 tbsp | 15g<br>1 tbsp | 25g<br>2 tbsp | 15g<br>1 tbsp |
| salt | ¼ tsp | ¼ tsp | ¼ tsp | ¼ tsp | ¼ tsp | ¼ tsp |
| xanthan gum | / | ¼ tsp* | / | / | / | ¼ tsp* |
| milk, room temp [2] | 280g<br>1 cup + 2½ tbsp | 280g<br>1 cup + 2½ tbsp | 280g<br>1 cup + 2½ tbsp | 340g<br>1⅓ cups + 1½ tbsp | 340g<br>1⅓ cups + 1½ tbsp | 255g<br>1 cup + 1 tbsp |
| eggs, room temp [3] | 2 | 2 | 2 | / | / | / |
| unsalted butter, melted [4] | 15g<br>1 tbsp | 15g<br>1 tbsp | 15g<br>1 tbsp | 15g<br>1 tbsp | 15g<br>1 tbsp | 15g<br>1 tbsp |
| vegan condensed milk [5] | / | / | / | / | / | 85g<br>¼ cup + ½ tbsp |
| Cook time on first side | 45–60 secs | 45–60 secs | 45–60 secs | 45–60 secs | 45–60 secs | 2–3 mins |

[1] Either plain (all-purpose) wheat flour or plain gluten-free flour blend. For the latter, use shop-bought or make your own (see page 24).

[2] Either whole dairy or dairy-free milk, excluding canned coconut milk.

[3] UK medium eggs (US large).

[4] Either dairy or vegan butter.

[5] Either dairy condensed milk or vegan, such as condensed coconut or oat milk. For vegan, use shop-bought or make your own (see pages 26 and 27).

* Omit if your gluten-free flour blend already contains xanthan gum or other binders.

1. In a large bowl, whisk together the flour, sugar, salt, and xanthan gum (if using).

2. In a separate bowl or jug, whisk together the milk, eggs (if using), melted butter, and vegan condensed milk (if using).

3. Add approximately ⅓ of the wet ingredients to the dry, whisking well until you get a smooth, paste-like batter with no flour clumps.

4. Gradually add the rest of the wet ingredients, whisking constantly, until you get a smooth, runny batter with no flour clumps. You can add 1–2 tablespoons of extra milk if your pancake batter is slightly too thick.

5. Heat a frying pan over medium heat until a drop of water sizzles on its surface. Lightly butter the pan and wipe away any excess with kitchen paper.

6. Add a ladleful, or about ⅓ cup, of batter to the hot pan and, as you're pouring it, swirl the pan to get an even, thin coating.

7. Cook over medium heat for about 45–60 seconds (for gluten-free, dairy-free, egg-free and vegan variations) or for about 2–3 minutes (for gluten-free vegan crêpes), or until the crêpe loosens from the pan and is golden brown underneath.

8. Flip and cook the crêpe on the other side for a further 45–60 seconds, or until dark brown spots appear. Then, place it on a plate or wire rack while you repeat the process with the remaining batter. The recipe makes about 6–7 crêpes, depending on their thickness and the size of your pan. (Optional for gluten-free vegan crêpes: to prevent them for developing a slightly crisp edge, you can cover the cooked hot crêpes with a clean tea towel to trap in some of the steam.)

9. Serve immediately with toppings and fillings of choice.

Regular

Gluten-free

Dairy-free

Egg-free

Vegan

Gluten-free vegan

**Rules for adapting fluffy pancakes**

↓

**p.79**

# Case Study 13:
# Fluffy American-style Pancakes

This case study starts with the softest, fluffiest American-style pancakes you could possibly make: they're satisfyingly plush and fairly thick (about 1.5cm/½in) and, importantly, very easy to rustle up. You don't need to whip up the egg whites separately or anything like that – because, let's be honest, simple and fuss-free is definitely the way to go when it comes to breakfast.

The ingredients are simple: regular plain (all-purpose) wheat flour, sugar, baking powder, a pinch of salt, dairy milk, eggs and some melted unsalted dairy butter for extra richness. When making the pancake batter, it's very important that you mix all the ingredients together until only just combined with some small lumps still remaining.

With most other batters – be that crêpe batter or cake batter – the aim is usually to get it smooth and lump-free, typically by gradually adding the wet ingredients to the dry. But that's not the case here – the ideal pancake batter for American-style fluffy pancakes is actually fairly lumpy, which ensures that your pancakes will be perfectly pillowy-soft and thick – so the preparation method is different as well.

The best method to prepare these fluffy pancakes is to whisk together all the dry ingredients and all the wet ingredients separately, and then add the dry ingredients to the wet. Mix or fold them together with a rubber spatula – don't whisk the batter and don't over-mix it, and definitely resist the ingrained bakers' temptation to get rid of all the clumps. Over-mixing the batter will actually make it too runny, and the resulting pancakes can end up flat, dense and verging on rubbery. As long as you get the batter consistency right, your pancakes will be absolutely gorgeous.

Lumpy vs Smooth

# Gluten-free

To make gluten-free fluffy American-style pancakes, you need to tweak the amount of flour the same way you would with a cake (see page 96). That is, you need to reduce the amount of flour by 10% to account for the greater moisture-absorption capacity of the gluten-free flour blend. In practice, this means multiplying the weight of flour by 0.9, or reducing its volume by 1½ tablespoons per cup of flour in the recipe.

Furthermore, in order to achieve a similar batter consistency to the regular version (and therefore a similar texture and thickness of the final, cooked pancakes), you need to use a slightly larger amount of xanthan gum: ½ teaspoon per 120g (1 cup) of gluten-free flour blend. If your blend already contains xanthan gum or other binders, add only ¼ teaspoon.

This is crucial, because when it comes to fluffy pancakes, it's really all about getting just the right batter consistency – you want to ensure that the batter is thick enough so that it doesn't spread out too much when you scoop or ladle it into the frying pan. In the regular version, it's the gluten in the regular wheat flour that gives the batter some viscosity and controls its spread in the pan. In the gluten-free version, we can achieve a similar effect with a slightly larger quantity of xanthan gum. In this case, we're focusing primarily on the thickening properties of xanthan gum (that is, its ability to increase the viscosity of liquids and batters) rather than its ability to add flexibility and elasticity, although the latter helps to ensure that the gluten-free pancakes aren't in any way too delicate or too crumbly.

Now, in theory, you could also make the pancake batter thicker by increasing the amount of gluten-free flour blend – but that would result in denser, drier pancakes. Increasing the amount of xanthan gum is definitely the better option.

The preparation method is the same as for the regular version: add the dry ingredients to the wet, and then mix them together with a rubber spatula (not a whisk) until you get a slightly lumpy batter. It's best to allow the gluten-free batter to stand for about 5 minutes before you start cooking the pancakes. This gives both the gluten-free flour blend and the xanthan gum time to absorb some of the moisture, so that the batter reaches its optimal consistency. At this point, you can loosen it with a small amount of extra milk, if necessary – this can depend on the gluten-free flour blend you're using, as different brands can vary quite widely in terms of how much moisture they absorb.

The optimized gluten-free pancakes are virtually indistinguishable from the regular equivalent: they're just as soft and fluffy, and they have the same thickness of about 1.5cm (½in).

**NOTE**

The greater quantity of xanthan gum is necessary only if you're using milk to make your pancakes. If you're using a thicker liquid, such as buttermilk, you can use ¼ teaspoon of xanthan per 120g (1 cup) of gluten-free flour blend (and if your blend already contains binders, there's no need to add any extra).

# Dairy-free

The adjustments for dairy-free American-style fluffy pancakes are straightforward: you just need to replace the dairy milk with an equal weight or volume of an unsweetened dairy-free milk (almond, rice, soy or oat milk work great; avoid using canned coconut milk due to its high fat content, which can make the pancakes too heavy and dense) and substitute the dairy butter with an equal weight or volume of a vegan butter block.

You can also use a neutral-tasting oil as a butter alternative, such as sunflower, vegetable or rapeseed (canola) oil. You'll just need to use slightly less of it, as oil is essentially 100% fat whereas butter is only about 80% fat (note that the quantity of butter that you're replacing is fairly small in most pancake recipes, so you don't have to account for the difference in the moisture content between butter and oil). In fact, oil will give you slightly softer, fluffier and thicker pancakes. The reason for this is the same as with the buttery vanilla cake on page 95: oil is naturally a liquid fat at and around room temperature, which results in a softer and airier crumb (that also stays that way for longer).

The dairy-free pancakes are noticeably paler in colour with less browning than the regular version because of the absence of the dairy milk solids in both the milk and the butter. To make up for this difference, we can tweak two things:

- **Cook the pancakes on a slightly higher heat to help them achieve a greater amount of browning and caramelization in the time it takes them to fully cook through.**

- **Add about 10g (1 tablespoon) of extra sugar per 240g (1 cup) of dairy-free milk to promote browning and caramelization.**

Because we're using unsweetened dairy-free milk, the pancakes lack some of the sweetness that's naturally present in dairy ingredients, especially milk. That means that, in addition to promoting browning and caramelization, the extra sugar brings the dairy-free pancakes to a similar level of sweetness as the regular ones.

The resulting dairy-free pancakes are beautifully golden brown, satisfyingly thick and perfectly soft and fluffy.

In order to be able to substitute eggs in the pancake batter, first consider the role that they play in this fluffy pancake recipe: they're a structure-providing ingredient, a moisture source and an aerating ingredient that (together with the baking powder) helps to achieve a perfectly soft, fluffy pancake texture.

Knowing all of this makes adapting the recipe to be egg-free straightforward. So, to make up for the absence of eggs, we need to increase the amount of the only other structure-providing ingredient (the flour), increase the amount of milk to account for the loss of moisture, increase the amount of baking powder, and also add some apple cider vinegar to boost the activity of the raising agent. Don't worry – you can't actually taste the vinegar in the final, cooked pancakes.

More precisely, for each egg removed, you need to:

- **Increase the amount of flour by 10g (1½ tablespoons) – true for wheat flour and gluten-free flour blend.**
- **Add 30g (2 tablespoons) of milk (true for dairy and dairy-free milk).**
- **Add ¼ teaspoon of baking powder and ½ teaspoon of apple cider vinegar.**

The resulting egg-free pancake batter has the perfect consistency and it gives pancakes that are beautifully soft and fluffy, and just as thick as the regular ones.

# Vegan

The vegan version is just a simple combination of all the dairy-free and egg-free adjustments – and that's all there really is to it. So, you need to account for the absence of eggs by increasing the amount of flour, adding extra milk, increasing the amount of baking powder and adding some apple cider vinegar. On the dairy-free end, you need to replace all the dairy ingredients with their dairy-free equivalents. Just like with the dairy-free version, you can replace the regular dairy butter either with melted vegan butter or with a neutral-tasting oil – the latter will give you slightly softer, fluffier and thicker pancakes but it's not a huge difference and both options work great.

Additionally, to get a similar amount of browning and caramelization as with the regular version, you need to increase the amount of sugar by 10g (1 tablespoon) per 240g (1 cup) of dairy-free milk. This extra sugar does two things: first, it accounts for the absence of the natural sugars present in the dairy ingredients, so that you get a similar level of sweetness as in the regular pancakes; and, second, it helps to achieve a similar amount of browning, which would otherwise have been reduced in the absence of the dairy milk solids (see page 97).

Just as with the dairy-free version, it's best to cook the vegan pancakes on a slightly higher heat to achieve a greater amount of browning and caramelization to bring them closer to the regular version.

The final vegan pancakes are deliciously soft, squishy and fluffy, with a thickness of about 1.5cm (½in) – and truthfully, it's almost impossible to tell that they're made without any eggs or dairy. They keep very well and they stay beautifully soft for hours, even without reheating.

## Gluten-free vegan

As you might expect, the gluten-free vegan version of these fluffy pancakes was by far the trickiest one to figure out and optimize. If you simply combine all the gluten-free and vegan adjustments without any additional tweaks, the pancakes end up far too doughy and strangely gummy, as well as very pale with only negligible browning. The solution, as it turns out, is almond flour – just as it was with the gluten-free vegan version of the buttery vanilla cake recipe on pages 101–2, which had similar gumminess issues.

Adding just 20g (3½ tablespoons) of almond flour per 120g (1 cup) of gluten-free flour blend transforms the doughy gluten-free vegan pancakes into perfectly soft, fluffy ones. (This is actually true for both gluten-free vegan and for gluten- and egg-free pancakes.) If you're allergic to nuts, you can replace the almond flour with an equal weight of finely ground sunflower seeds – they work perfectly as a substitute.

The pancakes made with the extra almond flour (as well as all the combined gluten-free and vegan adjustments) are wonderfully soft and fluffy, with just the right amount of squishiness and sponginess. They're just as thick as the regular ones, and they're no longer in any way gummy or unpleasantly doughy.

Even with the larger amount of sugar and cooking them on a higher heat (as we did with the dairy-free and the vegan versions), the gluten-free vegan pancakes show less browning and caramelization. The almond flour does help slightly, but you still can't get quite the same golden brown colour as you did with the regular, original recipe. You can, however, "cheat" a bit and use golden caster (superfine) sugar or light brown soft sugar to give them more of a golden hue.

The extra almond flour will make the pancake batter slightly thicker, but don't be tempted to add more milk – the thicker batter doesn't mean that the end results will be too dense or too dry in any way. It just means that as you scoop or ladle the batter into the frying pan, you might need to gently nudge it around to help spread it out a bit more.

A final note: the gummy pancake texture in the absence of almond flour is especially noticeable with gluten-free flour blends with a very high starch content. Most shop-bought blends fall into that category. However, if you use a homemade blend that's lower in starches, you might get away with not using the almond flour, or you might need to use less of it. In that case, prepare the batter without any almond flour, then cook one "test" pancake to see how it turns out. Then, add the almond flour as needed.

# Fluffy American-style pancakes: recipe

**This recipe makes 10–12 perfectly fluffy pancakes.**

| | DIET | | | | | |
|---|---|---|---|---|---|---|
| | **Regular** | **Gluten-free** | **Dairy-free** | **Egg-free** | **Vegan** | **GF Vegan** |
| plain flour [1] | 240g<br>2 cups | 220g<br>1¾ cups + 1 tbsp | 240g<br>2 cups | 260g<br>2 cups + 2½ tbsp | 260g<br>2 cups + 2½ tbsp | 240g<br>2 cups |
| almond flour [2] | / | / | / | / | / | 40g<br>¼ cup + 2½ tbsp |
| caster or granulated sugar | 30g<br>2½ tbsp | 30g<br>2½ tbsp | 50g<br>¼ cup | 30g<br>2½ tbsp | 50g<br>¼ cup | 50g<br>¼ cup |
| baking powder | 4 tsp | 4 tsp | 4 tsp | 4½ tsp | 4½ tsp | 4½ tsp |
| salt | ½ tsp | ½ tsp | ½ tsp | ½ tsp | ½ tsp | ½ tsp |
| xanthan gum | / | 1 tsp* | / | / | / | 1 tsp* |
| milk, room temp [3] | 300g<br>1¼ cups | 300g<br>1¼ cups | 300g<br>1¼ cups | 360g<br>1½ cups | 360g<br>1½ cups | 360g<br>1½ cups |
| eggs, room temp [4] | 2 | 2 | 2 | / | / | / |
| unsalted butter, melted [5] | 30g<br>¼ stick | 30g<br>¼ stick | 30g<br>¼ stick | 30g<br>¼ stick | 30g<br>¼ stick | 30g<br>¼ stick |
| apple cider vinegar | / | / | / | 1 tsp | 1 tsp | 1 tsp |

[1] Either plain (all-purpose) wheat flour or plain gluten-free flour blend. For the latter, use shop-bought or make your own (see page 24).

[2] Or use an equal weight of finely ground sunflower seeds.

[3] Either whole dairy or dairy-free milk, excluding canned coconut milk.

[4] UK medium eggs (US large).

[5] Either dairy or vegan butter.

* If your gluten-free flour blend already contains binders, use only ½ teaspoon.

1. In a bowl, whisk together the flour, almond flour (if using), sugar, baking powder, salt, and xanthan gum (if using).

2. In a separate large bowl, whisk together the milk, eggs (if using), melted butter, and apple cider vinegar (if using).

3. Add the dry ingredients to the wet and, with a rubber spatula or a wooden spoon, mix everything together until only just combined – your batter should be slightly lumpy, not completely smooth. You can adjust the consistency of the batter, if needed, by adding a tablespoon or two of extra milk.

4. Heat a frying pan over medium heat and butter it lightly, wiping away any excess with kitchen paper.

5. Dollop the pancake batter into the frying pan, about a ladleful or ⅓ cup per pancake. You can cook several pancakes at once, depending on the size of your frying pan.

6. Cook the pancakes over medium heat for about 2 minutes, or until you see bubbles appearing on the top surface, the edges are set and the bottom is a golden brown colour.

7. Flip the pancakes and cook them for a further 2 minutes, or until the other side is golden brown as well.

8. Transfer the cooked pancakes to a plate or wire rack and continue with the rest of the batter. The recipe makes about 10–12 pancakes, depending on their size.

9. Serve immediately with toppings of choice.

Regular

Dairy-free

Egg-free

Vegan

Rules for adapting
a baked cheesecake

↓

p.82

# Case Study 14:
# Baked New York-style Cheesecake

My love of cheesecake has always been there – but it grew exponentially once I realized that it's possible (and very easy, as it turns out) to bake perfectly creamy cheesecakes that don't crack – without a water bath. Because, let's be honest, fussing about with boiling hot water in the oven isn't much fun, and neither is the thought of a soggy crust if the water bath manages to find its way into your springform tin.

The idea behind the water bath is simple: it controls the temperature around the cheesecake so that it doesn't exceed 100°C/212°F, which bakes the cheesecake slowly and in a controlled manner, thus preventing cracking. And it makes sense, considering that over-baking is the main reason for why a cheesecake might crack.

However, you can just as easily control the temperature around the cheesecake by adjusting the oven temperature – and that's exactly what my go-to, "no-water-bath" baking method does. Instead of baking the cheesecake at the most common baking temperature of 180°C/350°F, we'll reduce the oven temperature all the way down to 140°C/275°F. This, along with a few other tricks, ensures that your cheesecake will come out of the oven with a perfectly smooth, crack-free top and a decadently creamy centre – every single time.

So, to prevent your (regular) cheesecake from cracking without a water bath:

- **Use room-temperature ingredients.** This is particularly important for the cream cheese, yogurt and eggs. It's better to avoid rapid temperature changes if you want to achieve cheesecake perfection.

- **Don't aerate or over-mix the cheesecake filling.** Incorporate as little air into your cheesecake filling as possible. That means that you shouldn't intensively whisk the filling if you're making it by hand, using a balloon whisk. I also don't recommend using a hand mixer, as it tends to introduce too much air into the mixture. If using a stand mixer, use the paddle attachment and set the mixer to the lowest speed setting.

- **Bake your cheesecake at a relatively low oven temperature of 140°C/275°F.** This bakes the cheesecake very slowly, which allows you to control its texture precisely and it prevents the filling from over-baking, which is the most common cause of cracking.

- **Turn off the oven while the cheesecake is still wobbly in the middle.** The cheesecake will continue to bake as a result of "carryover cooking", even after you've turned off the oven. A wobbly middle will – eventually – result in a perfectly set, yet still creamy centre. You don't want an intense jiggle in the centre, just a gentle wobble. If the centre of the cheesecake is completely set when you turn off the oven, it's possible that the cheesecake is over-baked and it might crack as it cools.

- **Leave the cheesecake to cool in a turned-off oven with the oven door ajar.** This slow cooling process prevents another rapid temperature change, further guarding against cracks during baking.

Other than that, the regular cheesecake starting point contains all of the usual ingredients: full-fat cream cheese, plain yogurt (although sour cream works as well), caster (superfine) or granulated sugar, cornflour (cornstarch), eggs and a generous dose of vanilla. The cheesecake crust is composed of crushed-up digestive biscuits (graham crackers work, too) and melted butter.

The regular cheesecake of our starting point is rich and creamy, with a silky smooth filling that is neither dense nor claggy – after all, there's nothing appealing about a mouthful of cheesecake tasting like straight-up cream cheese. Instead, through the process of baking and largely because of the presence of eggs, the baked filling is ever so slightly aerated, with teeny tiny air pockets visible throughout in a cut slice. This results in a lighter cheesecake texture that's a real pleasure to eat.

**NOTE: ALL ABOUT THE FILLING**

**In this case study, we'll focus only on adapting the cheesecake filling rather than the crust itself. The latter is easily adapted to gluten-free by using a gluten-free biscuit alternative (either shop-bought or homemade) and to dairy-free or vegan by using vegan biscuits and melted vegan butter. (The majority of digestive biscuits and graham crackers are already egg-free – just check the packet ingredients before you buy.)**

## Dairy-free

The key to a delicious dairy-free cheesecake lies in choosing the correct dairy-free equivalents for the cream cheese and the yogurt. There are two things that you should look for:

- **A texture that's as similar as possible to the dairy-containing versions.** This is especially important for the cream cheese: the dairy-free cream cheese should be fairly firm and not too soft or runny – it should have a consistency that's as close as possible to that of regular dairy, full-fat cream cheese.

- **As low a water content as possible – they shouldn't be too watery.** That's why I recommend using a Greek-style dairy-free yogurt rather than a plain one. Your dairy-free cream cheese also shouldn't be too watery, otherwise your cheesecake can end up rather bland and is more likely to crack during baking and cooling.

If you can find only fairly soft vegan cream cheese in your local grocery store (with a high water content), you can still get away with it – there's just one extra step you need to take. You need to remove some of the excess water by straining the vegan cream cheese. To do this, place a strainer or colander over a bowl, line it with cheesecloth, add the vegan cream cheese and allow the excess water to drip out over the course of a few hours. To speed things up, you can make a closed pouch with the cheesecloth and then weigh it down gently with a plate or similar – the added weight will help the water drain a bit faster. (It's best to place the whole straining set-up in the fridge, to avoid keeping the cream cheese out at room temperature or in a warm kitchen for a prolonged period of time.)

Once your vegan cream cheese has noticeably thickened, you can use it in your cheesecake. Even just removing a tablespoon or two of water will drastically improve the texture and flavour of your dairy-free cheesecake and it'll greatly reduce the chances of it cracking.

Once you have the correct dairy-free equivalents, simply replace the dairy cream cheese and yogurt in the regular recipe with an equal weight or volume of the dairy-free/vegan versions. Although there is one more adjustment you need to make.

All dairy-free/vegan ingredients, even if they are optimized, still have a higher moisture content than the dairy-containing versions. To account for this, you need to add 5g (2 teaspoons) of cornflour (cornstarch) per about 225g (1 cup) of vegan cream cheese in the recipe (you can round this off as necessary). The cornflour (cornstarch) will act as a "sponge" for some of the extra moisture, thereby thickening the cheesecake filling to bring it closer to the texture of the regular cheesecake.

All of these modifications result in a wonderfully creamy dairy-free cheesecake that's very similar in appearance to the regular, dairy-containing recipe. It'll be a bit softer in texture and not quite as rich, especially immediately on the day of baking. However, after it's been chilled in the fridge overnight, it firms up beautifully and its texture becomes much more comparable to that of a regular cheesecake. It also slices beautifully into clean, neat slices.

## What about the flavour?

Vegan cream cheeses and yogurts have a discernibly different flavour to regular dairy versions. Consequently, the flavour of the dairy-free cheesecake will differ from the original, regular recipe – and there's not much you can do about that. This doesn't mean that it will taste bad in any way, it's just different.

So, in addition to choosing dairy-free/vegan alternatives with the correct texture and composition, make sure you choose those whose flavour you like. I also recommend playing around with additional flavourings that will help to make the dairy-free cheesecake taste richer and more well-rounded, despite the different taste of the dairy-free/vegan equivalents. A generous dose of good-quality vanilla or a pinch or two of lemon zest are good options. And, of course, you can incorporate various fruits (blueberries or raspberries are a delicious choice), or add melted chocolate, or peanut butter or other intense flavours.

The result will be an incredibly delicious cheesecake that even non-dairy-free folks will enjoy.

**NOTE**

Because of the higher moisture content of vegan ingredients, dairy-free cheesecakes typically require a longer baking time (the same is true for vegan cheesecakes). Whenever you're baking a cheesecake, pay attention to the physical indicators, especially to how wobbly or jiggly the centre is.

# Egg-free

The egg-free cheesecake variation is all about understanding the role that eggs play in a typical cheesecake recipe. First, they're structure-providing ingredients in that they help the cheesecake to set properly. Second, they're a moisture source (which is rather self-explanatory). And, third, they're also an aerating or lift-providing ingredient. Like I've mentioned before on page 248, there's a small amount of aeration present in the final, baked regular cheesecake, and it's visible in the form of tiny air pockets evenly distributed throughout. This is what gives the cheesecake a slightly lighter, more elegant texture and a mouthfeel that doesn't resemble just straight-up cream cheese (as that would make it rather claggy and unpleasant).

The next step is to determine which ingredients can fulfil the same roles – be that additional ingredients, or larger quantities of ingredients that are already present in the recipe. In practice, for each egg removed, you need to:

- **Increase the amount of cornflour (cornstarch) by 5g (2 teaspoons) – this acts as an alternative structure-providing setting agent.**

- **Add 20g (1½ tablespoons) of milk and 20g (1½ tablespoons) of yogurt as an alternative moisture source.**

As you've probably noticed, we didn't add an alternative aerating ingredient to make up for the absence of the eggs. That's because you can get just enough lightness and aeration from the moisture in the other ingredients (cream cheese, yogurt and milk) turning into steam. And, as you'll see below, this is also why it's best to bake egg-free (and vegan) cheesecakes at a slightly higher oven temperature.

When it comes to choosing the alternative moisture source, a 50:50 mixture of yogurt and milk outperforms either milk or yogurt on its own. (Note that this is in addition to the cream cheese and the yogurt already in the recipe.) Using only milk results in a cheesecake that's slightly too soft; using only extra yogurt gives a cheesecake that's slightly too dense, especially after an overnight chill in the fridge. Using a 50:50 mixture of both, on the other hand, gives a creamy yet stable texture that's much closer to that of a regular cheesecake.

Adding the milk, extra yogurt and extra cornflour (cornstarch) also helps to maintain a similar volume of the egg-free cheesecake filling and therefore a similar height of the baked result compared to its regular equivalent.

However, all these tweaks combined are still not quite enough to completely mimic the effect of eggs. The final piece of the puzzle lies in the oven temperature. While the regular (and all egg-containing) cheesecakes are best baked at the low oven temperature of 140°C/275°F (without a water bath!) to prevent over-baking and cracking, the danger of cracking is actually greatly reduced in egg-free cheesecakes. That's because eggs are definitely the main culprit when it comes to those pesky cracks!

So, with cracking being less of a concern, we can bake the egg-free cheesecake at the slightly higher oven temperature of 160°C/325°F, which results in the cheesecake puffing up a bit more during baking and therefore achieving a greater aeration. I still don't recommend baking at 180°C/350°F, as that can result in the edges of the cheesecake aerating too much, resulting in a rather comical shape with greatly puffed-up edges and a sunken centre.

All of these changes result in an egg-free cheesecake that's absolutely phenomenal: wonderfully rich and creamy, with an incredibly delicious flavour and just the right amount of aeration that adds a hint of lightness. In terms of its appearance, it's very similar to the regular, egg-containing cheesecake: it's of the same height but whiter in colour (whereas the regular version has a light golden hue, especially on top, owing to the presence of the eggs).

**NOTE**

Depending on how firm your cream cheese is (for example, if you're using cream cheese in block form rather than from a tub), you might need to adjust the milk-to-yogurt ratio (for example, use a 60:40 or even a 70:30 mixture). Furthermore, if you're using vegan ingredients (so, if you're going from a dairy-free to a vegan cheesecake by removing the eggs), then it's better to use only yogurt rather than the 50:50 mixture – see opposite.

# Vegan

As with many other recipes in this chapter, the vegan New York-style baked cheesecake is just a straightforward combination of the dairy- and egg-free adjustments. First, you need to replace the dairy cream cheese and yogurt with an equal weight or volume of their dairy-free equivalents. And, just as with the dairy-free version, it's very important to choose the best possible dairy-free products – ones that are similar in texture to their regular equivalents and that don't have too high a moisture (water) content. In fact, that's even more important in the vegan variation as there are no eggs to act as a failsafe to ensure a good cheesecake texture.

Like I've mentioned, it's important that you use dairy-free alternatives whose flavour you actually like, as these will determine the flavour of the final, baked cheesecake. As the taste of vegan cream cheese and yogurt tends to be milder and not quite as rich as that of the dairy ingredients, it's a good idea to be extra generous with any flavourings you're using, such as vanilla or citrus zest.

In this vegan version, cornflour (cornstarch) plays two different roles and so its quantity requires a slightly more complex adjustment:

- **It absorbs some of the excess moisture that comes along with the dairy-free ingredients. To account for that, you need to add 5g (2 teaspoons) per 225g (1 cup) of vegan cream cheese used.**
- **It also acts as an alternative structure-providing, setting agent in the absence of eggs. For this, you need to add 5g (2 teaspoons) for each egg removed.**

While a 50:50 mixture of milk and yogurt turned out to be the best alternative moisture source in the egg-free cheesecake, here it's best to use only extra yogurt – specifically, you need to add 40g (3 tablespoons) of vegan yogurt for each egg removed. That's because vegan yogurt has a greater water content than its regular counterpart, so it'll result in the perfect cheesecake batter consistency with no milk necessary. (This is also why I recommend using a Greek-style vegan yogurt, as it tends to have a lower moisture content.) And, just like with the egg-free cheesecake, it's best to bake this vegan cheesecake at the slightly higher oven temperature of 160°C/325°F to achieve a similar degree of aeration and lightness as with the regular cheesecake.

The final result, after an overnight chill, is a wonderfully creamy cheesecake that simply melts in your mouth. It's very easy to cut the cheesecake into neat, clean slices and it holds its shape beautifully – which is rather amazing when you consider that we've removed both eggs and dairy cream cheese from the recipe.

*Regular*

*Dairy-free*

*Egg-free*

*Vegan*

*Regular*

*Dairy-free*

*Egg-free*

*Vegan*

# Baked New York-style cheesecake: recipe

**This recipe makes one 20cm (8in) cheesecake that serves about 12 people.**

| | DIET | | | |
|---|---|---|---|---|
| | **Regular** | **Dairy-free** | **Egg-free** | **Vegan** |
| crushed digestives or graham crackers [1] | 220g<br>2¼ cups | 220g<br>2¼ cups | 220g<br>2¼ cups | 220g<br>2¼ cups |
| unsalted butter, melted [2] | 70g<br>½ stick + 1 tbsp | 70g<br>½ stick + 1 tbsp | 70g<br>½ stick + 1 tbsp | 70g<br>½ stick + 1 tbsp |
| cream cheese, room temp [3] | 600g<br>2⅔ cups | 600g<br>2⅔ cups | 600g<br>2⅔ cups | 600g<br>2⅔ cups |
| yogurt, room temp [4] | 115g<br>½ cup | 115g<br>½ cup | 175g<br>¾ cup | 230g<br>1 cup |
| milk, room temp [5] | / | / | 60g<br>¼ cup | / |
| caster or granulated sugar | 150g<br>¾ cup | 150g<br>¾ cup | 150g<br>¾ cup | 150g<br>¾ cup |
| cornflour (cornstarch) | 15g<br>2 tbsp | 30g<br>4 tbsp | 30g<br>4 tbsp | 45g<br>6 tbsp |
| vanilla paste [6] | 1 tsp | 1 tsp | 1 tsp | 1 tsp |
| eggs, room temp [7] | 3 | 3 | / | / |
| **Oven temp** | 140°C/275°F | 140°C/275°F | 160°C/325°F | 160°C/325°F |
| **Baking time** | 50–60 mins | 65–75 mins | 45–55 mins | 60–70 mins |

[1] Use cookies that suit your dietary requirements.

[2] Either dairy or vegan butter. For the latter, use a firm vegan butter block, not a soft spread.

[3] Either dairy or dairy-free cream cheese (see also page 248).

[4] Either unsweetened plain or Greek-style dairy or vegan yogurt.

[5] Either whole dairy or dairy-free milk, excluding canned coconut milk.

[6] Double the quantity if using vanilla extract.

[7] UK medium eggs (US large).

### Cheesecake base

1. Adjust the oven rack to the middle position, pre-heat the oven to 180°C/350°F and line the bottom and sides of a 20cm (8in) springform tin with baking paper.

2. Mix together the crushed digestive biscuits or graham crackers and melted butter, until you get a mixture resembling wet sand. Transfer the mixture into the lined springform tin and, using the flat bottom of a glass or measuring cup, compress them into an even layer with an approximately 4cm (1½in) rim around the edge.

3. Bake for 10 minutes, then remove from the oven and leave to cool until warm.

### Cheesecake filling & baking

1. Reduce the oven temperature to 140°C/275°F (for regular and dairy-free cheesecake) or 160°C/325°F (for egg-free and vegan cheesecake).

2. In a large bowl using a balloon whisk or using a stand mixer fitted with the paddle on the lowest speed setting, mix the cream cheese, yogurt, and milk (if using) together until smooth. Make sure to mix rather than whisk or aerate – you don't want to incorporate too much air into the mixture.

3. Mix together the sugar and cornflour (cornstarch), and add them to the cream-cheese mixture. Mix well until combined and smooth.

4. Add the vanilla and mix well until combined.

5. Add the eggs (if using), one at a time, mixing well after each addition, until smooth.

6. Transfer the cheesecake filling into the slightly cooled cheesecake crust and smooth out the top. If your springform tin isn't 100% leakproof, get a large baking sheet and place the cheesecake on it before it goes into the oven, so that the baking sheet can catch any small butter leaks.

7. Bake at 140°C/275°F for about 50–60 minutes (regular) or 65–75 minutes (dairy-free), or at 160°C/325°F for 45–55 minutes (egg-free) or 60–70 minutes (vegan), until the edges are slightly puffed up, and the middle is still wobbly when you gently shake the springform tin. Note that these baking times are guidelines – always judge the doneness of a cheesecake based on its physical indicators (the wobbliness of the centre and how set the edges are; see page 247) rather than on the baking time, especially as each oven behaves slightly differently. Start checking your cheesecake about 10 minutes before the end of the recommended baking time.

8. Turn off the oven and leave the cheesecake to cool to room temperature in the turned-off oven with the oven door ajar.

9. Once it's cooled to room temperature, transfer the cheesecake into the fridge for at least 4 hours or preferably overnight. Once chilled, remove it from the springform tin on to a serving plate and slice it into individual portions to serve.

# Gf

**Gluten-free**

# What Is Gluten? (And How to Replace It)

**Before we delve into the science of (successful) gluten-free baking, we first need to understand what gluten actually is and what role it plays in regular, wheat-based baking. Gluten is a mixture of two proteins (gliadin and glutenin) found in cereal grains (primarily wheat) and it's responsible for the elasticity and flexibility of bakes made with wheat flour – it is a "glue" that prevents bakes from crumbling apart.**

In practical terms, gluten ensures that your cakes and cookies aren't too delicate and that your pastry is flexible enough that you can roll it out without it tearing. It gives regular bread dough enough elasticity and extensibility that it's easy to shape and so that it can prove efficiently, easily doubling in size. The gluten is also responsible for the characteristic, chewy crumb of a loaf of bread.

So, in order to create amazing gluten-free bakes that are nearly indistinguishable from their regular, wheat-based equivalents, we need to mimic the effects of gluten. That's where binders come in: ingredients such as xanthan gum and psyllium husk that give gluten-free bakes some elasticity and flexibility.

There are also other things to consider, such as which gluten-free flours or blends to use, which binder (and how much of it) is best suited for different types of bake, the fact that gluten-free flours absorb more moisture than regular wheat flour – and much more. This chapter has a lot to cover!

It's worth noting that there is an advantage to gluten-free baking: you don't have to worry about over-working or over-mixing your batter or dough, as there's no gluten present that could make your bakes too tough or rubbery. When prepared correctly, gluten-free cakes, cookies and similar bakes will have a more tender, delicate, melt-in-the-mouth crumb – so much so that many non-gluten-free folks actually end up preferring them.

# Starchy & Protein Gluten-free Flours

When you first embark on your gluten-free baking journey, the sheer number of gluten-free flours available can be rather overwhelming. Sorghum flour, tapioca starch, buckwheat flour, teff flour, potato starch... it can seem almost impossible to keep track of all of them.

However, things get much easier when you realise that you can group these flours into three different categories within which you can make swaps:

| Starchy flours | "Lighter" protein flours | "Heavier" protein flours |
|---|---|---|
| • **cornflour (cornstarch)**<br>• **potato starch**<br>• **tapioca starch**<br>• **arrowroot starch** | • **brown rice flour**<br>• **millet flour** | • **sorghum flour**<br>• **light buckwheat flour**<br>• **white teff flour**<br>• **maize flour (corn flour in the USA)**<br>• **oat flour**<br>• **quinoa flour** |

So, if you encounter one of these flours in a recipe or a homemade gluten-free flour blend and you don't have it to hand, you can always substitute it with an equal weight of another flour from the same group. Note that this is a non-exhaustive list – there are more gluten-free flours out there, these are just the ones that will crop up most commonly in my recipes.

Keep in mind that you can make these 1:1 substitutions by weight, but not by volume. So, while you can replace 150g of potato starch with 150g of tapioca starch, you can't replace 1 cup of potato starch with 1 cup of tapioca starch. That's because different gluten-free flours have widely different densities. As a case in point, 1 cup of potato starch weighs about 165g, whereas 1 cup of tapioca starch weighs about 115g. If you don't account for it, that 50g difference could have disastrous consequences for your recipe.

In general, white rice flour behaves more like a starchy flour, so I don't recommend substituting it with brown rice flour. However, I also haven't grouped it with the other starches because its composition and properties are different enough from things like cornflour (cornstarch) or potato starch that you can't reliably substitute them for each other either. So, if a recipe lists white rice flour as an ingredient, I don't really recommend substituting it with anything else (unless absolutely necessary).

Now that we've defined the different groupings, let's have a look at what they actually mean and what their crucial properties are.

**Starchy gluten-free flours** are, as the name suggests, starches. They're extracted from their base plant component (for example, corn kernels for cornflour/cornstarch, or roots of the cassava plant for tapioca starch) in such a way that nothing remains except for the starch element. These flours don't impart any flavour to the bakes and they don't contribute much to their structure. Instead, they're there to make the gluten-free bakes softer, fluffier and airier. They have a low protein content (because of the extraction process that eliminates everything apart from the starch or carbohydrate component) and a lower water-absorption capacity (that is, they don't absorb a lot of water). We use them to give gluten-free cakes and similar bakes a plush, open crumb and to ensure that gluten-free pastry isn't too tough or too gummy.

**Protein gluten-free flours**, on the other hand, are the flavour- and structure-providing elements of a gluten-free bake. While they don't contain any gluten, they do contribute a very small amount of elasticity to bakes, preventing them from being too fragile or crumbly. They have a higher water-absorption capacity (that is, they absorb more moisture). Consequently, bakes with a higher protein-flour content are slower to dry out.

## "Lighter" and "heavier" protein flours

This distinction is a personal one, following years of observation during my baking with the various gluten-free flours. "Lighter" protein flours (millet and brown rice flour) give an airier crumb and don't impart as much flavour. "Heavier" flours give a slightly denser, heartier crumb and they're also more intense in flavour. The difference between the two is especially obvious in bakes like bread or vanilla cake, where there aren't many other prominent flavourings.

The distinction is also important when it comes to swapping different "heavier" protein flours. They all have their very distinct flavours and while they all give delicious results, you may eventually find that you prefer one over the other. But that will come with time and experience – do experiment until you find your favourites.

## Favourite flour combinations

My personal favourite flour combination, especially when it comes to gluten-free bread, is a mixture of tapioca starch (starchy), millet flour ("lighter" protein) and sorghum flour ("heavier" protein). I've found that this gives a flavour that's most like regular wheat flour.

Once you've found your favourites, you'll also realize that it's not necessary to have twenty different types of gluten-free flour in your pantry at all times. Three or four go-to flours will usually be enough.

NOTE: FINELY GROUND FLOURS

It's important that you use finely ground gluten-free flours (and blends) – they should have a powdery texture rather than a coarse one, like polenta. Using coarse flours can inhibit moisture absorption (which can, for example, result in sticky bread dough, and cookies that spread out too much) and give your bakes an unpleasantly gritty mouthfeel. A fine texture is especially important in rice flour – always use superfine white or brown rice flour.

# Almond Flour & Other "Additional" Flours

In addition to starchy and protein gluten-free flours, there are also what I like to call "additional" flours – those that don't really fit into either of those groups but are still frequently used in gluten-free baking. These include almond flour, coconut flour, chickpea flour and other nut flours.

**Almond flour** is a great way to ensure that your gluten-free cakes, cupcakes and muffins turn out moist, and stay that way for longer. Because of its higher fat content compared to other gluten-free flours, almond flour gives a richer mouthfeel. I often substitute up to 25% (one quarter) of the total flour content with an equal weight of almond flour in my cakes. Almond flour is also a crucial ingredient in many gluten-free vegan bakes: for example, it ensures that the gluten-free vegan buttery vanilla cake (see pages 101–102) and the gluten-free vegan fluffy American-style pancakes (page 243) aren't too gummy, and that the gluten-free vegan shortcrust pastry (page 182) is pleasantly crisp and crumbly rather than tooth-breakingly hard.

However, if you're allergic to nuts and you encounter a gluten-free recipe that uses almond flour, you have two options. First, if the almond flour isn't 100% essential to the recipe, you can substitute it with an equal weight of the gluten-free flour blend. Your bakes might dry out a tiny bit faster, but they will still be delicious. Second, if almond flour is a crucial ingredient that makes the recipe work (this is especially true with gluten-free vegan recipes), you can substitute it with an equal weight of finely ground sunflower seeds. I've found them to be a wonderful nut-free alternative that adds a gorgeous, subtle flavour and richness to bakes.

**Avoid using coconut flour**. Coconut flour absorbs a lot of moisture (and I do mean *a lot*), so unless you're making a recipe that's been specifically optimized to work with it, it's best avoided. Don't replace other gluten-free flours (like sorghum flour, tapioca starch or almond flour) with coconut flour, otherwise you'll be left with a dry, crumbly mess.

**Use chickpea flour only in savoury bakes**. Because of its quite intense flavour, chickpea flour doesn't work so well in most sweet bakes. However, it can be a great option for savoury.

# Gluten Substitutes: Binders

Of course, the most obvious distinction between baking with gluten-free flours and wheat flour is the absence of gluten – and therefore, the absence of the structure, elasticity and flexibility that gluten brings to bakes.

While you might think that you don't need any elasticity in bakes such as cakes or cookies – think again. If you want to be able to handle cake sponges, trim them and stack them when making a layer cake, you need them to have some degree of elasticity, otherwise they'll crack all over the place. The same goes for cookies: without the gluten (and without anything to replace it), they can be so crumbly that they fall apart when you try to pick them up.

You're probably familiar with the importance of gluten (or, more specifically, "developing gluten") when it comes to making regular bread. Through prolonged kneading or by hydrating the flour, the developed gluten allows you to shape and prove the bread and gives the final baked loaf its characteristic chewy, springy crumb. Thankfully, there's a straightforward way to mimic the effects of gluten in gluten-free baking: binders. These are ingredients that act as gluten replacements or substitutes, and they give gluten-free bakes some elasticity and flexibility, preventing them from being too fragile and crumbly.

There are two main binders in gluten-free baking: xanthan gum and psyllium husk. Both are amazing, even indispensable, and, on the surface, they carry out similar functions. They are hydrocolloids, which absorb water to form a sticky, extensible gel. But, in terms of application and of what kinds of bake they're best suited to, there are some important differences.

# Xanthan gum: best for non-bread recipes

**NOTE**

Xanthan gum isn't a 1:1 gluten substitute and it most certainly doesn't provide the same degree of elasticity as gluten. However, in the case of its preferred bakes, that's not a problem at all. After all, you don't need much elasticity in a cake – you just need enough binding power to prevent it from being too crumbly. And that's exactly what xanthan gum provides.

Xanthan gum is the best binder to use in cake, cupcake, muffin, cookie, brownie and pastry recipes. That is, it's the best binder for pretty much all gluten-free bakes that aren't bread (although it does have its uses in gluten-free enriched bread recipes; more on that on page 274). It holds the bakes together, gives them some flexibility, prevents them from being too crumbly and greatly improves their texture.

In terms of its composition, xanthan gum is a polysaccharide (that is, its chemical structure comprises several smaller sugar units bonded together) and it's produced through a fermentation process by the *Xanthomonas campestris* bacteria.

Many shop-bought gluten-free flour blends, especially those available in the USA, already contain binders (usually xanthan gum or guar gum). These commercial blends are formulated to work well for your average cake or cookie recipe. So, if your gluten-free flour blend already contains xanthan gum or other binders, you need to reduce the amount of xanthan gum added separately by ¼ teaspoon per 120g (1 cup) of gluten-free flour blend with respect to the amount listed in the recipe.

Here's a very general overview of how much xanthan gum you typically need to add (per 120g/1 cup of gluten-free flour blend), depending on what kind of bake you're making (note that you need more xanthan gum for bakes that require more elasticity, such as pastry and Swiss rolls):

| Bake | Amount of xanthan gum per 120g (1 cup) of gluten-free flour blend | |
|---|---|---|
| | blend without binders | blend with binders |
| cakes & cupcakes | ¼ teaspoon | none |
| muffins | ½ teaspoon | ¼ teaspoon |
| Swiss rolls | ¾ teaspoon | ½ teaspoon |
| brownies | ¼ teaspoon | none |
| cookies | ¼ teaspoon | none |
| pastry (shortcrust or flaky pie crust) | ½ teaspoon | ¼ teaspoon |
| thin pancakes & crêpes | ¼ teaspoon | none |
| fluffy pancakes | ½ teaspoon | ¼ teaspoon |

All of these amounts are based on a rule of thumb – they are just a good starting point for most recipes. However, there will always be exceptions. Sometimes, if your bake contains a tenderizing ingredient, such as melted chocolate (see page 108), which will make it more delicate, you'll need to use more xanthan gum than these general guidelines predict. Gluten-free vegan bakes also require adjusted quantities of xanthan gum (see pages 428–9).

Finally, always treat xanthan gum as a dry ingredient. Add it to your batter or dough along with all the other dry ingredients, such as gluten-free flours or blends, raising agents and salt.

## Xanthan gum myth-busting

For whatever reason, there's quite a lot of misinformation out there about xanthan gum. So, let's clear some things up.

**Myth 1: You can substitute xanthan gum with cornflour (cornstarch).** Unfortunately not. Both xanthan gum and cornflour make good thickeners for sauces and soups, but only xanthan gum makes a good binder in gluten-free baking (whereas cornflour is a starchy gluten-free flour; see page 260).

**Myth 2: Xanthan gum and baking powder or bicarbonate of soda (baking soda) have the same function.** I'm not sure where or how the idea originated that these are somehow interchangeable (maybe it's because they're all white powders that you use in small-ish amounts?), but xanthan gum and baking powder or bicarbonate of soda couldn't have more different roles in gluten-free baking. Xanthan gum is a binder, providing structure, texture and flexibility. Baking powder and bicarbonate of soda are raising or leavening agents that ensure that your bakes are fluffy and aerated. You definitely can't use one instead of the other.

## Psyllium husk: best for bread recipes

If you are baking gluten-free bread, there's no doubt about it: psyllium husk is the star of the show. It's the ingredient that gives you a gluten-free dough that you can actually handle, knead and shape, and that gives gluten-free bread enough extensibility to expand properly during proving.

Without psyllium husk, you'd have to make do with gluten-free bread "batter" that's poured into a loaf tin and that bakes up into more of a savoury cake-like texture. With psyllium husk, however, you can enjoy proper gluten-free bread, with a soft, chewy interior and a crisp, crunchy, caramelized crust. The kind that's so good you actually have to fight non-gluten-free folks for the last slice.

Psyllium husk is the outer coating (the husk, hence the name) of the psyllium seeds from the *Plantago ovata* plant, which is a herb grown mainly in India. It's a rich source of fibre, and it's therefore frequently used as a dietary supplement for improving gut health. Just like xanthan gum, psyllium husk is a hydrocolloid – it binds water, and even at very low concentrations can cause a significant increase in the viscosity of a liquid. That is: it forms an elastic, extensible, slightly sticky gel. And it's this hydrocolloid property that makes it so brilliant at transforming what would otherwise be a loose batter into a kneadable, springy, extensible dough.

This means that you're no longer restricted to bread baked in a loaf tin. Instead, you can make proper artisan-style bread (boules), smaller bread rolls, baguettes, and even bakes that require more complex dough shaping, like cinnamon rolls, braided challah bread, and babka.

Furthermore, making the gluten-free dough elastic and extensible allows it to expand during proving. We all know that yeast action (that is, yeast consuming the sugars present in the dough and releasing gases) is responsible for wheat bread increasing in volume as it proves. But that's only possible because gluten gives the dough the elasticity required to trap those gases. When you remove the gluten, you're removing the dough's ability to expand without cracking or tearing – unless, of course, you replace it with something that can provide a

**GLUTEN-FREE TROUBLESHOOTING**

If you make a gluten-free bake and it's much too crumbly, without also being too dry, likelihood is that it doesn't contain enough binders. Try increasing the amount of xanthan gum by ¼ teaspoon to help.

similar elasticity and extensibility. That "something" is psyllium husk. And it works like a dream, allowing gluten-free bread to go through one or two rounds of proving, during which it can double in size without any problems whatsoever.

And finally, psyllium husk is responsible for giving gluten-free bread that wonderful chewy crumb that you're familiar with from regular wheat bread. Essentially, it gives gluten-free bread that "there's-no-way-this-is-gluten-free" quality. It truly is a magical ingredient.

## Whole husk vs powder

Psyllium husk comes in two forms: whole (or rough) psyllium husk and psyllium husk powder. The powdered form is just the ground-up whole husk. Either form will work well in gluten-free recipes that call for psyllium husk, but I prefer the whole husk version, which, in my experience, gives a slightly nicer, more open bread crumb. Whole psyllium husk is also less likely to form clumps when you mix it with water to make the psyllium gel (see page 266), and it's therefore easier to incorporate into gluten-free bread dough.

**Whole psyllium husk**                    **Psyllium husk powder**

If you do want to use powder rather than whole husk, note that you will need to use only 85% of the weight listed in the recipe – that is, reduce the weight by 15%. Because psyllium husk powder comprises smaller particles and therefore has a larger surface area, it absorbs more water and forms a stiffer gel. So, to get the same effect as with the whole psyllium husk, you need to use a smaller quantity. As a worked example, if a recipe calls for 10g (2 tablespoons) of whole psyllium husk, you need to use only 8.5g (1 tablespoon) of the powder.

You'll notice that the volume (the tablespoon measure) has reduced by 50%, while the weight has reduced only by 15%. That's because the two forms of psyllium husk have different densities: 1 tablespoon of whole psyllium husk weighs 5g, whereas 1 tablespoon of psyllium husk powder weighs 8.5g. That means that while you reduce the weight by 15%, you actually need to reduce the volume by half.

Regardless of whether you are using whole or powdered psyllium husk, make sure to use "blond" psyllium husk, which doesn't add any colour or flavour to your bakes. Other varieties can sometimes add both an aftertaste as well as a dark brownish or even purple colour to gluten-free bread. Many brands don't specify the variety, in which case I recommend having a look at the reviews, if they're available. Avoid brands whose reviews mention they turned the bake a strange colour.

---

**NOTE: BINDERS IN BREAD**

In general, you need to use about 5–6 b% (baker's percentage; see page 272) of whole psyllium husk when making gluten-free bread (5–6g per 100g of total gluten-free flour blend). When making non-enriched bread, psyllium husk is typically the only binder you need to use. When making enriched, brioche-like dough, it's best to substitute 25–30% of the psyllium husk with an equal weight of xanthan gum. You can read more about the reasons for this in the "Gluten-free bread 101" section on pages 272–5.

---

## Psyllium gel

In terms of actual practical application, I like to use psyllium husk in a gel form. That is, I don't add it directly to the dry ingredients as a "dry" husk – instead, I first mix it with water, wait for a short while for the gel to form, and then add it to the dough along with all the wet ingredients.

Whether you use psyllium husk in its dry form or as a gel doesn't really affect the texture, flavour or appearance of the final gluten-free bread. However, using it as a gel is both faster and more practical.

If you add psyllium husk in its dry form to the dry ingredients, the initial dough (after all the ingredients have been thoroughly combined) will be fairly loose and sticky. You then need to wait anywhere from 15 to 45 minutes for both the gluten-free flours and the psyllium husk to hydrate (to absorb some of the water) before you get a dough that you can easily handle. And that's a significant waiting time that I like to avoid – I confess, I am a rather impatient baker.

Psyllium husk in gel form gives you a workable dough that's easy to handle straight away. And considering that any bread recipe will include at least one round of rising and a relatively long time in the oven anyway, shaving away that extra waiting time is a big advantage in my book.

Now, the psyllium gel will look a bit odd, especially if you're not used to working with it. Think: slightly sticky, somewhat elastic gloop. But that's how it's supposed to look, so don't worry – you'll get the most amazing gluten-free bread thanks to its gloopy properties.

## Xanthan and psyllium: swaps won't work

While both xanthan gum and psyllium husk function as binders in gluten-free baking, they're not interchangeable. You can't replace the psyllium husk in gluten-free bread recipes with xanthan gum – it won't give you the same supple, springy dough that's easy to handle, knead and shape. Instead, the dough made only with xanthan gum will be much looser, stickier and more difficult to handle, and the final baked loaf also won't have the correct texture.

Similarly, you can't replace the xanthan gum in gluten-free cake, cookie, brownie or pastry recipes with psyllium husk, as the latter tends to give a chewy texture to bakes, which is great in bread but not so much in other bakes. Psyllium husk also tends to hold on to moisture a bit more than xanthan gum, which could make any cakes that use it a bit gummy, and pastry slightly rubbery or leathery.

## Other binders

Xanthan gum and psyllium husk are my go-to binders for gluten-free baking. Although other binders – such as guar gum, flax seeds and chia seeds – exist, they tend to give rather disappointing results when compared to xanthan gum and psyllium husk. Flax and chia seeds are particularly unsuccessful.

### Guar gum

A binder similar to xanthan gum, guar gum is best suited to non-bread gluten-free recipes, such as cakes, cupcakes, muffins, brownies, cookies and pastry. Just like xanthan gum, it's a hydrocolloid that binds water to form a sticky, slightly elastic gel. It doesn't add any flavour, affecting only a bake's texture to prevent it from being too delicate and crumbly; it gives bakes some elasticity and flexibility.

However, I don't use it. I've found that xanthan gum gives gluten-free bakes a much better crumb and texture – one that's closer to that of regular bakes made with wheat flour. But, guar gum is a good alternative for anyone intolerant to corn and soy (as xanthan gum is produced via a fermentation process by the *Xanthomonas campestris* bacteria that often feed on a corn- or soy-based medium). Guar gum, on the other hand, is derived from the ground endosperm of guar beans, so it's completely gluten-, corn- and soy-free.

In my experience, you can use guar gum as a 1:1 replacement for xanthan in most gluten-free bakes that don't require much elasticity, such as buttery cakes, cupcakes, muffins, brownies and cookies. In bakes that require more flexibility, such as Swiss rolls and pastry (both shortcrust and flaky pastry), using the same amount of guar gum as you would xanthan gum typically isn't sufficient. In such cases, you need to add about ¼–½ teaspoon more per 120g (1 cup) of gluten-free flour blend. So, for example, if a gluten-free Swiss roll recipe calls for ¾ teaspoon of xanthan gum per 120g (1 cup) of gluten-free flour blend, it's best to use 1–1¼ teaspoons of guar gum to get enough flexibility to roll the sponge with minimal cracking.

### Flax and chia seeds

These are often suggested as alternatives for psyllium husk but, unfortunately, they simply don't have the same binding power as psyllium husk. Consequently, they don't work as well when it comes to producing a supple, elastic and kneadable gluten-free dough.

### Ground flax seeds

Also known as linseeds, ground flax seeds can form a gel once mixed with water. However, the gel formation is rather sluggish and ineffective if you use cold or room-temperature water, and it improves only marginally with hot water. In all of these cases, you get only a very, very runny gel and even for that, you need to wait quite a long time compared to psyllium husk (which forms a thick, firm, elastic gel in about 15–30 seconds even with cold water).

You'll get the best flax-seed gel (and with minimal waiting time) if you combine the ground flax seeds with water in a saucepan and then boil them on the stovetop, with occasional stirring, for about 5–10 minutes, until you get a thick, viscous gel-like mixture. However, the texture of this flax-seed gel is still much looser than the texture of an equivalent psyllium gel. That is, if we compare such a flax-seed gel, made from 10g of ground flax seeds in 100g of water, to a psyllium gel made from 10g of whole psyllium husk in 100g of water, the former will be much looser. In fact, we'd need to use double the amount of flax seeds to achieve a similar gel texture.

Furthermore, while this flax-seed gel may look promising at first, it's completely ineffective at giving you a workable gluten-free bread dough. Where the dough made with psyllium husk will be beautifully supple, elastic and flexible, the dough made with the flax-seed gel isn't much of a bread dough at all. Instead, it's much more paste-like or like a very thick, sticky batter: it has no elasticity, you can't knead it, and it's impossible to roll out and shape without copious amounts of extra flour – and even then, you'll get lots of sticking and tearing.

## Ground chia seeds

These are much quicker to form a gel than flax seeds. The gel formation is again accelerated by using hot rather than cold water, but unlike with flax seeds, there's no need to cook or boil the mixture on the stovetop. Just like with flax seeds, chia seeds form a much looser gel compared to psyllium husk: you'd need double the amount of chia seeds to get a somewhat similar gel thickness.

Interestingly, boiled flax seeds form a stiffer, firmer and more elastic gel than chia seeds mixed with hot water – but when it comes to forming a somewhat supple dough by mixing the gel with gluten-free flour, chia seeds are actually better. The dough made with chia seeds is definitely less paste-like but, unfortunately, there's little elasticity to it. So, while you can in principle roll it out and shape it, it's very quick to tear and therefore a bit of a nightmare to handle. There's also a further disadvantage to using chia seeds: they add a very dark colour to bakes, which is distinctly noticeable in an otherwise pale dough.

**IN SUMMARY**

While flax and chia seeds can form a gel, they're simply not a suitable replacement for psyllium husk in gluten-free bread baking – not even if you use a greater quantity of them. They simply don't have the same binding power. First of all, they give you a dough that's impossible to handle. And, second, this also translates into inefficient proving and problems at other stages of the baking process. That's why I always recommend using psyllium husk in my gluten-free bread recipes – and don't be tempted to replace it with another ingredient (no matter what you read online).

# Gluten-free Flour Blends

**NOTE**

A good gluten-free flour blend should work across pretty much any type of bake: from cakes, cookies, cupcakes and muffins to pancakes, brownies and all sorts of pastry. After all, any reasonably well-stocked gluten-free pantry will always contain quite a number of different flours and binders, so also having to store several different gluten-free flour blends would quickly become rather inconvenient. That's why you need to have a good "all-purpose" kind of blend.

As a general rule in gluten-free baking, it's best to use a blend of several different gluten-free flours, rather than a single gluten-free flour. For example, I don't recommend trying to make a cake or cookie recipe with only tapioca starch or only buckwheat flour, as you'll end up with a rather disappointing result. Instead, you need a combination that gives just the right flour profile: the best ratio of starchy, "lighter" protein and "heavier" protein flours. This ratio affects both the texture and the flavour of your gluten-free bakes, so it's important to get it just right.

That's where gluten-free flour blends – a mixture of gluten-free flours and sometimes other additives, like binders or raising agents in the case of self-raising blends – come in.

You should be able to find them online and in pretty much any grocery store, but you can also mix up your own using the recipe on page 24. A good-quality, reliable gluten-free flour blend is absolutely crucial for success in gluten-free baking, as it strongly influences the texture, flavour and appearance of your bakes.

And just like with the individual gluten-free flours, I recommend testing out different gluten-free flour blends that are available to you, at least until you find a favourite. It's bound to become your constant companion in the kitchen, so make sure it's a good and reliable one.

The great thing about the homemade gluten-free flour blend is that you can easily modify it further, depending on which flours are available to you and if you have any additional dietary requirements, such as a nightshade or a corn allergy. As long as you keep the ratio of the starchy, "lighter" protein and "heavier" protein flours within the blend the same, you can easily swap them out for an equal weight of another flour within the same group (see page 260).

I recommend using gluten-free flour blends that don't contain any binders or raising agents. I'm something of a perfectionist (actually, that might be putting it lightly), so I like to control the amounts of binder and raising agent in my bakes quite precisely, and that's just not possible with a blend that already contains them.

That said, I am aware that you might have no option but to use a blend with gums or binders already added. In that case, you need to reduce the amount of xanthan gum that you add separately by ¼ teaspoon per 120g (1 cup) of gluten-free flour blend. So, for example, if the recipe originally calls for ¾ teaspoon of xanthan gum and uses 240g (2 cups) of gluten-free flour blend, you'll need to reduce this to ¼ teaspoon of xanthan gum if your blend already contains any binders or gums.

**NOTE: GLUTEN-FREE FLOUR BLENDS AND BREAD**

While "all-purpose" gluten-free flour blends are brilliant in cake, cupcake, muffin, brownie, cookie and pastry recipes, I don't recommend using them to make gluten-free bread. Depending on what type of bread you're making, you need to be able to control the exact ratio of starchy to protein flours very precisely. For example, this ratio will be different for an artisan loaf and for a brioche-like recipe, such as cinnamon rolls or doughnuts. Furthermore, most commercial gluten-free flour blends have a starch content that's too high to work well for gluten-free bread recipes. You can read more about the flour requirements of gluten-free bread in the "Gluten-free bread 101" section (see pages 272–5).

# The Issue of Density: Use a Scale

I've said it before, but I'll say it again: you should really be using a digital food or kitchen scale in your baking. It's infinitely more precise and reliable, and it gives better and more consistent results than using volume measurements, such as cups and tablespoons. Plus, there's less washing up to do – you don't have to wash a scale after every baking session but you most certainly do need to wash all those measuring cups and spoons.

Using a kitchen scale is particularly important when it comes to gluten-free baking, where all the gluten-free flours have vastly different densities. That is, the weight per unit volume (for example, per one US measuring cup) can vary widely. For example, 1 cup of buckwheat flour weighs 150g and 1 cup of tapioca starch weighs only 115g. That's an enormous difference, and it carries through to gluten-free flour blends as well.

For many commercial gluten-free flour blends, 1 cup weighs about 120–130g. However, homemade gluten-free flour blends tend to vary a lot more in density. For example, 1 cup of my homemade gluten-free flour blend weighs about 115–120g, but if you substitute any of the flours, the density (weight per unit volume) will automatically change – and it can change by quite a large amount.

So, if you use volume measurements and something goes wrong with your recipes – getting a digital food scale and weighing your ingredients is the first fix I would recommend.

# Moisture & Fat Response

In addition to the obvious difference of lacking gluten, gluten-free flours have very different moisture and fat responses compared to wheat flour. In simple terms, when it comes to their interaction with wet ingredients (eggs, water, milk and so on) and fat (butter or oil), gluten-free flours and blends behave rather differently from regular wheat flour.

## The moisture response

Gluten-free flours have a higher moisture-absorption capacity than wheat flour. That is, they absorb more moisture – be that in the form of eggs, milk, yogurt, water or some other wet ingredient. Consequently, if you were to make a 1:1 substitution of regular flour with a gluten-free flour blend, you'd probably get a dry, crumbly end result (no matter what claims are made by gluten-free-blend manufacturers).

For most cake, cupcake and muffin recipes, you need to account for the higher moisture-absorption capacity of gluten-free flours and blends by reducing the amount of flour by 10% when you convert a regular recipe to gluten-free.

This very simple tweak makes a huge difference when it comes to the texture of these bakes. Instead of a dry crumb and crumbly texture, this small decrease in the amount of flour produces perfectly moist bakes.

## The fat response

This is the exact opposite of the moisture response. While gluten-free flours can take on more moisture than regular wheat flour, they can actually tolerate a smaller amount of fat. That's because gluten-free bakes lack the structure-providing ingredient (gluten). Fat (butter or oil) has tenderizing or "structure-destroying" properties – it makes bakes more tender, delicate and crumbly, or stodgy and dense, depending on the type of bake we're considering.

This lower fat tolerance of gluten-free flours and blends is especially relevant for bakes where we want to control the crumbliness and spread, like shortbread biscuits (where we want to minimize spread and prevent them from being too crumbly), chocolate chip cookies (where we want to achieve just the right amount of spread) and shortcrust pastry (where we need a certain degree of sturdiness).

In such cases, where the fat response is more important than the moisture response, you typically need to reduce the amount of butter (or oil) by 20–30% when converting a regular recipe to gluten-free.

Because the moisture and the fat response work in opposite directions, they can also cancel each other out – as is the case with gluten-free brownies (see page 136).

Here's a quick overview of which response is the more important for different types of bake:

| Bake | More important response |
|---|---|
| cakes, cupcakes & muffins | moisture response |
| thin pancakes (crêpes) & fluffy American-style pancakes | moisture response |
| brownies (egg-containing) | neither – they cancel each other out |
| brownies (eggless) | fat response |
| cookies that hold their shape (such as cut-out sugar cookies, shortbread or gingerbread) | fat response |
| cookies that spread (such as chocolate chip cookies) | fat response |
| cakey cookies (such as crinkle cookies or whoopie pies) | moisture response |
| shortcrust pastry | fat response |
| flaky pastry (pie crust & puff pastry) | moisture response |
| bread | moisture response |

To see these guidelines in action, take a look at the gluten-free (and also some gluten-free vegan) sections of the case studies in Chapter 4. You can also read more about the moisture and fat response of gluten-free flours and blends on page 42 in Chapter 2.

# Gluten-free Bread 101

Gluten plays many important roles in regular, wheat-based bread recipes:

- **It creates an intricate, interwoven network of protein strands, which captures the gases produced by the yeast action during the proving (rising) stages. The elasticity it provides allows the dough to expand in volume without cracking or tearing.**

- **It gives the dough elasticity and extensibility, so you can shape the bread into whatever form you fancy.**

- **It gives the baked bread its characteristic chewy crumb.**

- **And, finally, it also helps with moisture retention, preventing the bread from drying out too quickly.**

In order to make amazing gluten-free bread, we therefore need to find ways to mimic the effects of gluten. This is where the magical ingredient that is psyllium husk comes in – but before we get to that, let's first introduce a concept that's incredibly helpful when describing the composition of (both gluten-free and wheat-based) bread: baker's percentage.

## Baker's percentage (b%)

This is a useful way to express the proportion of the different ingredients (or groups of ingredients) in a bread recipe. Specifically, the amount of each ingredient is expressed as a percentage of the flour weight, where the flour weight is always 100 b%. That is:

**Ingredient b% = (weight of ingredient ÷ weight of flour) x 100%**

For example, if a recipe uses 5 b% of psyllium husk, that means that it uses 5g of psyllium husk per 100g of the total flour content.

This comes in handy when you want to compare different bread recipes, because baker's percentage stays the same even if you scale a recipe up or down. As you'll soon see, the science behind successful gluten-free bread is all about ingredient ratios, and baker's percentage is the perfect way to keep track of them.

## Psyllium husk

I've mentioned the importance of psyllium husk before on pages 264–6, but it bears repeating: psyllium husk is what makes gluten-free bread work, and work well. It should be the only, or at least the main binder when making gluten-free bread. While xanthan gum is amazing, it's the psyllium husk that's responsible for giving you a gluten-free dough that you can knead and shape, and that proves efficiently, easily doubling in volume. Without the psyllium husk, your dough would be more of a batter. With psyllium husk, however, you can shape it into artisan loaves, baguettes, burger buns, bagels or cinnamon rolls without any issues whatsoever. Psyllium husk is also what gives gluten-free bread a chewy crumb similar to that of regular wheat-based bread.

Now, while there is no proper gluten-free bread without psyllium husk, there are also other factors at play. The texture of gluten-free bread is determined, for the most part, by four things: the starch content of the gluten-free flour blend, the hydration (the amount of water or other liquid in the dough), the amount of binder, and the ratio of psyllium husk to xanthan gum.

## Starch content

The starch content of your gluten-free bread determines how soft and squishy it'll be. The higher the starch content, the fluffier the bread – but don't go overboard! Starches don't provide much (or any) structure to gluten-free bread, so using too much of them can result in a rather gummy, sticky, unpleasant crumb. Here's an overview of the recommended starch content, depending on what kind of bread you're making:

| Type of bread | Recommended starch content |
|---|---|
| **non-enriched bread,**<br>such as artisan loaves, baguettes, bagels and similar | 40–45 b% |
| **enriched brioche dough,**<br>such as burger buns, dinner rolls, cinnamon rolls, doughnuts, babka and similar | around 50 b% |

When you make gluten-free bread, it's best to prepare your own gluten-free flour mixture from the individual gluten-free flours. Most shop-bought blends are too high in starches to work well for gluten-free bread recipes, and they also don't allow you to control the exact starch content. While it might be tempting to rely on a pre-mixed blend, you'll get a much, much better result if you mix the individual gluten-free flours together yourself.

## The hydration

On average, the hydration of gluten-free bread will be about 20–30 b% higher than that of a similar bread made with regular wheat flour. That's because both the gluten-free flours and the psyllium husk absorb a lot of moisture. And especially in the case of psyllium husk, you'll use some of that extra liquid (usually water) to make the psyllium gel (see page 266). While most regular bread recipes have a hydration in the range of 55–80 b%, the hydration of gluten-free bread recipes can be as high as 115 b%.

So, don't panic when you see that a gluten-free bread recipe uses a surprisingly large amount of water – it's not a misprint, you really do need that much! For example, the honey and sesame artisan loaf on page 297 uses 460g (1¾ cups + 2½ tablespoons) of water, which might seem like a lot, but you definitely need it if you want to get a beautifully pliable, springy dough and a gorgeous final crumb.

As a good rule of thumb, the hydration of non-enriched gluten-free bread that doesn't contain any eggs should be about 105–115 b%. The hydration of enriched, brioche-like bread with eggs in the dough should be around 75–90 b%.

## Binder content

Use about 5–6 b% of binders – that is, 5–6g per 100g of total gluten-free flour mix. This is a good general principle that applies widely to everything from artisan loaves and pizza dough to things like cinnamon rolls, or burger buns made with an enriched, brioche-like dough. This will give you a dough that's easy to handle and the final, baked bread will have the perfect texture that has just the right balance between soft and chewy.

Using a smaller quantity of binders can result in a dough that's looser and stickier, and therefore more difficult to handle. Using a much larger amount, on the other hand, can give you a dough that's too firm and too dry (as binders also absorb a lot of moisture) and a bread that's too dense and gummy. It's all about getting the amount just right, and using 5–6 b% works really well across a wide range of different bread and dough recipes.

## When to use xanthan gum

While psyllium husk is undoubtedly the most important binder when it comes to gluten-free breads, xanthan gum can still come in handy with certain types of bread recipe:

- **Use only psyllium husk when making non-enriched bread, like artisan loaves, baguettes, tortillas and other flatbreads, pizza dough and similar.** Psyllium husk is perfect for achieving a chewy interior crumb and a crisp, crunchy crust.

- **Use a mixture of psyllium husk and xanthan gum when making enriched brioche dough, like burger buns, cinnamon rolls, doughnuts and similar.** When you want to achieve a pillowy-soft, squishy, plush texture, use a mixture of both binders. For most recipes, the psyllium husk:xanthan gum ratio should be in the range from 2:1 to 3:1.

## Baking powder in gluten-free brioche dough

For the softest, fluffiest gluten-free brioche texture, use a combination of yeast and baking powder. Typically, there is no baking powder in regular brioche dough made with wheat flour – instead, the dough relies entirely on yeast for its fluffy, soft texture and open crumb. However, we're in the realm of gluten-free baking and, sometimes, in order to achieve a texture that's virtually indistinguishable from that of a regular wheat-based equivalent... well, we need to "cheat" a bit.

That's where the baking powder comes in. The baking powder helps to make the gluten-free brioche dough (and any bakes made from it) even fluffier and squishier, and therefore closer in texture to their regular equivalents made with wheat flour. It's a small trick – but it makes a huge difference.

## Proving gluten-free bread

With gluten-free bread, you have the option to choose either one or two rounds of rising. While wheat bread definitely benefits from both the first (bulk fermentation) and the second round of rising (the final prove), I've found that you can achieve amazing results with just a single prove when it comes to gluten-free bread. That means that you can prepare the dough, shape the bread, prove it straight away and then bake it according to the recipe.

The single prove produces a bread that's just as delicious and gorgeous as one that's gone through two rounds of rising (both the flavour and the crumb are absolutely spot on), with the added advantage of a shorter waiting time. And if you're an impatient baker like me, that's a very good thing indeed.

## Weight (moisture) loss during baking

I recommend weighing gluten-free bread to see if it's fully baked. While the usual indicators (an internal temperature of about 90–95°C/195–205°F, a hollow sound when you tap on the bottom of a loaf, and a deep, golden brown crust) are all helpful, they don't account for the fact that gluten-free bread needs to lose a certain amount of moisture during baking in order to have a pleasantly chewy, open crumb. If it doesn't lose enough moisture, the centre of the bread can end up sticky and dense. And the best way to determine whether or not a loaf of gluten-free bread has lost enough moisture is to weigh it – look for a weight loss of about 10–25%, depending on the type of bread you're making.

Note that this method works great for bakes such as artisan loaves, baguettes, burger buns, bread rolls and similar, but it's not suitable for filled bakes, such as cinnamon rolls or babka, for pull-apart-style bakes such as dinner rolls or pull-apart bread, for boiled breads such as bagels, or for fried doughs such as doughnuts.

## Two recipes with endless options

You'll find two fundamental gluten-free bread recipes on the next couple of pages: one for a basic gluten-free non-enriched bread and one for my go-to gluten-free brioche dough. Because it's impossible to establish a simple set of rules for converting regular wheat bread into gluten-free, you can instead use these two simple recipes and shape them, flavour them and fill them in whatever way you fancy – the options are endless.

For example, I used the basic gluten-free non-enriched dough as the basis for the honey and sesame artisan loaf on page 297; and the basic gluten-free brioche dough as the basis for the chocolate-stuffed braided brioche muffins on page 301 and the cheesy garlic pull-apart bread on page 305.

Furthermore, if you combine these basic recipes with the "to make vegan" bread modification rules on page 85, you can easily transform them into gluten-free vegan recipes. That way, I've created the gluten-free vegan cinnamon rolls on page 457 and the gluten-free vegan pesto rolls on page 461.

**NOTE**

Gluten-free bread recipes are super-versatile, so you can easily tweak them to work with whatever gluten-free flours you have on hand and also according to any other food sensitivities or allergies you might have. All of the gluten-free bread recipes in this book offer plenty of substitution options – I've put them in the notes of each recipe.

# Basic non-enriched bread dough

25g (5 tablespoons) whole psyllium husk [1]

460g (1¾ cups + 2½ tablespoons) lukewarm water

180g (1½ cups + 1 tablespoon) tapioca starch [2]

180g (1⅓ cups) millet flour, plus extra for flouring the surface [3]

60g (⅓ cup + 2 tablespoons) sorghum flour [4]

25g (2 tablespoons) caster (superfine) or granulated sugar

10g (2 teaspoons) salt

8g (2½ teaspoons) instant yeast [5]

10g (2 teaspoons) apple cider vinegar

20g (1½ tablespoons) olive oil, or neutral-tasting oil like sunflower or vegetable oil (optional)

........................................................

**Notes**

[1] If using psyllium husk powder, use 21g (2½ tablespoons).

[2] Or use an equal weight of arrowroot starch, cornflour (cornstarch) or potato starch instead.

[3] Or use an equal weight of finely milled/ground brown rice flour instead.

[4] Or use an equal weight of light buckwheat flour, white teff flour or oat flour instead.

[5] If using active dry yeast, use 10g (3 teaspoons), and activate it first. Mix together the active dry yeast, half of the sugar listed in the recipe and about 120g (½ cup) of the warm water (use the remaining water to make the psyllium gel). Set aside for 10–15 minutes, until frothing. Add to the dry ingredients along with the psyllium gel, vinegar and oil.

**This fundamental recipe can make all sorts of artisan-style loaves (like the honey and sesame loaf on page 297) or, made in a loaf tin, a bread that's perfect for slicing to turn into toast or sandwiches. Adding oil results in a slightly more open crumb and a bread that stays softer for longer, but you can omit it if you prefer an oil-free recipe. Flavour-wise, this bread is closer to white bread than to wholemeal.**

**To make baguettes, add 20g (1½ tablespoons) of extra water, raising the hydration to 114 b% (baker's percent). This will give a more open crumb, typical of a baguette.**

### Making the dough

*Prepare the dough using a stand mixer fitted with the dough hook or by hand. The mixer makes the process much easier and results in a smoother dough.*

1. In a bowl, mix together the psyllium husk and lukewarm water. After about 30–45 seconds, a gel will form.

2. In a large bowl or the bowl of the stand mixer, whisk together the tapioca starch, millet flour, sorghum flour, sugar, salt and instant yeast. Make a well in the middle of the dry ingredients and add the psyllium gel, vinegar, and oil (if using).

3. Knead the dough until smooth and it starts coming away from the inside of the bowl, about 4–5 minutes with a stand mixer or 6–8 minutes by hand. The final dough should be pliable and supple, and not too sticky to the touch.

### Tips for shaping, proving & baking the bread

- If you want to include any extras, such as seeds, chopped nuts or dried fruit, add them either with the dry ingredients or to the finished dough before shaping.

- Give the dough a gentle knead on a lightly floured surface before you shape it, that'll make it even easier to handle.

- In general, this bread needs to prove for about 1 hour to double in size.

- To get maximum oven spring and therefore a very open crumb in the baked bread, pre-heat the oven to 240–250°C/450–475°F and bake with steam for about 10–20 minutes (say, by adding ice cubes to a pre-heated cast-iron skillet on the bottom of the oven). Then, remove the steam source (or open the Dutch oven/combo cooker, if using), reduce the oven temperature to about 200–220°C/400–425°F and bake until done.

| Composition of the basic gluten-free non-enriched bread | |
|---|---|
| **Quantity name** | **Value** |
| Hydration | 110 b% |
| Starch content | 43 b% |
| Binder content | 6 b% |

# Basic brioche dough

15g (3 tablespoons) whole psyllium husk [1]

180g (¾ cup) lukewarm water

160g (1⅓ cups + 1 tablespoon) tapioca starch [2]

135g (1 cup) millet flour, plus extra for flouring the surface [3]

25g (3 tablespoons) sorghum flour [4]

25–50g (2 tablespoons–¼ cup) caster (superfine) or granulated sugar

6g (2 teaspoons) instant yeast [5]

6g (1½ teaspoons) baking powder

5g (2 teaspoons) xanthan gum

5g (1 teaspoon) salt

100g (⅓ cup + 1½ tablespoons) whole milk, lukewarm

1 medium egg (US large), room temperature

35g (2½ tablespoons) unsalted butter, melted

**Notes**

[1] If using psyllium husk powder, use 13g (1½ tablespoons; whole psyllium husk and the powder form have different densities).

[2] Or use an equal weight of arrowroot starch, cornflour (cornstarch) or potato starch instead.

[3] Or use an equal weight of finely milled/ground brown rice flour instead, but your brioche might be slightly less fluffy.

[4] Or use an equal weight of light buckwheat flour, white teff flour or oat flour instead.

[5] If using active dry yeast, use 8g (2½ teaspoons), and activate it first. Mix together the active dry yeast, 1 tablespoon of the sugar and the warm milk. Set aside for 10–15 minutes, or until frothing. Add to the dry ingredients along with the psyllium gel, egg and melted butter.

**Use this recipe to make bakes that call for a brioche or enriched dough, such as burger buns, cinnamon rolls, and doughnuts. If you're making a sweet brioche dough, use 50g (¼ cup) of sugar; for a savoury brioche, use 25g (2 tablespoons).**

**This recipe forms the basis for the gluten-free chocolate-stuffed braided brioche muffins on page 301 and gluten-free cheesy garlic pull-apart bread on page 305.**

### Making the dough

*Prepare the dough using a stand mixer fitted with the dough hook or by hand. The mixer makes the process much easier and results in a smoother dough.*

1. In a bowl, mix together the psyllium husk and lukewarm water. After about 30–45 seconds, a gel will form.

2. In a large bowl or the bowl of the stand mixer, whisk together the tapioca starch, millet flour, sorghum flour, sugar, instant yeast, baking powder, xanthan gum and salt. Make a well in the middle and add the psyllium gel, lukewarm milk, egg and melted butter.

3. Knead until smooth and evenly incorporated, then knead for a further 4–5 minutes with a stand mixer or 6–8 minutes by hand. Use a rubber spatula to occasionally scrape along the bottom and inside of the bowl to prevent any dry patches of unmixed flour.

4. The final dough will be slightly sticky to the touch – that's okay, you'll be working on a lightly floured surface so it shouldn't be a problem. Resist the temptation to add more flour to the dough, as that can make the bread too dense and dry.

### Tips for shaping, proving & baking (or frying) the dough

- Gently knead the dough on a lightly floured surface before shaping. If the dough feels too soft and sticky to handle easily, chill it in the fridge for about 1 hour, then proceed.

- In general, this gluten-free brioche dough needs to prove for about 1 hour 15 minutes to 1 hour 30 minutes to double in size.

- For most bakes using this dough, an oven temperature of 180°C/350°F works best. For fried doughnuts, use an oil temperature of around 160°C/325°F.

| Composition of the basic gluten-free brioche dough | |
| --- | --- |
| **Quantity name** | **Value** |
| Hydration | 88 b% |
| Starch content | 50 b% |
| Binder content | 6 b% |
| Psyllium:xanthan ratio | 3:1 |

# Chocolate chip banana upside-down cake

**Serves 10–12 / Prep time 30 mins / Cook time 10 mins / Bake time 40 mins**

## Caramel layer

100g (½ cup) caster (superfine)
   or granulated sugar

40g (3 tablespoons) double
   (heavy) cream, warm

½ teaspoon vanilla paste

4–5 bananas

## Chocolate chip banana cake

1 banana, finely mashed
   (115–125g peeled weight,
   ½ cup mashed)

115g (½ cup) unsweetened
   plain or Greek-style yogurt,
   room temperature

100g (½ cup) light brown
   soft sugar

55g (½ stick) unsalted butter,
   melted

40g (3 tablespoons) sunflower
   oil, or other neutral oil

2 medium eggs (US large),
   room temperature

½ teaspoon vanilla paste
   (or 1 teaspoon vanilla extract)

200g (1⅔ cups) plain gluten-free
   flour blend [1]

2 teaspoons baking powder

½ teaspoon xanthan gum [2]

¼ teaspoon salt

½ teaspoon cinnamon

90g (½ cup) chopped dark
   chocolate (60–70% cocoa
   solids) or dark chocolate chips

### Notes

[1] Use a shop-bought gluten-free flour blend or mix your own (see page 24).

[2] If your gluten-free flour blend already contains binders, omit the xanthan gum.

[3] A light-coloured saucepan allows you to keep track of the colour of the caramel.

[4] Because this recipe uses the "dry caramel method" (without water), you can stir the caramel without it crystallizing.

## Storage

2–3 days in an airtight container in a cool, dry place.

---

If you have any ripe bananas lying around, don't make banana bread – make this instead. It's a total showstopper, but incredibly easy. The cake itself is moist with a soft, plush crumb and it's topped with perfectly tender (but not mushy!) caramelized bananas. Its sweetness is partially tempered by the acidity of the yogurt in the batter, which results in a really well-balanced dessert.

*This recipe follows the rules for adapting buttery cakes on page 52 – use them to adapt it to any free-from variation. In the caramel layer, you can replace the double (heavy) cream with an equal amount of a dairy-free alternative.*

### Caramel layer

1. Adjust the oven rack to the middle position and pre-heat the oven to 180°C/350°F. Lightly butter a 23cm (9in) round cake tin and line the bottom with baking paper.

2. In a light-coloured or stainless-steel saucepan, cook the sugar over medium heat, with occasional stirring, until it's fully melted. [3] The sugar will initially clump together – don't worry, that doesn't mean that it's crystallizing. Stir until it's fully melted. If there are any persistent sugar clumps, reduce the heat to low and stir until they all disappear. [4]

3. Continue cooking the caramel (melted sugar) with constant stirring over medium heat until it reaches an amber colour.

4. Once you reach the desired colour, remove the caramel from the heat and pour in the warm cream, mixing constantly. Be careful: adding cream releases lots of hot steam and it might bubble up quite violently. (If your caramel clumps up after you've added the cream, return it to the heat and stir until smooth.)

5. Stir in the vanilla, then pour the caramel into the lined cake tin and smooth it out into an even layer.

6. Cut the bananas in half lengthways and arrange them on top of the caramel, cut side down, as close to each other as possible. Set aside until needed.

### Chocolate chip banana cake

1. In a large bowl, whisk together the mashed banana, yogurt, light brown sugar, melted butter, oil, eggs and vanilla.

2. In a separate bowl, whisk together the gluten-free flour blend, baking powder, xanthan gum, salt and cinnamon.

3. Add the dry ingredients to the wet, and whisk well until you get a smooth batter with no flour clumps. Add the chocolate and mix well until evenly distributed.

4. Transfer the batter on top of the caramel-banana layer and smooth out the top.

5. Bake for about 40–45 minutes, or until well risen, golden brown on top and an inserted toothpick or cake tester comes out clean. If the cake starts browning too quickly, cover with a sheet of foil (shiny side up) and bake until done.

6. Cool the cake in the tin for about 15–20 minutes. Then, run a knife or a small offset spatula around the edge of the cake to help release it from the tin, and turn it out on to a serving plate. If any caramel or banana pieces have stuck to the bottom of the tin, carefully scrape them off and arrange them on top of the cake. Serve warm, with a dollop of vanilla ice cream or lightly sweetened vanilla whipped cream.

# Coffee Swiss roll

**Serves 10–12  /  Prep time 1 hour  /  Cook time 5 mins  /  Bake time 10 mins / Cool time 1 hour / Chill time 1 hour**

## Coffee sponge

1–2 tablespoons sunflower or
    vegetable oil, for greasing
8g (2 tablespoons) instant
    coffee granules
20g (4 teaspoons) whole milk
3 medium eggs (US large),
    room temperature
125g (½ cup + 2 tablespoons)
    caster (superfine) or
    granulated sugar
½ teaspoon vanilla paste
    (or 1 teaspoon vanilla extract)
45g (3 tablespoons) unsalted
    butter, melted
80g (⅔ cup) plain gluten-free
    flour blend [1]
¾ teaspoon xanthan gum [2]
½ teaspoon baking powder
¼ teaspoon bicarbonate of soda
    (baking soda)
¼ teaspoon salt
icing (powdered) sugar, for
    dusting the sponge
1–2 tablespoons cocoa powder
chocolate shavings, to decorate

## Coffee soak

4g (1 tablespoon) instant coffee
    granules
15g (1 tablespoon) caster
    (superfine) or granulated
    sugar
45g (3 tablespoons) hot water

## Coffee mascarpone whipped
    cream

8g (2 tablespoons) instant coffee
    granules
300g (1⅓ cups) double (heavy)
    cream, chilled
120g (1 cup) icing (powdered)
    sugar, sifted
240g (1 cup) mascarpone
    cheese, chilled
1 teaspoon vanilla paste (or
    2 teaspoons vanilla extract)

This fabulous Swiss roll is definitive proof that there's no such thing as too much coffee in a single dessert. It's like eating a pillowy cloud of coffee goodness, filled with a rich, velvety coffee mascarpone whipped cream. The gluten-free sponge rolls like an absolute dream, so you don't need to worry about it cracking – you'll get a perfect swirl every time. And if you're avoiding caffeine, you can of course use decaf coffee instead.

*This recipe follows the rules for adapting Swiss rolls and sponge cakes on page 58 – use them to adapt this recipe to any free-from variation. In the filling, you can replace the double (heavy) cream and mascarpone cheese with equal amounts of dairy-free alternatives (in the latter case, I recommend a vegan cream cheese).*

### Coffee sponge

1. Adjust the oven rack to the middle position, pre-heat the oven to 180°C/350°F and line a 25x38cm (10x15in) rimmed baking sheet with baking paper. Lightly grease the baking paper and the sides of the baking sheet with oil (or spray it with non-stick baking spray) to ensure that it smoothly releases without sticking.

2. Mix the instant coffee granules with the milk and heat them (either in the microwave or on the stovetop) until the coffee is fully dissolved. Set aside to cool until lukewarm.

3. Using a stand mixer fitted with the whisk attachment or a hand-held mixer fitted with the double beaters, whisk the eggs and sugar together until pale, thick, fluffy and about tripled in volume (the ribbon stage). This should take about 5–7 minutes on a high speed.

4. Add the coffee-milk mixture, vanilla and melted butter, and whisk briefly to combine.

5. Sift in the gluten-free flour blend, xanthan gum, baking powder, bicarbonate of soda (baking soda) and salt, and whisk well for about 15–30 seconds until no flour clumps remain. Scrape down the bottom and inside of the bowl to prevent any unmixed patches.

6. Transfer the batter into the lined baking sheet and smooth it out into an even layer. You can tap it a few times on the counter to make it perfectly level and also to get rid of any large trapped air pockets.

7. Bake for about 10–12 minutes or until well risen, soft and spongy to the touch, and an inserted toothpick or cake tester comes out clean.

8. Immediately out of the oven, dust the top of the sponge with icing (powdered) sugar and cover the baking sheet first with a clean tea towel and then with a large sheet of foil. Allow to cool to room temperature or lukewarm – ideally, the temperature of the sponge shouldn't drop below about 22°C/72°F. [3]

### Coffee soak

1. Mix together the coffee granules, sugar and hot water, and mix well until the coffee and sugar are fully dissolved.

2. Allow to cool until warm or at room temperature.

→

**Notes**

[1] Use a shop-bought gluten-free flour blend or mix your own (see page 24).

[2] If your gluten-free flour blend already contains binders, reduce the amount to ½ teaspoon.

[3] Covering the sponge with foil traps the moisture within the sponge, making it much more pliable and flexible – and therefore less likely to crack when you roll it. This method was pioneered by Stella Parks (see page 113).

## Storage

3–4 days in a closed container in the fridge. Allow to stand at room temperature for 5–10 minutes before serving.

## Coffee mascarpone whipped cream

1. In a small saucepan (if cooking on the stovetop) or in a microwave-safe bowl (if using the microwave) heat together the instant coffee granules and 115g (about ½ cup) of the double (heavy) cream, with occasional stirring, until the coffee is completely dissolved. Set aside to cool completely.

2. Using a stand mixer fitted with the whisk or a hand-held mixer fitted with the double beaters, whisk together the remaining double (heavy) cream and the icing (powdered) sugar until soft peaks form.

3. In a separate bowl, whisk the mascarpone until it's smooth and looser in texture.

4. Add the mascarpone to the whipped cream along with the cooled coffee-cream and the vanilla, and whisk until well combined and firm peaks form.

## Assembling & decorating the Swiss roll

1. Once the sponge is sufficiently cooled, loosen it from the edges of the baking sheet with an offset spatula or a thin knife.

2. Turn it out on to a large sheet of baking paper, so that the caramelized "skin" side is facing down (so that it's on the outside of the Swiss roll when you roll it up). Peel away the baking paper that you used to line the baking sheet.

3. Use a pastry brush to gently brush the sponge with the coffee soak.

4. Spread just over half of the filling evenly across the sponge, all the way to the edges.

5. Turn the sponge so that a short edge is closest to you. Using the baking paper underneath to help you, roll up the sponge until you get a 25cm (10in) log. Make sure to keep the roll fairly tight from the very beginning, otherwise you'll be left with an empty hole in the centre of your Swiss roll.

6. Use the remaining coffee mascarpone whipped cream to cover the outside of the cake. Decorate the cake by creating swirls and swoops in the cream with a small offset spatula or the back of a spoon.

7. Chill the Swiss roll in the fridge for at least 1 hour.

8. Just before serving, dust the Swiss roll generously with cocoa powder and sprinkle some chocolate shavings over the top.

# Raspberry & almond muffins

**Makes 12 / Prep time 30 mins / Bake time 22 mins**

290g (2⅓ cups + 1 tablespoon)
plain gluten-free flour blend [1]

50g (½ cup) almond flour

200g (1 cup) caster (superfine)
or granulated sugar

1½ teaspoons baking powder [2]

1 teaspoon bicarbonate of soda
(baking soda)

1 teaspoon xanthan gum [3]

½ teaspoon salt

55g (½ stick) unsalted butter,
melted and cooled until warm

55g (¼ cup) sunflower or
vegetable oil

300g (1¼ cups + 1 tablespoon)
buttermilk, room temperature

2 medium eggs (US large), room
temperature

½ teaspoon vanilla paste (or
1 teaspoon vanilla extract)

a few drops of almond extract
(optional)

180g (1½ cups) fresh or frozen
raspberries [4]

60g (⅔ cup) flaked almonds

### Notes

[1] Use a shop-bought gluten-free flour blend or mix your own (see page 24).

[2] This recipe contains slightly less baking powder than the gluten-free chocolate chip muffin recipe on page 128 because here we are using buttermilk instead of yogurt and milk. Buttermilk is more acidic and so reacts more strongly with the raising agents, which in turn boosts their activity – so, you need less of them.

[3] If your gluten-free flour blend already contains binders, use only ½ teaspoon.

[4] If using frozen raspberries, don't thaw them.

### Storage

3–4 days in an airtight container in a cool, dry place.

**This recipe will give you bakery-worthy muffins every time – with minimal effort and minimal fuss. They're moist and fluffy, with a plush crumb and a gloriously domed, caramelized muffin top. The combination of the rich almond flavour and the fresh, slightly tart raspberries is divine, and the flaked almonds on top get all crunchy and toasty in the oven, which adds a wonderful textural contrast.**

*This recipe follows the rules for adapting buttery cakes on page 52 – use them to adapt this recipe to any free-from variation.*

1. Adjust the oven rack to the middle position and pre-heat the oven to 190°C/375°F. Line a 12-hole muffin tin with paper liners.

2. In a large bowl, whisk together the gluten-free flour blend, almond flour, sugar, baking powder, bicarbonate of soda (baking soda), xanthan gum and salt.

3. In a separate large bowl or jug, whisk together the melted butter, oil, buttermilk, eggs, vanilla and almond extract (if using).

4. Add the wet ingredients to the dry, and use a rubber spatula or a wooden spoon to fold them together into a smooth batter with no flour clumps.

5. Add the raspberries and mix briefly to evenly distribute throughout the batter.

6. Using an ice-cream or cookie scoop, or a spoon, divide the batter equally between the 12 liners, filling each to the brim.

7. Sprinkle the top of each muffin with about 1 tablespoon of flaked almonds.

8. Bake for about 22–24 minutes if using fresh raspberries, or 26–28 minutes if using frozen, or until well risen, golden brown on top with slightly darker edges, and an inserted toothpick comes out clean or with a few moist crumbs attached.

9. Allow to cool in the muffin tin for about 5–10 minutes, then transfer them out of the tin and on to a wire rack to cool. Serve warm or cooled completely to room temperature.

# Lemon curd cookies

**Makes 16 / Prep time 1 hour / Cook time 5 mins / Chill time 2 hours / Bake time 9 mins (x2)**

## Lemon curd

100g (½ cup) caster (superfine)
    or granulated sugar
zest of 1 unwaxed lemon
3 medium egg yolks (US large),
    room temperature
¼ teaspoon salt
60g (¼ cup) freshly squeezed
    lemon juice
55g (½ stick) unsalted butter,
    cubed

## Lemon cookie dough

150g (¾ cup) caster (superfine)
    or granulated sugar
zest of 2 unwaxed lemons
115g (1 stick) unsalted butter,
    melted and cooled until warm
2 medium eggs (US large),
    room temperature
30g (2 tablespoons) freshly
    squeezed lemon juice
½ teaspoon vanilla paste (or
    1 teaspoon vanilla extract)
240g (2 cups) plain gluten-free
    flour blend [1]
½ teaspoon xanthan gum [2]
½ teaspoon baking powder
¼ teaspoon salt
90g (¾ cup) icing (powdered)
    sugar, for rolling the cookies

These are the lemoniest of all lemon cookies. There's lemon zest and lemon juice in the dough, and they're baked with a generous dollop of tangy, creamy lemon curd in the centre – you seriously couldn't stuff more citrusy goodness in there! And the texture is incredible, they simply melt in your mouth.

*This recipe follows the rules for adapting cakey cookies on page 68 – use them to adapt this recipe to any free-from variation. Dairy-free, egg-free and vegan lemon curd recipe variations appear on page 478.*

### Lemon curd

1. Add the sugar and lemon zest to a bowl [3] and use your fingertips to rub the zest into the sugar, releasing essential oils from the zest to make your lemon curd extra fragrant.

2. Add the egg yolks and salt to the lemon-sugar, and mix or whip them together briefly by hand with a spatula or wooden spoon until pale and slightly fluffy.

3. In a saucepan over medium–high heat, cook the lemon juice until it just begins to boil.

4. Add the hot lemon juice to the egg yolk-sugar mixture in a slow drizzle, mixing constantly until you've added all the juice. [4]

5. Return the mixture to the saucepan and cook it over low heat with constant stirring until thickened so that it thickly coats the back of a spoon or spatula (about 4–5 minutes). Don't allow the lemon curd to come to a boil – you shouldn't see any bubbles forming.

6. Once thickened, remove it from the heat and stir in the butter until it's fully melted.

7. Pass the lemon curd through a fine-mesh sieve to remove the zest and make it perfectly smooth and creamy (skip this step if you don't mind the texture of the lemon zest). [5]

8. Pour the finished lemon curd into a bowl or heatproof container and cover it with a sheet of cling film. Make sure that the cling film is in direct contact with the surface of the lemon curd to prevent skin formation. Allow to cool completely to room temperature. (You can prepare the lemon curd a day or two in advance and keep it in the fridge until needed, if you like.)

### Lemon cookie dough

1. Add the sugar and lemon zest to a large bowl and use your fingertips to rub the zest into the sugar.

2. Add the melted butter, eggs, lemon juice and vanilla, and whisk well until combined.

3. In a separate bowl, whisk together the gluten-free flour blend, xanthan gum, baking powder and salt, and add them to the wet ingredients.

4. Mix with a wooden spoon or a rubber spatula until you get a smooth, batter-like cookie dough. (At this stage, the cookie dough will really be more like a batter – it will be very loose, soft and sticky, bordering on runny. That's how it should be. Don't add more flour!)

5. Chill the cookie dough in the fridge for at least 2 hours before proceeding; or keep it in the fridge overnight if you want to bake the cookies the next day. [6]

→

Notes

[1] Use a shop-bought gluten-free flour blend or mix your own (see page 24).

[2] If your gluten-free flour blend already contains binders, omit the xanthan gum.

[3] It's best to minimize contact with metal when preparing the lemon curd to prevent it from developing a metallic aftertaste. Avoid using a metal bowl, metal utensils (such as a metal whisk) or a metal/metal-coated saucepan. Instead, use a glass or ceramic bowl, a rubber spatula or a wooden spoon, and a non-metal saucepan such as one with a ceramic coating.

[4] This tempers the egg yolks and reduces the chances of your lemon curd splitting or curdling when you cook it.

[5] If possible, use a sieve with a plastic or silicone mesh to avoid the aftertaste you may get as a result of using a metal one (see note 3).

[6] In addition to firming up the cookie dough to make it easier to handle and shape, chilling ensures that the cookies won't melt into puddles during baking.

## Storage

1 week in an airtight container in the fridge. You'll have some lemon curd left over: store it in an airtight container in the fridge for up to 10 days.

## Assembling & baking the cookies

1. Adjust the oven rack to the middle position, pre-heat the oven to 180°C/350°F and line two large baking sheets with baking paper.

2. Use a 2-tablespoon cookie or ice-cream scoop to scoop out a portion of the cookie dough. Drop it directly into a bowl of icing (powdered) sugar and roll it around until it's evenly coated. The sugar coating will allow you to handle the cookie dough without it sticking, so you can roll it between your palms to form a perfectly round ball.

3. Repeat with the rest of the cookie dough; you should get 16 cookies in total.

4. Place the sugar-coated cookie-dough balls on the lined baking sheets, with plenty of space between them – about 8 per baking sheet (the cookies will spread during baking).

5. Use a ½-tablespoon measuring spoon to make an indent in the centre of each cookie dough ball (make sure that you press only halfway through each cookie dough ball, not all the way through).

6. Fill the cookies with about 1 (generous) teaspoon of lemon curd each.

7. Bake one baking sheet at a time for 9–12 minutes or until the cookies have spread and cracked around the edges and the lemon-curd centre is slightly puffed up but not visibly bubbling (this will ensure that it stays beautifully smooth and creamy). While the first batch of cookies is baking, keep the second batch in the fridge.

8. The cookies will be very soft and delicate immediately out of the oven. Allow them to cool on the baking sheet for about 5–10 minutes before transferring them to a wire rack to cool completely.

# Brown butter chocolate chip blondies

**Serves 12–16 / Prep time 30 mins / Cook time 6 mins / Bake time 28 mins**

200g (1¾ sticks) unsalted butter

150g (¾ cup) light brown
soft sugar

150g (¾ cup) caster (superfine)
or granulated sugar

3 medium eggs (US large),
room temperature

½ teaspoon vanilla paste (or
1 teaspoon vanilla extract)

200g (1⅔ cups) plain
gluten-free flour blend [1]

½ teaspoon xanthan gum [2]

½ teaspoon salt

120g (⅔ cup) chopped 60–70%
dark chocolate or dark
chocolate chips

### Notes

[1] Use a shop-bought gluten-free flour
blend or mix your own (see page 24).

[2] If your gluten-free flour blend already
contains binders, omit the xanthan gum.

[3] Baking at a slightly lower oven
temperature of 160°C/325°F gives a more
even bake, which results in perfectly fudgy
blondies all the way through. The lower
temperature also promotes the formation
of the glossy, crinkly crust all the way
across the top, even right at the edges.

[4] It's important that most of the sugar
dissolves – this helps to achieve the fudgy
texture and the gorgeous shiny, crinkly top

### Storage

3–4 days in an airtight container
in a cool, dry place.

Let's get one thing out of the way: blondies are not white chocolate brownies and
they're not exactly like cookie bars either. Instead, they have the soft, fudgy-gooey
texture and the gorgeous paper-thin, glossy, crinkly top of a brownie – just without
any melted chocolate (or cocoa powder) in the batter. These blondies have the
most incredible flavour thanks to the brown butter and light brown sugar, which
pairs beautifully with the bittersweet dark chocolate.

*This recipe follows the rules for adapting brownies on page 62 – use them to adapt
this recipe to any free-from variation. (Note that you can't buy brown vegan butter
– if you want to make a dairy-free version, use melted vegan butter instead.)*

1. Adjust the oven rack to the middle position, pre-heat the oven to 160°C/325°F and line
a 23cm (9in) square baking tin with baking paper. [3] Leave some overhang, which will
help you to remove the blondies from the tin later on.

2. To brown the butter, add the unsalted butter to a saucepan (preferably one with a
light-coloured interior that allows you to see the butter changing colour) and cook it over
medium heat with frequent stirring for 6–8 minutes in total. The butter will first melt and
then start bubbling and foaming. Finally, it will turn amber and smell nutty. You should
see specks of a deep brown/amber colour on the bottom of the saucepan (those are the
caramelized milk solids).

3. Pour the browned butter into a large bowl (make sure to scrape out all the caramelized
milk solids, they carry the most flavour), and allow it to cool until warm.

4. Add the light brown sugar, caster (superfine) or granulated sugar, eggs and vanilla,
and mix with a wooden spoon or rubber spatula until smooth and the sugar is mostly
dissolved (about 3–4 minutes). [4] Don't whisk or aerate the mixture, as that can make
the final blondies cakey.

5. In a separate bowl, whisk together the gluten-free flour blend, xanthan gum and salt,
and add them to the wet ingredients. Mix well until you get a fairly runny batter with no
flour clumps.

6. Add most of the chocolate to the batter (reserving some for sprinkling on top), and fold
it in until evenly distributed.

7. Transfer the batter into the lined baking tin, smooth out the top and sprinkle with the
reserved chocolate.

8. Bake for about 28–30 minutes or until an inserted toothpick or cake tester comes out
covered in a mixture of half-baked batter and moist crumbs.

9. Allow the blondies to cool completely to room temperature before you remove them
from the tin (use the overhanging baking paper to help you). Use a sharp knife to slice
them into individual portions – wipe the knife clean between cuts for neat slices.

# Blueberry crumble pie

Serves 8–10  /  Prep time 1 hour (excluding pastry prep)  /  Chill time 30 mins  /  Bake time 1 hour 25 mins

1 batch of **gluten-free flaky pie dough** (see pages 200–201)

## Crumble topping

125g (½ cup + 2 tablespoons) caster (superfine) or granulated sugar

zest of 1 unwaxed lemon

85g (¾ stick) unsalted butter, softened

½ teaspoon vanilla paste (or 1 teaspoon vanilla extract)

180g (1½ cups) plain gluten-free flour blend [1]

¼ teaspoon xanthan gum [2]

## Blueberry filling

1kg (2¼lb/7 cups) blueberries

150g (¾ cup) caster (superfine) or granulated sugar

35g (5 tablespoons) cornflour (cornstarch)

30g (2 tablespoons) lemon juice

1 teaspoon vanilla paste (or 2 teaspoons vanilla extract)

Notes

[1] Use a shop-bought gluten-free flour blend or mix your own (see page 24).

[2] If your gluten-free flour blend already contains binders, omit the xanthan gum.

[3] Rolling out the pie crust on a sheet of cling film or baking paper makes it much easier to transfer it into the pie dish without having to worry about it tearing.

[4] The baking sheet serves two purposes: it starts baking the bottom of the pie straight away to reduce the chance of a soggy bottom, and it catches any filling drips!

[5] The long cooling time makes for neat, clean slices. Cutting into a warm pie can be rather messy, as the filling won't have set.

This recipe combines two amazing desserts into one: blueberry pie and blueberry crumble. While I love a pretty lattice top as much as any pie lover – there's something so cosy and special about a buttery, crisp, golden brown crumble topping. And it's also much quicker and easier to make than the more traditional pie lattice. The pie crust is nicely crisp and flaky, with no sogginess thanks to the blind-baking step, and the blueberry filling is juicy and jammy without being too runny (after all, nobody wants blueberry soup as their pie filling). If you want to get perfectly neat slices, allow the pie to cool completely to room temperature before you cut into it... but I completely understand if you want to tuck in while it's still warm. Nothing beats a warm slice of blueberry crumble pie with a generous scoop of vanilla ice cream on top.

*The pie-crust dough follows the rules for adapting flaky pastry on page 72 and the crumble topping follows the rules for adapting cookies that hold their shape during baking on page 64 – use them to adapt this recipe to any free-from variation.*

### Flaky pie crust

1. Chill the pie-crust dough for at least 30 minutes before using. If you've made it a few days ahead and stored it in the fridge, allow it to come up to room temperature for 5–10 minutes until it's pliable (to prevent cracking during rolling).

2. Get a 23cm (9in) pie dish (about 4cm/1½in deep) on hand.

3. On a lightly floured large piece of cling film or baking paper, roll out the pie-crust dough to about 2–3mm (⅛in) thick and cut out a 30cm (12in) circle. [3]

4. Transfer the circle into the pie dish, making sure that it's snug against the bottom and sides. Trim the excess dough, leaving about a 2.5cm (1in) overhang.

5. Fold the overhanging dough under itself and crimp the edges: squeeze the pastry between the thumb and index finger of your non-dominant hand (forming a V shape) and press gently into the V using the index finger or thumb of your dominant hand.

6. Refrigerate the unbaked pie crust for at least 30 minutes.

### Crumble topping

1. Add the sugar and lemon zest to a large bowl and use your fingertips to rub the zest into the sugar. This releases essential oils from the zest, to make your crumble topping extra lemony and aromatic.

2. Add the butter and vanilla, and mix until combined (don't cream or aerate the mixture).

3. In a separate bowl, whisk together the gluten-free flour blend and xanthan gum.

4. Add the dry ingredients to the butter-sugar mixture and mix until it starts clumping together. Then, give it a knead until you get a fairly crumbly cookie dough. Store in the fridge until needed.

→

**Storage**

3–4 days in an airtight container in a cool, dry place.

**Blind baking the pie crust**

1. Place a large baking sheet on the lower-middle oven rack and pre-heat the oven to 200°C/400°F. [4]

2. Dock the base of the chilled pie crust all over with a fork, line it with a scrunched-up piece of baking paper and fill to the brim with baking beans or rice.

3. Place the pie on the hot baking sheet and bake for about 18–20 minutes until you can see the edges turning a light golden colour.

4. Remove the baking beans or rice and the baking paper, and bake for a further 3–4 minutes or until the bottom appears set and dry (but is still pale in colour with minimal browning).

5. Take the blind-baked pie crust out of the oven and set aside until needed (leave the oven at 200°C/400°F with the baking sheet on the middle-lower oven rack).

**Filling & baking the pie**

1. In a large bowl, mix together all the blueberry filling ingredients. Pour this into the blind-baked pie crust, smoothing it out into an even layer.

2. Sprinkle the crumble topping evenly over the blueberry filling, breaking up any large clumps as needed. You'll get quite a large mound of filling and crumble – that's okay, the filling will shrink slightly during baking.

3. Bake for about 1 hour to 1 hour 10 minutes or until the juices are visibly bubbling around the crumble topping and the internal temperature of the filling reaches about 90°C/195°F. If the pie crust or the crumble topping start browning too quickly, cover the pie with a sheet of foil (shiny side up) and continue baking until done.

4. Allow to cool for at least 4 hours before serving. [5]

> **NOTE: USING FROZEN FRUIT**
>
> If you prefer, you can use frozen blueberries. Thaw them first, then drain the juices and set the blueberries aside in a bowl. Pour the juices into a saucepan and reduce them on the stovetop over medium–high heat until they've thickened but are not quite jam-like. Leave the reduced juices to cool to room temperature, then add them to the blueberries along with the other filling ingredients, but use 30g (4 tablespoons) of cornflour (cornstarch) instead.

# Honey & sesame artisan loaf

**Makes 1 loaf  /  Cook time 3 mins  /  Prep time 45 mins  /  Prove time 1 hour  /  Bake time 50 mins**

90g (⅔ cup) sesame seeds

25g (5 tablespoons) whole psyllium husk [1]

460g (1¾ cups + 2½ tablespoons) lukewarm water

180g (1½ cups + 1 tablespoon) tapioca starch [2]

180g (1⅓ cups) millet flour, plus extra for flouring the surface [3]

60g (⅓ cup + 2 tablespoons) sorghum flour [4]

8g (2½ teaspoons) instant yeast [5]

10g (2 teaspoons) salt

30g (1½ tablespoons) runny honey

20g (1½ tablespoons) olive oil

10g (2 teaspoons) apple cider vinegar

### Notes

[1] If using psyllium husk powder, use only 21g (2½ tablespoons).

[2] Or use an equal weight of arrowroot starch, cornflour (cornstarch) or potato starch instead.

[3] Or use an equal weight of finely milled brown rice flour instead.

[4] Or use an equal weight of light buckwheat flour, white teff flour or oat flour instead.

[5] If using active dry yeast, use 10g (3½ teaspoons), and activate it first. Mix together the active dry yeast, 1 tablespoon of the honey and about 120g (½ cup) of the warm water (use the remaining water to make the psyllium gel). Set aside for 10–15 minutes, or until frothing. Add to the dry ingredients along with the psyllium gel, the remaining honey, olive oil and vinegar.

[6] Weighing the loaf tells you whether the bread has lost enough moisture to have a soft, open, non-sticky crumb (see page 275).

**This bread is so ridiculously flavourful you can easily eat it all by itself or just generously slathered with some salted butter. It has a deliciously soft, chewy open crumb, and the toasted sesame seeds in it give a wonderful nuttiness, which works incredibly well with the subtle flavours of honey and olive oil. Rolling the loaf in sesame seeds before proving makes it look (and taste) extra special.**

*This recipe is based on the basic gluten-free non-enriched bread dough on page 276. You can use maple syrup instead of honey to make it vegan.*

### Making the dough

*You can prepare the dough using a stand mixer fitted with the dough hook or by hand. The mixer makes it much easier and results in a smoother dough.*

1. In a saucepan over medium–high heat, toast half of the sesame seeds, stirring frequently, until golden brown (about 3–4 minutes). Set aside to cool completely.

2. In a bowl, mix together the psyllium husk and lukewarm water. After about 30–45 seconds, a gel will form.

3. In a large bowl or the bowl of the stand mixer, whisk together the tapioca starch, millet flour, sorghum flour, instant yeast, salt and the cooled toasted sesame seeds.

4. Make a well in the middle of the dry ingredients and add the psyllium gel, honey, olive oil and vinegar.

5. Knead the dough until smooth and it starts coming away from the inside of the bowl, about 4–5 minutes with a stand mixer or 6–8 minutes if kneading it by hand. The final dough should be pliable and supple, and not too sticky to the touch.

### Shaping & proving the loaf

1. Line a 25cm (10in) oval proving basket (banneton) with its liner or a clean tea towel. Set aside until needed.

2. Turn out the dough on to a lightly floured surface and give it a gentle knead to ensure it's perfectly smooth. Pat down the dough into an approximately 23cm (9in) circle about 2.5cm (1in) thick, then roll it up into an oval loaf that fits the shape and size of the proving basket. Pinch the seam together to seal it. (Don't over-flour your work surface – you want the surface of the bread to be slightly sticky and not covered in flour, so that the sesame seeds will stick to it.)

3. Place the remaining (untoasted) sesame seeds on a large plate, a baking sheet or a clean tea towel, and spread them out evenly. Place the shaped loaf on to the seeds, seam side up, and gently roll it around to completely cover its top and sides with seeds. (You can lightly spray the loaf with a bit of water to make the seeds stick better, if needed.)

4. Transfer the loaf, seam side up (so that the sesame-covered top faces down), into the lined proving basket. Cover with a clean tea towel or cling film or place it into a proving bag, and prove in a warm place for about 1 hour or until doubled in size. The bread will rise about 4cm (1½in) above the rim of the proving basket – that's okay, it won't overflow!

$\rightarrow$

Gluten-free recipes  297

## Storage

3–4 days in an airtight container (such as a bread box or similar) in a cool, dry place. Best toasted on days 3 and 4.

## The baking set-up

1. While the bread is proving, adjust the oven rack to the lower-middle position, so that it's in the bottom third of the oven with no rack above it.

2. Put a 25–30cm (10–12in) cast-iron skillet or a Dutch oven/combo cooker on the oven rack. If you're using a skillet, also place a metal baking tray or pan on the bottom rack of the oven. (Don't use a glass baking tray, as it could crack because of the rapid temperature change when you put in the ice cubes later on.)

3. Pre-heat the oven to 250°C/475°F for at least 45 minutes (the oven needs to be thoroughly pre-heated for maximum oven spring, so I recommend that you start pre-heating it after the loaf has been proving for about 15–20 minutes).

## Scoring & baking the loaf

1. Once the loaf has doubled in size, turn it out of the proving basket on to a piece of baking paper and score the top about 5mm–1cm (¼–½in) deep, using a bread lame or sharp knife. Take the hot cast-iron skillet or Dutch oven/combo cooker out of the oven and then transfer the bread along with the baking paper into it.

2. **If using a Dutch oven/combo cooker:** Add 4–5 ice cubes around the bread (between the baking paper and the walls of the Dutch oven/combo cooker) and close the Dutch oven, then place it into the pre-heated oven.

3. **If using a cast-iron skillet:** Place the skillet in the oven, add 4–5 ice cubes into the bottom baking tray and close the oven door.

4. Bake at 250°C/475°F with steam for 20 minutes – don't open the Dutch oven or the oven doors during this period, as that would allow the steam to escape out of the oven.

5. After the 20 minutes, remove the bottom tray with water from the oven (for cast-iron skillet) or uncover the Dutch oven/combo cooker, reduce the oven temperature to 220°C/425°F, and bake for a further 30–40 minutes in a steam-free environment. The final loaf should be of a deep golden-brown colour and weigh about 930g immediately out of the oven (about 12% weight loss). [6]

6. Transfer the loaf on to a wire cooling rack to cool completely, or at least until lukewarm, before cutting into it.

| Composition of the honey & sesame artisan loaf | |
| --- | --- |
| **Quantity name** | **Value** |
| Hydration | 110 b% |
| Starch content | 43 b% |
| Binder content | 6 b% |

# Chocolate-stuffed braided brioche muffins

**Makes 8 / Prep time 1 hour / Cook time 5 mins / Prove time 1 hour 15 mins / Bake time 15 mins**

## Chocolate pastry cream

240g (1 cup) whole milk

½ teaspoon vanilla paste
(or 1 teaspoon vanilla extract)

3 medium egg yolks (US large),
room temperature

75g (¼ cup + 2 tablespoons)
caster (superfine) or
granulated sugar

20g (3 tablespoons) cornflour
(cornstarch)

100g (3½oz) 60–70% dark
chocolate, chopped

30g (2 tablespoons) unsalted
butter, cubed

¼ teaspoon salt

## Brioche dough

15g (3 tablespoons) whole
psyllium husk [1]

180g (¾ cup) lukewarm water

160g (1⅓ cups + 1 tablespoon)
tapioca starch [2]

135g (1 cup) millet flour, plus extra
for flouring the surface [3]

25g (3 tablespoons) sorghum
flour [4]

50g (¼ cup) caster (superfine)
or granulated sugar

6g (2 teaspoons) instant yeast [5]

6g (1½ teaspoons) baking powder

5g (2 teaspoons) xanthan gum

5g (1 teaspoon) salt

100g (⅓ cup + 1½ tablespoons)
whole milk, lukewarm

1 medium egg (US large),
room temperature

35g (2½ tablespoons) unsalted
butter, melted, plus extra for
brushing the brioche muffins

½ teaspoon vanilla paste (or
1 teaspoon vanilla extract)

## Simple syrup

50g (¼ cup) caster (superfine)
or granulated sugar

20g (4 teaspoons) water

## Cinnamon sugar

100g (½ cup) caster (superfine)
or granulated sugar

½ tablespoon ground cinnamon

Pillowy brioche rolled in cinnamon sugar and filled with chocolate pastry cream – it doesn't get much better than that. These braided brioche muffins look impressive, but the braiding method is really easy, and the dough handles beautifully. If you're in a rush, use chocolate-hazelnut spread or jam for the filling.

*This recipe is based on the basic gluten-free brioche dough recipe on page 277. You can use the rules for adapting bread & yeasted bakes on page 84 to make it dairy-free, egg-free or vegan. Dairy-free, egg-free and vegan pastry cream recipe variations are on page 476.*

### Chocolate pastry cream

1. In a saucepan, cook the milk and vanilla over medium heat until the mixture only just comes to a boil.

2. While the milk is heating, whisk the egg yolks and sugar together in a bowl until pale and slightly fluffy. Add the cornflour (cornstarch) to the egg mixture and whisk well until combined and no clumps remain.

3. Pour the hot milk in a slow, thin stream into the egg mixture, whisking constantly. Return the mixture to the saucepan and cook over medium heat, with constant whisking, until thickened and it comes to a boil (about 2–3 minutes). Cook for about 1 minute more.

4. Remove from the heat and stir in the chocolate, butter and salt, mixing well until completely melted and incorporated. The pastry cream should be smooth and glossy.

5. Transfer the pastry cream to a bowl or heatproof container and cover it with a sheet of cling film. Make sure that the cling film is in direct contact with the surface of the pastry cream to prevent skin formation. Allow to cool completely to room temperature, then store in the fridge until needed (you can prepare it a day or two in advance).

### Brioche dough

*You can prepare the dough using a stand mixer fitted with the dough hook or by hand. The mixer makes it much easier and results in a smoother dough.*

1. In a bowl, mix together the psyllium husk and lukewarm water. After about 30–45 seconds, a gel will form.

2. In a large bowl or the bowl of the stand mixer, whisk together the tapioca starch, millet flour, sorghum flour, sugar, instant yeast, baking powder, xanthan gum and salt. Make a well in the middle and add the psyllium gel, lukewarm milk, egg, melted butter and vanilla.

3. Mix the dough until all the ingredients are evenly incorporated, then knead for 4–5 minutes if using a stand mixer, or 6–8 minutes by hand. Use a rubber spatula to occasionally scrape the inside of the bowl to prevent any patches of unmixed flour.

4. The final dough will be slightly sticky to the touch – that's okay, you'll be working on a lightly floured surface so it shouldn't be a problem. Resist the temptation to add more flour to the dough, as that can make the brioche too dense and dry. [6]

### Shaping & proving

1. Lightly butter 8 holes of a muffin tin. Divide the dough into 8 equal pieces; each should weigh about 96g. While you're working with one piece, keep the others covered with a damp tea towel or a piece of cling film to prevent them from drying out.

→

Notes

[1] If using psyllium husk powder, use only 13g (1½ tablespoons).

[2] Or use an equal weight of arrowroot starch, cornflour (cornstarch) or potato starch.

[3] Or use an equal weight of finely milled/ground brown rice flour, but your brioche muffins might be slightly less fluffy.

[4] Or use an equal weight of light buckwheat flour, white teff flour or oat flour.

[5] If using active dry yeast, use 8g (2½ teaspoons), and activate it first. Mix together the active dry yeast, 1 tablespoon of the sugar and the warm milk. Set aside for 10–15 minutes, or until frothing. Add it to the dry ingredients along with the psyllium gel, egg and melted butter.

[6] If you find the dough too sticky to handle easily, chill it in the fridge for about 1 hour before proceeding to the next step.

## Storage

2–3 days in a closed container in a cool, dry place. Reheat in the microwave for 15–20 seconds before serving. Store any leftover chocolate pastry cream in an airtight container in the fridge for about 3 days.

2. On a lightly floured surface, shape the piece of dough into a small, 15cm (6in) log, then use a rolling pin to roll it out into an approximately 20x8cm (8x3¼in) oval.

3. Use a sharp knife or a pizza cutter to divide the dough into three equal strips, leaving a 2cm (¾in) border on one end intact.

4. Braid the three strips together until you have a single braid. Starting at the end of the braid, roll it up toward the intact end. Place the rolled-up braid into the prepared muffin tin, so that one of the open ends faces upward. Repeat with the rest of the dough pieces.

5. Lightly cover the muffin tin with a sheet of cling film and prove the brioche muffins in a warm place for about 1 hour 15 minutes to 1 hour 30 minutes or until doubled in size.

### Baking the braided brioche muffins

1. While the brioche muffins are proving, adjust the oven rack to the middle position and pre-heat the oven to 180°C/350°F.

2. Once the muffins have doubled in size, brush the top of each gently with melted butter and bake for 15–20 minutes or until golden brown on top. Remove them immediately out of the muffin tin on to a wire rack. Allow to cool until warm.

### Make the sugar coatings

1. For the simple syrup, in a small saucepan on the stovetop or in a microwave-safe bowl or jug in the microwave, heat the sugar and water together until the sugar has completely dissolved.

2. For the cinnamon sugar, in a large bowl, mix together the sugar and cinnamon until well combined (the bowl should be large enough so that you can easily toss the muffins in the cinnamon sugar).

### Assemble the muffins

1. Brush the warm brioche muffins all over with the simple syrup and then toss them in the cinnamon sugar until completely coated.

2. Give the chocolate pastry cream a good whisk to smooth it out and transfer it into a piping bag fitted with a round nozzle.

3. Use the end of a wooden spoon or similar utensil to make a hole on top of each braided brioche muffin (in between the braids), this will make it easier to fill them. Fill the brioche muffins with a generous amount of the pastry cream – they're completely full when the pastry cream starts coming out of the hole. Serve warm or at room temperature.

| Composition of the braided brioche muffins | |
|---|---|
| Quantity name | Value |
| Hydration | 88 b% |
| Starch content | 50 b% |
| Binder content | 6 b% |
| Psyllium:xanthan ratio | 3:1 |

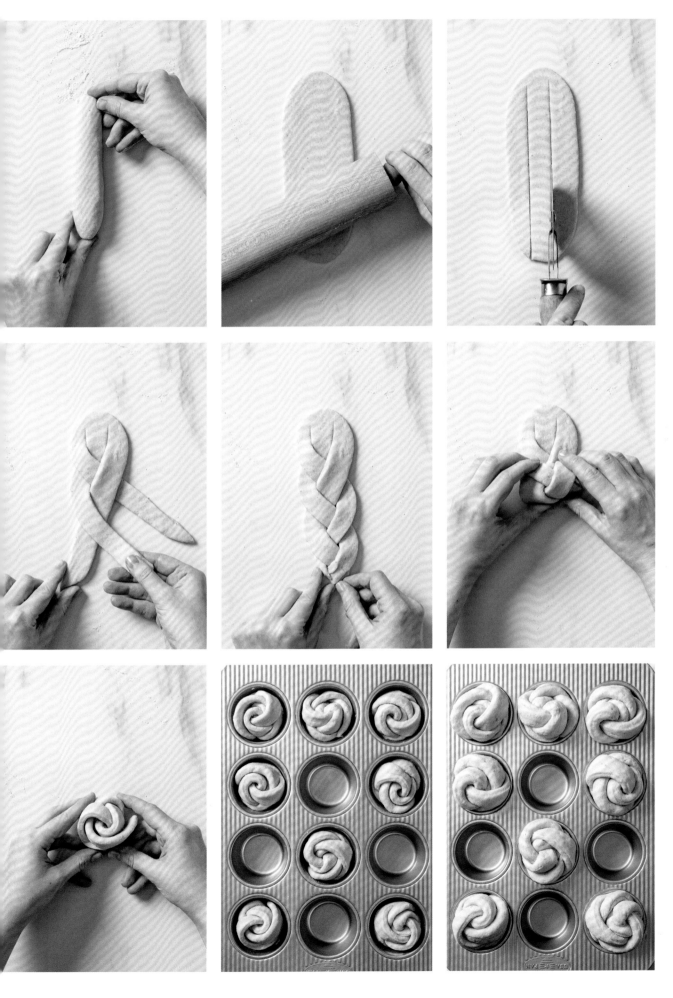

# Cheesy garlic pull-apart bread

**Serves 10–14  /  Prep time 1 hour  /  Prove time 1 hour 15 mins  /  Bake time 45 mins**

## Brioche dough

15g (3 tablespoons) whole psyllium husk [1]

180g (¾ cup) lukewarm water

160g (1⅓ cups + 1 tablespoon) tapioca starch [2]

135g (1 cup) millet flour, plus extra for flouring the surface [3]

25g (3 tablespoons) sorghum flour [4]

25g (2 tablespoons) caster (superfine) or granulated sugar

6g (2 teaspoons) instant yeast [5]

6g (1½ teaspoons) baking powder

5g (2 teaspoons) xanthan gum

5g (1 teaspoon) salt

100g (⅓ cup + 1½ tablespoons) whole milk, lukewarm

1 medium egg (US large), room temperature

35g (2½ tablespoons) unsalted butter, melted, plus optional 1–2 tablespoons (melted), to finish

flaky salt (optional)

## Filling

55g (½ stick) salted butter, softened

1–2 teaspoons garlic powder

2 tablespoons finely chopped fresh herbs, such as parsley, rosemary and oregano

¼ teaspoon pepper

80g (¾ cup) coarsely grated (shredded) cheddar

80g (¾ cup) coarsely grated (shredded) low-moisture mozzarella

This is one of the best things I've ever eaten (and I don't use these words lightly). The texture is perfect: soft and squishy, and you get that stunning stretchy cheese pull as you tear off individual pieces. The combination of the two cheeses gives the best of both worlds: the cheddar contributes a delicious saltiness and the mozzarella adds a melty creaminess. The filling also includes lots of garlic and herbs, and the whole thing is one giant cheesy, garlicky flavour explosion. Some of the butter and cheese will leak out slightly during baking – but this actually results in the best parts of this bread: the crispy, cheesy, caramelized bits around the sides and on the bottom.

*This recipe is based on the basic gluten-free brioche dough recipe on page 277. You can use the rules for adapting bread & yeasted bakes on page 84 to make it dairy-free, egg-free or vegan as well. For the dairy-free and vegan versions, replace the butter and cheese in the filling with vegan equivalents (or use the vegan pesto from page 461 as an alternative filling).*

### Brioche dough

*You can prepare the dough using a stand mixer fitted with the dough hook or by hand. The mixer makes it much easier and results in a smoother dough.*

1. In a bowl, mix together the psyllium husk and lukewarm water. After about 30–45 seconds, a gel will form.

2. In a large bowl or the bowl of the stand mixer, whisk together the tapioca starch, millet flour, sorghum flour, sugar, instant yeast, baking powder, xanthan gum and salt.

3. Make a well in the middle of the dry ingredients and add the psyllium gel, warm milk, egg and melted butter.

4. Mix the dough until smooth and all the ingredients are evenly incorporated, then knead for 4–5 minutes if using a stand mixer, or 6–8 minutes if kneading it by hand. Use a rubber spatula to occasionally scrape down the bottom and inside of the bowl to prevent any dry patches of unmixed flour.

5. The final dough will be slightly sticky to the touch – that's okay, you'll be working on a lightly floured surface so it shouldn't be a problem. Resist the temptation to add more flour to the dough, as that can make the bread too dense and dry. [6]

### Garlic butter filling

1. In a small bowl, mix together the softened butter, garlic powder, finely chopped fresh herbs and pepper until well combined. Set aside until needed.

### Assembling & proving

1. Lightly butter a 23x13cm (9x5in) loaf tin. You can also line it with baking paper, although it's not essential.

2. On a lightly floured surface, roll out the dough into a large 30cm (12in) square.

3. Spread the garlic butter filling in an even layer over the rolled-out dough, all the way to the edges.

→

## Notes

[1] If using psyllium husk powder, use only 13g (1½ tablespoons).

[2] Or use an equal weight of arrowroot starch, cornflour (cornstarch) or potato starch.

[3] Or use an equal weight of finely milled/ ground brown rice flour, but your pull-apart bread might be slightly less fluffy.

[4] Or use an equal weight of light buckwheat flour, white teff flour or oat flour.

[5] If using active dry yeast, use 8g (2½ teaspoons), and activate it first. Mix together the active dry yeast, 1 tablespoon of the sugar and the warm milk. Set aside for 10–15 minutes, or until frothing. Add it to the dry ingredients along with the psyllium gel, egg and melted butter.

[6] If you find the dough too sticky to handle easily, chill it in the fridge for about 1 hour before proceeding to the next step.

## Storage

Best served hot or warm, fresh from the oven. You can also store it for about 2 days in an airtight container at room temperature and reheat it before serving, in the microwave for 15–20 seconds or in a 180°C/ 350°F oven for 5–10 minutes.

4. Evenly scatter the grated cheddar and mozzarella over the garlic butter, and press down gently to make sure it sticks.

5. Using a pizza cutter or a sharp knife, divide the dough into 16 equal 7.5cm (3in) squares.

6. Stack eight of the squares, cheese side up, on top of each other, and carefully place them into the prepared loaf tin (so that a cheese-free square faces the end of the tin). Repeat with the other eight squares, but make sure that the top square faces cheese side down. Carefully place the second stack into the loaf tin; you might need to squeeze them a bit to make them all fit.

7. Lightly cover the loaf tin with cling film and leave the dough to prove in a warm place for about 1 hour 15 minutes to 1 hour 30 minutes or until about doubled in size.

## Baking

1. While the dough is proving, adjust the oven rack to the middle position and pre-heat the oven to 180°C/350°F.

2. Once doubled in size, place the bread on to a baking sheet (to catch any drips), then place it into the oven and bake for about 45 minutes or until evenly golden brown on top and an inserted toothpick comes out completely clean with no sticky, raw dough attached to it. If the top of the bread starts browning too quickly, cover it with a sheet of foil (shiny side up) and continue baking until done.

3. Remove the baked bread from the loaf tin straight away and allow it to cool on a wire rack for 5–10 minutes before serving. (Optional: brush with a bit of melted butter immediately out of the oven and sprinkle with flaky salt.)

| Composition of the pull-apart bread | |
|---|---|
| Quantity name | Value |
| Hydration | 88 b% |
| Starch content | 50 b% |
| Binder content | 6 b% |
| Psyllium:xanthan ratio | 3:1 |

# Chapter

## 6

# Df

## Dairy-free

# Dairy-free Baking: It's All in the Ingredients

Successful dairy-free baking is, for the most part, all about knowing how to select the best possible alternatives to the regular ingredients. Unlike with gluten-free (Chapter 5) and egg-free baking (Chapter 7), dairy-free baking is less about adjusting the ingredient quantities and more about understanding the composition of the dairy ingredients and their roles in the relevant bakes, and then using that understanding to choose dairy-free equivalents that mimic those properties as closely as possible.

And once you've picked the correct dairy-free equivalent, you're good to go. In most cases, you can simply replace the dairy ingredients with an equal weight or volume of dairy-free, with only minor additional tweaks.

Out of all the free-from adjustments, converting a recipe to be dairy-free is by far the simplest – with only a few exceptions. Without a doubt, choosing the best possible vegan butter when making flaky pastries (such as flaky pie crust or rough puff pastry) or other flaky or laminated bakes (such as American-style buttermilk biscuits) is the most significant consideration. In general, vegan butters have a lower melting point than dairy butter, which makes using them in flaky and laminated bakes quite tricky. You can read more about that on pages 43 and 314.

# Reduced Browning

An important difference between regular dairy ingredients and their dairy-free equivalents is the presence and absence of milk solids, respectively. As a consequence, your dairy-free bakes will, on average, show much less browning. That is, your dairy-free cakes, cupcakes, muffins, cookies and pastry will all come out of the oven noticeably paler.

That's because, in general, bakes get their deep golden colour from two processes: caramelization and browning (the Maillard reaction). While these two often occur simultaneously either in the oven or on the stovetop, and both result in the literal "browning" of foods, they're actually separate, distinct processes.

**Caramelization** is a chemical reaction that involves only sugars and heat. In this process, you heat a sugar until its molecules start breaking apart – this results in a colour change and also in the development of new, complex flavours and aromas. You may be familiar with this reaction from making a caramel or a caramel sauce, and also from creating the crunchy caramelized sugar topping on crème brûlée.

**Browning (Maillard reaction),** on the other hand, is a reaction that involves not only sugar and heat, but also the presence of amino acids (the building blocks of proteins). In the presence of heat, the amino acids react with the sugars, which results in browning and the evolution of new flavours – but different ones from those that you get with caramelization. This is a crucial reaction when it comes to grilling or roasting meat, getting a dark, flavourful crust on a loaf of artisan bread, or browning butter.

With bakes that use regular dairy ingredients, you usually get both of these processes working together to give a perfectly golden-brown result. There, the caramelization uses the sugars that you add to the batter or dough, and the Maillard reaction uses the same sugars (as well as the natural sugars present in dairy) and also the proteins present in dairy. These are the so-called "milk solids", largely composed of casein protein and whey protein.

You can easily see the Maillard reaction and these milk solids in action when you brown dairy butter. If you cook it for long enough, there is a visible change in colour from the initial pale yellow to a rich amber with brown specks in it. Those brown specks are the browned milk solids – and they're responsible not just for the colour change but also for the characteristic rich, nutty, almost caramel-like flavour of brown butter. And a similar process occurs in your bakes, albeit in a diluted state and mainly restricted to their crust or outer surface.

Of course, there are no such milk solids in any dairy-free ingredients. Consequently, dairy-free bakes can, for the most part, get that gorgeous golden-brown colour only through caramelization, as the proteins that make the Maillard reaction possible are largely absent. (That's also why you can't brown vegan butter!) In dairy-free bakes that use eggs, the latter do contribute some protein, so the Maillard reaction is not completely absent – but it is greatly reduced in importance and impact.

That means that when you take a regular recipe and convert it to be dairy-free, you'll inevitably lose some of the colour and also some of the flavour that would otherwise have been provided by the Maillard reaction. This is especially noticeable with light-coloured bakes that are fairly subtle in terms of flavour, such as vanilla cakes or cupcakes. In such cases, you can somewhat make up for this absence of colour and flavour by replacing part of the white sugar with light brown soft sugar or golden caster (superfine) sugar.

# Dairy-free Ingredients 101

We'll conquer the topic of dairy-free baking by looking at each of the different dairy-free substitutions in turn: from vegan butters, through dairy-free milk and cream substitutes, all the way to homemade vegan buttermilk and vegan condensed milk.

## Dairy-free (vegan) butter substitutes

Broadly speaking, we can divide vegan butter substitutes into two groups: liquid and solid fats.

### Liquid dairy-free fats

**NOTE**

**I don't include coconut oil in this grouping, as it's a solid fat at room temperature (where room temperature is around 22°C/72°F).**

These are, of course, the various oils, such as olive oil, sunflower oil, vegetable oil and rapeseed (canola) oil. They're all composed of 100% fat, whereas regular dairy butter contains only 80% fat (plus 15% water and 5% milk solids). That means that you can't just replace dairy butter with an equal amount of oil.

Instead, you need to replace the dairy butter with 80% of oil and 15% of dairy-free milk. In terms of weight, that means that you need to multiply the weight of the butter by 0.8 to get the weight of the oil and 0.15 to get the weight of the dairy-free milk. For example, you need to use 80g of oil and 15g of dairy-free milk if you want to replace 100g of dairy butter. If you're working in volume, you need to use 7 tablespoons (100ml) of oil and 1 tablespoon (15ml) of dairy-free milk for every stick (115g) of butter you're replacing. Note that if the recipe uses only a small amount of butter, you can omit the dairy-free milk.

Replacing dairy butter with oil is great for cakes, cupcakes and muffins, but I don't recommend it for bakes such as cookies or pastry. Those bakes perform much better with a solid type of fat. As a rule of thumb, use oil in cookies or pastry only if the recipe has been specifically developed to work with oil.

In cakes, cupcakes and muffins, oil gives a much lighter, fluffier crumb than butter. In fact, I often replace 50% of (dairy or dairy-free) butter with oil because it gives cakes a better rise and it results in beautifully domed muffins with a tall muffin top. Oil also keeps such bakes softer and moister for longer, compared to dairy butter. That's mainly because oil is a liquid fat at and around room temperature, whereas butter is a solid fat.

Another advantage of using oil in cakes is that even if you keep them in the fridge, they'll stay beautifully soft and spongy even when they're cold. In comparison, butter-based cakes (even if it's vegan butter) usually need to come up to room temperature to achieve their optimal, soft texture.

I recommend that you choose the oil you use based on flavour. You can either use neutral-tasting oils that won't add any flavour to your bakes, such as sunflower, vegetable or rapeseed (canola) oil, or use oils with a more intense flavour such as olive oil or walnut oil. The latter are great if you want to add another layer of complexity to your bakes; for example walnut oil would amp up the walnut flavour in a coffee and walnut cake.

### Solid dairy-free fats

These include firm vegan butter blocks, soft spreads, vegetable shortening and coconut oil.

First of all, let's talk about the difference between margarine and vegan butter (and whether there is any at all). In general, margarine and vegan (or dairy-free or plant-based) butter are very similar to each other. The key difference is that while vegan butter doesn't contain any dairy at all, margarine may contain traces of dairy products. Margarine is also often softer than vegan butter (closer to a soft spread), but its exact texture and consistency can vary depending on its exact composition.

And then there's the semantics. Margarine got a bad reputation because it used to contain hydrogenated oils (trans fats). While most products don't contain them anymore, the word "margarine" still has bad connotations for many – so it got rebranded to "vegan butter". I use the term "vegan butter" to mean firm vegan butters sold as sticks or blocks (not in tubs). Always check the ingredients to ensure that the products you're choosing don't contain dairy.

There is also a key distinction between soft spreads and firm vegan butter blocks. I always recommend using the latter in your dairy-free baking: their texture and composition is closer to that of dairy butter (they usually have a fat content of around 75–80%, which is very similar to that of regular butter) and they'll therefore give the best texture to your dairy-free bakes. If you have the option to choose between salted and unsalted vegan butter, always use unsalted – that gives you much better control over the amount of salt in your bakes.

**Firm vegan butter block** For the most part, you can replace regular dairy butter with an equal weight or volume of firm vegan butter block. However, it's important to remember that a large part of the composition of vegan butter is actually unsaturated fats (such as sunflower oil and rapeseed/canola oil) that are naturally liquid at and around room temperature. Consequently, vegan butter blocks have a lower melting point than regular dairy butter.

This is an important consideration when making bakes that contain discrete pieces of butter, such as flaky pie crust (or other flaky pastry). The lower melting point means that vegan butter has a greater tendency to leak out during baking. With bakes that use wheat flour, that's not much of a concern because the gluten-containing flour creates a strong, flexible "framework" that envelops the butter particles and therefore reduces the fat leakage.

However, if the bake uses gluten-free flour (such as in the gluten-free vegan pie crust on page 194), the lower melting point can result in a greasy, oily and quite hard or leathery baked pastry. To avoid that, adjust the way you incorporate the vegan butter into the dough: work it into the dry ingredients to a greater extent until you get smaller, pea-sized pieces. In comparison, you can leave the butter pieces approximately the size of walnut halves if using dairy butter and also if you're using vegan butter in combination with wheat flour.

NOTE: THE COMPOSITION OF FIRM VEGAN BUTTER BLOCKS
Not all vegan butter blocks are created equal. They can have different compositions and, importantly, different total fat and saturated fat contents. I've found that you get the best results if you use vegan butter with a high fat content, of 75% or higher, and a high saturated fat content, of 40% or higher. This is especially relevant with gluten-free vegan bakes – it's less important if you're using wheat flour. (You can get the information about the composition and fat content from the packaging or the relevant brand's website.)

**Vegetable shortening** Unlike vegan butter, shortening is 100% fat with no water content to speak of, so it behaves quite differently. It's especially useful when making flaky pastry, such as flaky pie crust (see page 192). There, you can use a combination of both vegan butter and vegetable shortening, and by adjusting the ratio of the two, you can control the tenderness of the pastry – this is especially helpful when making the gluten-free vegan pie crust (see page 194). Note that because vegetable shortening doesn't contain any water, any flaky pastry that uses it will puff up much less (or not at all) – I've explained why on page 193.

**Coconut oil** Although coconut oil is a popular vegan butter alternative, I don't use it much in my baking. Especially in cookies and pastry, it tends to give rather inconsistent results and it becomes solid when chilled, which makes any cookie or pastry dough rock hard if you keep it in the fridge for longer than 30 minutes. That can make any subsequent rolling and handling steps challenging – the final pastry tends to be much more prone to cracking and crumbling.

NOTE
Lard also belongs to the solid dairy-free fat category, but I don't use it in my baking, so I've omitted it from my explanations.

## Dairy-free milk

For the most part, you can easily substitute dairy milk with an equal weight or volume of a dairy-free milk, such as almond, rice, soy or oat milk. Although regular dairy and dairy-free milk have different compositions and fat contents, this amounts to a very small difference of only about 3–3.5g of fat per 100g of milk – so, we can safely and reliably 1:1 substitute one for the other in most situations.

You can also use the different dairy-free milks interchangeably, as they're predominantly composed of water, with only minor differences between them. When choosing your preferred dairy-free milk, choose one whose flavour you like and that fits within your diet and lifestyle (for example, if you have any additional food sensitivities or allergies). For baking, it's best to use unsweetened dairy-free milk with no flavourings added (or at least as few as possible) – this gives you more control over the sweetness and taste of your final bake.

However, avoid using canned coconut milk. It's much thicker and it has a very high fat content (much higher than that of dairy milk or other dairy-free milks) and it can make your bakes greasy, oily, heavy and dense. If you want to use coconut milk, use the kind from a carton, which is lower in fat and closer in texture and consistency to other dairy-free milks.

## Dairy-free (vegan) yogurt

Most vegan yogurts that you can find in shops will work great as a 1:1 substitution in dairy-free baking. That is, you can easily replace dairy yogurt with an equal weight or volume of the dairy-free equivalent.

In general for baking, use unsweetened plain or Greek-style vegan yogurt. This allows you to control the exact sweetness of your bakes. In some instances, Greek-style yogurt will work better than plain, and vice-versa – and I'll always specify which one you should use (and why) when that's the case.

The advantage of Greek-style vegan yogurt is that it has a lower water content, which is very helpful in bakes such as dairy-free cheesecake, where too much moisture could result in a split texture and a cracked top (see page 248).

## Dairy-free (vegan) buttermilk

I recommend making your own homemade version of vegan buttermilk using the recipe on page 25. It's super-quick and easy, and it mimics the acidity and consistency of shop-bought dairy buttermilk really well. It works great in all the typical buttermilk applications, such as in buttermilk pancakes and American-style flaky buttermilk biscuits, as well as in cakes, muffins and other bakes.

Once you've prepared your homemade vegan buttermilk, you can use it as a 1:1 substitute – that is, replace dairy buttermilk with an equal weight or volume of your dairy-free equivalent.

## Dairy-free (vegan) cream

The best dairy-free cream alternative depends to some extent on what you want to use it for.

In a frosting, it needs to be whippable. That means two things: **(1)** you need to be able to achieve a stiff, firm peak when you whip it with a stand or a hand mixer (regardless of whether or not you've added any icing/powdered sugar to it) and **(2)** it should maintain its whipped-up volume and hold its shape after you've piped it or spread it on to your bake – even if it stands at room temperature for an hour or two.

For such applications, I don't recommend using coconut cream as it can be temperamental and unpredictable (unless it's a specially formulated coconut whipping cream). Instead, you might need to test out a few different brands of dairy-free (or vegan or plant-based) double (heavy) cream to find your favourite – different brands can vary widely in terms of stability and how firm they are once whipped.

Using the vegan cream in a ganache or similar glaze or icing is a far more forgiving application, where most vegan double (heavy) creams will work well as long as they don't have too high a water content (too much water can result in a split ganache). Here, most shop-bought vegan double (heavy) cream alternatives should work well, as well as coconut cream.

When it comes to coconut cream, I recommend using the one you can get from canned coconut milk. Place a can of coconut milk into the fridge to chill overnight – this should make it separate into thick coconut cream and coconut water. Ideally, use a canned coconut milk without too many additives, otherwise it won't separate.

## Dairy-free (vegan) cream cheese

There are many vegan cream-cheese alternatives available, but ideally, use a vegan cream cheese with a low water content and a texture that's as close as possible to that of dairy (full-fat) cream cheese.

However, if the selection available to you is limited and the only vegan cream cheese you can find is slightly on the watery side, you can get away with it – you just need to remove some of that excess moisture first. To do this, place a strainer or colander over a bowl, line it with cheesecloth, add your vegan cream cheese to it, and then allow the excess water to drip out over the course of a few hours. To speed things up, you can make a closed pouch with the cheesecloth and then weigh it down gently with a plate or similar – the added weight will help the water drain a bit faster (it's best to place the whole straining set-up in the fridge, to avoid keeping the cream cheese out at room temperature or in a warm kitchen for a prolonged period of time).

Once your vegan cream cheese has noticeably thickened, you can use it as normal in your bake or frosting – even just removing a tablespoon or two of water will drastically improve the end result.

When you make dairy-free cheesecake, as well as opting for the lowest water content possible, you need to add some extra cornflour (cornstarch) – this is one of those rare times where a 1:1 substitution of dairy-free ingredients isn't enough for a perfect result. That's because even the best vegan cream cheese will contain more water than dairy cream cheese. And that extra moisture can result in a seemingly split or curdled cheesecake texture, as well as in a greater likelihood of it cracking during baking and cooling (see page 249).

## Dairy-free (vegan) condensed milk

There are many different vegan condensed milks available nowadays, and any one of them will work great in any recipe that calls for condensed milk – simply replace the dairy version with an equal weight or volume of the vegan equivalent.

You can, though, make your own homemade vegan condensed milk using the recipes on pages 26 and 27, as relevant. I've included recipes for condensed coconut milk as well as for coconut-free and dairy-free condensed milk – in case you prefer not to use coconut in your baking. Just like with the shop-bought versions, you can use these as 1:1 substitutes for dairy condensed milk.

While the texture, consistency and composition of the dairy-free (or vegan) ingredients, as well as how well they perform in bakes, are crucial to getting perfect results – we mustn't forget the importance of flavour.

Always pick dairy-free or vegan equivalents whose flavour you like. That's especially important in bakes where the flavour of other ingredients is fairly subtle, such as in vanilla cakes or cupcakes, and in recipes where the dairy-free ingredients are (one of) the main players, such as in cheesecakes, shortbread or buttercream. Dairy-free equivalents *will* taste different compared to their dairy equivalents, as will the bakes you use them in. There's not much you can do about that, but it doesn't mean that the flavour will be inferior – it will just be different.

Furthermore, you can experiment with additional flavourings that will make the taste of your dairy-free bakes richer and more well-rounded. A pinch of lemon zest, an extra dose of good-quality vanilla or a few drops of almond extract, for example, can make a huge difference.

# Dairy-free Fillings, Frostings, Icings and Glazes

As well as being fundamental to the various bakes themselves, dairy is a crucial component of numerous fillings (such as pastry cream or lemon curd), frostings (such as buttercream, whipped cream or cream cheese frosting), icings (such as cream cheese icing) and glazes (such as chocolate ganache).

In most cases, you can simply replace the dairy ingredients with an equal weight or volume of the relevant dairy-free equivalents (keeping in mind the advice so far).

There are, as always, exceptions. For example, to get a dairy-free pastry cream that's just as rich as its regular counterpart, I recommend replacing the dairy milk with a 50:50 mixture of vegan double (heavy) cream and dairy-free milk. By comparison, if you were to use dairy-free milk only, it would turn out a bit too watery and bland.

You can find dairy-free variations of the most frequently used fillings, frostings, icings and glazes on pages 469–79, as well as in the recipes in this chapter.

# Coffee & walnut cake

**Serves 10–12 / Prep time 45 mins / Cook time 5 mins / Bake time 30 mins**

120g (½ cup) dairy-free milk [1]

15g (3½ tablespoons) instant coffee granules

140g (1¼ sticks) unsalted vegan butter block, softened

100g (½ cup) light brown soft sugar

75g (¼ cup + 2 tablespoons) caster (superfine) or granulated sugar

½ teaspoon vanilla paste (or 1 teaspoon vanilla extract)

3 medium eggs (US large), room temperature

200g (1⅔ cups) plain (all-purpose) flour

60g (½ cup + 1½ tablespoons) ground walnuts

2½ teaspoons baking powder

¼ teaspoon salt

## Cappuccino frosting

230g (1 cup) vegan double (heavy) cream, chilled

14g (2 tablespoons) vegan instant cappuccino or latte powder [2]

2g (1½ teaspoons) instant coffee granules

90–120g (¾–1 cup) icing (powdered) sugar

½ teaspoon vanilla paste (or 1 teaspoon vanilla extract)

dark chocolate shavings

- - - - - - - - - - - - - - - - - - - - - -

### Notes

[1] Avoid using canned coconut milk, as it can make the cake too greasy and heavy.

[2] Or use more instant coffee granules: a total of 3.5–4.5g (2–3½ teaspoons).

- - - - - - - - - - - - - - - - - - - - - -

### Storage

3–4 days in an airtight container in the fridge. Allow to stand at room temperature for 5–10 minutes before serving.

**A coffee lover's dream come true, this cake has a tender coffee-walnut sponge and a truly magical cappuccino whipped-cream frosting. In fact, the frosting is the real star of this bake: it's velvety-smooth and fluffy, with the most incredible flavour.**

*This recipe follows the rules for adapting buttery cakes on page 52 – use them to adapt this recipe to any free-from variation.*

1. Adjust the oven rack to the middle position, pre-heat the oven to 180°C/350°F and line a 23cm (9in) round cake tin or springform pan with baking paper.

2. In a small saucepan on the stovetop or in a microwave-safe bowl in the microwave, heat together the milk and instant coffee, with occasional stirring, until the coffee is completely dissolved. Set aside to cool until lukewarm or at room temperature.

3. Using a stand mixer fitted with the paddle, a hand-held mixer with the double beaters or by hand using a large balloon whisk, cream together the vegan butter, light brown soft sugar, caster (superfine) or granulated sugar and vanilla until pale and fluffy. Add the eggs, one at a time, whisking well after each addition, until well combined.

4. In a separate bowl, whisk together the flour, ground walnuts, baking powder and salt.

5. Beginning and ending with the dry ingredients, alternately add the dry ingredients (in three batches) and the coffee-milk (in two batches) to the butter-sugar mixture, whisking well after each addition to a smooth, fluffy batter with no flour clumps. It might look a bit curdled or split after the addition of the coffee-milk (mostly owing to the acidic coffee), but don't worry, it should be silky smooth after the last portion of the dry ingredients. Transfer the cake batter into the lined cake tin and smooth out the top.

6. Bake for 30–35 minutes or until well risen, deep golden brown and an inserted toothpick comes out clean. If the top of the cake starts browning too quickly, cover it with foil (shiny side up) and continue baking until done. Cool in the cake tin for about 10 minutes, then remove from the tin on to a wire cooling rack to cool completely.

### Cappuccino frosting

1. In a small saucepan on the stovetop or in a microwave-safe bowl in the microwave, heat together 60g (¼ cup) of the vegan double (heavy) cream, the cappuccino powder and instant coffee, with occasional stirring, until the coffee and cappuccino powder are completely dissolved. Set aside to cool completely.

2. Using a stand mixer fitted with the whisk attachment or a hand-held mixer fitted with the double beaters, whisk together the remaining double (heavy) cream and icing (powdered) sugar until firm peaks form. (I recommend adding 90g/¾ cup of the icing sugar at first, then the remainder to taste, after the next step.)

3. Add the coffee-cream mixture to the whipped cream, about 1 tablespoon at a time, whisking well after each addition, until well combined. Add the vanilla and whisk well. The final frosting should be fluffy, smooth and hold a soft peak (if necessary, you can whisk it for a further 30 seconds or so, to thicken it a bit more).

4. Spoon the cappuccino frosting on top of the cooled cake and, using a small offset spatula or the back of the spoon, spread it out into an approximately even layer, creating decorative swirls. Sprinkle with chocolate shavings, slice and serve.

# Chocolate orange marbled loaf cake

**Serves 10 / Prep time 45 mins / Bake time 1 hour**

225g (1 cup + 2 tablespoons)
caster (superfine) or
granulated sugar

zest of 3 unwaxed oranges

170g (1½ sticks) unsalted vegan
butter block, softened

½ teaspoon vanilla paste (or
1 teaspoon vanilla extract)

4 medium eggs (US large),
room temperature

280g (2⅓ cups) plain
(all-purpose) flour

3 teaspoons baking powder

¼ teaspoon salt

160g (⅔ cup) orange juice,
freshly squeezed

20g (3 tablespoons)
Dutch-processed cocoa
powder, sifted

20g (4 teaspoons) dairy-free
milk, room temperature [1]

### Dark chocolate ganache glaze

80g (2¾oz) 60–70% dark
chocolate, chopped

115g (½ cup) vegan double
(heavy) cream

#### Notes

[1] Avoid using canned coconut milk, as it
can make the cake too greasy and heavy.

[2] Alternating dry and wet ingredients
helps to maintain the emulsion of the
butter, for a smooth batter and perfect
crumb. Always end with the dry.

[3] Adding milk with the cocoa powder
ensures that both batters have a similar
consistency.

#### Storage

3–4 days in an airtight container
in a cool, dry place.

With plenty of orange zest and juice in the batter, this moist, tender cake is
absolutely overflowing with orange goodness. The cocoa marbling effect is
incredibly easy to achieve and makes the cake look and taste extra special.

*This recipe follows the rules for adapting buttery cakes on page 52 – use them
to adapt this recipe to any free-from variation.*

1. Adjust the oven rack to the middle position, pre-heat the oven to 180°C/350°F and line
a 23x13cm (9x5in) loaf tin with baking paper.

2. Add the sugar and orange zest to a large bowl (or the bowl of a stand mixer) and use
your fingertips to rub the zest into the sugar (this helps to release the essential oils).

3. Add the vegan butter and the vanilla to the orange-sugar, and using a stand mixer
fitted with the paddle or a hand-held mixer with the double beaters, cream them
together until pale and fluffy. Add the eggs, one at a time, mixing well after each
addition, until well combined.

4. In a separate bowl, whisk together the flour, baking powder and salt.

5. Beginning and ending with the dry ingredients, alternately add the dry ingredients
(in three batches) and the orange juice (in two batches) to the butter-sugar mixture,
whisking after each addition, until you get a smooth batter with no flour clumps. The final
batter might look slightly split or curdled owing to the large amount of acidic orange
juice. Don't worry – you'll still get a soft, melt-in-the-mouth cake crumb in the end. [2]

6. Transfer about one third of the orange batter (about 350g) into a separate bowl, and
add the cocoa powder and milk. Mix until well combined. [3]

7. Spoon large dollops of the orange and the cocoa batter into the lined loaf tin, alternating
the two to create the marbled effect, until no batter remains. Use a knife or skewer to
swirl the batter around, making sure you reach all the way to the bottom of the tin.
Lightly tap the loaf tin on the work surface to level out the top.

8. Bake for about 1 hour to 1 hour 10 minutes or until risen, golden brown on top and
an inserted toothpick comes out clean. The loaf should have a crack along the centre.
If the cake starts browning too quickly, cover with foil (shiny side up) and bake until done.
Cool in the loaf tin for about 10 minutes, then transfer to a wire rack to cool completely.

#### Dark chocolate ganache glaze

1. Place the chopped chocolate into a heatproof bowl.

2. In a saucepan on the stovetop or in a microwave-safe bowl in the microwave, heat
the vegan double (heavy) cream until it only just comes to a boil, then pour it over the
chocolate. Allow to stand for 2–3 minutes, then stir together until smooth and glossy.

3. Allow the glaze to cool and thicken at room temperature, about 15–20 minutes, then
spoon or pour it over the top of the cooled cake. Use a small offset spatula or the back of
a spoon to spread the glaze evenly across the top and to guide it to drip down the sides.

4. Leave to set for at least 30 minutes at room temperature (or at least 15 minutes in the
fridge) before slicing and serving.

# Apple pie cupcakes

**Makes 12 / Prep time 1 hour / Cook time 5 mins / Bake time 22 mins**

## Apple pie filling

40g (3 tablespoons) unsalted vegan butter block

1kg (2¼lb) slightly tart, firm eating apples (about 6 apples), cored, peeled and diced into 1cm (½in) pieces

125g (½ cup + 2 tablespoons) light brown soft sugar

30g (2 tablespoons) lemon juice

1 teaspoon ground cinnamon

## Cinnamon cupcakes

210g (1¾ cups) plain (all-purpose) flour

100g (½ cup) caster (superfine) or granulated sugar

100g (½ cup) light brown soft sugar

2½ teaspoons baking powder

2 teaspoons cinnamon

½ teaspoon salt

55g (½ stick) unsalted vegan butter block, softened

55g (¼ cup) sunflower or vegetable oil

150g (½ cup + 2 tablespoons) dairy-free milk, room temperature

2 medium eggs (US large), room temperature

½ teaspoon vanilla paste (or 1 teaspoon vanilla extract)

## Cream cheese frosting

175g (¾ cup) vegan double (heavy) cream, chilled

90g (¾ cup) icing (powdered) sugar, sifted

170g (¾ cup) vegan cream cheese, chilled

½ teaspoon vanilla paste (or 1 teaspoon vanilla extract)

## Storage

3–4 days in an airtight container in the fridge. Allow to stand at room temperature for 5–10 minutes before serving.

Eating these is like biting into a fluffy cloud of cinnamon-y apple-pie goodness. The frosting uses whipped vegan cream instead of butter for lightness, and its tanginess balances out the sweetness of the spiced apple-pie filling.

*This recipe follows the rules for adapting buttery cakes on page 52 – use them to adapt this recipe to any free-from variation.*

### Apple pie filling

1. In a large saucepan or skillet over medium–high heat, melt the butter. Add the diced apples, sugar, lemon juice and cinnamon, and stir to combine.

2. Cook for 5–6 minutes with occasional stirring, until the apples have softened (but still have texture – they shouldn't be mushy) and the juices are a thick, syrupy consistency. Cool to room temperature and set aside until needed.

### Cinnamon cupcakes

1. Adjust the oven rack to the middle position, pre-heat the oven to 160°C/325°F, and line a 12-hole muffin tin with paper liners.

2. In a large bowl (or the bowl of a stand mixer), whisk together the flour, caster (superfine) or granulated sugar, light brown sugar, baking powder, cinnamon and salt.

3. Add the softened vegan butter and with a stand mixer fitted with the paddle or a hand-held mixer with the double beaters, work it into the dry ingredients until you get a mixture resembling breadcrumbs.

4. In a separate bowl, whisk together the oil, dairy-free milk, eggs and vanilla. Add them to the flour-butter mixture in 2–3 batches, mixing well after each addition, until smooth with no flour clumps. Scrape inside the bowl occasionally to prevent any unmixed patches.

5. Divide the batter equally between the paper liners, filling each about ⅔–¾ full.

6. Bake for about 22–24 minutes or until well risen with a gently rounded top and an inserted toothpick comes out clean. Cool in the tin for 5 minutes, then transfer the cupcakes on to a wire rack to cool completely.

### Cream cheese frosting

1. Using a stand mixer fitted with the whisk or a hand-held mixer with the double beaters, whip the vegan double (heavy) cream and icing (powdered) sugar together to stiff peaks.

2. In a separate bowl, whisk the vegan cream cheese until it's smooth and loosened.

3. Add the cream cheese and vanilla to the whipped cream, and whip for 30–60 seconds until well combined and stiff peaks form.

### Assembling the cupcakes

1. Use the wider end of a piping nozzle to create a hole in the middle of each cupcake. Fill each hole completely with the apple pie filling.

2. Transfer the frosting to a piping bag fitted with a large open star nozzle. Pipe a ring of frosting on top of each cupcake, leaving a hole in the centre. Fill each ring with a generous amount of apple-pie filling, so that some of it peeks over the top of the frosting. Drizzle with the syrupy apple-pie-filling juices, and serve.

# Salted peanut caramel brownie bars

**Makes 12  /  Prep time 1 hour  /  Bake time 16 mins  /  Cook time 15 mins  /  Chill time 2 hours 30 minutes**

### Chocolate brownies

160g (5½oz) 60–70% dark
chocolate, chopped

55g (½ stick) unsalted vegan
butter block

100g (½ cup) light brown
soft sugar

50g (¼ cup) caster (superfine)
or granulated sugar

2 medium eggs (US large),
room temperature

½ teaspoon vanilla paste (or
1 teaspoon vanilla extract)

100g (¾ cup + 1 tablespoon)
plain (all-purpose) flour

20g (3 tablespoons)
Dutch-processed
cocoa powder

¼ teaspoon salt

### Salted caramel peanut layer

270g (1 cup + 3 tablespoons)
vegan double (heavy) cream

45g (3 tablespoons) unsalted
vegan butter block

225g (1 cup + 2 tablespoons)
caster (superfine) or
granulated sugar

75g (3½ tablespoons) golden
syrup [1]

½ teaspoon salt

200g (1½ cups) salted roasted
peanuts

### Chocolate shell

500g (17½oz) 60–70% melted
dark chocolate

15–20g (1–1½ tablespoons)
coconut oil (optional)

flaky salt (optional)

With a fudgy, chocolate-brownie base, a chewy-gooey caramel layer studded
with salted peanuts and a crisp dark-chocolate shell, these bars are outrageously
delicious. I've optimized the recipe to give you the best possible flavours and
textures – so you'd never guess that these are dairy-free.

There are two heating stages when making the caramel in this recipe: the first
temperature determines the depth of caramelization and therefore the flavour,
and the second temperature determines the texture of the final caramel – how
hard or soft it'll be once cooled.

*This recipe follows the rules for adapting brownies on page 62 – use them to
adapt this recipe to any free-from variation.*

### Chocolate brownies

1. Adjust the oven rack to the middle position, pre-heat the oven to 160°C/325°F and line
a 23cm (9in) square baking tin with baking paper (leave some overhang, which will help
you with removing the brownies from the tin later on).

2. In a large heatproof bowl, either on the stovetop above a pot of simmering water or
in the microwave, melt the chocolate and butter together. Allow to cool until warm.

3. Add the light brown sugar and caster (superfine) or granulated sugar to the warm
chocolate-butter mixture and whisk well to combine.

4. Add the eggs, one at a time, whisking well after each addition, until smooth and glossy.
Add the vanilla and whisk to combine.

5. Sift in the flour, cocoa powder and salt, and whisk well until you get a smooth brownie
batter with no flour clumps.

6. Transfer to the prepared tin, smooth out the top and bake for about 16–18 minutes or
until an inserted toothpick comes out with some half-baked batter and moist crumbs
attached. Allow to cool completely in the baking tin. [2]

### Salted caramel peanut layer

1. In a saucepan on the stovetop or in a microwave-safe bowl in the microwave, heat the
cream and half of the butter together until hot and all the butter has melted. Set aside
until needed, making sure that the mixture stays warm.

2. In another saucepan, combine the sugar and golden syrup, and cook over medium–high
heat with frequent stirring until the mixture becomes a deep amber colour and reaches
160–170°C/320–340°F.

3. Remove from the heat, pour in the cream mixture and stir well until combined. Be
careful: adding the cream will release lots of hot steam and it might bubble up violently.

4. Return to the heat and cook with constant stirring until the mixture reaches 112–116°C/
235–240°F. Immediately remove from the heat and stir in the remaining butter and the
salt. [3]

5. Allow the caramel to cool until it reaches 60–70°C/140–160°F; it should be thicker but
still pourable.

→

## Notes

[1] Golden syrup helps to prevent crystallization, keeping the caramel perfectly smooth and not too hard. If you can't find golden syrup, use light corn syrup instead.

[2] These brownies are slightly firmer and denser rather than soft and gooey, so that you can easily slice them once they have the caramel layer on top. They contain more flour and less butter than the brownies on page 142, and are prepared without whipping the eggs and sugar together.

[3] In the 112–116°C/235–240°F temperature range, sugar is in the "softball stage". This means that once cooled to room temperature, the caramel will be pleasantly chewy, not too soft nor too hard.

[4] To get a glossy finished look on your chocolate-dipped bars with no white streaks ("blooming"), temper your chocolate. Melt about ¾ of the chocolate, finely chop up the remainder and add it to the melted. Mix to melt both together. This is the "seeding method", where the chopped chocolate (in temper) encourages the melted chocolate to crystallize correctly, to give a glossy finish with a "snap" to it. Make sure that your chocolate is cooled to about 30–32°C (86–90°F) before you start Step 4.

## Storage

3–4 days in an airtight container in the fridge. Allow to stand at room temperature for about 10–15 minutes before serving (straight from the fridge, the caramel is quite firm).

6. Add the salted roasted peanuts and mix well until they're evenly distributed throughout the caramel, then pour it over the cooled brownies and smooth out the top to create a fairly even layer.

7. Allow the caramel to cool to room temperature and then chill in the fridge for at least 2 hours to set.

### Assembling the bars

1. Line a large tray or baking sheet with cling film, baking paper or foil.

2. Remove the chilled brownies from the baking tin and slice them into twelve 11.5x4cm (4½x1½in) bars – slice them in half in one direction and into 6 in the other direction.

3. If your melted chocolate is too thick and viscous, add about 1–1½ tablespoons of melted coconut oil to loosen it up. You want to be able to achieve an even, fairly thin layer of chocolate on the bars. Ideally, use tempered chocolate at around 30–32°C (86–90°F). [4]

4. Dip the bars, one at a time, in the melted chocolate. Make sure that all sides are covered in chocolate. Shake off as much excess chocolate as you can – you want to get a thin chocolate coating (a thick shell can be a bit too hard when you bite into it).

5. Transfer the chocolate-covered bars on to the lined tray or baking sheet. As the bars are cold, the chocolate should set fairly quickly. (Optional: you can pipe any leftover melted chocolate in a zig-zag pattern on top of the bars and sprinkle on some flaky salt.)

6. Chill the chocolate-covered bars in the fridge for at least 30 minutes before serving.

# Double chocolate chip cookies

**Makes 12  /  Prep time 30 mins  /  Chill time 1 hour  /  Bake time 12 mins (x2)**

150g (1 stick + 2½ tablespoons)
  unsalted vegan butter block,
  melted and cooled until warm
150g (¾ cup) light brown
  soft sugar
50g (¼ cup) caster (superfine)
  or granulated sugar
½ teaspoon vanilla paste
  (or 1 teaspoon vanilla extract)
1 medium egg (US large),
  room temperature
180g (1½ cups) plain (all-purpose)
  flour
30g (¼ cup + 1 tablespoon)
  Dutch-processed cocoa
  powder
1 teaspoon baking powder
½ teaspoon bicarbonate of soda
  (baking soda)
½ teaspoon salt
140g (5oz/about ¾ cup) roughly
  chopped 60–70% dark
  chocolate or dark chocolate
  chips

### Note

[1] If you prepare the cookie dough in advance and chill it overnight, your cookies will spread less during baking and they'll be slightly thicker – this is ideal if you're a fan of cookies with crisp edges and a gooey, slightly underbaked centre. For thinner cookies, bake them on the same day.

### Storage

1 week in an airtight container in a cool, dry place.

**Chocoholics, rejoice. These cookies taste like brownies in cookie form – they're luxurious and ultra-chocolatey. They're quite thick (even if you bake them after just 1 hour of chilling), which ensures that they stay fudgy-gooey in the centre with deliciously crisp edges, especially when they're still warm from the oven. If you want to get those gorgeous, glossy puddles of chocolate on top of the baked cookies, top the dough balls with large chunks of chopped chocolate (rather than smaller chocolate chips) before baking.**

*This recipe follows the rules for adapting cookies that spread during baking on page 66 – use them to adapt this recipe to any free-from variation.*

1. In a large bowl, using a stand mixer fitted with the paddle or a hand-held mixer with the double beaters, or by hand using a large balloon whisk, mix together the vegan butter, both sugars and vanilla until well combined. You don't need to cream the mixture or incorporate any air into it at this stage.

2. Add the egg and whisk for a few minutes until the mixture has lightened in colour and is slightly fluffy.

3. Whisk together the flour, cocoa powder, baking powder, bicarbonate of soda (baking soda) and salt, and add them to the butter-sugar mixture. Mix well, either by hand with a wooden spoon or rubber spatula or with the stand or hand-held mixer, until you get a smooth and very soft cookie dough with no patches of unmixed flour.

4. Add in most of the chocolate chips or chopped chocolate (reserving some to add on top of the cookies just before baking) and mix well until evenly distributed.

5. Chill the cookie dough in the fridge for at least 1 hour until it's firm enough to scoop. You can also chill the cookie dough for a few hours or overnight. [1]

6. While the cookie dough is chilling, adjust the oven rack to the middle position, pre-heat the oven to 180°C/350°F and line two large baking sheets with baking paper.

7. Use a 3–tablespoon ice-cream or cookie scoop to portion out individual balls of cookie dough. You should get 12 cookies in total.

8. Place 6 cookies on each lined baking sheet. Make sure to leave plenty of space between them (at least 5cm/2in), as they'll spread during baking.

9. Before the cookies go into the oven, add a few extra pieces of chocolate to the top of each cookie dough ball. This will give you gorgeous puddles of melted chocolate on top of the baked cookies (the puddles are better with chopped chocolate than with chocolate chips).

10. Bake the cookies, one baking sheet at a time (keep the other sheet in the fridge while the first is baking), for 11–12 minutes (for very gooey centres) or 13–14 minutes (for fudgier cookies).

11. Immediately out of the oven while the cookies are still soft and malleable, use a round cookie cutter, slightly larger than the cookie diameter, to nudge the cookies into a more perfectly round shape.

12. Allow the cookies to cool on the baking sheet for about 5–10 minutes, then transfer them to a wire rack. Serve warm or cooled to room temperature.

# Blueberry meringue bars

**Serves 12–16 / Prep time 1 hour / Cook time 10 mins / Bake time 50 mins / Chill time 3 hours**

## Shortbread base

180g (1½ cups) plain (all-purpose) flour

75g (¼ cup + 2 tablespoons) caster (superfine) or granulated sugar

¼ teaspoon salt

140g (1¼ sticks) unsalted vegan butter block, cubed and chilled

## Blueberry curd

450g (3½ cups) fresh or frozen blueberries

90g (6 tablespoons) lemon juice, freshly squeezed

250g (1¼ cups) caster (superfine) or granulated sugar

3 medium eggs (US large), room temperature

3 medium egg yolks (US large), room temperature

¼ teaspoon salt

85g (¾ stick) unsalted vegan butter block, cubed

½ teaspoon vanilla paste (or 1 teaspoon vanilla extract)

## Blueberry meringue

12g (½ cup) freeze-dried blueberries

3 medium egg whites (US large)

150g (¾ cup) caster (superfine) or granulated sugar

¼ teaspoon cream of tartar

½ teaspoon vanilla paste (or 1 teaspoon vanilla extract)

These are the blueberry version of the more familiar lemon meringue bars – and they're incredible. If you've never tried blueberry curd before, it's a total revelation. It's refreshing, creamy and rich, and pairs beautifully with the buttery, melt-in-the-mouth shortbread base and the fluffy, marshmallow-like blueberry meringue. The blueberry flavour is added to the meringue in the form of finely ground freeze-dried blueberries, which don't add moisture that could otherwise make the meringue too runny. You can leave the meringue as it is, just swirled or piped on top of the bars, or you can toast it with a kitchen blow torch.

*The shortbread base follows the rules for adapting cookies that hold their shape on page 64 – use them to adapt this recipe to any free-from variation. To make an egg-free/vegan blueberry curd, use the egg-free raspberry curd recipe on page 375, replacing the raspberries with blueberries and using a vegan butter block if needed (but don't bake the egg-free curd in the oven, just pour it over the base and leave to set fully in the fridge). For a vegan meringue recipe, using aquafaba, see page 472.*

### Shortbread base

*You can prepare the shortbread base either by hand or using a food processor.*

1. Adjust the oven rack to the middle position, pre-heat the oven to 180°C/350°F and line a 23cm (9in) square baking tin with baking paper (leave some overhang, which will help you to remove the bars from the tin later on).

2. **By hand:** In a large bowl, whisk together the flour, sugar and salt. Add the cold cubed vegan butter and, using your fingertips, work it into the dry ingredients until you get a breadcrumb-like mixture that clumps together.

3. **With a food processor:** Add the flour, sugar and salt to the bowl of a food processor and pulse a few times to combine. Add the cold cubed vegan butter and pulse until you get a breadcrumb-like mixture that starts clumping together.

4. Transfer the mixture to the lined baking tin and press it down into an even layer, using your hands, the flat bottom of a glass or measuring cup or a small offset spatula.

5. Bake for about 30 minutes or until it's evenly golden brown. Remove from the oven and set aside to cool slightly while you prepare the blueberry curd.

### Blueberry curd

1. Reduce the oven temperature to 160°C/325°F.

2. Add the blueberries to a saucepan and cook them over medium heat until they've completely softened and released their juices.

3. Pass the softened blueberries through a sieve placed over a bowl or jug to collect the juices, you should get about 280–290g (just over 1 cup) of juice in total. Discard the solids left in the sieve.

4. Return the blueberry juices to the saucepan and add the lemon juice. Set aside off the heat until needed.

→

Notes

[1] This process is called "tempering" and it prevents your blueberry curd from splitting or curdling when you cook it.

[2] Heat-treating the blueberry curd twice (first cooking it on the stovetop and then baking it in the oven) gives it a wonderfully creamy yet sliceable texture.

[3] For extra-neat, clean slices, use a sharp knife and dip it into hot water between cuts (wiping it clean and dry before you cut again).

## Storage

Best served on the day of assembling, but you can keep the bars in an airtight container in the fridge for 3–4 days. Note that the meringue will soften slightly with time.

5. In a heatproof bowl, whisk together the sugar, eggs, egg yolks and salt until slightly fluffy and paler in colour. (No need to use a stand or a hand mixer for this – just whisk them together briefly by hand using a balloon whisk.)

6. Cook the blueberry-lemon juice mixture over medium heat until it only just comes to a boil (but don't allow too much moisture to evaporate; remove it from the heat as soon as it starts to bubble).

7. Add the hot blueberry juices to the egg-sugar mixture in a slow drizzle, whisking constantly until you've added all the juices. [1]

8. Return the mixture to the saucepan and cook it over low heat with constant stirring until thickened so that it thickly coats the back of a spoon or spatula. This should take about 5–10 minutes. Don't allow the blueberry curd to come to a boil – you shouldn't see any bubbles forming.

9. Once thickened, remove the curd from the heat and stir in the butter until it's fully melted. Add the vanilla and mix well.

10. Pour the blueberry curd over the shortbread base, smooth out the top and bake for about 20–25 minutes or until the edges have puffed up slightly but the centre is still wobbly when you shake the baking tin. [2]

11. Allow the blueberry bars to cool in the turned-off oven with the oven door ajar until they're at room temperature, then chill them in the fridge for at least 3 hours or preferably overnight.

### Blueberry meringue

*It's best to prepare the meringue and spread it on top of the blueberry bars close to serving, as it can soften slightly with time.*

1. In a food processor, blend the freeze-dried blueberries until they form a fine powder. Sift it to remove any large pieces.

2. Mix together the freeze-dried blueberry powder, egg whites, sugar and cream of tartar in a heatproof bowl above a pot of simmering water. Heat the meringue mixture with constant whisking until it reaches about 70°C/160°F and the sugar has fully dissolved.

3. Remove from the heat, transfer to a stand mixer with the whisk attachment (or use a hand-held mixer with the double beaters) and whisk for 5–7 minutes on high speed, until greatly increased in volume and stiff peaks form.

4. Add the vanilla and whisk until well combined.

### Assembling the blueberry meringue bars

1. Remove the chilled bars from the baking tin and dollop on the blueberry meringue. Spread it all the way to the edges, using a small offset spatula or the back of a spoon to add some decorative swirls and swoops. (Or, you could pipe it on using a piping nozzle of your choice.)

2. Toast the meringue with a kitchen blow torch, if you wish, then slice and serve. [3]

# Creamy mushroom galette

**Serves 4–6 / Prep time 45 mins (excluding pastry prep) / Cook time 20 mins / Bake time 35 mins**

1 batch of **vegan flaky pie dough** (see pages 200–201), chilled for at least 30 minutes before using, or thawed at room temperature for at least 1 hour if frozen

1 medium egg (US large), whisked, for egg wash

flat-leaf parsley or thyme leaves, chopped, to serve

## Mushroom filling

3 tablespoons olive oil, divided

3 red onions, thinly sliced

600g (1¼lb) chestnut or cremini mushrooms, sliced

1 teaspoon thyme leaves (or ½ teaspoon dried thyme)

75g (⅓ cup) vegan cream cheese

salt and pepper, to taste

### Notes

[1] Baking the galette on the lower middle oven rack ensures that the bottom of the pastry will be perfectly crisp and golden, without any sogginess whatsoever.

[2] Rolling out the pie crust and assembling the galette on the sheet of baking paper allows you to simply slide it on to the baking sheet without having to worry about the pastry tearing or cracking.

### Storage

Best served hot or warm, fresh from the oven.

Galettes have everything you know and love about pies, with the advantage of being much easier and more forgiving to make. They're "rustic", which means that it's okay if they're a bit wonky and rough around the edges. It's all part of their charm – along with their buttery, flaky pastry and flavour-packed filling. This savoury version features a rich and creamy mushroom filling (without any dairy!) and it'll be the highlight of any lunch or dinner.

*This recipe follows the rules for adapting flaky pastry on page 72 – use them to adapt this recipe to any free-from variation.*

### Mushroom filling

1. Heat 1½ tablespoons of olive oil in a large frying pan over medium heat. Add the sliced onions and season with salt and pepper. Cook for about 15–20 minutes with frequent stirring, until soft and caramelized. Remove them from the heat, transfer them to a bowl, and allow them to cool completely to room temperature.

2. Heat the remaining olive oil in the frying pan (no need to clean the pan in between) over medium–high heat. Add the sliced mushrooms and thyme, and season with salt and pepper. Cook for 5–10 minutes until softened, most of the moisture released by the mushrooms has evaporated, and the mushrooms only just start to brown. Remove from the heat and transfer to the same bowl as the caramelized onions. Allow to cool completely to room temperature.

3. Once cooled, stir in the vegan cream cheese until well combined and adjust the seasoning as necessary.

### Assembling & baking the galette

1. Adjust the oven rack to the lower middle position and pre-heat the oven to 200°C/400°F. [1] Make sure you have a large baking sheet to hand.

2. If your pie crust has been in the fridge for several hours or overnight, leave it out on the counter at room temperature for about 5 minutes until it's more pliable – that will make it easier to roll out without cracking.

3. Lightly flour a large sheet of baking paper and place the pie crust in the centre. Roll out the pastry into a rough circle, about 32–36cm (13–14in) in diameter. You can trim the edges to achieve a more perfectly round shape if you wish, but it's not essential. [2]

4. Arrange the mushroom filling in the centre of the rolled-out pie crust in an even layer, leaving a 5cm (2in) border around the edge.

5. Fold the edges of the pie crust over the filling, overlapping the pastry as necessary. Brush the pie crust with the whisked egg.

6. Trim the baking paper if necessary, so that it'll fit on to the baking sheet. Slide the assembled galette together with the baking paper on to the baking sheet.

7. Bake for 35–40 minutes until the pastry is puffed up and golden brown.

8. Transfer to a wire rack and allow to cool for 5–10 minutes before serving. Garnish with some chopped parsley or thyme, if you wish.

# Lemon poppy seed "buttermilk" pancakes

**Makes 12 pancakes / Prep time 10 mins / Cook time 20 mins**

260g (1 cup + 2 tablespoons) unsweetened plain or Greek-style vegan yogurt, room temperature

135g (½ cup + 1 tablespoon) dairy-free milk, room temperature [1]

20g (4 teaspoons) lemon juice

75g (¼ cup + 2 tablespoons) caster (superfine) or granulated sugar

zest of 2 unwaxed lemons

270g (2¼ cups) plain (all-purpose) flour

20g (2 tablespoons) poppy seeds

1 teaspoon baking powder

1 teaspoon bicarbonate of soda (baking soda)

½ teaspoon salt

2 medium eggs (US large), room temperature

40g (3 tablespoons) unsalted vegan butter block, melted and cooled until warm, plus extra for cooking

½ teaspoon vanilla paste (or 1 teaspoon vanilla extract)

maple syrup, honey, fresh berries or vegan yogurt, for serving

### Notes

[1] Avoid canned coconut milk, as it can make the pancakes too greasy and dense.

[2] Keeping the pancake batter fairly lumpy is key to perfectly thick and fluffy American-style pancakes (see pages 237–8).

### Storage

Best served warm, immediately after cooking, but they stay soft and fluffy for a few hours afterward. Or, keep them tightly covered with cling film or foil (or in an airtight container) until the next day, then microwave them for a few seconds to return them to their fluffy texture.

**These lemon poppy seed pancakes are a fun and delicious take on the classic, with plenty of zest in the pancake batter, along with a couple of tablespoons of poppy seeds. I'm using lemon juice instead of apple cider vinegar to make a quick homemade vegan buttermilk here, to really amp up the fresh lemon flavour.**

*This recipe follows the rules for adapting fluffy pancakes on page 79 – use them to adapt this recipe to any free-from variation.*

1. In a bowl or jug, whisk together the vegan yogurt, dairy-free milk, and lemon juice to make the vegan buttermilk. Set aside until needed.

2. Add the sugar and lemon zest to a large bowl and use your fingertips to rub the zest into the sugar. This helps to release the essential oils from the lemon zest and it'll make your pancakes extra fragrant.

3. Add the flour, poppy seeds, baking powder, bicarbonate of soda (baking soda) and salt to the lemon-sugar, and whisk until well combined.

4. Add the eggs, melted vegan butter and vanilla to the vegan "buttermilk" and whisk until well combined.

5. Add the wet ingredients to the dry and, with a rubber spatula or a wooden spoon, mix everything together until only just combined – your batter should be slightly lumpy, not completely smooth for perfect American-style pancakes. [2]

6. Heat a frying pan, skillet or griddle over medium–high heat and butter it lightly, wiping away any excess butter with kitchen paper.

7. Dollop the pancake batter on to the frying pan, about ⅓ cup per pancake. You can cook several pancakes at once, depending on the size of your pan.

8. Cook the pancakes for about 2–2½ minutes, or until you see bubbles appearing on the top surface, the edges are set and the bottom is a golden-brown colour. (Adjust the heat as needed, depending on how quickly the pancakes are cooking.)

9. Flip the pancakes and cook them for a further 2–2½ minutes, or until the other side is golden brown as well.

10. Transfer the cooked pancakes to a platter or wire rack and continue with the rest of the batter (be sure to butter the pan or griddle before you start cooking the next batch of pancakes). The recipe makes about 12 pancakes, depending on their size.

11. Serve warm with toppings of choice, such as maple syrup, honey, fresh fruit or a dollop of vegan yogurt.

# Burnt Basque cheesecake

**Serves 10–12 / Prep time 20 mins / Bake time 50 mins**

750g (3⅓ cups) vegan cream cheese, room temperature [1]

200g (1 cup) caster (superfine) or granulated sugar

5 medium eggs (US large), room temperature

1 teaspoon vanilla paste (or 2 teaspoons vanilla extract)

350g (1½ cups) vegan double (heavy) cream, room temperature [2]

55g (½ cup) cornflour (cornstarch)

#### Notes

[1] Use a vegan cream cheese with a low water content (it shouldn't be too watery) and a texture that's as close as possible to that of dairy (full-fat) cream cheese (see page 316).

[2] Or an equal weight of coconut cream. To skim off your coconut cream, place a couple of cans of full-fat coconut milk in the fridge overnight – the contents will separate into thick coconut cream and coconut water. Remove only the cream part to use. Heat it on the stovetop or in the microwave until fully melted, then cool until lukewarm and use as per the recipe.

[3] Mixing the starch into a small amount of cream first ensures that you won't get any clumps in your final cheesecake batter.

#### Storage

4–5 days in an airtight container in the fridge. You can serve it chilled directly from the fridge or allow it to come to room temperature first.

**This is one of the easiest (it not the easiest) cheesecakes you can possibly make – and definitely one of the most delicious. Basque cheesecake was developed by Santiago Riviera of La Viña in San Sebastián, Spain. It's known for its deeply caramelized, almost burnt top and a barely set, extremely creamy centre, which is achieved by baking it at a very high temperature. It's typically very dairy-heavy, with lots of cream cheese and cream in the batter, so it's honestly shocking just how delicious the dairy-free version is.**

**For the best results, choose the correct dairy-free ingredients (see pages 313–17) and increase the amount of starch in the recipe (compared to a regular version) to absorb some of the extra moisture from your chosen alternatives. Without the extra starch, your cheesecake can end up almost watery and with a split, curdled texture. But if you get those two things right, it will be perfectly rich and creamy, with a dramatically caramelized, deep amber crust.**

*This recipe follows the rules for adapting baked cheesecake on page 82 – use them to adapt this recipe to any free-from variation.*

1. Adjust the oven rack to the middle position and pre-heat the oven to 220°C/425°F. Butter the bottom and sides of a 20cm (8in) springform tin (at least 7cm/2¾in deep). Crumple up two large sheets of baking paper and use them to line the tin, so that they extend about 5cm/2in above the rim. Set aside until needed.

2. Add the vegan cream cheese and sugar to a large bowl (or the bowl of a stand mixer). Using a balloon whisk, a hand-held mixer with the double beaters or a stand mixer with the paddle attachment, whisk them together until smooth.

3. Add the eggs, one at the time, whisking well after each addition until well combined. Add the vanilla and whisk well.

4. In a separate bowl, whisk together about one quarter of the vegan double (heavy) cream and the cornflour (cornstarch) until smooth, then pour in the rest of the cream. [3]

5. Add the starch-cream mixture, in a slow stream, to the cheesecake batter, whisking constantly. The final cheesecake batter should be smooth and very runny.

6. Pour the cheesecake batter into the prepared tin (the pan will be fairly full). Gently tap the tin on the work surface a couple of times to get rid of any large trapped air pockets. Make sure that the overhanging baking paper isn't covering any of the batter: all batter should be visible and open to the heat of the oven, which ensures even and intense browning on top of the cheesecake.

7. Place the tin on a large baking sheet (to catch any drips) and bake the cheesecake for about 50–60 minutes or until it's very puffed up (even as much as 2.5–3cm/1–1¼in above the rim of the tin), dark brown on top and the edges are set, but the middle is still wobbly when you gently shake the tin.

8. Remove the cheesecake from the oven and allow it to cool in the tin to room temperature (it will collapse as it cools, but that's okay). Once it has cooled completely, remove it from the tin. Serve it either at room temperature (for a softer, gooier texture) or chilled from the fridge (for a more firmly set texture).

# Chapter

# 7

# Ef

## Egg-free

# Replacing Eggs: Overcoming the Obstacle

Eggs are, without a doubt, the trickiest ingredient to eliminate from and replace in any recipe. And that's because they play so many incredibly important roles: from being a source of moisture and structure to providing lift and aeration.

It should therefore come as no surprise that we need to get a bit creative when it comes to egg-free baking. But don't worry, while it is slightly trickier, replacing eggs is still very much possible – you just need to go about it in a systematic (and scientific) way.

## Egg = egg white + egg yolk

Yes, I know that you know that an egg is composed of an egg white and an egg yolk. Still, I wanted to emphasize this (very obvious) fact because it's at the very core of successfully converting recipes to be egg-free. You have to treat the yolks and the whites as separate ingredients – because they have very different properties and they contribute different things to a bake. And, often, it's just one of them (usually the egg white) that you actually need to focus on and replace with another ingredient or ingredients.

And this is true in baking even when you're not looking to eliminate eggs from a recipe. Consider, for example, a recipe that includes one egg – say, a cookie recipe that makes 12 cookies. And you want to halve it. But how exactly do you halve an egg?

To repeat something that I said many, many pages ago, way back at the start of the book (but that is so worth repeating here): many would say that you should whisk the egg yolk and egg white together, and measure out half of that mixture. Here's the problem with that: how do you know that the mixture you've measured out contains the yolk and the white in the right proportion, so as to be representative of the egg as a whole? You don't, not really. Many times, your halved mixture will contain a larger proportion of either the egg yolk or the egg white.

Instead, separate the egg into the yolk and the white, and measure out half of each. (Ideally with a digital food scale, for absolute precision.) Voilà! You can now make only 6 cookies, knowing that they'll have the perfect texture and flavour, indistinguishable from those of the original recipe for a dozen cookies.

# The Many Functions of an Egg

Eggs are an incredibly complex ingredient and, at first glance, trying to understand what they contribute to a bake and how to replace them can seem rather overwhelming. But if we break this process down into analyzing the egg white and the egg yolk separately, and use the concept of the four ingredient categories introduced in Chapter 2 (see page 38), it all becomes much more manageable and straightforward. (Note that the following is just a very simplistic overview – for example, egg yolks can also provide some lift, but it's significantly less than that provided by the egg whites, so we can ignore it.)

## Egg whites provide structure, lift and moisture

Egg whites are a structure-providing and aerating (lift-providing) ingredient, as well as a moisture source. They give structure or a framework to a bake, which prevents it from collapsing, losing shape and being too crumbly. They also add a certain degree of elasticity and flexibility. As an aerating ingredient, they make bakes fluffy – which is true even if you incorporate them as they are, without first whipping them up. Of course, if you do whip them up (with or without sugar) until they've greatly increased in volume and can hold either a soft or a firm peak, you trap a huge amount of air in them and maximize their aerating capabilities. And then, when you fold them into a batter, for example, all these tiny air pockets get incorporated into the batter, which makes it extra fluffy and light, and that will, in turn, result in a much airier, softer and fluffier final bake. As a source of moisture, egg whites prevent bakes from being too dry (especially in the case of cakes, cupcakes, muffins and brownies) and they help to bind ingredients into a workable dough (in the case of cookies and shortcrust pastry).

## Egg yolks are tenderizing and provide moisture

In many ways, egg yolks are the exact opposite of egg whites. While egg whites provide structure, egg yolks behave much like butter and other fats in that they make bakes more tender and delicate, and they give them that delicious melt-in-the-mouth quality that we love in everything from cakes to cookies. In effect, they destroy some of the framework that the egg whites (and the flour) give to bakes. Additionally, because of their fat content, egg yolks provide a certain richness – although we can often ignore that when it comes to replacing them in egg-free baking, simply because their contribution in this sense is negligible in comparison to that made by butter or oil.

## Whites vs yolks: who's in charge?

While both egg whites and egg yolks act as sources of moisture, egg whites are far more important in that respect. That's because egg whites make up about ⅔ of the weight of an egg and they're about 90% water (the rest is mostly protein) whereas the egg yolks' water content is only about 50% (the rest is fat and protein).

As a general rule, when you're adapting recipes to be egg-free, you mostly have to focus on replacing the egg whites. That's because, on balance, the effects of the egg whites are far more significant.

There are exceptions to this, of course. Most notably, egg yolks are crucial when it comes to making any sort of pastry cream or curd (where egg whites are actually only rarely used). In such cases, we're mostly interested in the egg yolks' thickening capabilities and the richness that they bring. You can find my go-to recipes for egg-free pastry cream on page 476 and egg-free lemon curd on page 478.

> **NOTE**
>
> Both egg whites and egg yolks are important in the egg wash that you use for glazing pastry or enriched bread before baking. You can read all about the various egg-free egg wash options on page 359.

# The Egg-replacement Conundrum

I'm just going to put this out there: I'm not a fan of so-called "egg replacements". You know which ones I mean – the one-size-fits-all substitutes like chia "eggs", flax "eggs", mashed bananas or apple sauce. Don't get me wrong: some of these are valuable ingredients in their own right – instead, my problem is with the very concept of a singular "egg replacement".

As I'm sure you've realized by now, the functions that eggs play in baking are numerous, varied and all very important. The problem with all these "egg replacements" is that they mostly focus on just one or two of these functions (usually the structure-providing and the moisture parts) and ignore the others, usually to the detriment of the texture of your bake.

For example, chia and flax eggs are binders that also provide moisture (they're like a slightly weaker form of a psyllium gel; see pages 266–8) but they don't provide any lift or aeration. Mashed bananas and apple sauce, on the other hand, are mostly just moisture sources – so they really only fulfil one of the three main functions of an egg in baking.

What's more, both mashed bananas and apple sauce will noticeably change the flavour of your bakes, and that's something you want to avoid when it comes to successful recipe modification. Whenever you're adapting any recipe to be any kind of free-from, the aim should always be to make your bake as similar to the original as possible, in texture, appearance and flavour. If you replace eggs in a vanilla cake with mashed bananas... well, all of the sudden you're making a banana-flavoured cake instead.

I've had mixed results with chia and flax eggs. They can have a tendency to give bakes a somewhat gloopy, gluey texture, which isn't a huge problem with fudgy brownies or gooey chocolate chip cookies, but can be annoying with bakes like cakes, cupcakes and muffins. That's why I don't use them in my egg-free and vegan baking, although I know that some bakers have achieved great results with them.

Instead of using any of the popular "egg replacements", my method for creating egg-free recipes relies on understanding the roles that eggs play in a recipe and then mimicking that same effect primarily by adjusting the quantities of the other ingredients already present, or by adding extra ingredients if necessary. All these adjustments vary depending on the specific type of bake I'm making.

Yes, I'm sorry to say that there's really no such thing as a one-size-fits-all egg replacement. But don't worry: that doesn't mean that replacing eggs is in any way scary or impossible. As I said at the start of this chapter, it just means that we need to go about it in a systematic and scientific manner. The rules for adapting recipes in Chapter 3 and the case studies in Chapter 4 will help you, and we'll also look at all the various different bakes and the roles that eggs play in them in the next few sections. But, first, over the page you'll find a general overview on replacing eggs, and then we'll look at them bake by bake.

# Replacing eggs: a (very) general overview

In the table below, you'll find a brief overview of the main functions that eggs carry out in bakes and the alternative ingredients you can use to achieve the same or a similar effect. It's important to keep in mind that, in most cases, you need to use a combination of several ingredients that mimic different egg functions to get the best possible result.

A small disclaimer: this table specifically applies to baked recipes – cakes, cookies, brownies, pastry and so on. The table doesn't apply to things like pastry cream and curds (for these, see page 357), meringue and meringue-based frostings (page 358) or egg wash (page 359).

| Egg function | Replacement ingredients |
| --- | --- |
| Structure | Regular wheat flour or gluten-free flour blend, binders (xanthan gum) |
| Aeration (lift) | Raising agents (baking powder), apple cider vinegar or lemon juice* |
| Moisture | Water, milk, yogurt |

* Note that you don't mix the baking powder and the vinegar or lemon juice together before adding them to the recipe. Instead, you add the extra baking powder to the dry ingredients and the vinegar or lemon juice to the wet ingredients.

Noticeably, the table makes no mention of the tenderizing effect of the egg yolks. That's because that effect is only minor compared to that of fats (butter or oil) present in a recipe. So, to make the process of recipe modification more straightforward, you can ignore it.

## Structure

This may sound odd, but for structure the best egg substitute is just a bit of extra flour. In most regular baking recipes, eggs and flour are the two main structure-providing ingredients. And in the absence of the former, it makes sense to increase the latter. This simple modification works incredibly well in everything from cakes to brownies. For example, adding the extra flour prevents egg-free cakes from collapsing and becoming stodgy, and with egg-free brownies the extra flour ensures that they won't turn into a gloopy chocolate soup.

## Aeration (lift)

Making up for the loss of the aeration and lift that would've been provided by the eggs is just as straightforward: you need to increase the amount of the chemical raising agents (usually baking powder) and, to boost their activity even further, add an acidic ingredient such as apple cider vinegar or lemon juice. This reacts with the baking powder to result in an increased evolution of gases. And that, in turn, makes your bakes much softer and fluffier. But don't worry: the amount of vinegar you need to add is very small, only about ½ teaspoon per egg removed, so you can't actually taste it in the final, baked product.

Now, I've already mentioned this in the footnote to the table above but *don't mix the baking powder and the vinegar or lemon juice together before you add them to the batter!* I've seen this done far too many times and it never fails to both horrify and amuse me.

Mixing the baking powder and the vinegar or lemon juice together in a bowl or cup until the mixture starts frothing and bubbling before you add it to the batter destroys all the activity of the baking powder before you actually need it. All that lovely bubbling and frothing is the baking powder reacting with the acidic vinegar or lemon juice to release gas – and that's something you want to happen in the batter, in the oven. So, if you mix the two together beforehand, you lose all those gases that make your bakes light and fluffy, and all that will remain for you to add to the batter are the products of the acid-base reaction: water and salt.

Instead, here's what you should do to guarantee the best possible egg-free result: add the baking powder to the dry ingredients, mix the vinegar or lemon juice into the wet ingredients, and only then combine everything together as per the recipe.

### Moisture

There are three main alternative moisture sources to choose from: water, milk and yogurt. Depending on what kind of recipe you're making, sometimes one of these will perform better than the others because of the differences in their consistency and viscosity. In most cases, both milk and yogurt will work great – the main exception being brownies, where water and milk give much better results. That's because, with brownies, you need the sugar to dissolve in the alternative moisture source to form a highly concentrated sugar syrup (see page 136) and that naturally works best in water or milk. Out of the two, I'll usually choose milk over water, simply because the former adds some extra richness.

### Preserving the recipe yield

It might seem counterintuitive to be adding both a dry ingredient (flour) and a wet ingredient (water, milk or yogurt) to a recipe when you're converting it to be egg-free. But this actually serves two purposes. First, it allows you to achieve the correct balance between structure- and moisture-providing ingredients. And, second, it helps to maintain a similar recipe yield by keeping the amount of batter or dough similar to that of the egg-containing version.

Remember: the aim with modifying recipes to be free-from isn't just to successfully replicate the texture, flavour and appearance of the regular originals. It's also to ensure that your free-from cakes are of a similar height and your free-from cookie recipe gives the same number of cookies, and so on.

## Replacing eggs: bake by bake

Now, this has been just a general overview of the different ingredients that will help you to create egg-free recipes that are nearly indistinguishable from the egg-containing equivalents. But because the role of eggs varies so much depending on the exact bake you're making (cakes, cookies, brownies, pastry and so on), it's best to look at all the various recipe categories individually.

# Cakes, Cupcakes & Muffins

| Egg function | Adjustments (per egg removed) |
|---|---|
| **Structure** | Add 20g (2½ tablespoons) of flour |
| **Aeration (lift)** | Add ¼ teaspoon of baking powder and ½ teaspoon of apple cider vinegar* |
| **Moisture** | Add 30g (2 tablespoons) of milk or yogurt |

* Note that you don't mix the baking powder and the vinegar together before adding them to the recipe. Instead, you add the extra baking powder to the dry ingredients and the vinegar to the wet ingredients.

In cake, cupcake and muffin recipes, eggs are crucial for ensuring a soft, fluffy texture and plush crumb in the final bake. We need to make quite a few changes to make up for their absence in the egg-free versions.

For the most part, the changes follow our general overview: you need to add extra flour to make up for the absence of the structure-providing egg whites, increase the amount of wet ingredients (milk or yogurt) to account for the loss of moisture, and add some baking powder and vinegar to make the cakes, cupcakes or muffins nicely soft and fluffy.

## Preparation method

The preparation method is just as important. Specifically, when it comes to egg-free cake, cupcake and muffin recipes, it's better to use melted rather than softened butter (along with oil, if using) as well as a simple wet+dry mixing method, which is a variation of the all-in-one mixing method (see page 98). Here, you combine all the dry ingredients in one bowl, all the wet ingredients in another bowl, and then gently whisk them together into a smooth, runny batter with no flour clumps – being very careful not to over-mix it.

**NOTE**

**Using melted butter (or using oil) gives you a highly fluid, very runny batter that rises very easily in the oven and will give you an airier, fluffier crumb in egg-free cakes, cupcakes and muffins (compared to softened butter, which would give a thicker, stiffer batter).**

This method avoids excessive gluten development, which is a greater issue for egg-free cakes, cupcakes and muffins compared to their egg-free equivalents. That's because milk and yogurt, as alternative moisture sources, are much better at promoting gluten development in regular wheat flour than eggs are. Because the wet+dry mixing method requires less mixing than the standard and the reverse creaming methods, the gluten development is greatly reduced (see also page 99).

There are some exceptions to the general rules in the table above:

- **Cakes, cupcakes and muffins that contain acidic ingredients in the batter, such as lemon juice (or other citrus juice), buttermilk or coffee** You don't need to add any vinegar, just the extra baking powder. The acidity already present in the batter is sufficient to increase the activity of the raising agents.

- **Chocolate cakes, cupcakes and muffins with melted chocolate in the batter** You don't need to add the extra baking powder or the vinegar because of the natural acidity and tenderizing effects of the chocolate.

- **Swiss rolls and sponge cakes that rely on whipped eggs or egg whites for their texture** Read on!

# Swiss Rolls

| Egg function | Adjustments (per egg removed) |
|---|---|
| Structure | Add 10g (1½ tablespoons) of flour. Also, add ½ teaspoon of xanthan gum per 120g (1 cup) of flour in the recipe |
| Aeration (lift) | Add ⅛ teaspoon of baking powder and ¼ teaspoon of apple cider vinegar* |
| Moisture | Add 40g (2½ tablespoons) of milk and 15g (2½ teaspoons) of condensed milk (and reduce the sugar by half of the total weight of condensed milk) |

*Note that you don't mix the baking powder and the vinegar together before adding them to the recipe. Instead, you add the extra baking powder to the dry ingredients and the vinegar to the wet ingredients.

Swiss rolls are a tricky bake to make egg-free because you want the sponge to be not only soft and fluffy but also flexible enough so that you can roll it up with minimal (or, ideally, no) cracking. With regular, egg-containing Swiss rolls, it's the eggs that give the sponge this flexibility – with egg-free Swiss rolls, on the other hand, we need quite a few tricks up our sleeve to achieve a similar result.

## Structure and flexibility

Just like with buttery cakes on the previous page, we need to increase the amount of the only other structure-providing ingredient present (the flour), but that doesn't actually improve the sponge's elasticity. Instead, it's the xanthan gum that provides some extra flexibility – it's rarely used outside of the realm of gluten-free baking but it's absolutely indispensable when it comes to making egg-free Swiss rolls (see page 116).

## Aeration and lift

To achieve the aeration and lift that regular Swiss rolls get from the whipped eggs or egg whites, you might think that aquafaba is the obvious choice – after all, you can whip it up just like egg whites. However, while whipped eggs and egg whites maintain much of their structure and fluffiness after they've been incorporated into the batter and throughout baking, aquafaba is quick to collapse, especially in contact with fat and once it enters the hot oven. It's simply not as stable and sturdy as whipped eggs. Instead, it's best to use the combination of baking powder and vinegar that we've discussed previously.

## Moisture

For moisture, use a combination of milk and condensed milk. The former acts simply as a moisture source, whereas the latter also contributes some much-needed extra structure and flexibility – possibly due to its "sticky" viscosity. Interestingly, the condensed milk doesn't make the sponge gluey or stodgy at all – instead, it's perfectly soft and tender and, thanks to the extra flexibility, easy to handle and roll up with no or minimal cracking.

Because condensed milk is very sweet, you will need to reduce the amount of sugar you use in the recipe to account for the extra sweetness. You can read more about the science behind egg-free Swiss rolls on page 115.

**NOTE**

If you're starting out with a gluten-free Swiss roll and you want to make it egg-free as well, you should use ¾ teaspoon of xanthan gum per 120g (1 cup) of gluten-free flour blend (or ½ teaspoon if your blend already contains binders).

# Brownies

| Egg function | Adjustments (per egg removed) |
|:---:|:---:|
| **Structure** | **For chocolate brownies and blondies**<br>add 20g (3 tablespoons) of cornflour (cornstarch)<br>or cocoa powder per 120g (1 cup) of flour |
| **Aeration (lift)** | Add ⅛ teaspoon baking powder* |
| **Moisture** | Add 40g (2½ tablespoons)<br>of water or milk |

* You can omit the baking powder if you prefer denser, extra-fudgy brownies.

**NOTE**

**If you're starting out with gluten-free brownies and you want to make them egg-free as well, make two further changes: reduce the amount of butter by 30% and use ½ teaspoon of xanthan gum per 120g (1 cup) of gluten-free flour blend (or ¼ teaspoon if your blend already contains binders). For more details, see the gluten-free vegan section of the cocoa brownies case study (page 138).**

In egg-containing brownies (both those that contain melted chocolate and those that contain just cocoa powder), the eggs primarily function as a source of moisture for the sugar to dissolve in. This is what gives you that gorgeous paper-thin, glossy top. They also function as a structure-providing ingredient, although that function is less important as we're aiming for a fudgy, gooey and/or chewy texture – we need just enough structure to help the brownies to set. And, although we're interested in fudgy rather than cakey brownies, the eggs still provide a tiny amount of aeration.

We can easily replace the structure-providing aspect of the eggs by increasing the amount of flour in the recipe, and a small amount of baking powder will prevent the brownies from being too dense (although you can omit it if you prefer extra fudgy, dense brownies). Specifically for chocolate brownies that contain melted chocolate in the batter, you also need to add 20g (3 tablespoons) of cornflour (cornstarch) or cocoa powder per 120g (1 cup) of flour in the recipe. This helps to deal with the extra fat you introduce when you add the melted chocolate, and ensures that the brownies come out of the oven fudgy without being greasy or oily.

Water or milk acts as an alternative moisture source. To get the sugar to fully dissolve in either one of them, create a simple sugar syrup by heating the water or milk together with the sugar until the sugar is fully dissolved (alternatively, just pour boiling hot water or milk over the sugar and mix until it dissolves). For more details, check out the cocoa brownie case study (see page 136) and the recipes on pages 140 and 142.

Using a sugar syrup as an egg replacement works incredibly well, giving the brownies a gorgeous fudgy, gooey texture and a stunning shiny, crinkly top. Both water and milk work great for the syrup, but milk adds slightly more richness and depth of flavour to the final bake. If you're a fan of the chocolate-coffee combination, you could use hot brewed coffee instead. However, avoid using dairy milk to make the sugar syrup when your recipe uses only brown sugar – the acidic molasses in the brown sugar will cause your milk to split and curdle.

## Preparation method

This is very similar for both egg-free chocolate and cocoa-only brownies: you make the sugar syrup using water or milk, add the melted butter and melted chocolate (if using), sift in the dry ingredients, whisk everything together into a glossy brownie batter, and bake.

# Cookies

| Egg function | Adjustments (per egg removed) |
|---|---|
| **Structure** | **For cut-out cookies**<br>Add 10g (1½ tablespoons) of cornflour (cornstarch) per 120g (1 cup) of flour |
| **Aeration (lift)** | / |
| **Moisture** | **For cookies that hold their shape**<br>Add 40g (2½ tablespoons) of milk<br><br>**For cookies that spread**<br>Add 50g (3½ tablespoons) of milk or yogurt<br><br>**For cakey cookies**<br>Add 40g (2½ tablespoons) of milk |

In cookies, eggs function primarily as a source of moisture that helps to bind all the other ingredients (usually butter, sugar, and dry ingredients such as flour, raising agents and salt) together into a workable dough. This is easily replicated in egg-free cookies by adding some milk or yogurt instead.

The eggs do provide a small amount of structure, but it's largely negligible considering the high proportion of the structure-providing flour in the cookie dough. The structure-providing aspect is only really relevant with cut-out cookies, where eggs help to control the shape and the spread. In the egg-free version, a small amount of cornflour (cornstarch) or another starch helps to achieve a similar effect – adding just 10g (1½ tablespoons) of cornflour (cornstarch) per 120g (1 cup) of flour ensures that cut-out cookies hold their shape beautifully in the oven and that they maintain their straight, neat edges, which is ideal when making something like sugar cookies for decorating.

**NOTE**

If you're starting out with gluten-free cookies and you want to make them egg-free as well, you may need a slightly large amount of xanthan gum – refer to the relevant rules for adapting recipes and case studies in chapters 3 and 4, respectively.

# Shortcrust Pastry

| Egg function | Adjustments (per egg removed) |
| :---: | :---: |
| Structure | / |
| Aeration (lift) | / |
| Moisture | Add 50g (3½ tablespoons) of milk |

As types of pastry such as flaky pie crust or puff pastry largely don't contain eggs, let's just focus on shortcrust. Just like with cookies, the eggs in shortcrust pastry are primarily a source of moisture that helps to bind all the other ingredients (flour, salt, sugar and butter) together into a workable dough. Milk is an excellent alternative moisture source that produces a delicious pastry with the perfect texture.

However, egg-free shortcrust pastry can sometimes be too tough and/or crunchy – largely because milk and yogurt are better at promoting gluten development than eggs are. To mitigate this, you can replace 20% of the wheat flour with an equal weight of a starch, such as cornflour (cornstarch), arrowroot starch, potato starch or tapioca starch. This will ensure that the egg-free shortcrust pastry has just the right balance between sturdy and melt-in-the-mouth tender.

# Pancakes

| Egg function | Adjustments (per egg removed) |
|:---:|:---:|
| Structure | Add 10g (1½ tablespoons) of flour |
| Aeration (lift) | **For fluffy pancakes**<br>Add ¼ teaspoon of baking powder and<br>½ teaspoon of apple cider vinegar* |
| Moisture | Add 30g (2 tablespoons) of milk |

\* Note that you don't mix the baking powder and the vinegar together before adding them to the recipe. Instead, you add the extra baking powder to the dry ingredients and the vinegar to the wet ingredients.

Making egg-free pancakes requires very similar adjustments to those necessary to make egg-free cakes. For both thin French-style crêpes and American-style fluffy pancakes, you need to add extra flour to make up for the lack of the structure-providing eggs, and to add some extra milk as an alternative moisture source.

However, when it comes to fluffy pancakes, you also need to consider aeration. Even when you add the eggs to pancake batter without any whipping, they contribute to the final fluffy, airy texture. To account for their absence in the egg-free version, you need to add some baking powder and vinegar (the latter isn't necessary for buttermilk pancakes because of the acidity of the buttermilk).

As with egg-free cakes, note that you mustn't mix the baking powder and the vinegar together before you add them to the batter. Instead, add the baking powder to the dry ingredients and the vinegar to the wet ingredients – and then mix the wet with the dry as instructed in the recipe.

# Cheesecake

| Egg function | Adjustments (per egg removed) |
|---|---|
| Structure & thickening/setting | Add 5g (2 teaspoons) of cornflour (cornstarch) |
| Aeration (lift) | / |
| Moisture | Add 20g (1½ tablespoons) of milk and 20g (1½ tablespoons) of yogurt* |

* If you're adapting a dairy-free cheesecake, it's best to use 40g (3 tablespoons) of unsweetened Greek-style vegan yogurt instead (see page 251).

The function of eggs in (baked) cheesecake recipes is slightly different, but it follows a very similar logic to the bakes so far – which might be slightly surprising, considering how different a cheesecake might seem at first glance.

While we talk about the structure-providing function of eggs in bakes like cakes or cupcakes, they play more of a thickening or setting role in cheesecakes. They ensure that the cheesecake isn't too soft or runny, so that you can cut it into neat slices. You can easily achieve the same effect in egg-free cheesecakes by adding a small amount of extra cornflour (cornstarch).

We don't typically think about aeration when it comes to baked cheesecakes – you'd certainly never describe a cheesecake as "fluffy" like you would, for example, a cake or a muffin. However, aeration provided by the eggs in the regular cheesecake batter is still an important consideration. It's what ensures that the cheesecake filling, once baked, isn't too dense or claggy, or like eating straight-up cream cheese. Instead, it's wonderfully creamy and just light enough to be a real pleasure to eat – and that's largely thanks to the aeration provided by the eggs. In fact, if you look closely, you can actually see teeny tiny air pockets visible throughout the filling when you cut a slice.

However, you don't actually need to add any raising agents to the egg-free cheesecake filling to achieve a similar amount of aeration as in an egg-containing cheesecake. Instead, you can get just enough lightness and aeration from the moisture in the other ingredients (cream cheese, yogurt and milk) turning into steam. As you'll see below, this is also why it's best to bake egg-free cheesecakes at a slightly higher oven temperature.

Finally, eggs also provide moisture – and you can replace them by adding milk and/or yogurt. It's best to use a 50:50 mixture of milk and yogurt when making dairy cheesecake, as this will give you an egg-free batter that's closest in texture to the egg-containing equivalent.

## Oven temperature

While I recommend baking egg-containing cheesecakes at quite a low oven temperature of 140°C/275°F to prevent cracking, it's actually better to bake egg-free cheesecakes at 160°C/325°F. Without the eggs, the likelihood of cracking is greatly reduced, and the higher oven temperature will result in the cheesecake puffing up a bit more during baking and therefore give an airier, lighter texture.

# Enriched Bread & Brioche Dough

In enriched bread and brioche recipes, such as cinnamon rolls, burger buns, dinner rolls, doughnuts, babka and similar, eggs are mainly a source of moisture, tenderness and richness. Along with butter (or oil), they make the bread softer and more tender in texture, as well as richer in flavour. Where non-enriched bread (like artisan loaves or baguettes) are chewier with a more robust crumb, enriched bread has a characteristic pillowy, squishy texture – and a lot of that is thanks to the eggs.

You can mimic the effects of the eggs by adding some extra milk and butter (or oil) to the dough. The exact quantities vary slightly depending on whether you're using wheat flour or gluten-free flours, as summarized below.

| Egg function | Adjustments (per egg removed) | |
| --- | --- | --- |
| | **For wheat bread** | **For gluten-free bread** |
| **Moisture** | Add 20g (1½ tablespoons) of milk | Add 30–40g (2–2½ tablespoons) of milk |
| **Richness** | Add 15g (1 tablespoon) of butter (or 12g/ 1 tablespoon of oil) | Add 15g (1 tablespoon) of butter (or 12g/1 tablespoon of oil) |

If your bread recipe calls for egg wash (as many do), take a look at the egg-free egg wash options on page 359.

# Pastry Cream & Curds

In pastry cream and various curds, while some recipes call for the whole egg, it's really the egg yolks that make the recipe work.

The egg yolks carry out three main functions: they're a source of moisture, they're a thickening agent and they add richness. They also help with emulsification, but we won't focus on that here.

Knowing this, the adjustments needed to create egg-free pastry cream and the various curds are very straightforward, as summarized in the table below.

| Egg function | Adjustments (per egg yolk removed) |
|---|---|
| Thickening | Add 5g (2 teaspoons) of cornflour (cornstarch) |
| Moisture | Add 15g (1 tablespoon) of the base liquid (such as milk in pastry cream)* |
| Richness | Add 5–10g (1–2 teaspoons) of butter |

* Note that if you're making lemon curd or a similar curd with a highly acidic ingredient, you need to replace half of the total lemon juice content with an equal amount of water.

## Egg-free pastry cream

To make egg-free pastry cream, just follow the rules in the table and you're good to go. Your pastry cream will turn out perfectly silky smooth and just thick enough – incredibly similar in texture and richness to the egg-containing version.

## Egg-free citrus curd

The presence of large amounts of strong acids (such as lemon juice when making lemon curd) inhibits the thickening power of cornflour (cornstarch), which can make the final texture of the curd far too loose (that is, too runny).

To work around this issue, you need to replace half of the total citrus-juice content with an equal amount of water to raise the pH a bit higher, toward neutrality (that is, use a 50:50 mixture of citrus juice and water instead). This way, your final egg-free citrus curd will be deliciously tart and citrussy with the perfect thick, creamy, smooth and spreadable texture.

## Preparing egg-free creams and curds

Here, you need to follow the same method for most egg-free pastry cream and curd recipes: combine all the ingredients except butter in a saucepan, cook over medium heat until thickened and the mixture comes to a boil, and then cook for at least 30–60 seconds longer. This last step is important because the liquid needs to come to a boil and stay there for a short amount of time for the cornflour (cornstarch) to achieve its full thickening power. Finally, remove the cooked pastry cream or curd from the heat and whisk in the butter.

After you've added the butter, your egg-free pastry cream or curd may initially look split because the fat won't immediately emulsify with the rest of the mixture. But don't worry – just keep on mixing and it'll eventually come together, especially as it cools down.

You can find the recipes for egg-free pastry cream and lemon curd, based on all these tips and guidelines, on pages 476 and 478, respectively.

**NOTE**

Egg yolks also add colour – for example, they give lemon curd its characteristic rich, vibrant golden yellowness. Without the yolks, your curd will be much paler, but you can add a drop or two of food colouring (or, in the case of lemon curd, a pinch of turmeric) to achieve a similar gorgeously appropriate hue, if you wish.

# Meringue & Meringue-based Frostings

There's really only one ingredient that can successfully, reliably and convincingly replace egg whites in meringue and meringue-based recipes. We're talking, of course, about the one and only: aquafaba.

If you're not familiar with it, aquafaba is the viscous water that you get from a can of chickpeas/garbanzos (or you can use the water from cooking your own chickpeas, but you might need to reduce it slightly in that case to make it more concentrated). Aquafaba has the special property in that you can whip it up to create a fairly stable foam, much like you would egg whites. You could use the water from other types of beans, but aquafaba from a can of chickpeas tends to form the most stable foam and it also has the most mellow flavour (so it's easy to mask using flavourings such as vanilla).

The thing that makes aquafaba fluff up is the presence of proteins that are also found in egg whites (albumins and globulins), in addition to saponins, which are naturally occurring compounds found in legumes that also have the ability to form stable, soap-like foams. All of these work together to make aquafaba a truly amazing egg-free alternative to egg whites when it comes to making meringue.

## How much aquafaba?

In general, use about 30g (2 tablespoons) of aquafaba for each egg white you're replacing. And then, use it as you would egg whites: add the sugar and cream of tartar (more on that below) and whip it up, either using a stand mixer fitted with a whisk attachment or a hand-held mixer fitted with the double beaters, until it forms firm, stiff peaks. On average, you need to whip the aquafaba slightly longer than you would egg whites (the exact time will depend on the volume/amount you're using), so I definitely don't recommend doing it by hand.

## Stabilizing the aquafaba meringue

Much like meringue made from egg whites, egg-free aquafaba meringue can be greatly stabilized by adding a small amount of an acidic ingredient such as cream of tartar. Adding about ¼ teaspoon of cream of tartar per 90g (⅓ cup + 1 tablespoon) of aquafaba – which is equivalent to about 3 medium (US large) egg whites – helps the egg-free meringue to hold its shape over a longer period of time with minimal (or no) liquid weeping out of it. This is very important if you're, for example, using it on a dessert that you won't serve straight away or if there are any leftovers that you want to store for a day or two.

## Aquafaba in frostings

I use aquafaba as the basis for the raspberry meringue topping on the egg-free raspberry meringue tart on page 375 and to decorate the gluten-free vegan lemon meringue cake on page 439. It toasts wonderfully with a kitchen blow torch, and it cuts beautifully to give neat slices. I also used it to make a vegan "meringue" buttercream in the vegan tiramisu cupcakes on page 406. You can find the general recipes for egg-free aquafaba meringue and for egg-free aquafaba "meringue" buttercream on pages 472 and 470, respectively.

## Aquafaba's one exception

I don't use whipped aquafaba for folding into cake batters, as you would whipped eggs or egg whites. Whipped aquafaba tends to deflate quite easily when it comes into contact with fat in the presence of heat. Unlike whipped egg whites, aquafaba doesn't add any structure to cakes and similar bakes, so there's nothing to maintain any extra lift or aeration you might get from it. While the batter might look fluffy initially, it will quickly collapse in the oven.

**NOTE**
Unlike egg whites, you don't need to heat-treat aquafaba to make it safe to eat – there's no need to heat it over a pot of simmering water (as you would for Swiss meringue made from egg whites) or to add a hot sugar syrup to it (as you would for Italian meringue made from egg whites). While heating the aquafaba can slightly reduce its beany flavour, the difference is marginal, especially when the flavour is so subtle anyway. I don't find the extra heating step necessary or useful.

# Replacing Egg Wash

The aims behind a regular egg wash are threefold:

- **To promote browning and add a richer golden brown colour to bakes.**

- **To make the crust of enriched breads and brioche (or similar) glossy and shiny.**

- **To ensure that any toppings (such as seeds, flaky salt or sugar) stick to the crust of your bread or pastry.**

There are numerous egg-free egg washes available, and which one you should choose depends on your primary aim – that is, on whether you're primarily interested in the golden brown colour, the shine or the sticking power (or a combination of them). Below, you'll find an overview of the possible egg-free egg washes and their properties.

**Aquafaba** (see opposite) adds only a slight shine to the crust and it has very little effect on the browning or the colour of the bakes. However, it does ensure that any toppings, such as seeds or flaky salt, stick well to the crust even after baking.

**Regular dairy milk** gives a very evenly glossy, shiny crust and it also promotes browning (thanks to the presence of the milk solids). It's great for ensuring that any toppings stick to the crust of your bakes.

**Melted dairy butter** doesn't add any glossiness or shine, but it does promote browning (thanks to the presence of the milk solids). It has no sticking power – any toppings that you sprinkle on top of the bake will easily fall off after baking. However, it does make the crust of enriched bread or brioche much softer.

**Oil, such as sunflower or olive oil,** doesn't add any shine and it also has a negligible effect on the browning. Just like melted butter, it has no sticking power, so I don't recommend using it if you wish any toppings to stick to the crust of your bake. The only real benefit to using oil as an egg wash alternative is that it does make the crust of any enriched bread noticeably softer.

**Mixed aquafaba and condensed milk** is great for adding a slight shine to your bakes and very effectively promotes browning (largely through caramelization rather than the Maillard reaction). It also has great sticking power – any toppings will stay put even after baking. I usually use a mixture of 30g (2 tablespoons) of aquafaba and 20g (1 tablespoon) of condensed milk. With this alternative, keep in mind that condensed milk will add a hint of sweetness, but I personally don't mind it as it's hardly noticeable even on burger buns or dinner rolls. A more important point is that the condensed milk can make the surface of your bakes slightly sticky if you store them in a closed container for a longer period of time.

**Mixed aquafaba and maple syrup** similarly promotes browning through caramelization but it doesn't add much shine or glossiness. It does have great sticking power, but it will add a slight hint of sweetness to the crust of your bakes. I usually use a mix of 30g (2 tablespoons) of aquafaba and 20g (1 tablespoon) of maple syrup.

I've summarized all of this information in the table on the following page, as a handy reference.

| Egg-wash alternative | Shine/ glossiness | Promotes browning | Helps any toppings to stick | Softens the bread crust | Extra notes |
|---|---|---|---|---|---|
| aquafaba | yes | no | yes | no | / |
| dairy milk | yes | yes | yes | no | / |
| melted dairy butter | no | yes | no | yes | / |
| oil | no | no | no | yes | / |
| aquafaba + condensed milk | yes | yes | yes | no | adds a hint of sweetness |
| aquafaba + maple syrup | no | yes | yes | no | adds a hint of sweetness |

It's worth noting that this egg-wash-alternative information applies mostly to pastry and bread recipes that use wheat flour. Wheat-based bread has a natural tendency toward a smooth, golden brown, slightly glossy crust even in the absence of any egg wash – especially if it contains any sort of fat like butter or oil in the dough. Therefore, finding an egg-free egg wash is far more forgiving when you're dealing with wheat flour.

Gluten-free bread, on the other hand, will often form a dull, matte, white-ish crust in the absence of steam and/or an egg wash (or an egg-wash alternative). That's because the crust of the gluten-free bread has a greater tendency to dry out once it encounters the high heat of the oven. Even regular egg wash gives much less shine to gluten-free bread compared to its regular, wheat-containing equivalent – the gluten-free bread will always have a duller and slightly more uneven crust. That means that choosing the best possible egg-wash alternative is both more important and more challenging when it comes to gluten-free bread. You can read more about this in the gluten-free vegan chapter on page 432.

Finally, this section deals specifically with egg-free egg washes – not vegan ones (although there is some crossover between them). For vegan egg washes, see page 397.

Aquafaba

Milk

Melted butter

Oil

Aquafaba & condensed milk

Aquafaba & maple syrup

# Apple crumble cake

Serves 12–16  /  Prep time 1 hour  /  Bake time 1 hour

## Crumble topping

160g (1⅓ cups) plain
(all-purpose) flour
100g (½ cup) light brown
soft sugar
¼ teaspoon salt
115g (1 stick) unsalted butter,
cubed and chilled
90g (¾ cup) walnut halves,
roughly chopped
icing (powdered) sugar, to serve

## Apple layer

800g (1¾lb) sweet-tart, firm
eating apples (about 5 apples)
30g (2 tablespoons) lemon juice
50g (¼ cup) caster (superfine)
or granulated sugar
2 teaspoons ground cinnamon
½ teaspoon ground ginger
¼ teaspoon ground nutmeg

## Cake layer

240g (2 cups) plain (all-purpose)
flour
150g (¾ cup) caster (superfine)
or granulated sugar
2 teaspoons baking powder
1 teaspoon ground cinnamon
¼ teaspoon salt
85g (¾ stick) unsalted butter,
melted and cooled until warm
25g (2 tablespoons) sunflower or
vegetable oil
120g (½ cup) whole milk, room
temperature
75g (⅓ cup) full-fat plain or
Greek-style yogurt, room
temperature
1 teaspoon apple cider vinegar
½ teaspoon vanilla paste (or
1 teaspoon vanilla extract)

This cake comprises three layers of deliciousness: a cinnamon sponge with a plush, buttery crumb, a thick layer of generously spiced, perfectly tender sliced apples, and a crisp, golden crumble on top. It's the ultimate cosy autumn dessert and it's incredibly easy to whip up. The apples get nicely soft (but not mushy) during baking – don't worry if they feel firm when you take them out of the oven because they'll keep cooking in the residual heat. Just make sure they're not crisp: a toothpick or cake tester should be able to easily pass through them.

*The cake part of this recipe follows the rules for adapting buttery cakes on page 52 and the crumble follows the rules for adapting cookies that hold their shape on page 64 – use them to adapt this recipe to any free-from variation.*

### Crumble topping

1. Adjust the oven rack to the middle position, pre-heat the oven to 180°C/350°F and line a 23cm (9in) square baking tin, at least 6cm (2¼in) deep, with baking paper, leaving some overhang (this will help you with removing the cake from the tin later on).

2. In a large bowl, whisk together the flour, light brown sugar and salt.

3. Add the cold butter and, using your fingertips, work it into the dry ingredients until you get a crumbly mixture that clumps together. (You can use a food processor for this step.)

4. Add the chopped walnuts and mix well, using a wooden spoon or spatula, until they're evenly distributed throughout the crumble. Store in the fridge until needed.

### Apple layer

1. Peel and core the apples, then cut them into 4–6mm (⅛–¼in) slices.

2. Add the sliced apples and the lemon juice to a large bowl, and toss them together to ensure that the apple slices are evenly coated with the lemon juice. Set aside until needed.

### Cake layer

1. In a large bowl, whisk together the flour, sugar, baking powder, cinnamon and salt.

2. In a separate bowl or jug, whisk together the melted butter, oil, milk, yogurt, vinegar and vanilla.

3. Add the wet ingredients to the dry and, using a rubber spatula or a wooden spoon, mix everything together into a fairly thick, smooth batter with no flour clumps. [1]

4. Transfer the batter into the lined baking tin and smooth it out into an even layer.

### Assembling the cake

1. Add the sugar, cinnamon, ginger and nutmeg to the sliced apples and toss well until all the apple slices are evenly coated.

2. Arrange the apples in an even layer on top of the batter. [2]

→

Notes

[1] The batter is fairly thick to ensure that the apple layer won't sink. The relatively low proportion of wet ingredients also means that the batter can handle the moisture that the apples release during baking.

[2] It's best to toss the apples with the sugar and spices just before you arrange them on top of the batter so that they don't release too much of their juice, which could make the cake layer below and the crumble above slightly too soggy.

## Storage

3–4 days loosely covered in a cool, dry place (an airtight container would soften the otherwise crisp crumble topping).

3. Sprinkle over the crumble topping, so that it forms an even layer on top of the apple. Don't worry if the cake looks very tall or thick at this point. As the apples soften during baking, the apple layer will become more compacted.

4. Bake the crumble cake for 1 hour to 1 hour 10 minutes, or until the crumble topping is golden brown, there are juices visibly bubbling around the edges of the cake, and an inserted toothpick or cake tester comes out clean and doesn't hit any crisp apple pieces. If the top of the cake starts browning too quickly, cover with a sheet of foil (shiny side up) and continue baking until done.

5. Cool the cake in the baking tin until warm, then carefully remove it from the tin (with the help of the overhanging baking paper) on to a wire rack to cool completely. Dust with some icing (powdered) sugar, slice and serve.

# Strawberry Swiss roll

Serves 10–12 / Prep time 1 hour / Bake time 12 mins / Cool time 1 hour / Chill time 1 hour 20 mins

**Vanilla sponge**

120g (½ cup + 1½ tablespoons)
caster (superfine) or
granulated sugar

45g (3½ tablespoons) sunflower
or vegetable oil

160g (⅔ cup) whole milk, room
temperature

60g (3 tablespoons) condensed
milk

1 teaspoon apple cider vinegar

1 teaspoon vanilla paste (or
2 teaspoons vanilla extract)

160g (1⅓ cups) plain
(all-purpose) flour

1¼ teaspoons baking powder

¼ teaspoon bicarbonate of
soda (baking soda)

¼ teaspoon salt

½ teaspoon xanthan gum

icing (powdered) sugar, for
dusting

**Macerated strawberries**

200g (about 1½ cups)
strawberries, cut into about
1cm (½in) pieces

25g (2 tablespoons) caster
(superfine) or granulated sugar

1 teaspoon lemon juice

½ teaspoon vanilla paste (or
1 teaspoon vanilla extract)

**Whipped cream filling**

175g (¾ cup) double (heavy)
cream, chilled

60g (½ cup) icing (powdered)
sugar

75g (⅓ cup) full-fat cream
cheese, chilled [1]

1 teaspoon vanilla paste (or
2 teaspoons vanilla extract)

**Chocolate ganache glaze**

120g (4¼oz) 60–70% dark
chocolate, chopped, plus
extra shavings to decorate

175g (¾ cup) double (heavy) cream

An egg-free Swiss roll with the perfect swirl and minimal cracking may sound impossible to achieve – but it's actually surprisingly straightforward. In this version, a soft and airy sponge is joined by a fluffy whipped-cream filling, an abundance of juicy strawberries and a glossy, rich dark-chocolate ganache. And to make sure that you get a good dose of strawberry flavour in every single bite, the sponge is also soaked with syrupy strawberry juices.

*This recipe follows the rules for adapting Swiss rolls & sponge cakes on page 58 – use them to adapt this recipe to any free-from variation you wish. In the filling and ganache glaze, you can replace the double (heavy) cream and cream cheese with equal amounts of their vegan equivalents.*

**Vanilla sponge**

1. Adjust the oven rack to the middle position, pre-heat the oven to 160°C/325°F and line a 25x38cm (10x15in) rimmed baking sheet with baking paper (don't grease the paper).

2. In a large bowl, whisk together the sugar, oil, milk, condensed milk, vinegar and vanilla.

3. In a separate bowl, sift together the flour, baking powder, bicarbonate of soda (baking soda), salt and xanthan gum.

4. Add the dry ingredients to the wet and whisk until you get a smooth batter with no flour clumps. Be careful not to over-mix – whisk until all the ingredients are combined and there are no clumps, but for no longer.

5. Transfer the batter to the lined baking sheet and smooth it out into a fairly thin, even layer. Tap it a few times on the counter to make it perfectly level and also to get rid of any large trapped air pockets.

6. Bake for about 12–14 minutes or until the sponge is light golden brown on top, well risen, soft and springy to the touch, and an inserted toothpick or cake tester comes out clean.

7. Immediately out of the oven, dust the top of the sponge with icing (powdered) sugar and cover the baking sheet with a clean tea towel (if your tea towel is fairly thin, use two tea towels on top of each other). Allow the sponge to cool to room temperature or lukewarm – ideally, the temperature of the sponge shouldn't drop below 22°C/72°F. [2]

**Macerated strawberries**

1. Combine the chopped strawberries, sugar, lemon juice and vanilla in a large bowl, and mix well to combine. Cover the bowl and place it on the counter (at room temperature) to macerate for at least 30 minutes or until needed. [3]

**Whipped cream filling**

1. Using a stand mixer fitted with the whisk attachment or a hand-held mixer fitted with the double beaters, whisk together the double (heavy) cream and the icing (powdered) sugar until soft peaks form.

2. In a separate bowl, whisk the cream cheese until it's smooth and looser in texture.

3. Add the cream cheese to the whipped cream along with the vanilla, and whisk until well combined and firm peaks form.

→

## Notes

[1] If you're using a firmer cream cheese (one that comes in block form, not in a tub), soften it at room temperature to make it easier to incorporate for a smoother filling.

[2] Covering the sponge with a tea towel traps some of the moisture within the sponge, making it less likely to crack when you roll it. This method was inspired by the one pioneered by Stella Parks (see page 113).

[3] Maceration is the process where sliced fruit softens and releases its juices with the help of sugar, which is hygroscopic (it attracts water): the sugar draws the moisture out of the fruit. Here, this also amps up the strawberry flavour.

[4] To get neat slices, use a sharp serrated knife that you dip into hot water between slices (wipe it dry before you cut).

## Storage

3–4 days in an airtight container in the fridge.

## Assembling the Swiss roll

1. Drain the syrupy strawberry juices released during the maceration process by transferring the macerated strawberries to a sieve placed over a bowl or a jug. Don't discard the juices!

2. Once the sponge is sufficiently cooled, loosen it from the edges of the baking sheet with an offset spatula or a thin knife.

3. Turn it out on to a large sheet of baking paper, so that the caramelized "skin" side is facing down (it will be on the outside of the rolled Swiss roll). Peel away the baking paper that you used to line the baking sheet.

4. Use a pastry brush to gently brush the sponge with the strawberry juices – be sure to use them all up.

5. Spread the whipped cream filling evenly across the sponge, all the way to the edges, and scatter over the chopped strawberries.

6. Turn the sponge so that a short edge is closest to you. Using the baking paper underneath to help you, roll up the sponge until you get a 25cm (10in) log. Make sure to keep the roll fairly tight from the very beginning, otherwise you'll be left with an empty hole in the centre of your Swiss roll.

7. Wrap the Swiss roll in baking paper and chill it in the fridge for at least 1 hour.

## Chocolate ganache glaze

1. Place the chopped chocolate into a heatproof bowl.

2. In a saucepan on the stovetop or in a microwave-safe bowl in the microwave, heat the double (heavy) cream until it only just comes to a boil, then pour it over the chocolate. Allow to stand for 2–3 minutes, then stir together until smooth and glossy.

3. To achieve a generous layer of ganache on your Swiss roll, it's best to cool it until it's slightly thicker but still pourable (at around 24–25°C/75–77°F). You can use a cold water bath or chill it in the fridge, with occasional stirring, for about 10 minutes.

4. Transfer the chilled Swiss roll to a wire rack and place it over a rimmed baking sheet – this will catch any excess chocolate ganache as it drips off the cake.

5. Pour the ganache over the chilled Swiss roll, making sure that it covers the cake completely. Sprinkle on the chocolate shavings.

6. Chill the glazed and decorated Swiss roll for about 20–30 minutes until the ganache sets and is no longer sticky to the touch, then slice and serve. [4]

# Brown butter cinnamon banana muffins

**Makes 12 / Prep time 30 mins / Cook time 6 mins / Bake time 20 mins**

115g (1 stick) unsalted butter, melted and cooled until lukewarm

3 bananas, mashed (about 350g peeled weight, 1½ cups mashed)

75g (¼ cup + 2 tablespoons) light brown soft sugar

75g (¼ cup + 2 tablespoons) caster (superfine) or granulated sugar

115g (½ cup) unsweetened plain or Greek-style yogurt, room temperature

15g (1 tablespoon) lemon juice

½ teaspoon vanilla paste (or 1 teaspoon vanilla extract)

300g (2½ cups) plain (all-purpose) flour

2½ teaspoons baking powder

1 teaspoon bicarbonate of soda (baking soda)

½ teaspoon salt

## Cinnamon-sugar topping

50g (¼ cup) caster (superfine) or granulated sugar

1 teaspoon ground cinnamon

## Storage

3–4 days in an airtight container in a cool, dry place.

**These muffins taste like a warm, cosy hug. They're perfectly fluffy, with beautifully domed tops and a slightly crunchy, crackly cinnamon-sugar topping. You'll also add a layer of cinnamon sugar to the centre of each muffin, which creates a gorgeous cinnamon-y ribbon and ensures that you'll get plenty of sugar and spice in every single bite.**

*This recipe follows the rules for adapting buttery cakes on page 52 – use them to adapt this recipe to any free-from variation.*

1. Adjust the oven rack to the middle position and pre-heat the oven to 190°C/375°F. Line a 12–hole muffin tin with paper liners.

2. To brown the butter, add the unsalted butter to a saucepan (preferably one with a light-coloured interior that allows you to see the butter changing colour) and cook it over medium–high heat with frequent stirring for about 6–8 minutes in total. The butter will first melt and then start bubbling and foaming. Finally, it will turn amber and smell nutty. You should see specks of a deep brown/amber colour on the bottom of the saucepan (those are the caramelized milk solids).

3. Pour the browned butter into a large bowl (make sure to scrape out all the caramelized milk solids, as they carry the most flavour), and allow it to cool until warm.

4. Add the mashed bananas, light brown sugar, caster (superfine) or granulated sugar, yogurt, lemon juice and vanilla, and whisk well to combine.

5. In a separate large bowl, whisk together the flour, baking powder, bicarbonate of soda (baking soda) and salt.

6. Add the wet ingredients to the dry and use a rubber spatula or a wooden spoon to mix them together into a smooth and fairly thick batter with no flour clumps. Be careful not to over-mix the batter.

7. In a separate small bowl, prepare the cinnamon-sugar topping by mixing together the caster (superfine) or granulated sugar and the ground cinnamon.

8. Fill each muffin liner halfway with the batter and sprinkle about ½ teaspoon of the cinnamon-sugar evenly over it. Divide the remaining batter equally between the 12 muffin liners, filling each to the brim. Sprinkle about ½ teaspoon of the cinnamon-sugar evenly on top of each muffin.

9. Bake for about 20–22 minutes or until well risen, golden brown on top and an inserted toothpick or cake tester comes out clean or with a few moist crumbs attached.

10. Allow the muffins to cool in the muffin tin for about 5–10 minutes, then transfer them out of the tin and on to a wire rack to cool further. Serve warm or at room temperature.

# No-chill blueberry muffin cookies

**Makes 12  /  Prep time 30 mins  /  Bake time 14 mins (x2)**

## Streusel

35g (2½ tablespoons) unsalted butter, softened

25g (2 tablespoons) caster (superfine) or granulated sugar

60g (½ cup) plain (all-purpose) flour

## Blueberry muffin cookies

150g (¾ cup) caster (superfine) or granulated sugar

zest of 1 unwaxed lemon

150g (1 stick + 2½ tablespoons) unsalted butter, softened

½ teaspoon vanilla paste (or 1 teaspoon vanilla extract)

50g (3½ tablespoons) full-fat yogurt, room temperature

240g (2 cups) plain (all-purpose) flour

¾ teaspoon baking powder

¼ teaspoon bicarbonate of soda (baking soda)

½ teaspoon salt

150g (1 cup) blueberries, plus extra for the topping [1]

2–3 tablespoons blueberry jam [2]

### Notes

[1] Avoid frozen blueberries. The extra moisture they release will result in soggy cookies.

[2] Resist the temptation to add too much jam, which can make the cookies spread too much and give them a soggy texture.

[3] Don't leave the cooling cookies on the baking sheet for too long – the condensation that forms beneath them can make them soggy.

## Storage

3–4 days in a loosely covered container in a cool, dry place. The cookies will soften and become slightly cakier with time, as they absorb the moisture from the jam and the blueberries.

Blueberry muffins in cookie form (with jammy, juicy blueberries and a crisp, buttery streusel topping), these aren't your typical chewy-fudgy cookies. They're thicker and cakier with a slight doming, to capture the essence of a muffin top.

As this is a no-chill recipe, you can bake the cookies straight away – but using the correct ingredients in the correct form and quantity is crucial: compared to the egg-free chocolate chip cookie recipe on page 166, this one contains more flour, less raising agent and less white sugar to better control the spread. It uses yogurt to replace the eggs, and softened instead of melted butter to give thicker cookies.

*This recipe follows the rules for adapting cookies that spread during baking on page 66 – use them to adapt this recipe to any free-from variation. The streusel follows the rules for adapting cookies that hold their shape on page 64.*

### Streusel

1. In a bowl, using a rubber spatula or a wooden spoon, mix together the butter and sugar until combined. Add the flour and mix well until you get a crumbly mixture that forms clumps when you press it together. Set aside until needed.

### Blueberry muffin cookies

1. Adjust the oven rack to the middle position, pre-heat the oven to 180°C/350°F and line two large baking sheets with baking paper.

2. Add the sugar and lemon zest to a large bowl or the bowl of a stand mixer, and use your fingertips to rub the zest into the sugar (to release the essential oils from the zest).

3. Add the butter and vanilla, and (by hand with a balloon whisk, or with a stand mixer fitted with the paddle or a hand-held mixer with the double beaters) cream everything together until pale and fluffy. Add the yogurt and mix until combined.

4. In a separate bowl, whisk together the flour, baking powder, bicarbonate of soda (baking soda) and salt.

5. Add the dry ingredients to the butter-sugar mixture, and mix until just combined with no flour streaks. Be careful not to over-mix. The final dough will be fairly soft and sticky.

6. Add the blueberries and, using a wooden spoon or a rubber spatula, gently fold them into the dough until they're evenly distributed throughout.

7. Drop small dollops of the blueberry jam into the dough. Use a wooden spoon or a rubber spatula to fold the dough over once or twice – do not over-mix; you want to keep large, visible streaks of jam in your cookie dough.

8. Use a 3-tablespoon ice-cream or cookie scoop to scoop out 6 cookies per baking sheet (12 in total), leaving plenty of space around them, as they will spread during baking.

9. Top each cookie with one or two extra blueberries and about 1 tablespoon of the streusel, pressing down gently to make sure that it sticks to the cookie dough.

10. Bake, one baking sheet at a time, for 14–16 minutes or until the cookies have spread and the edges are golden brown but the centres are still slightly soft.

11. Allow the cookies to cool on the baking sheet for 5–10 minutes before transferring them to a wire rack to cool completely. [3] The cookies will be very soft and delicate initially, so allow them to cool completely to room temperature before serving.

# Pistachio biscotti

**Makes 20 / Prep time 30 mins / Chill time 15 mins / Bake time 55 mins**

115g (1 stick) unsalted butter,
melted and cooled until warm

125g (½ cup + 2 tablespoons)
light brown soft sugar

80g (⅓ cup) whole milk,
room temperature

½ teaspoon vanilla paste (or
1 teaspoon vanilla extract)

270g (2¼ cups) plain
(all-purpose) flour

30g (¼ cup) cornflour
(cornstarch)

1 teaspoon baking powder

¼ teaspoon salt

125g (1 cup) whole, raw pistachio
kernels [1]

....................................................

Notes

[1] If you can't find raw pistachio kernels,
you can use salted roasted ones instead,
but omit the salt in the recipe.

[2] Chilling firms up the butter in the dough
and therefore the dough itself. It also
gives the flour in the dough some time to
properly hydrate, making the dough easier
to handle.

[3] Don't be tempted to slice the log into
individual biscotti while it's still hot. It'll be
too fragile, and the biscotti will break and
crumble as you try to cut them.

[4] This second bake dries out the
biscotti, which is why we use a low oven
temperature. Flipping them ensures even
moisture evaporation from both sides. If
you want slightly softer cookies, dry them
for only 20 minutes. For extra-dry and
crunchy cookies, dry them for 40 minutes.

....................................................

## Storage

1–2 weeks in an airtight
container in a cool, dry place.

---

**Biscotti, known as cantuccini when made with almonds, originated in Tuscany, Italy. The word** *biscotti* **means "twice cooked", referring to the double baking in the recipe, which gives them a super-crisp and crunchy texture. This egg-free version is straightforward, using milk as the moisture source in the absence of eggs and replacing some of the flour with cornflour (cornstarch) to prevent the biscotti from being too hard or tough. Feel free to use other favourite nuts (or even dried fruit), if you prefer, or even dip the biscotti in chocolate.**

*Perhaps surprisingly, I categorize biscotti as "cakey cookies", so this recipe follows the rules for adapting cakey cookies on page 68 – use them to adapt this recipe to any free-from variation you wish.*

### Cookie dough

1. In a large bowl using a balloon whisk, whisk together the melted butter, light brown sugar, milk and vanilla until well combined.

2. In a separate bowl, whisk together the flour, cornflour (cornstarch), baking powder and salt, and add them to the wet ingredients. Mix well with a rubber spatula or a wooden spoon until you get a smooth cookie dough. It'll be very soft at this stage but it shouldn't be sticky.

3. Add the pistachios and mix briefly until they're evenly distributed. Chill the cookie dough in the fridge for about 15–30 minutes, until it's easier to handle and shape. [2]

4. While the cookie dough is chilling, adjust the oven rack to the middle position, pre-heat the oven to 180°C/350°F and line a large baking sheet with baking paper.

### Shaping the log

1. Transfer the chilled cookie dough on to a lightly floured surface and shape it into a short log – don't worry about its exact size or shape at this point. Transfer the log on to the lined baking sheet and use a pastry brush to remove any excess flour.

2. Use your hands to shape the dough into a roughly 35x9cm (14x3½in) log, about 2cm (¾in) thick. It's best to arrange it so that it lies along the diagonal of the baking sheet, as it will spread slightly and increase in size during baking. (Or, you can shape it into two 18x9cm (7x3½in) logs, if you find that easier.)

### First bake

1. Bake the log(s) for 25–30 minutes or until evenly golden brown, fully baked through and firm to the touch. Remove the biscotti log(s) from the oven and allow to cool on the baking sheet for about 15–20 minutes, or until warm or lukewarm to the touch. [3]

2. In the meantime, reduce the oven temperature to 130°C/265°F.

### Slicing & second bake (drying out)

1. Once warm or lukewarm, use a sharp serrated knife to cut the log into about 1–2cm (½–¾in) slices. Use a sawing motion to give the cleanest slices and the least amount of breakage. You should get around 20–22 biscotti in total.

2. Arrange the sliced biscotti (cut sides down) on the lined baking sheet and bake them for 30 minutes, flipping them over halfway through. [4] Immediately transfer the baked biscotti to a wire rack to cool completely.

# Raspberry meringue tart

Serves 10–12 / Prep 1 hour 15 mins (excluding pastry prep) / Chill 4 hours 30 mins / Bake 30 mins / Cook 15 mins

1 batch of **egg-free shortcrust dough** (see pages 184–5)

**Raspberry curd filling**
450g (about 3¾ cups) fresh or frozen raspberries
30g (¼ cup) cornflour (cornstarch)
160g (⅔ cup) water [1]
175g (¾ cup + 2 tablespoons) caster (superfine) or granulated sugar
¼ teaspoon salt
150g (1 stick + 2½ tablespoons) unsalted butter, cubed
½ teaspoon vanilla paste (or 1 teaspoon vanilla extract)

**Raspberry aquafaba meringue**
30g (1 cup) freeze-dried raspberries
15g (2 tablespoons) icing (powdered) sugar
120g (½ cup) aquafaba [2]
150g (¾ cup) caster (superfine) or granulated sugar
¼ teaspoon cream of tartar [3]
1 teaspoon vanilla paste (or 2 teaspoons vanilla extract)

Perfect shortcrust pastry, a refreshingly zingy raspberry curd with just the right amount of sweetness, and a towering mound of fluffy, marshmallow-like raspberry aquafaba meringue on top – this tart is a real showstopper. The curd sets beautifully: it's stable enough so you can cut neat, clean slices but it's not in any way gummy or rubbery – instead, it's perfectly melt-in-the-mouth creamy. But the real star of the show is the raspberry aquafaba meringue, which gets its gorgeous flavour and colour from freeze-dried raspberries.

*This recipe follows the rules for adapting shortcrust pastry on page 70 – use them to adapt this recipe to any free-from variation. For a vegan variation, replace the dairy butter in the raspberry curd with an equal amount of a firm vegan butter block.*

### Shortcrust pastry

1. Chill the pastry dough for at least 30 minutes before using. If you've made it a few days ahead and stored it in the fridge, leave it to come up to room temperature for 5–10 minutes; if it's been frozen, thaw it at room temperature for 45 minutes to 1 hour, until pliable.

2. Pre-heat the oven to 180°C/350°F with a large baking sheet on the middle rack. Get a 23cm (9in) loose-bottom tart tin with a fluted edge (about 3.5cm/1⅓in deep) on hand.

3. On a lightly floured surface, roll out the pastry into a large circle about 3mm (⅛in) thick and about 4–5cm (1½–2in) larger than the tin diameter.

4. Transfer it into the tart tin and make sure that it's snug against the bottom and sides. Roll the rolling pin across the tart tin to cut away any excess, and gently press the pastry into the grooves of the fluted edge. Chill the pastry in the fridge for at least 30 minutes.

5. Once chilled, dock the bottom of the pastry with a fork, line it with a sheet of baking paper and fill it to the brim with baking beans (rice or dried beans work too). Place the tart tin directly on the hot baking sheet and blind bake for 18–20 minutes or until the edges are light golden.

6. Remove the baking beans and paper, and bake for a further 8–10 minutes or until the pastry is evenly golden (with slightly darker edges), fully baked through and crisp.

7. Allow the pastry to cool completely in the tart tin.

### Raspberry curd filling

1. Add the raspberries to a saucepan and cook them over medium heat until they've completely softened and released their juices.

2. Pass the softened raspberries through a sieve placed over a bowl or jug to collect the juices – you should get about 280–300g (about 1⅛–1¼ cups) of juice in total. Return the juices to the saucepan and discard the solids left in the sieve.

3. In a small cup, mix the cornflour (cornstarch) with about 3–4 tablespoons of the water until you get a smooth slurry with no clumps.

4. Add the cornflour (cornstarch) slurry, the remaining water, and the sugar and salt to the raspberry juices, and cook over medium heat with constant whisking until thickened and the mixture comes to a boil. Then, cook for 1 minute longer with constant whisking. [4]

→

Notes

[1] High acidity (low pH) inhibits the thickening power of cornflour (cornstarch). In order to get an egg-free raspberry curd that isn't too runny, you need to use a mixture of raspberry juices and water to reduce its acidity.

[2] Aquafaba is the viscous water in a can of chickpeas (garbanzos). It whips into a stable foam, which makes it a great substitute for egg whites in meringue (see page 358). This amount of aquafaba is equivalent to 4 UK medium/US large egg whites.

[3] Cream of tartar stabilizes the aquafaba meringue (see page 358).

[4] Cornflour (cornstarch) achieves maximum thickening power and stability when the mixture comes to a boil and stays at boiling point for a while (about 1 minute in this case).

[5] For extra-neat, clean slices, use a sharp knife and dip it into hot water between cuts (wiping it clean and dry before each cut).

## Storage

3–4 days in an airtight container in the fridge.

5. Remove from the heat and whisk in the butter and vanilla. Whisk well with a large balloon whisk for about 1 minute, until the butter has fully melted and the curd becomes noticeably lighter in colour (it doesn't need to be fluffy, you just want to incorporate a small amount of air into it).

6. Pour the finished raspberry curd into the cooled shortcrust pastry shell while it's still hot and smooth it out into an even layer (you might have a tablespoon or two left over). Place a sheet of cling film over the curd, so that it's in direct contact with the surface of the curd to prevent skin formation.

7. Allow it to cool completely to room temperature, then chill it in the fridge for at least 4 hours or preferably overnight.

## Raspberry aquafaba meringue

*It's best to prepare the aquafaba meringue and spread it on top of the tart close to serving, as it can soften slightly with time.*

1. In a food processor, blend the freeze-dried raspberries and icing (powdered) sugar until they form a fine powder. Pass it through a sieve to remove any seeds or other solids, and set aside until needed.

2. In the bowl of a stand mixer fitted with the whisk, or in a large bowl if using a hand-held mixer with the double beaters, combine the aquafaba, sugar and cream of tartar. Whisk for about 10–15 minutes on high speed, until greatly increased in volume and stiff peaks form. Add the freeze-dried raspberry powder and vanilla, and whisk well until combined.

## Assembling the tart

1. Peel away the sheet of cling film on top of the curd. Remove the chilled tart from the tart tin and place it on to a serving plate.

2. Spoon the raspberry aquafaba meringue on top of the tart and, using a small offset spatula or the back of a spoon, shape it into a mound with some decorative swirls.

3. Toast the meringue with a kitchen blow torch, then slice and serve. [5]

# Milk chocolate & hazelnut crêpe cake

**Serves 10–12 / Prep time 2 hours / Chill time 1 hour 30 mins / Cook time 35 mins**

### Chocolate crêpes

360g (3 cups) plain (all-purpose) flour

65g (⅔ cup) Dutch-processed cocoa powder

100g (½ cup) caster (superfine) or granulated sugar

½ teaspoon salt

1kg (4¼ cups) whole milk

1 teaspoon vanilla paste (or 2 teaspoons vanilla extract)

### Milk chocolate ganache

350g (12½oz) milk chocolate, chopped

400g (1¾ cups) double (heavy) cream

### Assembling & decorating

100g (1 cup) ground toasted hazelnuts

230g (1 cup) double (heavy) cream, chilled

60g (½ cup) icing (powdered) sugar, sifted

½ teaspoon vanilla paste (or 1 teaspoon vanilla extract)

toasted hazelnuts, roughly chopped, for sprinkling

**A crêpe cake may seem overwhelming to make – after all, this one comprises 17 delicately thin crêpes, 16 layers of rich milk chocolate ganache, and ground toasted hazelnuts scattered throughout – but trust me, you've got this. There's nothing complicated about this recipe; you just need to take some time to cook up all those crêpes. The crêpe batter here is slightly runnier than a usual batter: it makes very thin crêpes, which ensures that the assembled cake is wonderfully elegant, and delicate enough that you can easily cut through it with a fork.**

*This recipe follows the rules for adapting thin pancakes and crêpes on page 77 – use them to adapt this recipe to any free-from variation. To make the crêpe cake vegan, use the vegan dark chocolate ganache recipe on page 475 for the filling, and use vegan double (heavy) cream for the decorations on top.*

### Chocolate crêpes

*You can prepare the crêpe batter using a high-speed food blender or a hand immersion blender or by hand using a large balloon whisk.* [1]

1. In a large bowl, whisk together the flour, cocoa powder, sugar and salt. (If using a food blender, add the dry ingredients to the jug of the blender.)

2. Add the milk and vanilla, and blend or whisk everything together until you get a smooth, very runny crêpe batter with no flour clumps. If you have a few clumps, you can pass it through a sieve to remove them. [2]

3. Heat up a 25cm (10in) crêpe pan, frying pan or skillet over medium heat. Lightly butter the pan and wipe away any excess with kitchen paper.

4. Once the pan is hot, add a ladleful, or about ⅓ cup, of batter to the hot pan and, as you're pouring it, swirl the pan to get an even, thin coating.

5. Cook over medium heat for about 45–60 seconds or until the edges of the crêpe start loosening from the pan and the surface looks set (it will be matte/no longer glossy).

6. Flip and cook on the other side for 45–60 seconds, or until dark brown spots appear. Then, place the crêpe on a plate or wire rack while you repeat with the remaining batter. The recipe makes about 17–18 crêpes, depending on their thickness and the size of your pan or skillet. [3] Cover the hot crêpes with a clean tea towel to trap some steam and prevent the edges from drying out and getting crisp. Allow the crêpes to cool completely before assembling the cake.

### Milk chocolate ganache

1. Place the chopped milk chocolate into a heatproof bowl.

2. In a saucepan on the stovetop or in a microwave-safe bowl in the microwave, heat the double (heavy) cream until it only just comes to a boil, then pour it over the chocolate, making sure that the cream covers the chocolate as much as possible. Allow to stand for 2–3 minutes, then stir together until smooth and glossy.

3. Allow the ganache to cool to room temperature, then chill it in the fridge for about 1 hour until it's thickened to a spoonable consistency.

4. Using a stand mixer fitted with the whisk or a hand-held mixer with the double beaters, whisk the chilled ganache for 30–45 seconds on medium–high speed until it's paler in colour and fluffy. Be careful not to over-whip it, which can cause it to split and curdle.

→

Notes

[1] A high-speed food blender will give you the smoothest batter with minimal gluten development – and that, in turn, will result in the most tender, delicate crêpes.

[2] If making the batter by hand with a balloon whisk, you can minimize lump formation by first adding one third of the milk to the dry ingredients. Whisk to a smooth, paste-like batter with no flour clumps, then gradually add the rest of the milk and vanilla with constant whisking.

[3] Treat the first crêpe as a test run to determine if the batter consistency needs adjusting. If it does, add a small amount of extra flour or milk, as relevant.

## Storage

3 days in an airtight container in the fridge. Allow to stand at room temperature for 10–15 minutes before serving.

## Assembling the crêpe cake

1. For an extra-neat crêpe cake, trim each individual crêpe into a perfectly round 23cm (9in) circle. I recommend using a 23cm (9in) plate, cake tin or similar as a template and cutting around it with a sharp knife or a pizza cutter.

2. Place a crêpe on a cake stand or serving plate of choice, and dollop on about 3 tablespoons of the whipped milk chocolate ganache. Use a large offset spatula to smooth it out into an even layer, all the way to the edges. Evenly sprinkle on about 1 tablespoon of the ground toasted hazelnuts.

3. Place another crêpe on top (make sure that it's perfectly centred on top of the one below, otherwise you'll get a wonky crêpe cake), spread another 3 tablespoons of whipped ganache on top and sprinkle on about 1 tablespoon of ground toasted hazelnuts.

4. Repeat with the remaining crêpes, whipped ganache and ground hazelnuts. Make sure to keep your crêpe cake as straight as possible. The final layer should be a crêpe with no ganache on top.

5. Chill the assembled cake in the fridge for about 30 minutes. This will firm up the ganache and make the cake easier to cut into neat slices. (There's no need to cover the cake if you're only chilling it for 30 minutes. If you intend to chill it for longer than that, it's best to keep it covered or in a closed container to prevent it from drying out.)

6. Whip the chilled double (heavy) cream, icing (powdered) sugar and vanilla until soft peaks form. Spoon the whipped cream on top of the crêpe cake, and use the back of a spoon to create a few decorative swirls and swoops. Sprinkle on the chopped toasted hazelnuts, slice and serve.

# Lemon swirl cheesecake bars

**Serves 12–16 / Prep time 45 mins / Cook time 5 mins / Bake time 45 mins / Chill time 4 hours**

## Lemon curd

100g (½ cup) caster (superfine) or granulated sugar

zest of 1 unwaxed lemon

15g (2 tablespoons) cornflour (cornstarch)

50g (3½ tablespoons) water [1]

50g (3½ tablespoons) lemon juice, freshly squeezed

¼ teaspoon salt

70g (½ stick + 1 tablespoon) unsalted butter, cubed

yellow food colouring or a pinch of ground turmeric (optional) [2]

## Cheesecake crust

150g (1½ cups) crushed digestive biscuits or graham crackers [3]

45g (3 tablespoons) unsalted butter, melted

## Lemon cheesecake filling

150g (¾ cup) caster (superfine) or granulated sugar

zest of 2 unwaxed lemons

30g (¼ cup) cornflour (cornstarch)

600g (2⅔ cups) full-fat cream cheese, room temperature

115g (½ cup) full-fat unsweetened plain or Greek-style yogurt, room temperature

60g (¼ cup) whole milk, room temperature

1 teaspoon vanilla paste (or 2 teaspoons vanilla extract)

There's so much lemony goodness in these cheesecake bars, with plenty of lemon zest in the cheesecake filling and generous dollops of tangy, creamy lemon curd swirled on top before baking. Even in the absence of eggs, the cheesecake filling has a light and creamy texture, thanks to the slightly higher oven temperature (see page 250). The final result is a bright and zesty dessert that absolutely everyone will love.

*This recipe follows the rules for adapting a baked cheesecake on page 82 – use them to adapt this recipe to any free-from variation. If you want to make the lemon curd vegan as well, replace the unsalted butter with an equal amount of a firm vegan butter block.*

### Lemon curd

1. Combine the sugar and lemon zest in a bowl and use your fingertips to rub the zest into the sugar. This helps to release more essential oils from the zest and it will make your lemon curd extra fragrant.

2. In a small cup, mix the cornflour (cornstarch) with about 1–2 tablespoons of the water until you get a smooth slurry with no clumps.

3. Add the lemon-sugar, the cornflour (cornstarch) slurry, the lemon juice, the remaining water and the salt to a saucepan, and cook over medium heat with constant stirring until thickened and the mixture comes to a boil. Then, cook for 15–30 seconds longer with constant stirring. [4]

4. Remove from the heat and add the butter, stirring until fully melted. The mixture might initially look split (the melted butter won't fully incorporate into the curd straight away) but just continue stirring it – it will emulsify and come together after a few minutes and once the lemon curd has cooled slightly. (Optional: you can pass the lemon curd through a sieve to remove the lemon zest if you want it to be completely smooth.)

5. At this point, you can add a few drops of yellow food colouring or a pinch of ground turmeric to achieve a vibrant yellow colour. Whichever option you choose, add only a very small amount at a time and stir well after each addition, until you reach the desired colour. Remember: you can always add more, but you can't take it away!

6. Pour the finished lemon curd into a bowl or heatproof container and cover it with a sheet of cling film. Make sure that the cling film is in direct contact with the surface of the lemon curd to prevent skin formation. Allow to cool to room temperature. (You can prepare the lemon curd a day or two in advance and keep it in the fridge until needed. Before you swirl it into the cheesecake filling, allow it to come up to room temperature.)

### Cheesecake crust

1. Adjust the oven rack to the middle position, pre-heat the oven to 180°C/350°F and line a 23cm (9in) square baking tin with baking paper. (leave some overhang, which will help you to remove the cheesecake bars from the baking tin later on).

2. Mix together the crushed digestive biscuits or graham crackers and melted butter, until you get a mixture resembling wet sand. Transfer the mixture into the lined baking tin and compress it into an even layer with the help of a small offset spatula or the bottom of a glass or measuring cup.

3. Bake for 10 minutes, then remove from the oven and allow to cool until warm.

→

## Notes

[1] High acidity (low pH) inhibits the thickening power of cornflour (cornstarch). That's why it's best to use a 1:1 ratio of lemon juice to water when making an egg-free lemon curd (see pages 478–9).

[2] Regular, egg-containing lemon curd gets its vibrant yellow colour from the egg yolks. Egg-free lemon curd is almost off-white with only a tinge of yellow from the butter. Food colouring or a pinch of turmeric puts back that gorgeous lemon-yellow colour.

[3] Both digestive biscuits and graham crackers are typically egg-free, but always check the manufacturer's ingredients.

[4] Cornflour (cornstarch) achieves maximum thickening power and stability when the mixture comes to a boil and stays at boiling point for a while: 15–30 seconds is enough in this case.

[5] This slow cooling ensures a perfectly smooth cheesecake top with no cracking.

## Storage

3–4 days in an airtight container in the fridge.

## Lemon cheesecake filling

1. Reduce the oven temperature to 160°C/325°F.

2. Combine the sugar and lemon zest in a bowl and use your fingertips to rub the zest into the sugar. This helps to release more essential oils from the zest and it will make your cheesecake filling extra lemony.

3. Add the cornflour (cornstarch) to the lemon-sugar and whisk to get rid of any clumps.

4. In a separate large bowl or the bowl of a stand mixer (if using), combine the cream cheese and yogurt. Mix well until smooth, either by hand with a large balloon whisk, or in a stand mixer fitted with the paddle on the lowest speed setting.

5. Add the milk and vanilla, and mix until well combined.

6. Add the lemon-sugar mixture and combine to a smooth, fairly thick cheesecake filling.

## Assembling & baking the cheesecake bars

1. Transfer the cheesecake filling on to the slightly cooled cheesecake crust and smooth it out into an even layer.

2. Dollop about ⅔ of the lemon curd evenly over the cheesecake filling. (You can use the rest of the lemon curd for serving with the cheesecake.)

3. Use a knife, the handle of a spoon or a skewer to swirl the lemon curd around. Be careful not to over-swirl it – you want to see prominent streaks of lemon curd.

4. Bake for about 35–40 minutes or until the edges are slightly puffed up, and the middle is still wobbly when you gently shake the baking tin. Note that this time range is merely a guideline – you should always judge the doneness of a cheesecake based on its physical indicators (the wobbliness of the centre, how set the edges are, and so on), especially as each oven behaves slightly differently. You should start checking your cheesecake about 10 minutes before the end of the recommended baking time.

5. Turn off the oven and allow the cheesecake bars to cool to room temperature in the turned-off oven with the oven door ajar. [5]

6. Once cooled to room temperature, transfer the cheesecake bars into the fridge for at least 4 hours or preferably overnight, before removing them from the baking tin and slicing them into individual portions. Serve them with an extra dollop of lemon curd.

# Almond swirl brioche buns

**Makes 6 / Prep time 1 hour / Proof time 2 hours / Bake time 18 mins**

**Brioche dough**

150g (½ cup + 2 tablespoons) whole milk, lukewarm

25g (2 tablespoons) caster (superfine) or granulated sugar

240g (2 cups) bread flour, plus extra for flouring the surface

6g (2 teaspoons) instant yeast [1]

3g (½ teaspoon) salt

45g (3 tablespoons) unsalted butter, softened

**Almond frangipane**

50g (¼ cup) caster (superfine) or granulated sugar

45g (3 tablespoons) unsalted butter, softened

35g (2 tablespoons) condensed milk [2]

½ teaspoon vanilla paste (or 1 teaspoon vanilla extract)

¼ teaspoon almond extract (optional)

100g (1 cup) almond flour

15g (1 tablespoon) whole milk, room temperature

**To assemble the buns**

20g (1 tablespoon) condensed milk

30g (2 tablespoons) aquafaba [3]

30g (⅓ cup) flaked almonds

icing (powdered) sugar, to serve (optional)

**These stunning almond swirl buns combine a fluffy brioche dough with a rich, gooey frangipane filling. The flaked almonds on top get beautifully toasty and crunchy during baking. Your kitchen will smell divine while these are in the oven!**

*This recipe follows the rules for adapting bread and yeasted bakes on page 84 – use them to adapt this recipe to be vegan as well. If you want to make a gluten-free version, use the basic gluten-free brioche dough recipe on page 277 (in combination with the rules on page 84, if required).*

**Brioche dough**

1. Add all the brioche dough ingredients to the bowl of a stand mixer fitted with the dough hook.

2. Knead on a low speed for 15–20 minutes or until you get a smooth dough that comes away from the sides of the bowl (the sides of the mixing bowl should be completely clean at this point, with no dough sticking to them). The dough should pass the windowpane test and it shouldn't be too sticky or tacky to the touch.

3. Shape the dough into a smooth ball and place it into a lightly greased bowl, seam side down.

4. Cover the bowl with cling film or a clean, damp tea towel and prove in a warm spot for about 1 hour to 1 hour 15 minutes or until doubled in size. While the dough is proving, prepare the frangipane filling.

**Almond frangipane**

1. In a bowl, mix together the sugar and softened butter with a wooden spoon or a rubber spatula until combined and smooth. Don't cream, whisk or aerate the mixture – you don't want to incorporate too much air into it.

2. Add the condensed milk, vanilla and almond extract (if using), and mix until well combined.

3. Add the almond flour and mix well until you get a fairly thick frangipane mixture.

4. Add the milk, about a teaspoon at a time, until you get a spreadable yet thick frangipane: 15g (1 tablespoon) of milk should be sufficient to make it easily spreadable, but you can add about 5g (1 teaspoon) extra if necessary. [4] Set aside until needed.

**Assembling & proving the buns**

1. Line a large baking sheet with baking paper, and set aside until needed.

2. Once the dough has doubled in size, turn it out on to a lightly floured surface and roll it out into a 30x35cm (12x14in) rectangle, with the shorter 30cm (12in) side closest to you.

3. Spread the frangipane filling in an even layer over the bottom ⅔ of the dough rectangle, all the way to the edges, leaving the top ⅓ of the dough without filling.

4. Fold the dough like you would a letter. First, fold the top third (the one without the filling) over the middle third of the dough. Then, fold the bottom third over that. You'll get a 10x35cm (4x14in) rectangle comprising three dough layers.

→

Notes

[1] If using active dry yeast, use 8g (2½ teaspoons) instead. Activate it first: combine it with the warm milk and sugar, and let it stand for about 5 minutes until frothing, then add it to the other ingredients.

[2] The condensed milk adds a gooey richness to the egg-free frangipane, which, in a regular version, would have come from the egg yolks.

[3] Aquafaba is the viscous water in a can of chickpeas (garbanzos). Here, the mixture of aquafaba and condensed milk acts as an egg-free egg wash to help with browning, add a sheen and make sure that the flaked almonds stick. (See also pages 359–61.)

[4] The frangipane should be spreadable but not soft or runny, which can make shaping the buns more tricky.

### Storage

Best served on the day of baking, but they keep well for 2–3 days in an airtight container in a cool, dry place. You can reheat them in the microwave for 15–20 seconds to make them just as pillowy-soft as they were on the first day.

5. Gently roll over the folded dough with the rolling pin, rolling it to a width of about 14–15cm (5½–6in).

6. Use a pizza cutter or a sharp knife to cut the folded dough rectangle lengthways into 6 equal strips, about 2–2.5cm (¾–1in) wide and 35cm (14in) long.

7. Roll up each strip from one end to the other, tucking the tail end underneath the bun.

8. Arrange the rolled-up buns on the lined baking sheet, spacing them out as much as possible (as they'll expand during proving and baking). Press down gently on top of each bun to flatten it slightly.

9. Lightly cover the buns with a sheet of cling film or a clean tea towel and prove in a warm spot for about 1 hour to 1 hour 15 minutes or until doubled in size.

### Baking the buns

1. While the buns are proving, adjust the oven rack to the middle position and pre-heat the oven to 180°C/350°F.

2. In a small bowl, whisk together the condensed milk and aquafaba (as an egg-free alternative to egg wash).

3. Once doubled in size, brush the buns gently with the condensed milk-aquafaba mixture and sprinkle generously with the flaked almonds.

4. Bake for about 18–20 minutes or until golden brown.

5. Allow to cool slightly and then serve, either warm or at room temperature, with a light dusting of icing (powdered) sugar, if you wish.

# Chapter

## 8

# V

## Vegan

# A Simple Sum: Egg-free + Dairy-free

Once you have egg-free and dairy-free baking figured out, vegan baking becomes easy. And that's because vegan modification rules are just a simple sum of all the egg-free and dairy-free adjustments, with no additional tweaks or changes necessary.

In fact, if you read through the case studies in Chapter 4, you'll see the following sentence crop up again and again in various iterations: "The vegan version is just a simple combination of all the dairy-free and egg-free adjustments – and that's all there really is to it."

So, if you want to understand the science behind successful vegan baking, the best idea is to read through the introductory sections to chapters 6 and 7 (dairy-free and egg-free, respectively). But, I'll give you a brief overview of all the most important points here as well.

## Choosing the Correct Ingredients

When it comes to replacing regular dairy ingredients, we're mostly dealing with simple 1:1 substitutions. That is, for the most part, you can easily replace the dairy ingredients with an equal weight or volume of their dairy-free equivalents. And, apart from in cheesecake recipes, you don't need to adjust the quantities of the other ingredients present in any way. (With cheesecakes, you need to increase the amount of cornflour/cornstarch slightly in order to account for the higher moisture content of vegan cream cheese; see page 251.) Instead, replacing dairy ingredients is all about choosing the best vegan options.

**Use a firm vegan butter block (not a soft spread)** Ideally, use one with a high fat content, of 75% or higher.

**Use vegetable shortening to tailor your flaky pastry** By adjusting the ratio of vegetable shortening to vegan butter you can tailor how tender your pastry will be: the larger the proportion of shortening, the more tender and delicate the end result (see pages 192–3).

**Replace regular butter with 80% of oil and 15% of dairy-free milk** If you want to replace regular dairy butter with oil, you need to take into account that oil is 100% fat, whereas butter is only 80% fat (plus 15% water and 5% milk solids). Using oil is especially helpful in cakes, cupcakes and muffins, as it gives them a softer, fluffier crumb and it keeps them moister for longer. That's largely because oil is a liquid fat at and around room temperature, whereas butter is a solid fat.

**Most dairy-free milk alternatives work well – but not canned coconut milk** Avoid canned coconut milk because of its high fat content, which can make your bakes greasy, oily, dense and/or heavy. If you want to use coconut milk, use the kind from a carton, which is lower in fat and closer in texture and consistency to other dairy-free milk alternatives. The only exception when it comes to replacing regular dairy milk is in vegan pastry cream (see page 476). In that case, instead of replacing the full-fat dairy milk with an equal amount of a dairy-free milk, you need to replace it with a 50:50 mixture of dairy-free milk and vegan double (heavy) cream. Using dairy-free milk only would give you a very bland, watery vegan pastry cream. Adding the vegan cream, on the other hand, gives it all of that wonderful richness that we're familiar with from the regular, non-vegan version.

**Most unsweetened plain or Greek-style vegan yogurts work well** In some recipes, the thicker Greek-style yogurt works better because of its lower moisture content – but if that's the case, I'll always specify in the modification rule or recipe.

**Make your own vegan buttermilk (see page 25)** I haven't found a good shop-bought vegan buttermilk yet but, luckily, making your own homemade version is super easy and it takes just a couple of minutes.

**When you choose a vegan double (heavy) cream, consider its purpose** If you want to use your vegan cream for things like ganache, then most vegan options will work well, including coconut cream. However, if you want to whip it up to use for frosting, then make sure to use one that's whippable – you need to be able to achieve a stiff, firm peak when you whip it with a stand or a hand mixer, and it should maintain its whipped-up volume and hold its shape after you've piped it or spread it on to your bake. For such frosting applications, I don't recommend using coconut cream as it can be rather unreliable and unpredictable (unless it's a specially formulated coconut whipping cream).

**Use a vegan cream cheese that's quite thick and firm, with a low water content** Your vegan cream cheese shouldn't be too watery and its texture should be as close as possible to that of dairy cream cheese. However, if you have only a limited selection available to you and you can only find vegan cream cheese that's fairly soft and watery, you can remove some of the excess water by straining it with a cheesecloth before you use it (see page 316).

**You should be able to find vegan condensed milks online or in store** Shop-bought condensed coconut milk and condensed oat milk both work well in my experience, but if you can't find them, you can make your own dairy-free condensed milk using either of the recipes on pages 26 and 27. I've included two homemade vegan condensed milk options in this book: one using coconut milk and one that's coconut-free.

---

**NOTE: FIND YOUR FAVOURITES**

In practice, you might need to test out a few different brands of vegan ingredients before you find your favourites. Consider not just their texture and content, but also their flavour (choose one that tastes good to you). This is especially important in recipes where the relevant vegan alternative is present in a large quantity, and also in bakes that are otherwise fairly mellow in flavour (such as in vanilla cakes).

# Replacing the Eggs

While many vegan recipes rely on "one-size-fits-all" egg replacements, such as chia or flax eggs, mashed bananas or apple sauce, I don't use them. At best, they're not necessary. At worst, they don't work at all and they can give your bakes an odd texture or change the flavour profile, as would be the case with mashed bananas and apple sauce.

Eggs play many different roles in baking and they contribute many different properties to your bakes (see pages 346–356 for a full explanation of this). In order to successfully eliminate and replace them, you first need to understand what these roles and properties are. It's best to think of eggs as two separate ingredients: egg whites and egg yolks. Often, egg whites have a larger effect on the bake as a whole, so much of egg-free and vegan baking actually focuses on how to replace the egg whites (there are some exceptions to this, of course, most notably in pastry cream and various curds; see page 396).

- **Egg whites are a structure-providing and aerating (lift-providing) ingredient, as well as a moisture source.** They give structure to bakes, preventing them from collapsing, losing their shape or being too crumbly, and they make them soft and fluffy. As a moisture source, they prevent bakes from being too dry and, in the case of cookies and shortcrust pastry they help to bind other ingredients together into a manageable dough.

- **Egg yolks are a tenderizing (structure-destroying) ingredient and a moisture source.** Yolks make bakes more tender and delicate, giving them a melt-in-the-mouth quality. They also contribute some richness thanks to their fat content, but that's usually negligible compared to the richness added by the butter or oil.

So, if you want to replace eggs in a cake recipe, you need to somehow mimic their structure-providing and aerating effects, as well as add an alternative moisture source. In practice, this means that you need to increase the amount of the only other structure-providing ingredient present (the flour), increase the quantities of the raising agents and also boost their activity by adding an acidic ingredient (apple cider vinegar or lemon juice), and add some dairy-free milk or yogurt as the alternative moisture source. This is all summarized in the table below:

* Note that you don't mix the baking powder and the vinegar or lemon juice together before adding them to the recipe. Instead, you add the extra baking powder to the dry ingredients and the vinegar or lemon juice to the wet ingredients.

| Egg function | Replacement ingredients |
|---|---|
| Structure | Wheat plain (all-purpose) flour or gluten-free flour blend, binders (xanthan gum) |
| Aeration (lift) | Raising agents (baking powder), apple cider vinegar or lemon juice* |
| Moisture | Water, dairy-free milk, vegan yogurt |

Remember that the exact adjustments you need to make will vary depending on the type of recipe you're modifying: adjustments for a cake recipe will be different from those for a cookie recipe and those, in turn, will be different from the changes necessary to adapt a brownie recipe. And even within the cake family, you'll need to make different adjustments depending on whether or not the cake contains melted chocolate in the batter, and Swiss rolls also require different tweaks.

The table on page 395 also illustrates, once again, why one-size-fits-all egg replacements don't work. They focus on just one or two aspects of what the eggs actually bring to a recipe. For example, chia and flax eggs add only structure and moisture; mashed bananas and apple sauce are even less helpful, being only a source of moisture. That's simply not enough to successfully mimic the texture you'd get with eggs. Using the knowledge in this book, on the other hand, like the table on the previous page and the tables in the egg-free chapter, along with the rules for adapting recipes in Chapter 3, allows you to do exactly that: substitute the eggs in a systematic and scientific manner with guaranteed success.

## Pastry cream and curds

In pastry cream and curds, we mostly focus on the thickening power of the egg yolks and on the richness that they bring to the recipe. We can easily mimic this with a mixture of cornflour (cornstarch) and a bit of extra liquid and butter. The starch allows you to achieve the same thick, creamy texture as you would in a regular, egg-containing recipe and the extra butter makes it perfectly rich and luxurious (see also page 357).

Note that in vegan citrus curds, such as vegan lemon curd, the high acidity (low pH) inhibits the thickening power of cornflour (cornstarch). So, if you don't want your vegan curd to turn out super runny, you need to replace half of the citrus juice with water (that is, use a 50:50 mixture of juice and water). This reduces the acidity and results in a perfectly thick, creamy and spreadable lemon curd that has just the right amount of tart, intense citrus flavour.

You can find the recipes for vegan pastry cream and lemon curd, based on all these tips and guidelines, on pages 476 and 478, respectively.

## Meringue

In meringue recipes, aquafaba is your best friend. This is the viscous liquid from a can of chickpeas (garbanzos) and it's a magical ingredient in that you can easily whip it up into a very stable foam, much like you would egg whites. About 30g (2 tablespoons) of aquafaba is equivalent to one medium (US large) egg white. And, just like with egg whites, aquafaba is also stabilized by the addition of the acidic cream of tartar. Adding just ¼ teaspoon makes sure that the whipped aquafaba holds its shape better and for a longer period of time.

Remember that whipped-up aquafaba is great for applications such as meringue or meringue buttercream, but it's not stable in the presence of fats when exposed to high heat. Consequently, there's not much use folding it into a batter like you would whipped egg whites – while the batter might look fluffy initially, it will quickly collapse in the oven.

# Vegan Egg Washes

Vegan egg washes are the same as the egg-free ones (see page 359), just with dairy-free versions substituted where relevant. They're all outlined below. We're primarily interested in three aspects of these egg-wash alternatives: whether they add any shine or glossiness to bakes; how they affect the browning and colour; and if they have any sticking power – that is, if they help any toppings to stick to whatever bake you're making.

**Aquafaba** adds only a slight shine to a crust and it has very little effect on the browning or the colour of a bake. However, it does ensure that any toppings, such as seeds or flaky salt, stick well without falling off once baked.

**Dairy-free milk alternatives,** such as almond, rice and oat milk, add only a minimal amount of glossiness or shine to a crust, and they also have little effect on the browning or the colour. But just like aquafaba, they do make sure that any toppings stick to the surface of your bakes.

**Soy milk** makes a crust noticeably glossier – not quite as much as regular egg wash, but it's definitely a great vegan alternative. It also makes sure that any toppings stay put and, unlike the other dairy-free milks, it promotes browning.

**Melted vegan butter** doesn't add any glossiness or shine and doesn't affect the amount of browning. It has no sticking power – any toppings that you sprinkle over the bake will easily fall off after baking. However, it does make the crust of enriched bread or brioche much softer.

**Oil, such as sunflower or olive oil,** doesn't add any shine and has a negligible effect on browning. Just like melted butter, it has no sticking power. It will, though, make the crust of any enriched bread noticeably softer.

**A mixture of aquafaba or dairy-free milk and vegan condensed milk** is great for adding a slight shine to your bakes and it also very effectively promotes browning (largely through caramelization rather than the Maillard reaction). It also has great sticking power. I usually use a mixture of 30g (2 tablespoons) of aquafaba or dairy-free milk and 20g (1 tablespoon) of vegan condensed milk. Keep in mind that condensed milk will add a hint of sweetness, but I don't mind it as it's hardly noticeable. A more important point is that the condensed milk can make the surface of your bakes slightly sticky if you store them in a closed container for a longer period of time.

**A mixture of aquafaba or dairy-free milk and maple syrup** promotes browning through caramelization but it doesn't add much shine or glossiness. It does have great sticking power, but it will add a slight hint of sweetness to the crust of your bakes. I usually use a mixture of 30g (2 tablespoons) of aquafaba or dairy-free milk and 20g (1 tablespoon) of maple syrup.

The table on the following page will help you to quickly choose the best vegan egg wash for your bake.

| Egg-wash alternative | Shine/ glossiness | Promotes browning | Helps any toppings to stick | Softens the bread crust | Extra notes |
|---|---|---|---|---|---|
| aquafaba | yes | no | yes | no | / |
| dairy-free milk, such as almond, rice or oat milk | no | no | yes | no | / |
| soy milk | yes | yes | yes | no | / |
| melted vegan butter | no | no | no | yes | / |
| oil | no | no | no | yes | / |
| aquafaba or dairy-free milk + condensed milk | yes | yes | yes | no | adds a hint of sweetness |
| aquafaba or dairy-free milk + maple syrup | no | yes | yes | no | adds a hint of sweetness |

All of this applies mostly to recipes that use wheat flour. Gluten-free vegan bakes (especially bread) are trickier, as they're more prone to forming a dull, matte, white-ish crust. That means that choosing the best possible egg-wash alternative for gluten-free vegan bakes is both more important and more challenging. You can read more about this on page 432.

# Keeping It Simple

Once you combine all the dairy- and egg-free adjustments, that's pretty much the end of the story as far as vegan baking goes. It really is as simple as that.

However, note that this is only true when we talk about vegan baking that uses wheat plain (all-purpose) flour. Gluten-free vegan baking throws up a few extra complications – you can read more about that in the next chapter.

True egg wash

Aqualaba

Almond milk

Soy milk

Vegan butter

Oil

Aqualaba & condensed milk

Aqualaba & maple syrup

# Lemon poppy seed loaf cake

**Serves 10–12 / Prep time 30 mins / Bake time 1 hour**

### Lemon poppy seed loaf cake

200g (1 cup) caster (superfine)
   or granulated sugar
zest of 3 unwaxed lemons
180g (¾ cup) dairy-free milk,
   room temperature [1]
110g (½ cup) sunflower or
   vegetable oil
60g (4 tablespoons) lemon
   juice [2]
½ teaspoon vanilla paste (or
   1 teaspoon vanilla extract)
300g (2½ cups) plain
   (all-purpose) flour
25g (¼ cup) almond flour [3]
3 teaspoons baking powder
½ teaspoon salt
20g (2 tablespoons) poppy
   seeds, plus optional extra
   for sprinkling

### Lemon icing

120g (1 cup) icing (powdered)
   sugar, sifted
6–7 teaspoons lemon juice
½ teaspoon vanilla paste

#### Notes

[1] Avoid canned coconut milk, as it can make the cake too greasy and dense.

[2] Acidic lemon juice boosts the activity of the baking powder to make up for the "lift" lost because of the absence of eggs.

[3] Almond flour adds richness and a more tender, delicate crumb. You can replace it with an equal weight of extra plain (all-purpose) flour or finely ground sunflower seeds (the latter will result in a slightly darker final colour).

[4] Make the icing slightly thicker than you might think is necessary to give a generous layer on top of the cake, along with thick drips running down the sides.

### Storage

3–4 days in an airtight container in a cool, dry place.

The texture of this simple loaf cake is absolutely perfect. Even though the recipe doesn't include any eggs or dairy, the cake isn't doughy or dense in any way. This is largely because the recipe uses oil and the wet+dry (all-in-one) mixing method (see pages 98–9), which contribute to a very fluid batter with minimal gluten development (which is crucial in egg-free and vegan baking).

The flavour is incredible: there's the zest of three whole lemons, plenty of lemon juice and poppy seeds in the batter, and the simple lemon icing on top adds an extra tangy kick. This vegan version isn't quite as domed as egg-containing loaf cakes will be, but it still has a rounded top just waiting for that drizzle of icing.

*This recipe follows the rules for adapting buttery cakes on page 52 – use them to adapt this recipe to any free-from variation.*

### Lemon poppy seed loaf cake

1. Adjust the oven rack to the middle position, pre-heat the oven to 180°C/350°F, and line a 23x13cm (9x5in) loaf tin with baking paper.

2. Add the sugar and lemon zest to a large bowl and use your fingertips to rub the zest into the sugar. This helps to release essential oils from the zest to make your cake extra lemony and fragrant.

3. Add the dairy-free milk, oil, lemon juice and vanilla, and whisk until combined. The mixture might curdle slightly owing to the acidic lemon juice, but that's okay.

4. In a separate large bowl, whisk together the flour, almond flour, baking powder, salt and poppy seeds.

5. Add the wet ingredients to the dry and whisk well until you get a smooth cake batter with no flour clumps. Be careful not to over-mix the batter.

6. Transfer the batter into the prepared loaf tin and smooth out the top.

7. Bake for about 1 hour or until well risen, golden brown on top and an inserted toothpick or cake tester comes out clean. If the cake starts browning too quickly, cover it with foil (shiny side up) and continue baking until done.

8. Allow the cake to cool in the tin for about 10 minutes, then transfer it out of the tin and on to a wire rack to cool completely.

### Lemon icing

1. Stir together the icing (powdered) sugar, 6 teaspoons of lemon juice, and the vanilla to a thick icing with no clumps. If it is too thick, add an extra 1 teaspoon of juice. [4]

2. Drizzle the lemon icing over the cooled cake, spreading it evenly across the top with the back of a spoon, and letting it drip down the sides. You can sprinkle on some extra poppy seeds for decoration, if you wish.

3. Allow the icing to set and dry out slightly (at least for 30 minutes at room temperature) before slicing and serving.

# Carrot cake

**Serves 10–12  /  Prep time 45 minutes  /  Bake time 25 mins**

## Carrot cake

360g (3 cups) plain
  (all-purpose) flour
2 teaspoons baking powder
1 teaspoon bicarbonate of soda
  (baking soda)
½ teaspoon salt
2 teaspoons ground cinnamon
1 teaspoon ground ginger
½ teaspoon ground nutmeg
300g (1½ cups) light brown
  soft sugar
160g (¾ cup) sunflower or
  vegetable oil
120g (½ cup) dairy-free milk,
  room temperature [1]
2 teaspoons apple cider
  vinegar [2]
½ teaspoon vanilla paste (or
  1 teaspoon vanilla extract)
300g (about 3 cups) peeled
  and coarsely grated carrots
  (3–4 medium carrots) [3]
90g (¾ cup) pecans or walnuts,
  roughly chopped (optional),
  plus extra for sprinkling

## Cream cheese frosting

175g (¾ cup) vegan double
  (heavy) cream, chilled [4]
80g (⅔ cup) icing (powdered)
  sugar, sifted
170g (¾ cup) vegan cream
  cheese, chilled [5]
1 teaspoon vanilla paste (or
  2 teaspoons vanilla extract)
¼ teaspoon salt

**This vegan take on a classic has everything you know and love about carrot cake: it's wonderfully moist, rich, generously spiced and, in a single word: cosy. The carrot cake sponges are beautifully soft and tender. It's important that you use coarsely grated carrots rather than finely grated ones, as the latter can release too much moisture during baking, which can result in a denser crumb. The vegan cream cheese frosting uses whipped cream instead of butter, which gives it a much lighter and fluffier texture, and it's also not too sweet.**

*This recipe follows the rules for adapting buttery cakes on page 52 – use them to adapt this recipe to any free-from variation you wish.*

### Carrot cake

1. Adjust the oven rack to the middle position and pre-heat the oven to 180°C/350°F. Lightly butter two 20cm (8in) round cake tins and line their bottoms with rounds of baking paper.

2. In a large bowl, whisk together the flour, baking powder, bicarbonate of soda (baking soda), salt, cinnamon, ginger and nutmeg.

3. In a separate bowl or large jug, whisk together the sugar, oil, dairy-free milk, vinegar and vanilla.

4. Add the wet ingredients to the dry and, using a rubber spatula or a wooden spoon, mix everything together into a smooth, fairly thick cake batter with no flour clumps.

5. Fold in the grated carrots and chopped nuts, if using, until they're evenly distributed throughout the batter.

6. Divide the batter evenly between the two prepared cake tins and smooth out the top.

7. Bake for about 25–30 minutes or until an inserted toothpick or cake tester comes out clean.

8. Allow the cakes to cool in the cake tins for about 10 minutes before turning them out on to a wire rack to cool completely.

### Cream cheese frosting

1. Using a stand mixer fitted with the whisk or a hand-held mixer with the double beaters, whip the vegan double (heavy) cream and icing (powdered) sugar together until stiff peaks form.

2. In a separate bowl, whip the vegan cream cheese until it's smooth and looser in texture.

3. Add the cream cheese, vanilla and salt to the whipped cream, and whip for 1–2 minutes until very stiff peaks form. Make sure that you whip the frosting for long enough – it needs to be stable enough to support the weight of the top sponge.

→

Notes

[1] Most dairy-free milks work well, but avoid using canned coconut milk, as it can make the cake too greasy and heavy.

[2] The vinegar (an acid) reacts with the alkaline bicarbonate of soda (baking soda) and the alkaline component of baking powder to boost their activity. This gives the cake extra lift that would've been otherwise provided by the eggs. You can't taste the vinegar in the final, baked cake.

[3] The volume of grated carrots can vary widely based on how tightly you pack them into the measuring cup. For best results, use a kitchen scale.

[4] Use a vegan cream that is stable and holds its shape when whipped.

[5] Use a dairy-free cream cheese with a low water content (not too watery) and a close-to-regular cream-cheese texture.

## Storage

3–4 days in a closed container in the fridge. Allow to stand at room temperature for 5–10 minutes before serving.

**Assembling the cake**

1. Place one of the cake layers on to a cake stand or serving plate of choice.

2. Spread half of the cream cheese frosting on top of the cake in an even layer, leaving a 1–1.5cm (about ½in) border around the edge (the weight of the top sponge will make it spread to the edges on its own).

3. Place the other cake layer on top and spread the remaining frosting on top of the cake. Use a small offset spatula or the back of a spoon to create decorative swirls and swoops in the frosting.

4. Sprinkle on some chopped nuts (I like them in a ring around the top edge of the frosting), then slice and serve.

# Tiramisu cupcakes

**Makes 12  /  Prep time 1 hour  /  Bake time 22 mins**

## Coffee cupcakes

210g (¾ cup + 2 tablespoons) dairy-free milk [1]

15g (3½ tablespoons) instant coffee granules

250g (2 cups + 1 tablespoon) plain (all-purpose) flour

200g (1 cup) caster (superfine) or granulated sugar

3 teaspoons baking powder

¼ teaspoon salt

55g (½ stick) unsalted vegan butter block, melted and cooled until warm

55g (¼ cup) sunflower oil or vegetable oil

½ teaspoon vanilla paste (or 1 teaspoon vanilla extract)

## Meringue buttercream

90g (¼ cup + 2 tablespoons) aquafaba [2]

125g (½ cup + 2 tablespoons) caster (superfine) or granulated sugar

¼ teaspoon cream of tartar [3]

200g (1¾ sticks) unsalted vegan butter block, softened

½ teaspoon vanilla paste (or 1 teaspoon vanilla extract)

¼ teaspoon salt

1–2 tablespoons cocoa powder, to decorate

### Notes

[1] Avoid canned coconut milk, as it can make the cupcakes too greasy and heavy.

[2] Aquafaba, the viscous water in a can of chickpeas (garbanzos), whips to a stable foam, like egg whites (see page 358).

[3] Cream of tartar stabilizes the aquafaba meringue (see page 358).

## Storage

3–4 days in an airtight container in the fridge. Allow to stand at room temperature for 10–15 minutes before serving.

I love taking the flavours of tiramisu and infusing them into other desserts. Here, the coffee cupcakes are topped with a light yet rich aquafaba meringue buttercream. A dusting of cocoa powder brings the whole dessert together and also highlights the shape of the piping to make the cupcakes look super elegant.

Unlike with the vegan vanilla cupcakes on page 126, you don't need to add any apple cider vinegar to the batter because the coffee is itself acidic and therefore sufficient to boost the activity of the baking powder.

*This recipe follows the rules for adapting buttery cakes on page 52 – use them to adapt this recipe to any free-from variation.*

### Coffee cupcakes

1. Adjust the oven rack to the middle position, pre-heat the oven to 160°C/325°F and line a 12-hole muffin tin with paper liners.

2. In a small saucepan (if cooking it on the stove) or in a microwave-safe bowl (if using the microwave) heat together the dairy-free milk and instant coffee, with occasional stirring, until the coffee is dissolved. Set aside to cool until warm or at room temperature.

3. In a large bowl, whisk together the flour, sugar, baking powder and salt.

4. In a separate bowl, whisk together the cooled coffee-milk, melted vegan butter, oil and vanilla.

5. Add the wet ingredients to the dry, and whisk until you get a smooth batter with no flour clumps. Be careful not to over-mix. Divide the batter equally between the paper liners, filling each about ⅔–¾ full.

6. Bake for about 22–24 minutes, or until well risen with a gently rounded top and an inserted toothpick comes out clean. Allow the cupcakes to cool in the tin for 5 minutes before transferring them to a wire rack to cool completely.

### Meringue buttercream

1. In the bowl of a stand mixer fitted with the whisk attachment, or in a large bowl if using a hand-held mixer fitted with the double beaters, combine the aquafaba, sugar and cream of tartar. Whisk for about 10–15 minutes on high speed, until stiff peaks form.

2. Add the softened vegan butter to the aquafaba meringue, about 1 tablespoon at a time. Whisk well after each addition to completely incorporate the butter before adding the next portion. The buttercream will go through a curdled stage (it'll look split and/or soupy). Just keep adding the butter and, once you've added all of it, continue whisking the buttercream for a further 3–5 minutes until it comes together. The final buttercream will be fluffy and silky-smooth. Add the vanilla and salt, and whisk to combine.

### Assembling the cupcakes

1. Transfer the buttercream into a piping bag fitted with an open star nozzle (such as a Wilton 1M; see photograph) and pipe it on top of the cooled cupcakes.

2. Dust generously with cocoa powder, and serve.

# Black Forest brownie cookies

**Makes 18 open or 9 sandwich cookies / Prep time 45 mins / Bake time 8 mins (x2) / Cook time 15 mins**

## Brownie cookies

150g (5⅓oz) 60–70% dark
chocolate, chopped

75g (½ stick + 1½ tablespoons)
unsalted vegan butter block

100g (½ cup) caster (superfine)
or granulated sugar

50g (¼ cup) light brown
soft sugar

80g (⅓ cup) boiling water

140g (1 cup + 2½ tablespoons)
plain (all-purpose) flour

40g (⅓ cup + 1 tablespoon)
Dutch-processed cocoa
powder

½ teaspoon salt

½ teaspoon baking powder

## Cherry filling

1 x 425g (15oz) can of pitted
sour/morello cherries in syrup,
drained (reserve the syrup) [1]

## Vanilla whipped cream

230g (1 cup) vegan double
(heavy) cream, chilled

30g (¼ cup) powdered (icing)
sugar, sifted

1 teaspoon vanilla paste (or
2 teaspoons vanilla extract)

### Notes

[1] If you can't find cherries in syrup,
use (sour) cherry jam or conserve.

[2] Scoop the batter straight away, even
if you bake the cookies in several batches,
otherwise you'll lose that gorgeous glossy
top. (Definitely don't refrigerate it.)

These Black Forest brownie cookies happened because I really fancied a slice of Black Forest gâteau – but I wanted it quickly and with minimal fuss. And these cookies definitely delivered, both in terms of delicious flavour and in terms of speed. The recipe is optimized to give gorgeous vegan brownie cookies with fudgy-gooey centres and a gloriously glossy, crackly top. And while they're delicious on their own, they become truly spectacular when you pair them with the lightly sweetened vanilla whipped cream and the syrupy cherry filling. You have two options when it comes to serving the cookies: you can assemble them as sandwich cookies, or leave them as open-faced desserts.

*The brownie cookies follow the rules for adapting brownies on page 62 – use them to adapt this recipe to any free-from variation.*

### Brownie cookies

1. Adjust the oven rack to the middle position, pre-heat the oven to 180°C/350°F, and line two large baking sheets with baking paper.

2. In a bowl, either on the stovetop over a pot of simmering water or in the microwave, melt the chocolate and butter together until smooth and glossy.

3. In a separate bowl, combine the caster (superfine) or granulated sugar and light brown sugar, and pour over the boiling water. Mix with a whisk or a rubber spatula until the sugars have completely dissolved.

4. Add the sugar syrup to the melted chocolate-butter mixture and whisk well to combine. Allow to cool until lukewarm or around 35–36°C/95–97°F.

5. Sift in the flour, cocoa powder, salt and baking powder, and whisk well until you get a glossy, fairly runny brownie batter.

6. Scoop the brownie cookies straight away, using a 2-tablespoon ice-cream or cookie scoop. Drop the individual cookies on the two prepared baking sheets, about 9 cookies per sheet. Make sure to leave enough space (at least 4cm/1½in) between them, as they will spread during baking. Scoop all the cookies at once. [2]

7. Bake the cookies, one baking sheet at the time, for about 8–10 minutes or until the cookies are set around the edges but still slightly underbaked in the centre – this will ensure a fudgy, slightly gooey texture. They'll have a glossy, shiny, crackly crust. (While the first batch of cookies is in the oven, leave the other baking sheet on the counter at room temperature – don't keep it in the fridge.)

8. Immediately out of the oven, while the cookies are still soft, use a round cookie cutter, slightly larger than the cookie diameter, to nudge the cookies into a more perfectly round shape.

9. Allow the cookies to cool on the baking sheet for at least 10 minutes before transferring them to a wire rack to cool completely.

→

### Storage

Assemble the cookies with the whipped cream and cherry filling just before serving, but you can store any leftovers for 3–4 days in an airtight container in the fridge. The brownie cookies on their own store well in an airtight container in a cool, dry place for 4–5 days.

### Cherry filling

1. Pour the reserved syrup (juices) from the cherries into a saucepan and cook over medium heat, with occasional stirring, until it has thickened and become syrupy, but not jam-like. This usually takes about 15–20 minutes.

2. Allow the reduced syrup to cool to room temperature, then add in the drained cherries and mix well to combine. Set aside until needed.

### Vanilla whipped cream

1. Using a stand mixer fitted with the whisk or a hand-held mixer fitted with the double beaters, whip the vegan double (heavy) cream, icing (powdered) sugar and vanilla together until stiff peaks form.

2. Transfer the whipped cream into a piping bag fitted with a large open star nozzle.

### Assembling the cookies

1. Turn one (completely cooled) cookie upside down, so that its bottom faces upwards. Pipe a generous layer of whipped cream on top of the cookie.

2. Spoon the cherry filling over the whipped cream, then top it with another cookie to sandwich. Repeat for all the remaining cookies. Alternatively, you can pipe the cream and spoon the filling on to the flat surface of every cookie and serve as an open dessert.

# Gingerbread cookies

**Makes 40–45  /  Prep time 1 hour  /  Chill time 1 hour  /  Bake time 8 mins (x3)**

## Gingerbread cookies

90g (½ stick + 2½ tablespoons)
   unsalted vegan butter
   block, softened

100g (½ cup) light brown
   soft sugar

150g (½ cup) molasses [1]

15g (1 tablespoon) dairy-free
   milk, room temperature [2]

½ teaspoon vanilla paste (or
   1 teaspoon vanilla extract)

260g (2 cups + 3 tablespoons)
   plain (all-purpose) flour

½ teaspoon bicarbonate of
   soda (baking soda)

¼ teaspoon salt

1 teaspoon ground cinnamon

1 teaspoon ground ginger

¼ teaspoon allspice

¼ teaspoon ground cloves

## Vegan royal icing

60g (¼ cup) aquafaba [3]

¼ teaspoon cream of tartar

300g (2½ cups) icing (powdered)
   sugar, sifted

### Notes

[1] For the best flavour, use unsulphured, pure cane molasses, not blackstrap.

[2] Avoid using canned coconut milk, as it can make the cookies too greasy.

[3] Aquafaba is the liquid in a can of chickpeas (garbanzos; see page 358). This amount of aquafaba is equivalent to 2 medium (US large) egg whites.

### Storage

1–2 weeks in an airtight container in a cool, dry place. Any unused vegan royal icing keeps well in an airtight container in the fridge for about 3–4 weeks (whip the mixture again to loosen it before using).

These gingerbread cookies are deliciously spiced, with a melt-in-the-mouth texture that you can vary between chewy and crisp by adjusting the baking time. In addition, they hold their shape beautifully (so they're perfect for decorating). The vegan royal icing is made from aquafaba and pipes beautifully.

*This recipe follows the rules for adapting cookies that hold their shape on page 64 – use them to adapt this recipe to any free-from variation.*

### Gingerbread cookies

1. In a large bowl (or the bowl of a stand mixer fitted with the paddle), mix together the butter and sugar until well combined and the mixture has slightly lightened in colour. There's no need to cream the mixture or incorporate a lot of air into it. Add the molasses, dairy-free milk and vanilla, and mix until well combined.

2. In a separate bowl, whisk together the flour, bicarbonate of soda (baking soda), salt and spices.

3. Add the dry ingredients to the wet, mixing well until the mixture comes together into a soft cookie dough that shouldn't be sticky to the touch. Shape the dough into a disc, wrap it in cling film and chill it in the fridge for at least 1 hour or until it's firm to the touch.

4. Adjust the oven rack to the middle position, pre-heat the oven to 180°C/350°F and line 2–3 large baking sheets with baking paper.

5. On a floured surface and with a lightly floured rolling pin, roll out the chilled cookie dough until it's about 5–6mm (¼in) thick. Cut out the cookies with cookie cutters of choice, gently re-rolling the scraps as necessary (try not to over-knead the cookie dough, as that can make the cookies tough). If your dough becomes too soft or sticky, chill it in the fridge for 15–30 minutes before proceeding. Cookie cutters with an approximately 6cm (2½in) diameter give about 40–45 cookies in total.

6. Place the cookies on the lined baking sheets, about 1–1.5cm (½in) apart. Bake, one baking sheet at a time, for 6–8 minutes for soft and chewy cookies or 9–10 minutes for crisper cookies. While one sheet of cookies is in the oven, keep the others in the fridge until ready to bake. (Larger cookies may need longer in the oven.)

7. Allow the cookies to cool on the baking sheet for 5–10 minutes before transferring them to a wire rack to cool completely.

### Vegan royal icing

1. Add the aquafaba and cream of tartar to a large bowl (if using a hand-held mixer with the double beaters) or the bowl of a stand mixer fitted with the whisk. Whisk until frothy.

2. One heaped tablespoon at a time, add the icing (powdered) sugar, whisking constantly on medium speed, until you get a thick, glossy mixture that leaves a trail as it falls off the whisk. Make sure to scrape down the bottom and inside of the bowl, to prevent unmixed patches. You've reached the correct consistency when the trail takes 8–10 seconds to disappear. Correct the consistency of the icing by adding more icing (powdered) sugar (about ½ tablespoon at a time) or a small amount of water (about ½ teaspoon at a time) to make it thicker or runnier, respectively. Add any food colourings at this point.

3. Transfer the royal icing to a piping bag fitted with a small round piping nozzle and decorate the cooled gingerbread cookies. Let the icing dry completely before storing the cookies (it will take 1–2 hours at room temperature).

# Veggie & hummus galette

**Serves 4–6 / Prep time 1 hour (excluding pastry prep) / Bake time 40 mins**

1 batch of **vegan flaky pie dough**
(see pages 200–201)

## Veggie filling

2–3 carrots, peeled and sliced
into ribbons with a knife
or peeler
2–3 courgettes (zucchini), cut
into 3mm (⅛in) thin rounds
2 red (bell) peppers, seeds
removed, cut into strips
1½ tablespoons olive oil
2–3 rosemary sprigs, leaves
picked and finely chopped
2–3 thyme sprigs, leaves only
salt and pepper, to taste

## To assemble

230g (1 cup) hummus
10–15 cherry tomatoes
1–2 tablespoons dairy-free milk,
for brushing the crust [1]
1 tablespoon sesame seeds,
for sprinkling
1 teaspoon flaky sea salt,
for sprinkling
flat-leaf parsley or thyme leaves,
chopped, to serve (optional)

### Notes

[1] The dairy-free milk ensures that the sesame seeds and flaky sea salt stick to the crust. Avoid using canned coconut milk.

[2] Baking the galette on the lower middle oven rack ensures that the bottom of the pastry will be crisp, without any sogginess.

[3] Rolling out the pie crust and assembling the galette on the sheet of baking paper means you can slide it on to the baking sheet without having to worry about the pastry tearing or cracking.

### Storage

Best served hot or warm, fresh from the oven.

This is the perfect clean-out-your-fridge recipe. My ingredients call for carrots, courgettes (zucchini), peppers and cherry tomatoes, but you can really use any veg that you have lying around (some, like butternut squash or broccoli, are best if you cook or bake them separately first, to soften them up). You can use shop-bought or homemade hummus, either a plain one or a flavoured one – this galette is incredibly versatile, but always delicious, particularly with its crisp, flaky crust. Honestly, I could have it for lunch and dinner all week long, and never get tired of it.

*This recipe follows the rules for adapting flaky pastry on page 72 – use them to adapt this recipe to any free-from variation.*

### Flaky pie crust

1. Chill the pie crust dough for at least 30 minutes before using. If you've made it a few days ahead and stored it in the fridge, bring it up to room temperature for 5–10 minutes; if it's been frozen, thaw it at room temperature for 45 minutes to 1 hour, until pliable.

### Veggie filling

1. Add the carrot ribbons, courgette (zucchini) rounds and pepper strips to a large bowl.

2. Drizzle over the olive oil, add the rosemary and thyme, and season with salt and pepper. Toss well to combine. Taste and adjust the seasoning as needed.

### Assembling & baking the galette

1. Adjust the oven rack to the lower middle position and pre-heat the oven to 200°C/400°F. Get a large baking sheet on hand. [2]

2. Lightly flour a large sheet of baking paper and place the pie crust in the centre. Roll out the pie crust into a rough circle, about 32–36cm (13–14in) in diameter. You can trim the edges to achieve a more perfectly round shape if you wish (it's not essential). [3]

3. Spread the hummus in an even layer on the rolled-out pie crust, leaving a 5cm (2in) border free of any filling.

4. Arrange the veggie filling on top of the hummus in an even layer.

5. Cut half of the cherry tomatoes in half and leave the rest whole. Arrange both whole and halved tomatoes on top of the veggie filling, evenly spaced out.

6. Fold the edges of the pie crust over the filling, overlapping the pastry as necessary. Slide the assembled galette together with the baking paper on to the baking sheet (trim the baking paper if necessary).

7. Brush the pie-crust edge with the dairy-free milk and sprinkle it with sesame seeds and sea salt. Bake for 40–45 minutes until the pastry is puffed up and golden brown.

8. Transfer to a wire rack and allow to cool for 5–10 minutes before serving. Garnish with some chopped parsley or thyme, if you wish.

# Apple frangipane tart

**Serves 10–12 / Prep time 1 hour (excluding pastry prep) / Chill time 30 mins / Bake time 55 mins**

1 batch of **vegan shortcrust dough** (see pages 184–5)

### Almond frangipane

85g (¾ stick) unsalted vegan butter block, softened

75g (¼ cup + 2 tablespoons) caster (superfine) or granulated sugar

75g (¼ cup) vegan condensed milk [1]

45g (3 tablespoons) dairy-free milk, room temperature [2]

½ teaspoon vanilla paste (or 1 teaspoon vanilla extract)

¼ teaspoon almond extract (optional)

150g (1½ cups) almond flour [3]

60g (½ cup) plain (all-purpose) flour

### To assemble

3–4 firm eating apples with a red, orange or pink skin, such as Pink Lady, Gala, Jazz or Braeburn

30g (2 tablespoons) freshly squeezed lemon juice

30g (⅓ cup) flaked almonds

Notes

[1] Use shop-bought or make your own using the recipes on pages 26 and 27.

[2] Avoid canned coconut milk, as it can make the frangipane too greasy.

[3] Or, use finely ground almonds.

[4] Baking the tart on the lower middle oven rack and on a hot baking sheet ensures a crisp bottom crust while the top doesn't brown too quickly.

[5] The relatively long baking time means that you don't have to blind bake the pastry to prevent a soggy bottom.

### Storage

3–4 days in an airtight container in a cool, dry place.

The secret to the perfect vegan frangipane lies in using vegan condensed milk: it makes it beautifully rich and gooey but still firm enough so you can cut neat slices. I recommend using apples with a reddish-orange skin: this will make the apple slices really shine, and the end result will look like something out of a fancy pâtissérie (when it's actually incredibly easy to make).

*This recipe follows the rules for adapting shortcrust pastry on page 70 – use them to adapt this recipe to any free-from variation.*

### Pastry tart case

1. Chill the shortcrust dough for at least 30 minutes before using. If you've made it a few days ahead and stored it in the fridge, bring it up to room temperature for 5–10 minutes; if it's been frozen, thaw it at room temperature for 45 minutes to 1 hour, until pliable.

2. Get a 23cm (9in) loose-bottom tart tin with a fluted edge (about 3.5cm/1⅜in deep) on hand.

3. On a lightly floured surface, roll out the pastry into a large circle about 3mm (⅛in) thick and about 4–5cm (1½–2in) larger than the tin diameter.

4. Transfer it into the tart tin and make sure that it's snug against the bottom and sides. Roll the rolling pin across the tart tin to cut away any excess, and press the pastry into the grooves of the fluted edge. Chill the tart case in the fridge for at least 30 minutes.

### Almond frangipane

1. In a large bowl, using a wooden spoon or a rubber spatula, mix together the softened vegan butter and sugar until combined (don't cream or aerate the mixture).

2. Add the vegan condensed milk, dairy-free milk, vanilla and almond extract (if using), and mix to evenly combine. Add the almond flour and plain flour, and mix to a fairly thick frangipane batter. Set aside until needed.

### Assembling the tart

1. Pre-heat the oven to 180°C/350°F with a large baking sheet on the lower middle rack. [4]

2. Core the apples and cut them into a mixture of halves and quarters (leave the skin on). Cut the apple pieces into about 3mm (⅛in) slices, keeping the slices grouped together in their quarters and halves. Place them in a bowl, pour over the lemon juice (to prevent oxidation) and set aside until needed.

3. Spread the frangipane filling on the bottom of the chilled pastry shell, smoothing it out into an even layer. Arrange the sliced apple quarters and halves on top, placing them snugly next to each other, until you've covered the whole tart (discard the lemon juice). Sprinkle the top generously with flaked almonds.

4. Place the tart tin on the hot baking sheet and bake for 55–60 minutes or until the shortcrust pastry is golden around the edges, the flaked almonds are crisp and golden brown, and the apples have softened (you can check their softness by inserting a toothpick or cake tester – it should pass through them easily). [5]

5. Allow the tart to cool until warm before taking it out of the tin. You can serve it either warm or cooled to room temperature.

# Quadruple chocolate cheesecake

**Serves 12 / Prep time 45 mins / Bake time 1 hour 10 mins / Chill time 4 hours**

## Chocolate crust

220g (2¼ cups) crushed vegan digestive biscuits or graham crackers [1]

30g (5 tablespoons) Dutch-processed cocoa powder

30g (2½ tablespoons) caster (superfine) or granulated sugar

70g (½ stick + 1 tablespoon) unsalted vegan butter block, melted

## Chocolate filling

600g (2⅔ cups) vegan cream cheese, room temperature [2]

230g (1 cup) unsweetened Greek-style vegan yogurt, room temperature

200g (1 cup) caster (superfine) or granulated sugar

45g (6 tablespoons) cornflour (cornstarch)

½ teaspoon vanilla paste (or 1 teaspoon vanilla extract)

225g (8oz) 60–70% dark chocolate, melted and cooled until warm

## Chocolate whipped cream

350g (1½ cups) vegan double (heavy) cream, chilled [3]

175g (6oz) 60–70% dark chocolate, chopped, plus extra shavings or curls, to decorate

40g (⅓ cup) icing (powdered) sugar, sifted

½ teaspoon vanilla paste (or 1 teaspoon vanilla extract)

**This cheesecake is one giant, glorious chocolate overload. There's cocoa powder in the cheesecake crust, melted chocolate in the cheesecake filling, and a fluffy cloud of chocolate whipped cream to top it all off. Then, it's also sprinkled with chocolate shavings because when it comes to chocolate, more is just more.**

*This recipe follows the rules for adapting a baked cheesecake on page 82 – use them to adapt this recipe to any free-from variation.*

### Chocolate crust

1. Adjust the oven rack to the middle position, pre-heat the oven to 180°C/350°F and line the bottom and sides of a 20cm (8in) springform tin (at least 7cm/2¾in deep) with baking paper.

2. Mix together the crushed digestive biscuits or graham crackers, cocoa powder, sugar and melted butter, until you get a mixture resembling wet sand.

3. Transfer the mixture into the lined springform tin and, using the flat bottom of a glass or measuring cup, compress them into an even layer with an approximately 4cm (1½in) rim around the edge.

4. Bake for 10 minutes, then remove from the oven and allow to cool until warm.

### Chocolate filling

1. Reduce the oven temperature to 160°C/325°F. If your springform tin isn't completely leak-proof, I recommend that you also get a large baking sheet ready – you'll place the cheesecake on it before it goes into the oven. This will catch any small leaks of butter from the cheesecake base, and prevent any smoking at the bottom of your oven.

2. In a large bowl using a balloon whisk, or using a stand mixer fitted with the paddle on the lowest speed setting, mix the cream cheese and yogurt together until smooth. Make sure to mix rather than whisk or aerate – you don't want to incorporate too much air into the mixture.

3. Mix together sugar and cornflour (cornstarch), and add them to the cream cheese mixture. Mix well until combined and smooth.

4. Add the vanilla and melted chocolate, and mix until well combined and smooth.

5. Transfer the cheesecake filling into the slightly cooled cheesecake crust and smooth out the top.

6. Bake for 1 hour to 1 hour 10 minutes or until the edges are slightly puffed up and the middle is still wobbly when you gently shake the springform tin. This baking time is a guideline – always judge the doneness of a cheesecake based on its physical indicators (the wobbliness of the centre, how set the edges are, and so on) rather than on the baking time, especially as each oven behaves slightly differently. Start checking your cheesecake about 10 minutes before the end of the recommended baking time.

7. Turn off the oven and allow the cheesecake to cool to room temperature in the turned-off oven with the oven door ajar. [4]

8. Once the cheesecake has cooled to room temperature, transfer it to the fridge for at least 4 hours or preferably overnight.

→

Notes

[1] Some brands of digestive biscuits and graham crackers aren't vegan, so always check the manufacturer's ingredients.

[2] Use a dairy-free cream cheese with a low water content (not too watery) and a close-to-regular cream-cheese texture.

[3] Use a vegan cream that is stable and holds its shape when whipped.

[4] Slow cooling ensures a smooth cheesecake top with no cracking.

[5] For extra-clean, neat cuts, dip your sharp knife into hot water between cuts, wiping it clean each time.

## Storage

3–4 days in an airtight container in the fridge.

### Chocolate whipped cream

1. Remove the chilled cheesecake from the springform tin and transfer it to a serving plate.

2. Pour 230g (1 cup) of the vegan double (heavy) cream into a large bowl or the bowl of a stand mixer (if using) and allow to stand at room temperature for 5–10 minutes while you prepare the ganache.

3. Place the chopped chocolate into a separate heatproof bowl.

4. In a saucepan on the stovetop or in a microwave-safe bowl in the microwave, heat the remaining double (heavy) cream until it only just comes to a boil, then pour it over the chocolate. Allow to stand for 2–3 minutes, then stir together until smooth and glossy. Cool until lukewarm.

5. Add the icing (powdered) sugar and vanilla to the room-temperature double (heavy) cream. Using a stand mixer fitted with the whisk or a hand-held mixer fitted with the double beaters, whip the cream on high speed until soft peaks form.

6. Pour the lukewarm ganache into the whipped cream and whip them together on medium speed for about 1–2 minutes until well combined and you get a smooth, silky, fluffy chocolate whipped cream. Be careful not to over-whip, as the cream can split.

7. Spoon the chocolate whipped cream on top of the cheesecake straight away and, using a small offset spatula or the back of a spoon, shape it into a mound with some decorative swirls and swoops.

8. Decorate with chocolate shavings or curls, then slice and serve. [5]

# Brioche burger buns

**Makes 6 / Prep time 30 mins / Prove time 2 hours / Bake time 15 mins**

## Brioche dough

180g (¾ cup) dairy-free milk, lukewarm [1]

25g (2 tablespoons) caster (superfine) or granulated sugar

300g (2½ cups) bread flour, plus extra for flouring the surface

8g (2½ teaspoons) instant yeast [2]

8g (1½ teaspoons) salt

55g (½ stick) unsalted vegan butter block, softened

## For assembling the buns

30g (2 tablespoons) soy milk [3]

1 tablespoon sesame seeds, for sprinkling the buns

### Notes

[1] Avoid using canned coconut milk, as it can make the buns too dense and heavy.

[2] If using active dry yeast, use 10g (3½ teaspoons) and activate it first: combine it with the warm milk and sugar, and let it stand for about 5 minutes until frothing, then add it to the other ingredients.

[3] Soy milk makes a great vegan egg wash, as it adds a bit of shine to the crust and it makes sure that the sesame seeds stick to the burger buns. (For other vegan alternatives to egg wash, see pages 397–9.)

## Storage

4–5 days in an airtight container in a cool, dry place.

**Absolutely everyone will love these burger buns – even non-vegan folks. They're perfectly pillowy-soft and squishy, with a plush crumb and a rich flavour typical of a good brioche bun. The vegan butter adds plenty of richness, so you won't even notice the absence of the eggs and dairy.**

*If you want to make a gluten-free version, use the basic gluten-free brioche dough recipe on page 277, in combination with the rules for adapting bread and yeasted bakes on page 84, if required.*

### Brioche dough

1. Add all the brioche dough ingredients to the bowl of a stand mixer fitted with the dough hook. Knead on a low speed for 15–20 minutes or until you get a smooth dough that comes away from the sides of the bowl (the sides of the mixing bowl should be completely clean at this point, with no dough sticking to them). The dough should pass the windowpane test, and it shouldn't be too sticky or tacky to the touch.

2. Shape the dough into a smooth ball and place it into a lightly greased bowl, seam side down. Cover the bowl with cling film or a clean, damp tea towel and leave to prove in a warm spot for about 1 hour to 1 hour 15 minutes or until doubled in size.

### Shaping & proving the buns

1. Line a large baking sheet with baking paper and it set aside until needed.

2. Once the dough has doubled in size, turn it out on to a lightly floured surface and divide it into 6 equal pieces, each weighing about 95g.

3. Shape each portion of dough into a smooth ball, creating enough surface tension so that the bun holds a perfectly round shape without spreading out or flattening too much. For this, fold the edges of the dough toward the centre and pinch them together to form a pouch. Place the dough ball, seam side down, on to an unfloured section of the worksurface, form your hand into a "claw" over the dough and rotate the dough in place to seal the seams and create a tight ball.

4. Arrange the shaped burger buns on the lined baking sheet, spacing them out as much as possible (they will expand during proving and baking).

5. Lightly cover the buns with a sheet of cling film or a clean tea towel and prove in a warm spot for about 1 hour to 1 hour 15 minutes or until doubled in size.

### Baking the buns

1. While the buns are proving, adjust the oven rack to the middle position and pre-heat the oven to 200°C/400°F.

2. Once the buns have doubled in size, brush them gently with the soy milk and sprinkle them with sesame seeds.

3. Bake for about 15–18 minutes or until deep golden brown, then transfer to a wire rack to cool completely before serving.

Chapter

**9**

# Gfv

Gluten-free
Vegan

# Solving the Trickiest Modification of All

**Gluten-free vegan baking is the most challenging out of all the free-from variations. After all, you're trying to eliminate the most important ingredients that make regular baking work: the structure-providing gluten and eggs, and the dairy ingredients that are often responsible for the flavour and richness of regular recipes.**

**However, thanks to all the science in the previous chapters, we know how to conquer this challenge. For the most part, gluten-free vegan baking is a just a simple combination of all the things we've discussed so far. So, if you want to get a thorough and in-depth understanding of the science, I recommend reading all the previous chapters: from the introduction all the way to the vegan chapter. The case studies in Chapter 4 show you the whole journey from a regular starting point to a delicious gluten-free vegan result for a whole host of recipes. And, of course, the rules in Chapter 3 show you how to apply these principles to whatever recipe you wish.**

In this chapter, rather than repeat it all again, I want to focus on the extra tweaks needed in gluten-free vegan baking to take it from good to amazing. To help those tweaks make sense, though, I'm going to start with just a quick recap of the crucial points in the rest of the book.

# First: A Quick Overview

**Gluten-free adjustments** are all about using a reliable gluten-free flour blend (see page 24), choosing the correct binders in the correct quantity (page 262) and understanding the opposing moisture and fat responses of gluten-free flours and blends (pages 42 and 270). Depending on the type of bake you're considering, either the moisture or the fat response will be more important (or they can cancel each other out). The moisture response refers to the fact that gluten-free flours absorb more moisture than wheat flour – if it's the dominant factor, you'll need to reduce the amount of flour when replacing wheat flour with a gluten-free flour blend. The fat response refers to the fact that gluten-free flours can take on less fat than regular wheat flour before it starts to negatively affect the texture of the bake – so, if this is the more important response, you'll need to reduce the amount of fat when going from a recipe that uses regular flour to one that uses a gluten-free flour blend.

**Dairy-free adjustments** are all about choosing the best possible dairy-free equivalents – this includes alternatives for ingredients such as dairy butter, milk, yogurt, cream cheese, double (heavy) cream, buttermilk and condensed milk. And then, once you've chosen them according to the guidelines on pages 22 and 313–17, using them as 1:1 substitutes for the dairy ingredients. Another thing to keep in mind here is that owing to the absence of the dairy milk solids, any dairy-free (or gluten-free vegan) bakes will be paler in colour (see page 312).

**Egg-free adjustments** are all about understanding the various roles that eggs play in different bakes, and then adding other ingredients that can mimic those roles. These can be ingredients already present in the recipe, such as flour or baking powder, where you simply need to increase their amounts; or ingredients that you need to add separately, such as (vegan) yogurt or apple cider vinegar. Keep in mind that eggs carry out three main functions: they provide structure, they aerate bakes to make them light and fluffy, and they're a source of moisture – so, we usually need several different ingredients to replace them. Furthermore, the roles that eggs play change depending on your chosen bake – that's why there's no such thing as a one-size-fits-all egg replacement. You can read more about this on pages 344–356.

# Extra Tweaks to Reach Perfection

Like I've emphasized already, gluten-free vegan baking often requires a few extra tweaks, in addition to combining all the gluten-free, dairy-free and egg-free adjustments. And it's these tweaks that will take it from good to "I-can't-believe-that-this-is-gluten-free-vegan."

## Gluten-free flour blends

You might find that some gluten-free flour blends work better than others – not just in terms of the texture that they give to bakes but also in terms of their flavour, which really stands out in the absence of both eggs and dairy. So, I strongly recommend trying out different brands of shop-bought gluten-free flour blends and also different compositions of the homemade blend (see page 24). For example, I love using the combination of tapioca starch, millet flour and sorghum flour in my go-to homemade gluten-free flour blend – it gives a wonderful crumb and texture, and has a flavour I really enjoy. You might also be a fan of it, or you might find that you prefer to swap sorghum flour for oat or light buckwheat flour. The world of gluten-free flours is expansive and it offers so much in terms of flavour – so make use of it.

## Vegan butter block

For best results, use a firm vegan butter block with a high fat content (75% or higher) and a high saturated fat content (40% or higher). In dairy-free and vegan baking, you can get away with using a vegan butter with a low saturated fat content. That's because those versions contain eggs and/or wheat flour, which essentially act as failsafes. But in gluten-free vegan baking, those failsafes are absent and the composition of your vegan butter block becomes infinitely more important, especially in bakes such as chocolate chip cookies (see page 164), flaky pie crust (page 194), scones (page 210) and flaky buttermilk biscuits (page 221).

In these cases, it's important to use a vegan butter alternative that's very similar to dairy butter. That means that you want to get as close as possible to its composition – and dairy butter has a fat content of about 80–82% and a saturated fat content of about 50–52%. You can find out all that nutritional information on the product packaging or the relevant brand's website.

## Quantities of xanthan gum

Certain gluten-free vegan bakes require more xanthan gum. In gluten-free vegan recipes, you need to account for the absence of two structure-providing ingredients: gluten and eggs. Consequently, you sometimes need to add a larger quantity of xanthan gum than is necessary in equivalent gluten-free bakes. This is primarily the case for chocolate cakes with melted chocolate in the batter (see page 109), brownies (page 138) and certain types of cookie (pages 151 and 172).

The table opposite summarizes these differences (highlighted in **bold**) – note that the amounts listed apply if your gluten-free flour blend doesn't contain xanthan gum or other binders. If it does contain them, reduce the amount listed by ¼ teaspoon per 120g (1 cup) of gluten-free flour blend.

| Bake | Amount of xanthan gum per 120g (1 cup) of gluten-free flour blend | |
| --- | --- | --- |
| | gluten-free | gluten-free vegan |
| cakes & cupcakes | ¼ tsp | ¼ tsp |
| muffins | ½ tsp | ½ tsp |
| chocolate cakes with melted chocolate in batter | ½ tsp | **1 tsp** |
| Swiss rolls | ¾ tsp | ¾ tsp |
| brownies | ¼ tsp | **½ tsp** |
| cookies | ¼ tsp | **¼–½ tsp\*** |
| pastry (shortcrust or flaky pie crust) | ½ tsp | ½ tsp |
| thin pancakes & crêpes | ¼ tsp | ¼ tsp |
| fluffy pancakes | ½ tsp | ½ tsp |

\* The exact amount depends on the type of cookie you're making.

## Almond flour

You might expect gluten-free vegan bakes to be very crumbly and too delicate because of the absence of both gluten and eggs – but that's not the case at all. Instead, gluten-free vegan bakes can quickly become too gummy (in the case of cakes, cupcakes, muffins and fluffy pancakes) or too hard and crunchy (in the case of shortcrust pastry).

Note that that's usually not an issue with gluten- and egg-free bakes that use dairy ingredients (nor for gluten- and dairy-free bakes that use eggs) – for the most part, this is specifically just a concern with gluten-free vegan bakes. The reason for this is not completely clear, but it's likely to do with the interactions between the oil-based vegan butter and the gluten-free flour blend where there are no eggs present to act as a failsafe.

The solution to this problem turns out to be very simple: you need to add some almond flour. Specifically, adding 20g (3½ tablespoons) of almond flour per 120g (1 cup) of gluten-free flour blend is enough to transform gluten-free cakes, cupcakes, muffins and fluffy pancakes from strangely gummy and rubbery to absolutely perfect, with a soft, tender, plush crumb that melts in your mouth. At the same time, it doesn't make the texture too delicate or too crumbly.

Adding almond flour is required only if the initial recipe doesn't contain any ground nuts or melted chocolate in the batter. If either of those two ingredients is present, however, the texture will be perfect even without the almond flour. You can read more about this in the gluten-free vegan sections of the buttery vanilla cake case study (see page 101) and the fluffy American-style pancakes case study (see page 243).

Adding the same amount of almond flour to gluten-free vegan shortcrust pastry transforms it from rock-hard and unpleasantly crunchy to deliciously crisp and crumbly. But with shortcrust pastry, you need one more thing to make it perfect: baking powder.

> **NOTE: NUT ALLERGIES**
>
> If you have a nut allergy or if you want to avoid almond flour for whatever reason, you can replace it with an equal weight of finely ground sunflower seeds. They're a great alternative to nuts and they won't affect the flavour of your bakes – but they will give your bakes a slightly darker colour. Note that you can't replace the almond flour with an equal weight of extra gluten-free flour blend in these instances.

## Using baking powder in shortcrust pastry

Adding ¼ teaspoon of baking powder per 120g (1 cup) of gluten-free flour blend in gluten-free vegan shortcrust pastry introduces a small amount of aeration (trapped air pockets) into the baked pastry, which gives it a more tender, delicate and just-crumbly-enough texture. That is, the baking powder prevents the pastry from becoming too hard and crunchy.

Of course, though, there is an exception: this adjustment isn't necessary if you're making a gluten- and egg-free or a gluten- and dairy-free pastry. You can read more about this in the gluten-free vegan section of the shortcrust pastry case study on page 182.

## When it comes to butter, size matters

When you make gluten-free or vegan flaky pastry (such as pie crust or rough puff pastry), you can leave the butter pieces fairly large – about the size of walnut halves – and you'll get a beautifully crisp, flaky and shatter-y end result. If you were to keep the fat pieces that large with gluten-free vegan pastry, however, you'd get a lot of fat leakage in the oven and your final pastry would be greasy, oily and tooth-breakingly hard.

To avoid this, you need to work the fat into the dry ingredients to a greater extent, until they're about pea-sized. This will still give you a good amount of flakiness, but it will also reduce the amount of fat leakage and your pastry will end up nicely crisp and tender. You can read more about this in the gluten-free vegan section of the flaky pie crust case study on page 194. In addition to this, your selection of dairy-free butter alternatives is very important – and I don't mean just the composition of your vegan butter block.

## Vegetable shortening in flaky pastry

Using a mixture of vegan butter and vegetable shortening in gluten-free vegan flaky pastry allows you to tailor just how tender it'll be. Using only vegan butter will often make the pastry too hard and crunchy.

Using only vegetable shortening, on the other hand, will make it far too delicate and crumbly, so much so that it'll crumble apart when you so much as touch it. Using a 1:1 ratio of the two therefore offers the perfect balance between sturdy, crisp and pleasantly tender. See the flaky pie crust case study on page 194 for all the details.

> **NOTE**
>
> If you find a firm vegan butter block that has a high saturated fat content and that's perfect for making flaky pastry, you can get away with not using any vegetable shortening at all.

## Go easy on the water (for pastry)

You often need less water (or dairy-free milk) to bring gluten-free vegan pastry together. Vegan butter has a lower melting point and therefore a softer texture. Furthermore, you need to work it into the dry ingredients to a greater extent in the case of gluten-free vegan pastry, as we've discussed earlier. Both of these things mean that you'll typically need less liquid to bring both gluten-free vegan shortcrust and flaky pastry together into a workable dough, as compared to their gluten-free or vegan counterparts. All the recipes and modification rules in this book include the recommended quantities that you should use, but as a general rule of thumb, always add the liquid slowly and mix well after each addition, until the pastry comes together in a ball and all the gluten-free flour blend has been hydrated.

## Gluten-free vegan brownies

In all egg-containing brownies, the moisture and the fat response of the gluten-free flour blend cancel each other out. This means that you can replace the wheat flour with an equal amount of a gluten-free flour blend (or vice versa) without having to change the amount of fat. For eggless brownies (both gluten- and egg-free, and gluten-free vegan ones), though, the fat response is the dominant factor. That's because fat has a tenderizing (structure-destroying) effect and, in the absence of eggs, that's strongly felt by the gluten-free flour blend.

So, in order to get the best possible gluten-free vegan (or gluten- and egg-free) brownie texture, you need to reduce the amount of fat by 30%. You can read more about this in the cocoa brownies case study on page 138.

## Gluten-free vegan crêpes

Vegan condensed milk is what makes gluten-free vegan crêpes work. This is quite an unusual (and highly specific) example, but it really highlights the fact that sometimes in gluten-free vegan baking, you need to think outside the box to get the best possible result. If you try to make gluten-free vegan crêpes (or another type of thin pancake) just by combining all the gluten-free, dairy-free and egg-free modification rules, the crêpes would be strangely gummy and they'll appear undercooked no matter how long you cook them for.

Replacing one quarter (25%) of the dairy-free milk in the batter with an equal weight of vegan condensed milk solves all these issues. The gluten-free vegan crêpes with the vegan condensed milk in the batter cook through beautifully, so that there's no more gumminess – instead, the texture is absolutely perfect: soft and tender, with deliciously crisp edges. You can read more about this on page 232.

## Gluten-free vegan bread

As I've said before, it's impossible to establish a simple set of rules for converting a regular bread recipe to gluten-free, simply because there are so many different variables. Consequently, there are also no rules for adapting a regular bread recipe to be gluten-free vegan in Chapter 3.

Instead, you can use the two fundamental gluten-free bread recipes (for a simple non-enriched loaf and for brioche dough) in the gluten-free chapter on pages 276–7 in combination with the rules for adapting bread and yeasted bakes on page 84 to create whatever gluten-free vegan bread masterpiece you wish. You'll also find two amazing bread recipes in this chapter: one for the softest, fluffiest gluten-free vegan cinnamon rolls (see pages 457–8) and one for gluten-free vegan pesto bread rolls, which just so happen to be one of my favourite recipes in this book (see pages 461–2).

# Egg-wash Alternatives

Choosing the best possible egg-wash alternative for gluten-free vegan (or gluten- and egg-free) bakes is far more challenging than it was with egg-free and vegan bakes that use wheat flour. That's because regular bakes made with wheat flour have a natural tendency to form a smooth, even, slightly glossy and perfectly caramelized crust – so that even in the absence of any egg wash or egg-wash alternatives, you'll still get a nice finish on your bakes.

Gluten-free bakes, however, are quick to form a dull, matte, white-ish crust in the absence of steam and/or an egg wash (or an egg-wash alternative). That's because the crust of gluten-free bread has a much greater tendency to dry out once it encounters the high heat of the oven. In fact, even regular egg wash doesn't produce the same perfectly shiny, even crust as it does with regular, wheat-based bakes – the gluten-free bread will always have a slightly duller and more uneven crust. So, it's clear that choosing the correct egg-wash alternative in gluten-free vegan baking is both more important and more challenging.

I've summarized the available egg-wash alternatives below – and I've included both the suitable and the unsuitable ones, so you'll know exactly which to use (and for what application) and which to avoid.

**Aquafaba** helps to avoid the dull, white-ish crust but it doesn't add any glossiness or shine, and it only negligibly affects browning. However, it does have some sticking power, so it'll make sure that any toppings stay in place.

**Dairy-free milk alternatives,** such as almond, rice and soy milk, act similarly to aquafaba, in that they help to prevent the formation of the dry, white-ish crust but they're unsuitable if you want to add any glossiness to your bakes or if you want to promote browning. However, they do have decent sticking power.

Aquafaba

Vegan butter

Aquafaba & condensed milk

Soy milk

Oil

Aquafaba & maple syrup

**Melted vegan butter** doesn't add any shine and it also doesn't have any sticking power, but it does help with the browning. And, importantly, it results in a very soft crust on bakes such as gluten-free vegan brioche buns or dinner rolls.

**Oil, such as sunflower or olive oil,** behaves fairly similarly to vegan butter: it doesn't add any glossiness and it doesn't help with making any toppings stick, but it does somewhat help with browning and it greatly softens the crust of gluten-free bread and yeasted bakes.

**A mixture of aquafaba or dairy-free milk and vegan condensed milk** is your best choice if you want to promote browning and add a small amount of shine or glossiness to your bakes. It also has great sticking power. I usually use a mixture of 30g (2 tablespoons) of aquafaba or dairy-free milk and 20g (1 tablespoon) of vegan condensed milk. Keep in mind that condensed milk will add a hint of sweetness, but I don't mind it as it's hardly noticeable.

**A mixture of aquafaba or dairy-free milk and maple syrup** promotes browning through caramelization but it doesn't add any shine or glossiness. It does have great sticking power, but it will add a slight hint of sweetness to the crust of your bakes. I usually use a mixture of 30g (2 tablespoons) of aquafaba or dairy-free milk and 20g (1 tablespoon) of maple syrup.

All this information is summarized in the table below, which should help you to select the best possible gluten-free vegan egg wash for your bake.

| Egg-wash alternative | Shine/ glossiness | Promotes browning | Helps any toppings to stick | Softens the bread crust | Extra notes |
|---|---|---|---|---|---|
| aquafaba | no | no | yes | no | / |
| dairy-free milk, such as almond, rice, soy or oat milk | no | no | yes | no | / |
| melted vegan butter | no | yes (minimal) | no | yes | / |
| oil | no | yes (minimal) | no | yes | / |
| aquafaba or dairy-free milk + condensed milk | yes (minimal) | yes | yes | no | adds a hint of sweetness |
| aquafaba or dairy-free milk + maple syrup | no | yes | yes | no | adds a hint of sweetness |

# Easy strawberry cake

**Serves 12–16  /  Prep time 30 mins  /  Bake time 1 hour**

500g (4 cups/1lb) strawberries,
 with tops removed

200g (1 cup) caster (superfine)
 or granulated sugar

zest of 2 unwaxed lemons

170g (1½ sticks) unsalted vegan
 butter block, melted and
 cooled until warm

180g (¾ cup) dairy-free milk,
 room temperature [1]

80g (⅓ cup) vegan unsweetened
 plain or Greek-style yogurt,
 room temperature

15g (1 tablespoon) lemon juice

½ teaspoon vanilla paste (or
 1 teaspoon vanilla extract)

270g (2¼ cups) plain gluten-free
 flour blend [2]

75g (¾ cup) almond flour

2¼ teaspoons baking powder

½ teaspoon bicarbonate of soda
 (baking soda)

½ teaspoon xanthan gum [3]

¼ teaspoon salt

icing (powdered) sugar,
 for serving

---

Notes

[1] Avoid canned coconut milk, as it can
make the cake too greasy and dense due
to its high fat content.

[2] Use shop-bought gluten-free flour
blend or mix your own (see page 24).

[3] If your gluten-free flour blend already
contains binders, omit the xanthan gum.

---

**Storage**

3–4 days in an airtight container
in a cool, dry place.

This is an incredibly easy, everyday kind of cake that you can whip up in about 30 minutes and then let it do its thing in the oven while it fills your kitchen with the tantalizing smell of lemon zest and juicy strawberries. It's deliciously soft and fluffy, and it's loaded with fruit – there are 500g (1lb) of strawberries in the batter and on top of the cake. You can enjoy the cake as a simple snack, but if you add a dollop of lightly sweetened vanilla whipped cream and a few extra fresh strawberries, it'll be a dessert perfectly suited to any special occasion.

*This recipe follows the rules for adapting buttery cakes on page 52 – use them to adapt this recipe to any free-from variation.*

1. Adjust the oven rack to the middle position, pre-heat the oven to 180°C/350°F and line a 23cm (9in) square baking tin with baking paper, leaving some overhang (this will help you to remove the cake from the tin later on).

2. Dice about one third of the strawberries into about 1cm (½in) pieces and slice the remaining strawberries in half. Set aside until needed.

3. Add the sugar and lemon zest to a large bowl and use your fingertips to rub the zest into the sugar. This releases more essential oils from the zest and will make your cake extra fragrant.

4. Add the melted vegan butter, dairy-free milk, vegan yogurt, lemon juice and vanilla, and whisk well to combine.

5. In a separate bowl, whisk together the gluten-free flour blend, almond flour, baking powder, bicarbonate of soda (baking soda), xanthan gum and salt.

6. Add the dry ingredients to the wet, and whisk everything together into a smooth cake batter with no flour clumps.

7. Transfer half of the batter into the lined baking tin and smooth it into an even layer.

8. Scatter the diced strawberries evenly on top, then pour over the remaining batter, making sure that you cover the strawberries as much as possible. Smooth out the top into an even layer.

9. Arrange the halved strawberries on top, making sure to pack them quite close together. You can arrange them cut side up or down, either way works (I recommend a mixture of both for more visual interest).

10. Bake for 1 hour to 1 hour 10 minutes or until the cake is golden on top and an inserted toothpick or cake tester comes out clean. If the cake starts browning too quickly, cover it with a sheet of foil (shiny side up) and bake until done.

11. Allow the cake to cool in the baking tin for about 15–20 minutes, then carefully remove it from the tin (with the help of the overhanging baking paper) on to a wire rack to cool completely.

12. Dust with icing (powdered) sugar, slice and serve.

# Double chocolate banana bread

**Serves 10 / Prep time 20 mins / Bake time 1 hour**

3 bananas, finely mashed (about 350g peeled weight, 1½ cups mashed)

115g (1 stick) unsalted vegan butter block, melted and cooled until warm

150g (¾ cup) light brown soft sugar

80g (⅓ cup) dairy-free milk, room temperature [1]

15g (1 tablespoon) lemon juice

½ teaspoon vanilla paste (or 1 teaspoon vanilla extract)

240g (2 cups) plain gluten-free flour blend [2]

35g (⅓ cup) Dutch-processed cocoa powder

2 teaspoons baking powder

¾ teaspoon bicarbonate of soda (baking soda)

½ teaspoon xanthan gum [3]

¼ teaspoon salt

120g (⅔ cup) chopped 60–70% dark chocolate or dark chocolate chips

### Notes

[1] Avoid canned coconut milk, as it can make the banana bread too greasy and heavy due to its high fat content.

[2] Use shop-bought gluten-free flour blend or mix your own (see page 24).

[3] If your gluten-free flour blend already contains binders, omit the xanthan gum.

### Storage

3–4 days in an airtight container in a cool, dry place.

**One of the easiest ways to take your banana bread to the next level is to add chocolate – and lots of it. The result is an ultra-moist, soft and incredibly chocolatey treat, which gets its richness from both the cocoa powder in the batter and from the abundance of chocolate pieces folded into it.**

*This recipe follows the rules for adapting buttery cakes on page 52 – use them to adapt this recipe to any free-from variation.*

1. Adjust the oven rack to the middle position, pre-heat the oven to 180°C/350°F and line a 23x13cm (9x5in) loaf tin with baking paper.

2. In a large bowl, whisk together the mashed bananas, melted vegan butter, light brown sugar, dairy-free milk, lemon juice and vanilla until well combined.

3. In a separate bowl, whisk together the gluten-free flour blend, cocoa powder, baking powder, bicarbonate of soda (baking soda), xanthan gum and salt.

4. Add the dry ingredients to the wet and whisk them together until you get a smooth batter with no flour clumps.

5. Add most of the chopped chocolate or chocolate chips, reserving some for sprinkling on top of the banana bread before baking, and mix well until they're evenly distributed.

6. Transfer the batter into the lined loaf tin, smooth out the top and sprinkle on the reserved chocolate.

7. Bake for about 1 hour to 1 hour 10 minutes or until well risen and an inserted toothpick or cake tester comes out clean or with a few moist crumbs attached. If the banana bread starts browning too quickly, cover it with a sheet of foil (shiny side up) to finish baking.

8. Allow the banana bread to cool in the loaf tin for about 10 minutes before transferring it out of the tin on to a wire rack to cool.

9. Serve warm or cooled to room temperature.

# Lemon meringue cake

Serves 10–12  /  Prep time 1 hour 30 mins  /  Cook time 5 mins  /  Chill time 2 hours  /  Bake time 15 mins

## Lemon curd

200g (1 cup) caster (superfine) or granulated sugar

zest of 2 unwaxed lemons

30g (4 tablespoons) cornflour (cornstarch)

100g (⅓ cup + 1½ tablespoons) water [1]

100g (⅓ cup + 1½ tablespoons) lemon juice, freshly squeezed

¼ teaspoon salt

150g (1 stick + 2½ tablespoons) unsalted vegan butter block, cubed

yellow food colouring or pinch of ground turmeric (optional) [2]

## Lemon sponge

200g (1 cup) caster (superfine) or granulated sugar

zest of 2 unwaxed lemons

85g (¾ stick) unsalted vegan butter block, melted and cooled until warm

255g (1 cup + 1 tablespoon) dairy-free milk, room temperature [3]

100g (⅓ cup) vegan condensed milk [4]

15g (1 tablespoon) lemon juice, freshly squeezed

1 teaspoon vanilla paste (or 2 teaspoons vanilla extract)

240g (2 cups) plain gluten-free flour blend [5]

40g (⅓ cup + 1 tablespoon) almond flour [6]

2 teaspoons baking powder

½ teaspoon bicarbonate of soda (baking soda)

1¼ teaspoons xanthan gum [7]

¼ teaspoon salt

icing (powdered) sugar, to dust

## Aquafaba meringue

120g (½ cup) aquafaba [8]

150g (¾ cup) caster (superfine) or granulated sugar

¼ teaspoon cream of tartar

1 teaspoon vanilla paste (or 2 teaspoons vanilla extract)

Every bite of this cake is like a lemony party in your mouth. The lemon sponges are sandwiched together with layers of smooth, creamy and perfectly tangy lemon curd, and the whole thing is enveloped in the fluffiest aquafaba meringue. The vegan lemon curd is optimized to be nicely spreadable and thick enough so that it doesn't squish out of the cake. And the aquafaba meringue is sheer perfection: fluffy and velvety, it gets beautifully toasted with the help of a kitchen blow torch and it's stable enough so you can cut neat slices. This is the perfect showstopper for any occasion, and nobody could ever guess that it's made without any gluten, eggs or dairy.

*This recipe follows the rules for adapting Swiss rolls and sponge cakes on page 58 – use them to adapt this recipe to any free-from variation.*

### Lemon curd

1. Combine the sugar and lemon zest in a bowl and use your fingertips to rub the zest into the sugar to release essential oils from the zest and make your lemon curd extra fragrant.

2. In a small cup, mix the cornflour (cornstarch) with about 3–4 tablespoons of the water until you get a smooth slurry with no clumps.

3. Add the lemon-sugar, the cornflour (cornstarch) slurry, the lemon juice, the remaining water and the salt to a saucepan, and cook over medium heat with constant stirring until thickened and the mixture comes to a boil. Then, cook for 15–30 seconds longer with constant stirring. [9]

4. Remove from the heat and add the vegan butter. Stir well until all the butter has fully melted. The mixture might initially look split (the melted butter won't fully incorporate into the curd straight away) but keep stirring – it will emulsify and come together after a few minutes and once the lemon curd has cooled slightly. (Optional: you can pass the lemon curd through a sieve to remove the lemon zest if you want it to be completely smooth.)

5. At this point, you can add a few drops of yellow food colouring or a pinch of ground turmeric to achieve a vibrant yellow colour. Whichever option you choose, add only a very small amount at a time and stir well after each addition, until you reach the desired colour. Remember: you can always add more, but you can't take it away!

6. Pour the finished lemon curd into a bowl or heatproof container and cover it with a sheet of cling film. Make sure that the cling film is in direct contact with the surface of the lemon curd to prevent skin formation. Allow to cool completely to room temperature, then chill it in the fridge for at least 1 hour or until needed. (You can prepare the lemon curd a day or two in advance, if you like.)

### Lemon sponge

1. Adjust the oven rack to the middle position, pre-heat the oven to 180°C/350°F and line a 25x38cm (10x15in) rimmed baking sheet with baking paper (don't grease the baking paper).

2. Combine the sugar and lemon zest in a large bowl and use your fingertips to rub the zest into the sugar (again, to release the essential oils).

→

## Notes

[1] High acidity (low pH) inhibits the thickening power of cornflour (cornstarch). A 1:1 ratio of lemon juice to water gives a vegan lemon curd that isn't too runny.

[2] Yellow food colouring or a pinch of turmeric bring the gorgeous yellow colour to the curd, in the absence of egg yolks.

[3] Avoid canned coconut milk, as it can make the sponge too greasy and dense.

[4] Use shop-bought vegan condensed milk or make your own (see pages 26 and 27).

[5] Use shop-bought gluten-free flour blend or mix your own (see page 24).

[6] Or use an equal weight of finely ground sunflower seeds.

[7] If your gluten-free flour blend already contains binders, add only ¾ teaspoon of xanthan gum.

[8] Aquafaba, the viscous water in a can of chickpeas (garbanzos), whips into a stable foam as a substitute for egg whites (see page 358). Here, the aquafaba amount is equivalent to 4 medium (US large) egg whites.

[9] Cornflour (cornstarch) achieves maximum thickening power and stability when the mixture comes to a boil and stays at boiling point for a while: 15–30 seconds in this case.

## Storage & serving

3–4 days in an airtight container in the fridge. Allow to stand at room temperature for 10–15 minutes before serving.

3. Add the melted vegan butter, dairy-free milk, vegan condensed milk, lemon juice and vanilla, and whisk well until combined.

4. In a separate bowl, sift together the flour, almond flour, baking powder, bicarbonate of soda (baking soda), xanthan gum and salt.

5. Add the dry ingredients to the wet and whisk well until you get a smooth cake batter with no flour clumps.

6. Transfer the batter to the lined baking sheet and smooth it out into an even layer. Tap it a few times on the counter to make it perfectly level and also to get rid of any large trapped air pockets.

7. Bake for about 15–18 minutes or until the sponge is light golden brown on top, well risen, soft and spongy to the touch, and an inserted toothpick or cake tester comes out clean.

8. Allow the sponge to cool completely in the baking sheet.

### Assembling the cake

1. Turn out the lemon sponge on to a large sheet of baking paper that you've lightly dusted with icing (powdered) sugar, to prevent sticking.

2. Cut the sponge widthways into three equal pieces, each measuring about 12x25cm (5x10in).

3. Place one of the sponge pieces on to a serving platter of choice.

4. Spread half of the cooled and thickened lemon curd on top of the bottom sponge in an even layer, all the way to the edges.

5. Place another sponge piece on top, and spread the remaining lemon curd on top in an even layer.

6. Place the final sponge piece on top, making sure that it's centred. Use an offset spatula to smooth out the edges of the cake, if needed.

7. Chill the assembled cake in the fridge for at least 1 hour. While the cake is chilling, prepare the aquafaba meringue.

### Aquafaba meringue

1. In the bowl of a stand mixer fitted with the whisk attachment, or in a large bowl if using a hand-held mixer fitted with the double beaters, combine the aquafaba, sugar and cream of tartar. Whisk for about 10–15 minutes on a high speed, until greatly increased in volume and stiff peaks form.

2. Add the vanilla and whisk well until evenly combined.

3. Use a small offset spatula or the back of a spoon to frost the top and sides of the chilled cake with the meringue, then create a few decorative swirls and swoops.

4. Toast the meringue with a kitchen blow torch, then slice and serve. (For extra-neat, clean slices, use a sharp knife and dip it into hot water between cuts, wiping it clean and dry before each cut.)

# PB&J muffins

**Makes 12 / Prep time 30 mins / Bake time 20 mins**

## Peanut butter muffins

300g (2½ cups) plain gluten-free
   flour blend [1]

175g (¾ cup + 2 tablespoons)
   light brown soft sugar

2½ teaspoons baking powder

¾ teaspoon bicarbonate of soda
   (baking soda)

1 teaspoon xanthan gum [2]

¼ teaspoon salt

145g (½ cup + 1 tablespoon)
   smooth natural peanut butter

50g (3½ tablespoons) sunflower
   or vegetable oil

200g (¾ cup + 1½ tablespoons)
   dairy-free milk [3]

135g (½ cup + 1½ tablespoons)
   unsweetened plain or
   Greek-style vegan yogurt

1 teaspoon apple cider vinegar

½ teaspoon vanilla paste (or
   1 teaspoon vanilla extract)

## PB&J swirl

160g (½ cup) seedless strawberry
   or raspberry jam, plus optional
   extra to serve

30g (2 tablespoons) peanut
   butter, plus optional extra
   to serve

### Notes

[1] Use a shop-bought gluten-free flour
blend, or mix your own (see page 24).

[2] If your gluten-free flour blend already
contains binders, add only ½ teaspoon of
xanthan gum.

[3] Avoid canned coconut milk, as it can
make the muffins too greasy and dense
owing to its high fat content.

### Storage

3–4 days in an airtight container
in a cool, dry place.

These peanut butter muffins are generously swirled through with jam to give them that classic "peanut butter and jelly" flavour. They're incredibly easy to whip up and the best part is definitely the crisp, caramelized muffin top. For an extra-pretty finish, I recommend swirling a spoonful of both jam and smooth peanut butter on top of each muffin before baking.

*This recipe follows the rules for adapting buttery cakes on page 52 – use them to adapt this recipe to any free-from variation.*

1. Adjust the oven rack to the middle position and pre-heat the oven to 190°C/375°F. Line a 12–hole muffin tin with paper liners.

2. In a large bowl, whisk together the gluten-free flour blend, sugar, baking powder, bicarbonate of soda (baking soda), xanthan gum and salt.

3. In a separate large bowl or jug, whisk together the peanut butter and oil until smooth. Add the milk, yogurt, vinegar and vanilla, and whisk until combined.

4. Add the wet ingredients to the dry, and use a rubber spatula or a wooden spoon to fold them together into a smooth, fairly thick batter with no flour clumps.

5. Fill each muffin liner halfway with the batter. Spoon about 1 teaspoon of the jam on top and use a toothpick, a skewer or the tip of a sharp knife to swirl it gently into the batter.

6. Divide the remaining batter evenly between the 12 paper liners, filling each to the brim.

7. Heat up the peanut butter briefly in the microwave, for about 15–20 seconds, until it's slightly looser and runnier (that way, it'll be easier to swirl into the muffin batter).

8. Spoon about 1 teaspoon of jam and ½ teaspoon of the warmed-up peanut butter on top of each muffin and use a toothpick, a skewer or the tip of a sharp knife to swirl them gently into the batter. Try to keep the jam concentrated toward the centre of the batter – any jam around the edges can bubble and burn during baking, and it can make the muffins stick to the tin.

9. Bake for about 20–22 minutes or until well risen, deep golden brown on top with slightly darker edges, and an inserted toothpick or cake tester comes out clean or with a few moist crumbs attached.

10. Allow to cool in the muffin tin for about 5–10 minutes, then transfer them out of the tin and on to a wire rack to cool.

11. Serve warm or cooled to room temperature, with extra dollops of peanut butter and jam, if you wish.

# Tahini shortbread cookie sticks

**Makes 30 / Prep time 45 mins / Chill time 30 mins / Bake time 14 mins (x2)**

140g (1¼ sticks) unsalted vegan
butter block, softened

125g (½ cup + 2 tablespoons)
light brown soft sugar

½ teaspoon vanilla paste (or
1 teaspoon vanilla extract)

120g (½ cup) tahini paste

280g (2⅓ cups) plain
gluten-free flour blend [1]

60g (½ cup) cornflour
(cornstarch) [2]

½ teaspoon xanthan gum [3]

½ teaspoon salt

60g (6 tablespoons) white
sesame seeds

30g (3 tablespoons) black
sesame seeds

### Notes

[1] Use a shop-bought gluten-free flour
blend, or mix your own (see page 24).

[2] Or use an equal weight of arrowroot
starch, potato starch or tapioca starch.

[3] If your gluten-free flour blend already
contains binders, omit the xanthan gum.

[4] Aerating your cookie dough (through
over-mixing or raising agents) can result
in cookies that spread too much.

[5] If your cookie dough is too crumbly
(it can depend on your tahini paste and
the gluten-free flour blend), add dairy-free
milk, 1 teaspoon at a time, until you get
a smooth dough that holds together.

[6] Rolling on baking paper means that
you don't need to flour your work surface,
removing the risk of incorporating too
much extra flour into the dough.

### Storage

1–2 weeks in an airtight
container in a cool, dry place.

**Cookie sticks are an underappreciated cookie shape – they're perfect for dunking into tea, coffee or hot cocoa. This tahini version has a melt-in-the-mouth texture with just the right balance between crumbly and crisp, and the tahini adds a gorgeous, slightly savoury flavour that's perfectly offset by the light brown sugar. Rolling the cookies in a mixture of black and white sesame seeds before baking is a really easy way to decorate them, making them look truly sensational.**

*This recipe follows the rules for adapting cookies that hold their shape on page 64 – use them to adapt this recipe to any free-from variation.*

1. In a large bowl, with a wooden spoon or a rubber spatula, mix together the butter, sugar and vanilla until smooth. Don't cream or aerate the mixture – you want to introduce as little air into it as possible. [4] Add the tahini and mix well to combine.

2. In a separate bowl, whisk together the gluten-free flour blend, cornflour (cornstarch), xanthan gum and salt.

3. Add the dry ingredients to the butter-sugar mixture and mix well until the cookie dough starts coming together. Give it a thorough knead (because it's gluten-free you don't need to worry about over-working the dough) until it comes together in a smooth ball. The cookie dough shouldn't be too crumbly, it will hold together well – but it also shouldn't be sticky to the touch. [5]

4. Divide the dough into two equal pieces, and roll out each piece between two sheets of baking paper into a 13x23cm (5x9in) rectangle about 1cm (½in) thick. [6] Press a bench scraper against the sides of the cookie-dough rectangles to make them straight.

5. Chill the rectangles in the fridge for at least 30–45 minutes or until they're very firm to the touch. While they are chilling, adjust the oven rack to the middle position, pre-heat the oven to 180°C/350°F and line two large baking sheets with baking paper.

6. Use a bench scraper or a sharp knife to cut the chilled cookie-dough rectangles widthways into 1.5cm-wide (½–⅔in) cookie sticks. You should get a total of 28–30 sticks.

7. In a shallow bowl or a deep plate, mix together the white and black sesame seeds.

8. Carefully pick up each cookie stick (use a small offset spatula to help you) and roll it in the sesame-seed mixture, so that it's evenly coated on all sides. Place the sesame-covered cookie sticks on the lined baking sheets, at least 2cm (¾in) apart.

9. One baking sheet at a time, bake for 14–15 minutes or until the cookies are evenly golden brown. While one baking sheet is in the oven, keep the other in the fridge until you're ready to bake that batch.

10. Allow the cookies to cool on the baking sheet for about 10 minutes, then transfer them to a wire cooling rack to cool completely.

# Double chocolate crinkle cookies

**Makes 12 / Prep time 30 mins / Chill time 1 hour / Bake time 10 mins (x2)**

150g (¾ cup) caster (superfine)
or granulated sugar

55g (¼ cup) sunflower or
vegetable oil

80g (⅓ cup) dairy-free milk,
room temperature [1]

½ teaspoon vanilla paste (or
1 teaspoon vanilla extract)

120g (1 cup) plain gluten-free
flour blend [2]

65g (⅔ cup) Dutch-processed
cocoa powder

1 teaspoon baking powder

½ teaspoon xanthan gum [3]

¼ teaspoon salt

90g (¾ cup) icing (powdered)
sugar, for rolling the cookies
before baking

12 large squares of 60–70%
dark chocolate, about
3–3.5cm (1¼in) in size

flaky sea salt, for sprinkling on
top of the baked cookies

### Notes

[1] Avoid using canned coconut milk,
as it can make the cookies too greasy.

[2] Use a shop-bought gluten-free flour
blend, or mix your own (see page 24).

[3] If your gluten-free flour blend already
contains binders, add only ¼ teaspoon of
xanthan gum.

[4] Before chilling, the cookie dough will be
very soft, like thick brownie batter. Chilling
firms it up and gives the gluten-free flour
blend time to absorb some of the moisture,
making the batter easier to handle and
preventing too much spread during baking.

[5] Skip this step for regular crinkle cookies
(with no molten chocolate centre).

### Storage & serving

About 1 week in an airtight
container in a cool, dry place.
Reheat briefly in the microwave
for 10–15 seconds for a gooey
molten chocolate centre.

**This is a simple (yet very effective) twist on the Christmas classic that are chocolate crinkle cookies. Immediately out of the oven, while the cookies are still hot and malleable, you press a large square of chocolate into the middle of each cookie – this gives them an incredibly decadent molten chocolate centre, and it makes them extra rich and chocolatey.**

***This recipe follows the rules for adapting cakey cookies on page 68 – use them to adapt this recipe to any free-from variation.***

1. In a large bowl, whisk together the sugar, oil, dairy-free milk and vanilla.

2. In a separate bowl, whisk together the gluten-free flour blend, cocoa powder, baking powder, xanthan gum and salt.

3. Add the dry ingredients to the wet, and mix everything together with a wooden spoon or a rubber spatula into a smooth, fairly soft, batter-like cookie dough.

4. Chill the cookie dough in the fridge for at least 1 hour or until it's firmed up sufficiently so that you can easily shape it into balls. [4]

5. Adjust the oven rack to the middle position, pre-heat the oven to 180°C/350°F and line two large baking sheets with baking paper.

6. Use a 2-tablespoon cookie or ice-cream scoop to scoop out a portion of the firmed-up cookie dough. Drop it directly into a bowl of icing (powdered) sugar and roll it around until it's evenly coated. The sugar coating will allow you to handle the cookie dough without it sticking, so you can roll it between your palms to form a perfectly round ball.

7. Repeat with the rest of the cookie dough – you should get 12 cookies in total.

8. Place about 6 of the sugar-coated cookie dough balls on to each lined baking sheet, with plenty of space between them (the cookies will spread during baking).

9. Use a ½-tablespoon semi-spherical measuring spoon to make an indent in the centre of each cookie dough ball (make sure that you press only halfway through each cookie dough ball, not all the way through). [5]

10. Bake the cookies, one baking sheet at a time, for about 10–12 minutes or until the cookies have spread and puffed up with cracks in their sugar coating. They should still be fairly soft to the touch. While the first batch of cookies is baking, keep the second baking sheet of cookies in the fridge until needed.

11. The indents you've made in the centre of each cookie will puff up during baking, giving the cookies a flat surface. Immediately out of the oven, press a square of chocolate in the centre of each cookie – the heat from the cookies and the baking sheet will melt the chocolate.

12. Sprinkle with some flaky sea salt and serve warm, while the chocolate centre is still molten and gooey.

# Fudgy walnut brownie pie

Serves 8–10 / Prep time 1 hour (excluding pastry prep) / Chill/freeze time 15 mins / Bake time 1 hour

1 batch of **gluten-free vegan flaky pie dough** (see pages 200–201)

200g (7oz) dark chocolate (60–70% cocoa solids), chopped

70g (½ stick + 1 tablespoon) unsalted vegan butter block

100g (½ cup) caster (superfine) or granulated sugar

100g (½ cup) light brown soft sugar

110g (⅓ cup + 2 tablespoons) boiling hot water

½ teaspoon vanilla paste (or 1 teaspoon vanilla extract)

200g (1⅔ cups) plain gluten-free flour blend [1]

45g (⅓ cup + 2 tablespoons) Dutch-processed cocoa powder

½ teaspoon salt

½ teaspoon xanthan gum [2]

90g (¾ cup) walnut halves, roughly chopped

Notes

[1] Use a shop-bought gluten-free flour blend, or mix your own (see page 24).

[2] If your gluten-free flour blend already contains binders, omit the xanthan gum.

[3] Using cling film or baking paper to roll out makes it easier to transfer the pastry into the pie dish without cracking or tearing.

[4] Chilling or freezing the pie crust before it goes into the oven minimizes the risk of fat leakage from the vegan butter.

[5] A hot baking sheet starts cooking the bottom of the pie straight away, reducing the risk of a soggy bottom, and it also catches any drips from the pie!

**Why choose between brownies and pie, when you can have both in a single dessert! The textural contrast between the crisp, flaky pie crust and the rich, fudgy-gooey brownie filling is simply amazing. The walnuts work incredibly well to add another layer of flavour and crunch. And while you'll definitely get the prettiest and neatest slices if you wait for the brownie pie to cool completely, I actually recommend serving it warm with a scoop of vegan vanilla ice cream. It's magical.**

*The pie crust follows the rules for adapting flaky pastry on page 72 and the brownie filling follows the rules for adapting brownies on page 62 – use them to adapt this recipe to any free-from variation.*

### Flaky pie crust

1. Chill the pie crust dough for at least 30 minutes before using. If you've made it a few days ahead and stored it in the fridge, bring it up to room temperature for 5–10 minutes; if it's been frozen, thaw it at room temperature for 45 minutes to 1 hour, until pliable.

2. Get a 23cm (9in) pie dish (about 4cm/1½in deep) on hand.

3. On a lightly floured large piece of cling film or baking paper, roll out the pie crust to about 2–3mm (⅛in) thick and cut out a 30cm (12in) circle. [3]

4. Transfer the pie crust into the pie dish, making sure that it's snug against the bottom and sides. Trim the excess dough, leaving about a 2.5cm (1in) overhang.

5. Fold the overhanging dough under itself and crimp the edges: squeeze the pastry between the thumb and index finger of your non-dominant hand (forming a V-shape) and press gently into the V using the index finger or thumb of your other hand.

6. Chill the pie crust in the fridge for at least 30 minutes or in the freezer for at least 15 minutes. [4]

### Par-baking (blind baking) the pie crust

1. Place a large baking sheet on the lower-middle oven rack and pre-heat the oven to 200°C/400°F. [5]

2. Dock the base of the chilled pie crust all over with a fork, then line the pie crust with a scrunched-up piece of baking paper and fill to the brim with baking beans or rice.

3. Place the pie on the hot baking sheet and bake for about 18–20 minutes until you can see the edges turning a light golden colour.

4. Remove the crust from the oven and take out the baking beans and baking paper. Don't worry if your pie crust looks oily at this point – the pastry will reabsorb the small amount of melted vegan butter.

5. Return the uncovered pie crust to the oven for a further 3–4 minutes or until the bottom appears set and dry (but still pale in colour with minimal browning).

6. Take the blind-baked pie crust out of the oven and set aside until needed. Reduce the oven temperature to 180°C/350°F, with the baking sheet still on the lower-middle rack.

→

## Storage & serving

3–4 days in an airtight container in a cool, dry place. Best served warm – you can reheat individual portions in the microwave for 15–20 seconds.

## Brownie filling

1. In a heatproof bowl, either over a pot of simmering water on the stovetop or in the microwave, melt the chocolate and vegan butter together until smooth and glossy. Set aside to cool until warm.

2. In a separate heatproof bowl, combine the caster (superfine) or granulated sugar, light brown sugar and the boiling hot water. Stir well until all the sugar has completely dissolved, then set aside to cool until warm.

3. Add the sugar syrup and vanilla to the melted chocolate mixture, and whisk well to combine.

4. Sift in the flour, cocoa powder, salt and xanthan gum, and whisk until you get a smooth, glossy brownie batter with no flour clumps. Add the chopped walnuts and fold them in until evenly distributed.

5. Transfer the brownie filling to the blind-baked pie crust and smooth out the top.

6. Bake for about 35–40 minutes or until the edge of the crust is golden brown and a toothpick inserted into the brownie filling comes out with some half-baked batter and moist crumbs attached. (It's better to under- rather than over-bake the filling if you want it to be deliciously fudgy and gooey.)

7. Allow the pie to cool until warm before slicing and serving, ideally with a scoop of vegan ice cream or a dollop of lightly sweetened vanilla vegan whipped cream.

# Pistachio strawberry tart

Serves 12 / Prep 2 hours (excluding pastry prep) / Chill 4 hours 30 mins / Bake time 30 mins / Cook time 15 mins

1 batch of **vegan shortcrust pastry dough** (see pages 184–5)

## Pistachio paste

250g (2 cups) raw unsalted pistachios

60g (½ cup) icing (powdered) sugar

60g (¼ cup) water

15g (1 tablespoon) sunflower or vegetable oil

¼ teaspoon salt

## Pistachio pastry cream

75g (½ cup + 2 tablespoons) cornflour (cornstarch)

240g (1 cup) dairy-free milk [1]

170g (¾ cup) vegan double (heavy) cream

150g (¾ cup) caster (superfine) or granulated sugar

1 teaspoon vanilla paste (or 2 teaspoons vanilla extract)

85g (¾ stick) unsalted vegan butter block, cubed

300g (1⅓ cups) pistachio paste (see above)

## Macerated strawberries

500g (4 cups/1lb) strawberries, with tops removed

25g (2 tablespoons) caster (superfine) or granulated sugar

1 teaspoon lemon juice

½ teaspoon vanilla paste (or 1 teaspoon vanilla extract)

Making your own homemade pistachio paste might sound like too much effort, but it's 100% worth it when the end result is something as gorgeous and outrageously delicious as this pistachio strawberry tart. What's more, the most difficult part of this recipe is actually peeling the blanched pistachios – not because it's in any way challenging but because it takes a bit of time and patience. Other than that, this recipe is incredibly straightforward – and the end result will look (and taste!) like something out of a super-fancy pâtissérie.

There are three elements to this tart: a crisp, melt-in-the-mouth shortcrust pastry, a flavour-packed, velvety-smooth pistachio pastry cream and a small mountain of macerated strawberries. The recipe is optimized to give a filling that's perfectly creamy and rich but also sets firmly enough so you can cut neat slices.

*This recipe follows the rules for adapting shortcrust pastry on page 70 – use them to adapt this recipe to any free-from variation. The pistachio pastry cream is loosely based on the vegan pastry cream recipe on page 476.*

### Shortcrust pastry

1. Chill the pastry dough for at least 30 minutes before using. If you've made it a few days ahead and stored it in the fridge, bring it up to room temperature for 5–10 minutes; if it's been frozen, thaw it at room temperature for 45 minutes to 1 hour, until pliable.

2. Pre-heat the oven to 180°C/350°F with a large baking sheet on the middle oven rack, and get a 23cm (9in) loose-bottom, fluted tart tin (about 3.5cm/1⅛in deep) on hand.

3. On a lightly floured surface, roll out the pastry into a large circle about 3mm (⅛in) thick and about 4–5cm (1½–2in) larger than the tin diameter.

4. Transfer it into the tart tin and make sure that it's snug against the bottom and sides. Roll the rolling pin across the tart tin to cut away any excess, and gently press the pastry into the grooves of the fluted edge. Chill the pastry in the fridge for at least 30 minutes.

5. Dock the bottom of the chilled pie crust with a fork, line it with a sheet of baking paper and fill it to the brim with baking beans or rice. Place the tart tin directly on the hot baking sheet and blind bake for 18–20 minutes or until the edges are light golden.

6. Remove the baking beans and baking paper, and bake for a further 8–10 minutes or until the pastry is evenly golden (with slightly darker edges), fully baked through and crisp. Allow the pastry to cool completely in the tart tin.

### Pistachio paste

1. Bring a pot of water to a boil (use enough water to completely cover the pistachios). Add the pistachios and boil them for 60 seconds, then drain them and rinse with cold water to quickly cool them. Place them on a clean tea towel to absorb some of the water.

2. Peel the pistachios, either one by one by hand, or by using the tea towel to rub off the skins (then, pick out the peeled pistachios and discard the skins).

3. Add 200g (1⅓ cups) of the peeled pistachios, the icing (powdered) sugar, water, oil and salt to the bowl of a food processor or high-speed food blender. Reserve the remaining pistachios – you'll use them to decorate the assembled tart.

→

## Storage

3–4 days in an airtight container in the fridge.

4. Blend everything together into a smooth, spreadable paste – depending on your food processor or blender, this can take 10–15 minutes in total. Make sure to scrape down the bottom and inside of the bowl as needed. If the mixture seems too thick, add 1–2 teaspoons of water.

### Pistachio pastry cream

1. In a small bowl, mix the cornflour (cornstarch) with about 80g (⅓ cup) of the dairy-free milk until you get a smooth slurry with no clumps.

2. Add the cornflour (cornstarch) slurry, the remaining dairy-free milk, vegan double (heavy) cream, sugar and vanilla to a saucepan, and cook over medium heat with constant whisking until thickened and the mixture comes to a boil (about 5–6 minutes). Then, cook for about 30 seconds longer with constant whisking. [2]

3. Remove from the heat and add the vegan butter. Whisk well until all the butter has fully melted. The mixture might initially look split (the melted butter won't fully incorporate into the pastry cream straight away) but just keep stirring – it will emulsify and come together after a few minutes and once the pastry cream has cooled slightly.

4. Add 300g (1⅓ cups) of the homemade pistachio paste and whisk well until evenly combined. The final pistachio pastry cream will be fairly thick – that's how it should be if you want it to set to a consistency that slices easily and holds its shape once chilled.

5. Pour the pistachio pastry cream into the cooled shortcrust pastry shell and smooth it out into an even layer (you might have a tablespoon or two left over). Place a sheet of cling film over the pastry cream, so that it's in direct contact with the surface of the cream to prevent skin formation.

6. Allow it to cool completely to room temperature, then chill it in the fridge for at least 4 hours or preferably overnight.

### Macerated strawberries

1. Prepare the macerated strawberries about 1 hour before you're ready to serve.

2. Slice the strawberries into halves and quarters (depending on their size) and add them to a large bowl. Add the sugar, lemon juice and vanilla, and mix well to combine.

3. Cover the bowl and macerate at room temperature for about 1 hour or until needed. [3]

### Assembling the tart

1. Peel away the sheet of cling film on top of the pastry cream. Remove the chilled tart from the tart tin and place it on to a serving plate.

2. Spoon the macerated strawberries over the filling along with some of their juices – reserve most of the juices for drizzling on top of the individual slices as you serve. (You can reduce the juices in a saucepan on the stovetop over medium-high heat to make them thicker and syrupy.)

3. Roughly chop the reserved peeled pistachios and sprinkle them on top of the strawberries, before slicing and serving.

# Cinnamon rolls

Makes 12  /  Prep time 1 hour  /  Prove time 1 hour 15 mins (or overnight; see box, page 458)  /  Bake time 35 mins

## Brioche dough

25g (5 tablespoons) whole
psyllium husk [1]

300g (1¼ cups) lukewarm water

270g (2⅓ cups) tapioca starch [2]

225g (1⅔ cups) millet flour, plus
extra for flouring [3]

40g (¼ cup + 1 tablespoon)
sorghum flour [4]

75g (¼ cup + 2 tablespoons)
caster (superfine) or
granulated sugar

10g (3 teaspoons) instant
yeast [5]

10g (2½ teaspoons) baking
powder

8g (3 teaspoons) xanthan gum

8g (1½ teaspoons) salt

240g (1 cup) dairy-free milk,
lukewarm [6]

70g (½ stick + 1 tablespoon)
unsalted vegan butter block,
melted

½ teaspoon vanilla paste (or
1 teaspoon vanilla extract)

75g (⅓ cup) vegan double
(heavy) cream, warmed

## Cinnamon filling

70g (½ stick + 1 tablespoon)
unsalted vegan butter block,
softened, plus extra for
greasing

100g (½ cup) light brown
soft sugar

1½ tablespoons ground
cinnamon

## Cream cheese icing

75g (⅓ cup) vegan cream
cheese, room temperature [7]

28g (2 tablespoons) unsalted
vegan butter block, softened

80g (⅔ cup) icing (powdered)
sugar

½ teaspoon vanilla paste (or
1 teaspoon vanilla extract)

The dough for these gluten-free vegan cinnamon rolls handles beautifully: you can knead it and roll it out without any problems. I recommend cutting the dough into strips before you roll them up into individual cinnamon rolls: this will give you perfect swirls with no squishing. Pouring vegan cream over the rolls before baking keeps them extra soft, and there's even an overnight option – so you can prep them ready to bake the day before you fancy extra-cosy breakfast in the morning.

There are two parts to the baking process: first, you bake the cinnamon rolls covered with a sheet of foil to trap any steam and prevent crust formation. It also lets the rolls expand for longer and by a greater amount. Then, you remove the foil and bake uncovered until golden brown, which helps with flavour development.

*This recipe is based on the basic gluten-free brioche dough recipe on page 277, in combination with the rules for adapting bread and yeasted bakes on page 84.*

### Brioche dough

*You can prepare the dough using a stand mixer fitted with the dough hook or by hand. Note that the mixer results in a smoother dough.*

1. In a bowl, mix together the psyllium husk and lukewarm water. After about 30–45 seconds, a gel will form.

2. In a large bowl or the bowl of the stand mixer, whisk together the tapioca starch, millet flour, sorghum flour, sugar, instant yeast, baking powder, xanthan gum and salt. Make a well in the middle of the dry ingredients and add the psyllium gel, lukewarm dairy-free milk, melted vegan butter and vanilla.

3. Knead the dough until smooth and all the ingredients are evenly incorporated, then knead for a further 4–5 minutes if using a stand mixer, or 6–8 minutes if kneading it by hand. Use a rubber spatula to occasionally scrape down the bottom and inside of the bowl to prevent any dry patches of unmixed flour.

4. The final dough will be slightly sticky to the touch – that's okay, you'll be working on a lightly floured surface so it shouldn't be a problem. Resist the temptation to add more flour to the dough, as that can make the cinnamon rolls too dense and dry. [8]

### Assembling & proving the cinnamon rolls

1. Lightly butter a 23x33cm (9x13in) rectangular deep baking tin or tray, and set aside.

2. Turn out the dough on to a lightly floured surface and shape it into a ball. Roll it out into a roughly 38x45cm (15x18in) rectangle. Spread on the softened vegan butter in an even layer, all the way to the edges.

3. Mix together the light brown sugar and cinnamon, and sprinkle the mixture evenly over the rolled-out dough.

4. Use a sharp knife or a pizza cutter to cut the rectangle widthways into twelve 3.5–4cm-wide (1½in) strips, each 38cm (15in) long. Roll up each individual strip all the way to the end – this will give you a perfect swirl.  Arrange the cinnamon rolls in the baking tin so that they only just touch each other.

5. Cover the tin with a sheet of cling film or a clean tea towel and prove the rolls in a warm place for about 1 hour 15 minutes to 1 hour 30 minutes or until doubled in size. (Alternatively, see over the page for an overnight proving option.)

→

## Notes

[1] If using psyllium husk powder, use 22g (2½ tablespoons).

[2] Or use an equal weight of arrowroot starch, cornflour (cornstarch) or potato starch.

[3] Or use an equal weight of finely milled brown rice flour (your rolls might be less fluffy).

[4] Or use an equal weight of light buckwheat flour, white teff flour or oat flour.

[5] If using active dry yeast, use 12g (4 teaspoons), and activate it first: mix together the active dry yeast, 1 tablespoon of the sugar and the warm dairy-free milk. Set aside for 10–15 minutes, until frothing. Then, add it to the dry ingredients with the psyllium gel and vegan butter.

[6] Avoid using canned coconut milk, as it can make the rolls too dense and heavy.

[7] Use vegan cream cheese with a low water content and texture close to that of dairy (full-fat) cream cheese.

[8] If the dough is too sticky to handle, chill it in the fridge for about 1 hour.

## Storage

Best served while warm. Store any leftovers in an airtight container in a cool, dry place for 2–3 days. Just before serving, re-heat the rolls briefly in the microwave for 15–20 seconds. This will return them to their original pillowy softness.

### Overnight proving option

Make the dough and shape the cinnamon rolls, and then (without proving) place the tightly covered baking tin in the fridge overnight. The next day, bring the rolls to room temperature. If they haven't doubled in size by the time they've reached room temperature, prove them for a while longer – and then, pour over the vegan double (heavy) cream and bake according to the recipe.

### Baking the rolls

1. While the rolls proving, adjust the oven rack to the middle position and pre-heat the oven to 180°C/350°F.

2. Once the cinnamon rolls have doubled in size, pour the warm vegan double (heavy) cream evenly all over them.

3. Cover the baking tin with a sheet of foil and bake the rolls, covered, for 15 minutes. You don't need to cover it very tightly, just enough so that most of the steam generated during baking will get trapped by the foil. After 15 minutes, remove the foil and continue baking until the cinnamon rolls are golden brown on top – about 20–25 minutes more.

4. Leave the cinnamon rolls to cool until warm while you make the cream cheese icing.

### Cream cheese icing

1. In a bowl, whisk together the cream cheese and butter until smooth. You can do this by hand with a balloon whisk, or in a stand mixer fitted with the whisk or with a hand-held mixer fitted with the double beaters.

2. Add the icing (powdered) sugar and vanilla, and whisk well until evenly combined, smooth and creamy.

3. Spread the cream cheese icing over the cinnamon rolls while they're warm. The warmth of the cinnamon rolls will make the icing partially melt into all the nooks and crannies, and it'll make the cinnamon rolls even more decadent and luxurious.

4. Enjoy the cinnamon rolls while they're still warm.

| Composition of the cinnamon rolls | |
| --- | --- |
| Quantity name | Value |
| hydration | 100 b% |
| starch content | 50 b% |
| binder content | 6 b% |
| psyllium:xanthan ratio | 3:1 |

# Pesto bread rolls

Makes 12 / Prep time 1 hour / Cook time 15 mins / Prove time 1 hour 15 mins / Bake time 22 mins

## Homemade pesto

4–6 garlic cloves, peeled

55g (¼ cup) olive oil, plus extra
  if needed

35g (about 1½ cups packed)
  basil leaves

100g (¾ cup) pine nuts

10g (2 teaspoons) lemon juice

salt and pepper, to taste

## Brioche dough

20g (4 tablespoons) whole
  psyllium husk [1]

240g (1 cup) lukewarm water

215g (1¾ cups + 2 tablespoons)
  tapioca starch [2]

180g (1⅓ cups) millet flour,
  plus extra for flouring
  the surface [3]

35g (4½ tablespoons)
  sorghum flour [4]

25g (2 tablespoons) caster
  (superfine) or granulated
  sugar

8g (2½ teaspoons) instant
  yeast [5]

8g (2 teaspoons) baking powder

6g (1 teaspoon) salt

5g (2 teaspoons) xanthan gum

180g (¾ cup) dairy-free milk,
  lukewarm [6]

40g (3 tablespoons) olive oil

These soft, squishy rolls, swirled together with an aromatic vegan pesto, are a real showstopper of a side dish. I like to make a quick garlic confit to use in the pesto – this is just a fancy word for garlic that's been slowly cooked in olive oil until it's soft and tender. The process makes the garlic flavour more mellow and less sharp, but you can easily use fresh garlic instead, if you prefer. And if you're in a rush, you could even use shop-bought vegan pesto (you'll need about 230g/1 cup for the recipe) but I definitely recommend making your own, the flavour is truly incredible and you can easily tailor it to your own taste.

*This recipe is based on the basic gluten-free brioche dough recipe on page 277, in combination with the rules for adapting bread and yeasted bakes on page 84.*

### Homemade pesto

1. Add the garlic and olive oil to a small saucepan. Make sure that the olive oil mostly covers the garlic cloves (add a little extra, if needed).

2. Cook over medium heat until the olive oil only just starts bubbling, then reduce the heat to low and cook until the garlic has softened and is tender enough so that a fork easily passes through it – about 15 minutes. Leave to cool slightly.

3. Combine the softened garlic, 40g (3 tablespoons) of the garlicky olive oil, and the basil, pine nuts, lemon juice, salt and pepper in the bowl of a food processor or high-speed blender. (Reserve the remaining garlicky olive oil for brushing the rolls. Store it in a closed airtight container in the fridge until needed.)

4. Blend to a smooth, creamy pesto. Adjust the salt and pepper to taste.

5. Transfer the pesto to an airtight container and set aside until needed. You can prepare the pesto a day in advance and store it in the fridge, if you like.

### Making the dough

*You can prepare the dough using a stand mixer fitted with the dough hook or by hand. Note that the mixer results in a smoother dough.*

1. Lightly grease a 23cm (9in) square baking tin with olive oil and set aside.

2. In a bowl, mix together the psyllium husk and lukewarm water. After about 30–45 seconds, a gel will form.

3. In a large bowl or the bowl of the stand mixer, whisk together the tapioca starch, millet flour, sorghum flour, sugar, yeast, baking powder, salt and xanthan gum.

4. Make a well in the middle of the dry ingredients and add the psyllium gel, the warm dairy-free milk and the olive oil.

5. Knead the dough until smooth and all the ingredients are evenly incorporated, then knead for a further 4–5 minutes if using a stand mixer; or 6–8 minutes if kneading it by hand. Use a rubber spatula to occasionally scrape down the bottom and inside of the bowl to prevent any dry patches of unmixed flour.

6. The final dough will be slightly sticky to the touch – that's okay, you'll be working on a lightly floured surface so it shouldn't be a problem. Resist the temptation to add more flour to the dough, as that can make the bread rolls too dense and dry. [7]

## Notes

[1] If using psyllium husk powder, use 17g (2 tablespoons).

[2] Or use an equal weight of arrowroot starch, cornflour (cornstarch) or potato starch.

[3] Or use an equal weight of finely milled brown rice flour (your rolls might be less fluffy).

[4] Or use an equal weight of light buckwheat flour, white teff flour or oat flour.

[5] If using active dry yeast, use 10g (3½ teaspoons), and activate it first: mix together the active dry yeast, 1 tablespoon of the sugar and the warm dairy-free milk. Set aside for 10–15 minutes, until frothing. Then, add it to the dry ingredients along with the psyllium gel and olive oil.

[6] Avoid using canned coconut milk, as it can make the rolls too dense and heavy.

[7] If the dough is too sticky to handle, chill it in the fridge for about 1 hour.

## Storage & serving

Best served warm, fresh from the oven. Or, you can store them until the next day in an airtight container at room temperature and reheat them before serving, either in the microwave for 15–20 seconds or in a 180°C/350°F oven for 5–10 minutes.

## Shaping & proving the bread rolls

1. Divide the dough into two equal pieces (each should weigh about 480g). While you're working with one piece, keep the other one covered with a damp tea towel or a piece of cling film to prevent it from drying out.

2. On a lightly floured surface, roll out one half of the dough into an approximately 36x22cm (15x9in) rectangle, about 6–7mm (¼in) thick.

3. Spread half of the pesto in an even, thin layer over the dough, all the way to the edges.

4. Use a sharp knife or a pizza cutter to cut the dough widthways into six 6cm-wide (2½in) strips, 22cm (9in) long. Roll up each individual strip all the way to the end.

5. Repeat with the rest of the dough and pesto to make 12 rolls in total.

6. Arrange the rolls seam side down in the prepared baking tin, in a 3x4 grid.

7. Cover the baking tin with a sheet of cling film or a clean tea towel and prove the rolls in a warm place for about 1 hour 15 minutes to 1 hour 30 minutes or until doubled in size.

## Baking the rolls

1. While the rolls are proving, adjust the oven rack to the middle position and pre-heat the oven to 180°C/350°F.

2. Brush the tops of the risen bread rolls gently with the leftover garlicky olive oil and bake for 22–24 minutes or until golden brown on top.

3. Immediately out of the oven, you can brush the hot rolls with extra garlicky olive oil to make them even richer. Serve warm.

| Composition of the pesto bread rolls | |
| --- | --- |
| Quantity name | Value |
| hydration | 98 b% |
| starch content | 50 b% |
| binder content | 6 b% |
| psyllium:xanthan ratio | 4:1 |

# Chapter
## 10

# Fr

## Frostings, Icings, Creams & Curds

**Adapting your favourite bakes to be X-free (where X = gluten, dairy, eggs or a combination of these) doesn't stop just at knowing how to make a perfectly soft and tender cake, a deliciously crisp and crumbly tart shell or a melt-in-the-mouth cookie. You also need to know how to adapt a wide variety of frosting, icings, glazes, creams and curds – after all, you do need something to fill your cakes, tarts and other bakes with (otherwise, life would be rather boring).**

In this section, you'll find all the most important, basic frosting, icing, glaze, cream and curd recipes that you can then adapt further by playing around with different flavourings. Just like with the case-study recipes in Chapter 4, these recipes include all the relevant free-from variations, so you can easily choose whichever you need.

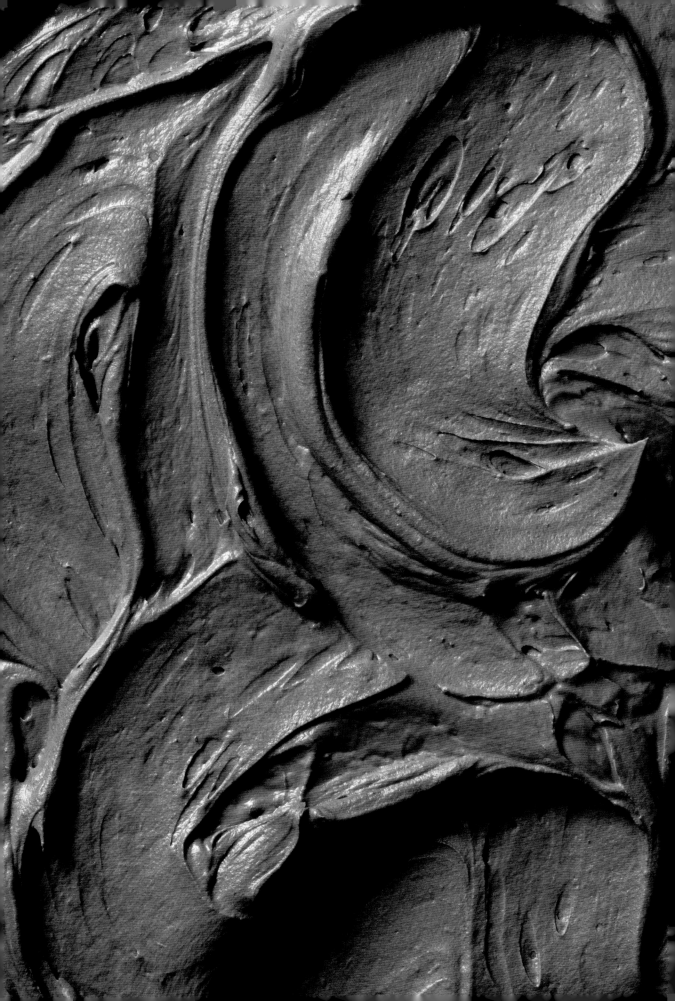

# American buttercream

250g (2¼ sticks) unsalted butter,
    softened [1]
500g (4 cups) icing (powdered)
    sugar
1 teaspoon vanilla paste
    (or 2 teaspoons vanilla extract)
¼ teaspoon salt
15–30g (1–2 tablespoons) double
    (heavy) cream (optional) [2]

**Notes**

[1] Either dairy or vegan butter. For the
latter, use a firm vegan butter block, not
a soft spread.

[2] Either dairy or vegan double (heavy)
cream.

**This recipe makes enough buttercream to frost about 12–16 cupcakes, a two-layer 15cm (6in) cake or a single-layer 20cm (8in) or 23cm (9in) cake. For a two-layer 20cm (8in) or 23cm (9in) cake, increase the amount of frosting by 50% – that is, multiply all the ingredient quantities by 1.5.**

1. In a stand mixer fitted with the paddle attachment or using a hand-held mixer fitted with the double beaters, beat the butter for 2–3 minutes.

2. Sift in the icing (powdered) sugar and whip for a further 5–7 minutes on a high speed setting until pale and fluffy.

3. Add the vanilla and salt, and whip briefly to combine.

4. If the buttercream is too thick, you can add 15–30g (1–2 tablespoons) of double (heavy) cream and whip briefly until evenly combined and you get a smooth, fluffy buttercream. Your buttercream is ready to use.

# Chocolate buttercream

250g (2¼ sticks) unsalted butter,
    softened [1]
180g (1½ cups) icing (powdered)
    sugar, sifted
65g (⅔ cup) Dutch-processed
    cocoa powder
1 teaspoon vanilla paste
    (or 2 teaspoons vanilla extract)
¼ teaspoon salt
120g (4¼oz) dark chocolate
    (60–70% cocoa solids), melted
    and cooled until warm

**Note**

[1] Either dairy or vegan butter. For the
latter, use a firm vegan butter block, not
a soft spread.

**This recipe makes enough chocolate buttercream to frost about 12–16 cupcakes, a two-layer 15cm (6in) cake or a single-layer 20cm (8in) or 23cm (9in) cake. For a two-layer 20cm (8in) or 23cm (9in) cake, increase the amount of frosting by 50% – that is, multiply all the ingredient quantities by 1.5.**

1. In a stand mixer fitted with the paddle attachment or using a hand-held mixer fitted with the double beaters, beat the butter for 2–3 minutes.

2. Sift in the icing (powdered) sugar and whip for a further 5–7 minutes on a high speed setting until pale and fluffy.

3. Sift in the cocoa powder and add the vanilla and salt. Whip until evenly combined.

4. Add in the melted chocolate and whip until you get a rich, fluffy chocolate buttercream with an even, deep chocolate-brown colour. Your buttercream is ready to use.

# Swiss meringue buttercream

This recipe makes enough Swiss meringue buttercream to frost about 12–16 cupcakes, a two-layer 15cm (6in) cake or a single-layer 20cm (8in) or 23cm (9in) cake. For a two-layer 20cm (8in) or 23cm (9in) cake, double the recipe.

| | DIET | | | |
|---|---|---|---|---|
| | **Regular** | **Dairy-free** | **Egg-free** | **Vegan** |
| egg whites [1] | 3 | 3 | / | / |
| aquafaba [2] | / | / | 90g<br>¼ cup + 2 tbsp | 90g<br>¼ cup + 2 tbsp |
| caster or granulated sugar | 150g<br>¾ cup | 150g<br>¾ cup | 150g<br>¾ cup | 150g<br>¾ cup |
| cream of tartar | ¼ tsp | ¼ tsp | ¼ tsp | ¼ tsp |
| unsalted butter, softened [3] | 200g<br>1¾ sticks | 200g<br>1¾ sticks | 200g<br>1¾ sticks | 200g<br>1¾ sticks |
| vanilla paste [4] | 1 tsp | 1 tsp | 1 tsp | 1 tsp |
| salt | ¼ tsp | ¼ tsp | ¼ tsp | ¼ tsp |
| Preparation method | Method 1: heating | Method 1: heating | Method 2: room temp | Method 2: room temp |

[1] UK medium eggs (US large).

[2] Aquafaba is the liquid in a can of chickpeas (garbanzos; see page 358). This amount of aquafaba is equivalent to 3 medium (US large) egg whites.

[3] Either dairy or vegan butter. For the latter, use a firm vegan butter block, not a soft spread.

[4] Double the quantity if using vanilla extract.

**METHOD 1: Heating method (egg-containing buttercream)**

1. Combine the egg whites, sugar and cream of tartar in a heatproof bowl above a pan of simmering water. Heat the meringue mixture with constant stirring or whisking until it reaches 70°C (160°F) and the sugar has fully dissolved – you shouldn't feel any graininess if you rub a small amount of the mixture between your fingertips.

2. Remove the meringue mixture from the heat, transfer it to a stand mixer fitted with the whisk (or use a hand-held mixer fitted with the double beaters) and whisk for 5–7 minutes on a high speed setting, until greatly increased in volume and stiff peaks form. Make sure that your meringue is at room temperature before you start adding the butter.

3. Add the butter, 1–2 tablespoons at a time, while whipping constantly on medium speed. Your buttercream might go through a "soupy" stage, where it's very runny and looks split or curdled – don't worry, just continue adding the butter and whipping and the buttercream will eventually come together.

4. Continue until you've used up all the butter and the buttercream looks smooth and fluffy. Add the vanilla and salt, and whisk briefly to evenly incorporate them. Your buttercream is ready to use.

**METHOD 2: Room temperature method (eggless buttercream)**

1. In the bowl of a stand mixer fitted with the whisk or in a large bowl using a hand-held mixer fitted with the double beaters, combine the aquafaba, sugar and cream of tartar. Whip for about 10–15 minutes on a high speed setting, until greatly increased in volume and stiff peaks form.

2. Add the softened butter to the aquafaba meringue, about 1 tablespoon at a time. Whisk well after each addition until the butter has been incorporated before adding the next portion. Your buttercream will go through a "soupy" stage, where it's very runny and looks split or curdled – don't worry, just continue adding the butter and whipping and the buttercream will come together.

3. Continue until you've used up all the butter and the buttercream looks smooth and fluffy. Add the vanilla and salt, and whisk until well combined. Your buttercream is ready to use.

# Swiss meringue

This recipe makes enough Swiss meringue to top a 23cm (9in) pie or tart or to frost about 12 cupcakes. You can vary the amount of sugar depending on how sweet you'd like the meringue to be.

| | DIET | |
| --- | --- | --- |
| | Regular | Egg-free/vegan |
| egg whites [1] | 4 | / |
| aquafaba [2] | / | 120g<br>½ cup |
| caster or granulated sugar | 150–200g<br>¾–1 cup | 150–200g<br>¾–1 cup |
| cream of tartar | ¼ tsp | ¼ tsp |
| vanilla paste [3] | 1 tsp | 1 tsp |
| **Preparation method** | Method 1: heating | Method 2: room temp |

[1] UK medium eggs (US large).

[2] Aquafaba is the liquid in a can of chickpeas (garbanzos; see page 358). This amount of aquafaba is equivalent to 4 medium (US large) egg whites.

[3] Double the quantity if using vanilla extract.

## METHOD 1: Heating method (egg-containing buttercream)

1. Combine the egg whites, sugar and cream of tartar in a heatproof bowl above a pan of simmering water. Heat the meringue mixture with constant stirring or whisking until it reaches 70°C (160°F) and the sugar has fully dissolved – you shouldn't feel any graininess if you rub a small amount of the mixture between your fingertips.

2. Remove the meringue mixture from the heat, transfer it to a stand mixer fitted with the whisk (or use a hand-held mixer fitted with the double beaters) and whisk for 5–7 minutes on a high speed setting, until greatly increased in volume and stiff peaks form.

3. Add the vanilla, whisk well and use it to top your pie or tart, or pipe on top of cupcakes. You can toast it with a kitchen blow torch, if you wish.

## METHOD 2: Room temperature method (eggless buttercream)

1. In the bowl of a stand mixer fitted with the whisk, or in a large bowl using a hand-held mixer fitted with the double beaters, combine the aquafaba, sugar and cream of tartar. Whip for about 10–15 minutes on a high speed setting, until greatly increased in volume and stiff peaks form.

2. Add the vanilla, whisk well and use it to top your pie or tart, or pipe on top of cupcakes. You can toast it with a kitchen blow torch, if you wish.

# Stabilized whipped cream

230g (1 cup) double (heavy) cream, chilled [1]

60g (½ cup) icing (powdered) sugar

75–115g (⅓–½ cup) full-fat cream cheese or mascarpone cheese, chilled [2] [3]

1 teaspoon vanilla paste (or 2 teaspoons vanilla extract)

### Notes

[1] Either dairy or vegan double (heavy) cream. For the latter, use a dairy-free cream that is stable once whipped and holds its shape well.

[2] Either dairy or vegan cream cheese. For firmer dairy cream cheeses (in a block, not in a tub), soften first at room temperature to make it easier to incorporate. For vegan cream cheese, choose one with a low water content (not too watery) and firm texture.

[3] For a vegan frosting, replace the mascarpone cheese with an equal amount of vegan cream cheese (see also note [2]).

**This recipe makes enough stabilized whipped cream to frost about 12–16 cupcakes, a two-layer 20cm (8in) or 23cm (9in) cake or thickly frost a single-layer 23cm (9in) cake. The benefit of stabilized whipped cream over standard whipped cream is that it's slightly firmer (so it better supports the weight of a layer cake, for example) and more stable, so it can hold its shape better and for a longer period of time, even at room temperature.**

1. Using a stand mixer fitted with the whisk or a hand-held mixer fitted with the double beaters, whip the double (heavy) cream and icing (powdered) sugar together until soft peaks form (if using dairy cream) or until stiff peaks form (if using vegan cream).

2. In a separate bowl, whip the cream cheese or mascarpone cheese until it's smooth and looser in texture.

3. Add the loosened cheese and the vanilla to the whipped cream, and whip for 30–60 seconds until stiff peaks form. The stabilized whipped cream is ready to use.

# Cream cheese frosting

175g (¾ cup) double (heavy)
    cream, cold from the fridge [1]
60–90g (½–¾ cup) icing
    (powdered) sugar, sifted
170g (¾ cup) full-fat cream
    cheese, cold from the fridge [2]
1 teaspoon vanilla paste
¼ teaspoon salt

**Notes**

[1] Either dairy or vegan double (heavy)
cream. For the latter, use a dairy-free
cream that is stable once whipped and
holds its shape well.

[2] Either dairy or vegan cream cheese. For
firmer dairy cream cheeses (in a block, not
in a tub), soften first at room temperature
to make it easier to incorporate. For vegan
cream cheese, choose one with a low water
content (not too watery) and firm texture.

**This recipe makes enough cream cheese frosting to frost about 12–16 cupcakes, a two-layer 20cm (8in) or 23cm (9in) cake or thickly frost a single-layer 23cm (9in) cake. Unlike many other cream-cheese-frosting recipes, this one uses double (heavy) whipped cream rather than butter. The result is a much lighter, fluffier frosting and it's also not as sweet, as you don't need to add a large amount of icing (powdered) sugar in order to stabilize it.**

1. Using a stand mixer fitted with the whisk or a hand-held mixer fitted with the double beaters, whip the double (heavy) cream and icing (powdered) sugar together until soft peaks form (if using dairy cream) or until stiff peaks form (if using vegan cream).

2. In a separate bowl, whip the cream cheese until it's smooth and looser in texture.

3. Add the cream cheese, vanilla and salt to the whipped cream, and whip for 30–60 seconds until stiff peaks form. Your frosting is ready to use.

# Cream cheese icing

115g (½ cup) full-fat cream
   cheese, room temperature [1]
40g (3 tablespoons) unsalted
   butter, softened [2]
90–120g (¾–1 cup) icing
   (powdered) sugar
½ teaspoon vanilla paste
   (or 1 teaspoon vanilla extract)

Notes

[1] Either dairy or vegan cream cheese.
For the latter, choose one with a low water
content (not too watery) and firm texture.

[2] Either dairy or vegan butter. For the
latter, use a firm vegan butter block, not
a soft spread.

**This recipe makes enough cream cheese icing to generously cover a batch of 12 cinnamon rolls. If you prefer a smaller quantity of icing on your cinnamon rolls (as on page 457), make only two thirds of the icing. You can adjust the amount of sugar depending on how sweet you'd like your icing to be.**

1. In a bowl, whisk together the cream cheese and butter until smooth. (You can do this by hand with a balloon whisk, with a hand-held mixer fitted with the double beaters, or with a stand mixer fitted with the whisk.)

2. Add 90g (¾ cup) of icing (powdered) sugar and whisk well until evenly combined, smooth
and creamy.

3. If you want your icing to be thicker and/or sweeter, you can add more icing (powdered) sugar (up to 30g/¼ cup extra).

4. Add the vanilla and whisk well until evenly combined. Spread the icing on your cinnamon rolls while they're still warm.

# Chocolate ganache glaze

120g (4¼oz) dark chocolate
   (60–70% cocoa solids),
   chopped
175g (¾ cup) double (heavy)
   cream [1]

Note

[1] Either dairy or vegan double
(heavy) cream.

**This recipe makes enough ganache to generously glaze one loaf cake or Swiss roll (such as those on pages 320 and 365).**

1. Place the chopped chocolate into a heatproof bowl.

2. In a saucepan on the stovetop or in a microwave-safe bowl in the microwave, heat the double (heavy) cream until it only just comes to a boil, then pour it over the chocolate. Allow to stand for 2–3 minutes, then stir together until smooth and glossy.

3. Allow the glaze to cool and thicken slightly at room temperature (about 15–20 minutes), then it's ready to use.

# Pastry cream

This recipe makes about 750g (2½ cups) of vanilla pastry cream.

When replacing regular milk with a vegan alternative in a pastry cream recipe, use a 50:50 mixture of dairy-free milk and vegan double (heavy) cream (instead of 100% dairy-free milk) to achieve the same richness as you'd get with dairy milk.

You can replace the egg yolks with a combination of extra milk, cornflour (cornstarch) and butter (see page 357).

| | DIET | | | |
|---|---|---|---|---|
| | **Regular** | **Dairy-free** | **Egg-free** | **Vegan** |
| milk [1] | 480g<br>2 cups | 240g<br>1 cup | 560g<br>2⅓ cups | 320g<br>1⅓ cups |
| double (heavy) cream [2] | / | 240g<br>1 cup | / | 240g<br>1 cup |
| vanilla paste [3] | 2 tsp | 2 tsp | 2 tsp | 2 tsp |
| egg yolks [4] | 6 | 6 | / | / |
| caster or granulated sugar | 150g<br>¾ cup | 150g<br>¾ cup | 150g<br>¾ cup | 150g<br>¾ cup |
| cornflour (cornstarch) | 45g<br>6 tbsp | 45g<br>6 tbsp | 75g<br>½ cup + 2 tbsp | 75g<br>½ cup + 2 tbsp |
| butter [5] | 55g<br>½ stick | 55g<br>½ stick | 85g<br>¾ stick | 85g<br>¾ stick |
| **Preparation method** | Method 1: egg-containing pastry cream | Method 1: egg-containing pastry cream | Method 2: eggless pastry cream | Method 2: eggless pastry cream |

[1] Either whole dairy or dairy-free milk, excluding canned coconut milk.

[2] Either dairy or vegan double (heavy) cream.

[3] Double the quantity if using vanilla extract.

[4] UK medium eggs (US large).

[5] Either dairy or vegan butter. For the latter, use a firm vegan butter block, not a soft spread.

**METHOD 1: Egg-containing pastry cream**

1. In a large saucepan, cook the milk, cream (if using) and vanilla over medium heat until the mixture only just comes to a boil.

2. While the milk is heating, whisk the egg yolks and sugar together in a bowl until pale and slightly fluffy. Add the cornflour (cornstarch) to the egg mixture and whisk well until combined and no clumps remain.

3. Pour the hot milk mixture in a slow, thin stream into the egg mixture, whisking constantly (this tempers the egg yolks and prevents the pastry cream from splitting or curdling when you cook it). Return the mixture to the saucepan and cook over medium heat, with constant whisking, until thickened and it comes to a boil. This will take about 2–3 minutes. Once the mixture comes to a boil, cook for about 1 minute more.

4. Remove from heat and stir in the butter, mixing well until the butter is completely melted and incorporated. The pastry cream should be smooth and glossy.

5. Transfer the finished pastry cream into a bowl or heatproof container and cover it with a sheet of cling film. Make sure that the cling film is in direct contact with the surface of the pastry cream – this will prevent skin formation. Allow to cool completely to room temperature, then chill it in the fridge for at least 1 hour or until needed. You can store it in an airtight container in the fridge for up to 3 days.

**METHOD 2: Eggless pastry cream**

1. In a small bowl, mix the cornflour (cornstarch) with about 60g (¼ cup) of the milk until you get a smooth slurry with no clumps.

2. Add the cornflour (cornstarch) slurry, the remaining milk, the cream (if using), sugar and vanilla to a large saucepan, and cook over medium heat with constant whisking until thickened and the mixture comes to a boil. This will take about 5–6 minutes. Then, cook for about 30 seconds longer with constant whisking. (This extra cooking time ensures that the cornflour achieves maximum thickening power and stability.)

3. Remove from the heat and add the butter. Whisk well until all the butter has fully melted. The mixture might initially look split (the melted butter won't fully incorporate into the pastry cream straight away) but just continue stirring it – it will emulsify and come together after a few minutes of stirring and once the pastry cream has cooled slightly.

4. Transfer the finished pastry cream into a bowl or heatproof container and cover it with a sheet of cling film. Make sure that the cling film is in direct contact with the surface of the pastry cream – this will prevent skin formation. Allow to cool completely to room temperature, then chill it in the fridge for at least 1 hour or until needed. You can store it in an airtight container in the fridge for up to 3 days.

# Lemon curd

This recipe makes about 260g (1 cup) of lemon curd. It's best to minimize contact with metal when making the lemon curd to prevent it from developing a metallic aftertaste. Therefore, I don't recommend using a metal bowl, metal utensils (such as a metal whisk) or a metal/metal-coated saucepan. Instead, use a glass or ceramic bowl, a rubber spatula or a wooden spoon, and a non-metal saucepan, such as one with a ceramic coating.

My method for making egg-containing (regular or dairy-free) lemon curd is slightly unusual in that it follows a similar technique to making pastry cream, where you whisk the egg yolks and sugar together and then temper them with a hot liquid (here, lemon juice). This prevents curdling or splitting when you cook the lemon curd, and results in an extra-smooth, perfectly creamy texture.

You can replace the egg yolks with a combination of extra liquid, cornflour (cornstarch) and butter. You also need to account for the fact that high acidity (low pH) inhibits the thickening power of cornflour (cornstarch) by using a 50:50 mixture of water and lemon juice (see page 357).

|  | DIET | | | |
|---|---|---|---|---|
|  | **Regular** | **Dairy-free** | **Egg-free** | **Vegan** |
| caster or granulated sugar | 125g<br>½ cup + 2 tbsp | 125g<br>½ cup + 2 tbsp | 125g<br>½ cup + 2 tbsp | 125g<br>½ cup + 2 tbsp |
| lemon zest | 2 lemons | 2 lemons | 2 lemons | 2 lemons |
| egg yolks [1] | 5 | 5 | / | / |
| salt | ¼ tsp | ¼ tsp | ¼ tsp | ¼ tsp |
| cornflour (cornstarch) | / | / | 25g<br>3½ tbsp | 25g<br>3½ tbsp |
| lemon juice | 80g<br>⅓ cup | 80g<br>⅓ cup | 80g<br>⅓ cup | 80g<br>⅓ cup |
| water | / | / | 80g<br>⅓ cup | 80g<br>⅓ cup |
| butter [2] | 70g<br>½ stick + 1 tbsp | 70g<br>½ stick + 1 tbsp | 115g<br>1 stick | 115g<br>1 stick |
| yellow food colouring | / | / | optional | optional |
| **Preparation method** | Method 1: egg-containing lemon curd | Method 1: egg-containing lemon curd | Method 2: eggless lemon curd | Method 2: eggless lemon curd |

[1] UK medium eggs (US large).

[2] Either dairy or vegan butter. For the latter, use a firm vegan butter block, not a soft spread.

**METHOD 1: Egg-containing lemon curd**

1. Add the sugar and lemon zest to a bowl and use your fingertips to rub the zest into the sugar. This helps to release more essential oils from the zest and it will make your lemon curd extra fragrant.

2. Add the egg yolks and salt to the lemon-sugar, and, by hand with a rubber spatula or a wooden spoon, mix or whip them briefly together until pale and slightly fluffy.

3. In a saucepan over medium–high heat, cook the lemon juice until it only just comes to a boil.

4. Add the hot lemon juice to the egg yolk-sugar mixture in a slow drizzle, mixing constantly until you've added all the juice. (This tempers the egg yolks and reduces the chances of your lemon curd splitting or curdling when you cook it.)

5. Return the mixture to the saucepan and cook it over low heat with constant stirring until thick enough to thickly coat the back of a spoon (about 4–5 minutes). Don't allow the lemon curd to come to a boil – you shouldn't see any bubbles forming.

6. Once thickened, remove the curd from the heat and stir in the butter until fully melted.

7. Pass the lemon curd through a fine-mesh sieve to remove the lemon zest – this will make it perfectly smooth (skip this step if you don't mind the texture of the zest).

8. Pour the curd into a bowl or heatproof container and cover it with a sheet of cling film. Make sure that the cling film is in direct contact with the surface of the curd – this will prevent skin formation. Allow to cool to room temperature, then chill in the fridge for at least 1 hour or until needed. Store in an airtight container in the fridge for up to 1 week.

**METHOD 2: Eggless lemon curd**

1. Combine the sugar and lemon zest in a bowl and use your fingertips to rub the zest into the sugar. This helps to release more essential oils from the zest and it will make your lemon curd extra fragrant.

2. In a small cup, mix the cornflour (cornstarch) with about 3–4 tablespoons of the water until you get a smooth slurry with no clumps.

3. Add the lemon-sugar, cornflour (cornstarch) slurry, lemon juice, remaining water and salt to a saucepan, and cook over medium heat with constant stirring until thickened and the mixture comes to a boil. Then, cook for 15–30 seconds longer with constant stirring. (This extra cooking time ensures that the cornflour/cornstarch achieves maximum thickening power and stability.)

4. Remove from the heat and add the butter, stirring until fully melted. The mixture might initially look split (the melted butter won't fully incorporate into the curd straight away) but just continue stirring – it will emulsify and come together after a few minutes and once the lemon curd has cooled slightly. (Optional: you can pass the lemon curd through a sieve to remove the lemon zest if you want it to be completely smooth.)

5. At this point, you can add a few drops of yellow food colouring or a pinch of ground turmeric to achieve a vibrant yellow colour. Whichever option you choose, add only a very small amount at a time and stir well after each addition, until you reach the desired colour. Remember: you can always add more, but you can't take it away!

6. Pour the finished lemon curd into a bowl or heatproof container and cover it with a sheet of cling film. Make sure that the cling film is in direct contact with the surface of the lemon curd – this will prevent skin formation. Allow to cool to room temperature, then chill in the fridge for at least 1 hour or until needed. Store the curd in an airtight container in the fridge for up to 1 week.

# Glossary

Words in **_bold italic_** are also listed in this glossary.

**Acidic**

Having a pH less than 7. Acidic ingredients react with **_basic_** (or alkaline) ingredients in an acid-base reaction. Acidic ingredients include lemon juice, vinegar, cream of tartar and buttermilk, and they have a sour, tart and/or tangy taste.

**Active dry yeast**

Yeast that comes in a dry, granular form and needs to be activated first in lukewarm water or milk (possibly in the presence of sugar or flour) before it's incorporated into the dough. Because of the way it's processed, it's less active than instant yeast: you need to use 20% more of it if replacing instant yeast in a recipe.

**Aerate**

To mechanically incorporate air into a batter or dough through the process of whisking, whipping or creaming.

**Aeration**

The presence of trapped air pockets in a batter, dough or the crumb of a finished bake, such as a cake, cupcake, muffin or similar.

**Alkaline**

See **_Basic_**

**All-in-one creaming method**

A creaming method used in cake-making where you put all the cake ingredients into a bowl, mix them together into a smooth batter and bake. Unlike the standard and reverse creaming methods, this method doesn't call for the gradual addition of ingredients.

**All-purpose flour (known as plain flour in the UK)**

Regular wheat flour that can be used in a wide range of different bakes, including cakes, cupcakes, muffins, cookies, brownies and pastry. Typically not used to make bread.

**Aquafaba**

The viscous liquid from a can of chickpeas (garbanzos; see also page 358).

**Baker's percentage (b%)**

A useful way to express proportions of ingredients in bread dough, where the amount of each ingredient is given as a percentage of the flour weight (the flour weight is always 100 b%). Baker's percentage stays constant even if you scale a bread recipe up or down. (See also page 272.)

**Basic**

Having a pH more than 7. Basic (or alkaline) ingredients react with acids or acidic ingredients in an acid-base reaction. The most common basic ingredient used in baking is baking soda (also known as bicarbonate of soda).

**Binder**

An ingredient used in gluten-free baking to mimic the effects of gluten, including the binding power, structure-providing properties, elasticity and flexibility. Binders prevent gluten-free bakes from being too delicate or crumbly. The most common binders used in gluten-free baking are xanthan gum and psyllium husk.

**Binder content**

The amount of a binder in a gluten-free bread recipe, expressed in terms of **_baker's percentage_** (b%).

**Blanch**

Briefly immerse in boiling water. Most commonly used as a technique when removing the skin from nuts, such as almonds or pistachios, or to scald vegetables or herbs to preserve their flavour, colour or texture.

**Blind baking**

The method by which you pre-bake a pie crust or a tart shell before you add any filling, typically by lining it with baking paper and filling it with baking beans, rice or dried beans to preserve its shape and prevent slumping. Blind baking typically refers to the process where the pastry is completely baked through and no further baking is necessary once the filling is added, although it may be used synonymously with **_par-baking_** (as it is in this book).

**Boil**

To cook in a liquid (typically water) that's been heated until it's visibly and vigorously bubbling (it's reached the boiling point). For water at sea level, the boiling point is at 100°C/212°F.

**Bread flour**

Regular wheat flour with a higher protein (gluten) content used to make bread.

**Browning**

Generally refers to the process of bakes becoming golden brown during baking or cooking. Often used specifically to refer to the **_Maillard reaction_**.

**Caramelization**

A chemical reaction where you heat sugar until its molecules start breaking apart, which results in a colour change to golden brown or dark amber and also in the development of new, complex flavours and aromas. This is a crucial reaction when making caramel or caramel sauce, and also for creating the crunchy caramelized sugar topping on crème brûlée.

**Carryover cooking**
The process where foods or bakes continue to cook even after you've removed them from the heat source, be that the oven or a pan on the stovetop. This happens because the outer layers of the food or bake are hotter than the centre, and that heat is partially transferred to the interior (the rest is lost to the surrounding air as the food or bake cools).

**Chill**
Cool in the fridge. Note the difference from *freeze*.

**Cocoa solids**
The components of cocoa beans that remain after the cocoa butter has been removed. Cocoa solids content is an easy way to convey how dark the chocolate is: milk chocolate typically has a cocoa solids content of about 25–50%, whereas dark chocolate can contain anywhere from 50 to 100% cocoa solids (the higher the cocoa-solid content, the darker and more bitter the chocolate; typical range is about 60–85%). White chocolate doesn't contain any cocoa solids.

**Cornflour (cornstarch in the US)**
The starch extracted from corn grain, specifically from the endosperm of the corn kernels. It's almost 100% starch, without any fibre, protein, fat or other components. It's a very fine white powder that's chalky in appearance and that "squeaks" when you rub it between your fingers. Often used as a thickening agent to thicken sauces and custards, like for example vanilla pastry cream. Note the difference from *maize flour (corn flour)*.

**Cream (verb)**
To mix butter and sugar together in a way which incorporates air into the mixture, until it's pale and fluffy (typically by whipping or whisking the two together either by hand with a wooden spoon, rubber spatula or whisk, or with a stand or hand-held mixer).

**Crimp**
To decorate the edge of a pie by pinching or pressing the pie crust between your fingers to create a fluted pattern.

**Crumb**
The interior texture of baked goods.

**Density**
Weight per unit volume.

**Dissolve**
To become incorporated into a liquid so as to create a solution. For example, sugar and salt dissolve in water. Note the difference from *melt*.

**Dock**
To poke evenly spaced holes in the surface of a dough or pastry to promote even baking and to prevent it from puffing up owing to trapped steam either underneath or within the dough or pastry.

**Doming**
When a cake, cupcake, muffin or similar bake has a noticeably domed top. This occurs when the edges of the batter set but the centre of the batter continues to rise.

**Dutch-processed cocoa powder**
Cocoa powder that's gone through an alkalizing process, which neutralizes the acidity of natural cocoa powder. It has a neutral pH, which means that it doesn't react with *basic* ingredients (unlike the acidic natural cocoa powder) and it tends to have a richer, deeper flavour.

**Emulsify**
To create an *emulsion*.

**Emulsion**
A fine dispersion of one liquid in another, where the two liquids otherwise aren't soluble or miscible (that is, they tend to separate). For example, mayonnaise is an oil-in-water emulsion. Similarly, cake batter is essentially an emulsion of water (coming from eggs and other wet ingredients) and butter.

**Fat response**
The way in which flours (wheat or gluten-free) interact with the fat present in the recipe (the fat most commonly being either butter or oil). This includes how well they absorb it and how much fat they can essentially "take on" before the bake turns stodgy, pudding-y, dense or, usually in the case of cookies or shortcrust pastry, too crumbly. (See also page 42.)

**Fluidity**
The ability of a substance to flow easily. In the context of cake batter, it refers to how runny the batter is.

**Fold (in)**
To gently combine two (or more) ingredients of different densities in such a way so as to preserve the lightness, fluffiness and aeration of the mixture as much as possible. For example, you'd fold whipped egg whites into cake batter, or melted chocolate into the whipped egg-sugar mixture when making brownies. In practice, you can use a rubber spatula to cut through the centre of the mixture, scrape along the bottom of the bowl and then fold the mixture from the bottom of the bowl over the top – and then repeat that motion until you get a light, airy homogeneous mixture.

**Free-from**
A single term that encompasses all the various different dietary requirements, including gluten-free, dairy-free, egg-free and vegan (and combinations of them).

**Freeze**
*Chill* or store in the freezer.

**Gluten-free flour**
A single, individual gluten-free flour, such as tapioca starch, brown rice flour, sorghum flour or millet flour. Note the difference compared to a *gluten-free flour blend*, which comprises two or more gluten-free flours.

**Gluten-free flour blend**
A mix of several gluten-free flours, sometimes also referred to as a "1-to-1 gluten-free flour" or a "gluten-free flour mix", which can be used to prepare a wide variety of bakes, such as cakes, cupcakes, muffins, cookies, brownies and pastry (typically not well suited for making gluten-free bread). You can find commercially available gluten-free flour blends in shops and online, or make your own homemade version using the recipe on page 24.

**Golden syrup**
An inverted sugar syrup also known as light treacle; a by-product of refining sugar cane to create sugar. It's a thick, amber-coloured syrup with a caramel-like, buttery flavour.

**Hydrate**
To absorb water.

**Hydration**
A term used in bread baking to describe the amount of water (or other liquid such as milk) in a bread recipe in terms of *baker's percentage* (b%).

**Instant yeast**
Yeast that comes in a dry, granular form and can be added directly to the dry ingredients without needing to be activated first. Because of the way it's processed, it's more active than *active dry yeast*: you need to use 20% less of it if replacing active dry yeast in a recipe.

**Lamination**
Alternating layers of dough and butter in pastry, such as puff pastry or croissant dough (also used to refer to the process of creating these butter-dough layers).

**Letter fold**
A lamination process where rolled-out dough is folded in thirds, as you would a letter: the top third toward the centre and the bottom third up and over it.

**Lukewarm**
Mildly warm, slightly warmer than body temperature, typically used to describe liquids such as water or milk. Generally means in the temperature range around 35–40°C/95–105°F.

**Maceration**
The process where (chopped or sliced) fruit softens and releases its natural juices with the help of sugar. Sugar is hygroscopic, which means that it attracts water – it essentially draws the moisture out of the fruit.

**Maillard reaction**
A chemical reaction between sugars and amino acids (the building blocks of proteins) in the presence of heat, which results in browning and the evolution of new flavours. This is a crucial reaction when it comes to grilling or roasting meat, browning butter, or getting a dark, flavourful crust on a loaf of bread.

**Maize flour (corn flour in the US)**
The flour obtained by grinding entire dried corn kernels into a fine powder, essentially very finely ground corn meal. In addition to the starch, it also contains fibre, protein and a small amount of fat. There are two types of corn flour: the more common yellow corn flour that's made from yellow corn, and white corn flour made from white corn kernels. Note the difference from *cornflour (cornstarch)*.

**Melt**
Heat a solid ingredient, such as butter or chocolate, until it's a liquid. Note the difference from *dissolve*.

**Milk solids**
The components of dairy ingredients, such as milk, butter, cream and similar, that would remain after all the water and fat have been removed. Milk solids consist of proteins (largely casein protein and whey protein), carbohydrates (primarily lactose) and minerals (such as calcium and phosphorus).

**Mix**
To combine two or more ingredients into a single, homogeneous mixture. Mix does not specify the way or manner in which the ingredients should be combined. Note differences with *cream*, *fold (in)*, *stir*, *whip* and *whisk*.

**Moisture (water) absorption capacity**
The amount of moisture or water that a flour (regular or gluten-free) can absorb.

**Moisture response**
The way in which flours (regular or gluten-free) interact with the moisture in the recipe – how well they absorb it and how well they hold on to it. This moisture can come from any of the moisture sources in the recipe, such as eggs, milk, yogurt or similar. (See also page 42.)

**Oven spring**

The rapid expansion of bread and other yeasted bakes as they enter the oven, owing to a combination of three things: the last burst of carbon dioxide generated by the yeast before it dies, some of the moisture in the dough quickly transforming into steam, and the gases in the dough expanding from the heat.

**Par-baking**

The method by which a pie crust or tart shell is only partially baked and requires further baking after filling, although this is also often referred to as *blind baking*.

**pH**

A measure of how *acidic* or *basic* something is: pH 7 is neutral, pH less than 7 is acidic and pH more than 7 is basic or alkaline.

**Plain flour**

Flour (regular or gluten-free) that doesn't contain any raising agents. Note the difference from *self-raising flour*. See also *all-purpose flour*.

**Pre-heat**

To heat the oven to the desired temperature before you place your bake into the oven. Typically, you want your oven to reach the desired temperature and stay at it for at least 10–15 minutes before you put in your bakes, so as to minimize any temperature fluctuations during baking.

**Psyllium husk**

The outer coating (the husk) of the psyllium seeds from the *Plantago ovata* plant, which is a herb grown mainly in India. It's a binder (gluten substitute) essential for making gluten-free bread owing to its ability to bind water and form a sticky, fairly elastic gel. (See also page 264.)

**Raising agents**

The collective name for baking powder and baking soda.

**Regular**

A term used throughout this book to describe non-free-from ingredients, such as wheat flour, dairy and eggs, as well as recipes that contain them (that is, recipes that don't belong to any of the free-from categories).

**Reverse creaming method**

A creaming method used in cake making, pioneered by Rose Levy Beranbaum, which involves working the butter into the dry ingredients and sugar until you get a texture resembling breadcrumbs, followed by the addition of wet ingredients to form a smooth cake batter. This method results in cakes with little doming and a very delicate, tender, melt-in-the-mouth crumb. (See also page 95.)

**Ribbon stage**

The stage in the process of whipping eggs with sugar when the mixture becomes thick enough so that it forms a ribbon on top of the bulk mixture when it falls off the whisk. The ribbon will last for a second or two and then disappear into the bulk. The whipped egg-sugar mixture will be very pale, fluffy and about tripled in volume at this point.

**Room temperature**

Around 22°C/72°F.

**Self-raising flour**

Flour (regular or gluten-free) that contains raising agents. Note the difference from *plain flour*.

**Sift**

To pass dry ingredients, such as flour, cocoa powder or icing (powdered) sugar, through a sieve or sifter to remove any clumps and also to aerate the ingredient(s).

**Simmer**

To heat a liquid to just below the boiling point, so that small bubbles rise below the surface. Also, to cook something in such a liquid (typically water).

**Soft peaks**

A stage in whipping or whisking where the mixture forms loose, rounded peaks that will bend or slump over to one side (to create a peak, lift the whisk or beaters straight up out of the mixture). Typically used to refer to double (heavy) or whipping cream, whipped egg whites, meringue or aquafaba. Note the difference from *stiff peaks*.

**Standard creaming method**

The most common creaming method used when preparing cakes, which involves creaming the butter and sugar together until pale and fluffy, adding the eggs one at a time and then adding the dry and the wet ingredients in alternating batches, starting and ending with the dry. (See also page 95.)

**Starch content**

A term used in gluten-free bread baking to describe the amount of starchy gluten-free flours in a recipe in terms of *baker's percentage* (b%).

**Stiff peaks**

A stage in whipping or whisking where the mixture forms very firm, pointed peaks that hold their shape without bending or slumping (to create a peak, lift the whisk or beaters straight up out of the mixture). Typically used to refer to double (heavy) or whipping cream, whipped egg whites, meringue or aquafaba. Note the difference from *soft peaks*.

### Stir

To mix two or more ingredients together without incorporating any air into the mixture, typically with a wooden spoon or a rubber spatula. Note the difference from *cream*, *whip* and *whisk*.

### Temper

**(1)** To melt and cool chocolate while precisely controlling its temperature at every stage of the process, in order to ensure a shiny, glossy end result and a solid texture that snaps when you break it. **(2)** To slowly raise the temperature of the egg-sugar mixture when making pastry cream (or similar) by gradually adding hot liquid (typically milk), in order to prevent the eggs or egg yolks from scrambling when you cook the pastry cream.

### Tenderizing

Having the ability to make bakes more tender by partially destroying the structural framework created by the gluten and eggs (specifically, egg whites). Tenderizing ingredients, such as butter, oil, egg yolks and even sugar, are responsible for giving bakes their characteristic tender, delicate, melt-in-the-mouth crumb. (See also page 38.)

### Toothpick test

A method of checking the doneness of a bake by inserting a toothpick, skewer or cake tester into the centre of the bake for about 2 seconds and then observing how it comes out. For most cake, cupcake and muffin recipes, you're looking for a clean toothpick or cake tester, possibly with a few moist crumbs attached. For fudgy or gooey brownies, you're looking for a toothpick or cake tester covered in a mixture of half-baked batter and many moist crumbs (if it's clean, you've probably overbaked your brownies).

### Toss

To lightly mix ingredients together by lifting and dropping them so as to ensure even coverage, typically with the help of spoons, forks or your fingertips. For example, you can toss a salad to evenly coat it with a dressing, or toss apple slices in cinnamon-sugar.

### Tunnelling

The formation of tunnels and very large air pockets inside cakes, cupcakes, muffins and similar bakes as a result of over-mixing a batter made from wheat flour.

### Whip

To mix ingredients rapidly with a balloon whisk, a stand mixer fitted with the paddle or whisk, or a hand-held mixer fitted with the double beaters, so as to incorporate air into the mixture and increase its volume.

### Whisk

To mix ingredients together using a balloon whisk until evenly combined, possibly also incorporating air into the mixture if it's specified in the recipe (in that case, you can also use a stand mixer fitted with the whisk or a hand-held mixer fitted with the double beaters).

### Windowpane test

A method of checking how strong and elastic your gluten-containing bread dough is, where you stretch a small amount of dough between your fingers to form a thin, translucent membrane that allows light to pass through it (a "windowpane"). The dough passes the windowpane test if it forms the translucent membrane without tearing or breaking.

### Xanthan gum

A polysaccharide (a type of complex sugar) produced through a fermentation process by the *Xanthomonas campestris* bacteria. It's a food thickening agent and a stabilizer, as well as a binder (gluten substitute) used in gluten-free baking. It prevents gluten-free bakes from being too delicate or too crumbly, and it greatly improves their texture. (See also page 263.)

---

**Basic Cook's Notes**

Use medium ingredients and fresh vegetables, fruit and herbs, unless specified otherwise. Oven temperatures vary. Always check the packaging for allergens. Use metric or imperial/volume measurements, but not a mixture of both (for precise results, I strongly recommend using metric weights with a digital scale for all ingredients; see page 15).

# UK / US Glossary

Depending on where in the world you are, different ingredients, tools and even methods might have different names – and the difference in baking terminology between the UK and US can be particularly confusing. Below, you can find an overview of the most common UK terminology used in the book and the "translations" into the US equivalents.

| UK | US | additional comments |
|---|---|---|
| baking beans | pie weights | / |
| baking paper | parchment paper | / |
| baking tin | baking pan | / |
| bicarbonate of soda | baking soda | / |
| cake tin | cake pan | / |
| caster sugar | superfine sugar | If you can't find superfine sugar, use granulated sugar instead. |
| cornflour | cornstarch | This is different from maize flour (UK) or corn flour (US). |
| double cream | heavy cream | Heavy cream has a lower fat content (about 36–38%) than double cream (about 48%), but it's a good alternative for most applications. |
| golden syrup | / | There is no ideal substitute for golden syrup – you should be able to find it in the US. If you can't find it, use corn syrup instead. |
| icing sugar | powdered (confectioner's) sugar | / |
| light brown soft sugar | light brown sugar | / |
| maize flour | corn flour | This is very finely milled/ground cornmeal, and different from cornflour (UK)/cornstarch (US). |
| medium eggs | large eggs | Average weight with shell about 60g; without shell about 50–52g |
| muffin tin | muffin pan | / |
| proving | proofing | / |

# Index

Note: page numbers in **bold** refer to illustrations.

# Recipe index

Note: page numbers in **bold** refer to illustrations.

# Acknowledgments

Writing and creating this book was an adventure and an ordeal – and I asked myself (daily, hourly) just how crazy I was for wanting to write a book that encompasses all of gluten-free, dairy-free, egg-free, vegan and gluten-free vegan baking. Luckily, I had a truly amazing team on my side, without whom this book would've been just a vague idea and not the beautiful (and rather heavy) thing you're holding in your hands right now.

But first, I have to thank all the readers and followers of The Loopy Whisk, who actually inspired it. This book would never have happened without you – in more ways than one. The number of questions I get on a daily basis about converting various recipes (from those on my blog to family favourites handed down through generations) into X-free is overwhelming in the best possible way. And because I can't answer each and every question that comes my way (although I so wish I could!), this book is my answer to you.

To my amazing editor Nicky Ross at Yellow Kite: thank you for seeing the potential in a rather bonkers proposal and for taking on this project that became so much more expansive and ambitious than any of us expected. The 200-or-so-page book somehow transformed into a 496-page beast, and you believed in it every step of the way.

Thank you also to Olivia Nightingall, who made sure that everything ran smoothly and that everyone knew what was going on when – which was really essential on this project.

I was lucky to once again work with the brilliant Judy Barratt, copyeditor extraordinaire, who speaks my (slightly nerdy and always nit-picky) language and made sure that this book is the very best it could be. Thank you for your patience in dealing with all my questions, text changes and also my tendency to overthink things that were probably perfectly fine to begin with.

As is probably evident from their vast number in this book, I adore tables and spreadsheets, and Nathan Burton, through his amazing design, made them look absolutely stunning. Thank you for transforming an information- and text-overload into a book that's so perfectly organized and a real joy to read and look at – and also for adding a sprinkling of Chemistry and the periodic table to the book design and cover in the most beautiful way.

Thank you also to my wonderful agent, Laurie Robertson at PFD, who believed in this book from the very start and is always on hand to answer my numerous questions and offer advice.

And finally: I always like to end with the best (and the most important) bit – the best bite of lunch or dinner, the gooiest middle part of a cinnamon roll and, in these acknowledgements, with my parents. Thank you for always supporting and encouraging me (even though I'm pretty sure you hoped I'd stop the insanity after just one book) and for your endless patience with my experiments, overthinking and double-checking the already double-checked things. I love you so, so much.

## About the Author

Katarina Cermelj (Kat for short) is an award-winning cookbook author, food writer, photographer and creator of the popular free-from baking blog The Loopy Whisk.

Originally from Slovenia, she moved to the UK for her undergraduate studies in Chemistry at the University of Oxford, and then stayed on for a PhD in Inorganic Chemistry (which she somehow managed to complete while writing her first book, *Baked to Perfection*). Being a science nerd, she loves to use a very scientific, analytical approach in her recipe development – and she's also a big believer in not only providing reliable, fail-proof (and always delicious) recipes, but also all the reasons why they work.

theloopywhisk.com

@theloopywhisk

Instagram  Facebook  TikTok

First published in Great Britain in 2024 by Yellow Kite
An imprint of Hodder & Stoughton
An Hachette UK company

10 9 8 7 6 5 4 3 2 1

A CIP catalogue record for this title is available from the British Library

Hardback ISBN 978 1 399 71289 7
eBook ISBN 978 1 399 71290 3

Editorial Director: Nicky Ross
Senior Project Editor: Liv Nightingall
Editor: Judy Barratt
Designer: Nathan Burton
Photography and styling: Katarina Cermelj
Production Controller: Katy Aries

Colour origination by Alta Image, London.
Printed and bound in China by C&C Offset Printing Co., Ltd.

Hodder & Stoughton policy is to use papers that are natural, renewable and recyclable products
and made from wood grown in sustainable forests. The logging and manufacturing processes
are expected to conform to the environmental regulations of the country of origin.

Yellow Kite
Hodder & Stoughton Ltd
Carmelite House
50 Victoria Embankment
London
EC4Y 0DZ

www.yellowkitebooks.co.uk
www.hodder.co.uk

**General disclaimer:** This book is not a substitute for the advice of any health professional. Always consult your doctor before eliminating any food group from your diet.

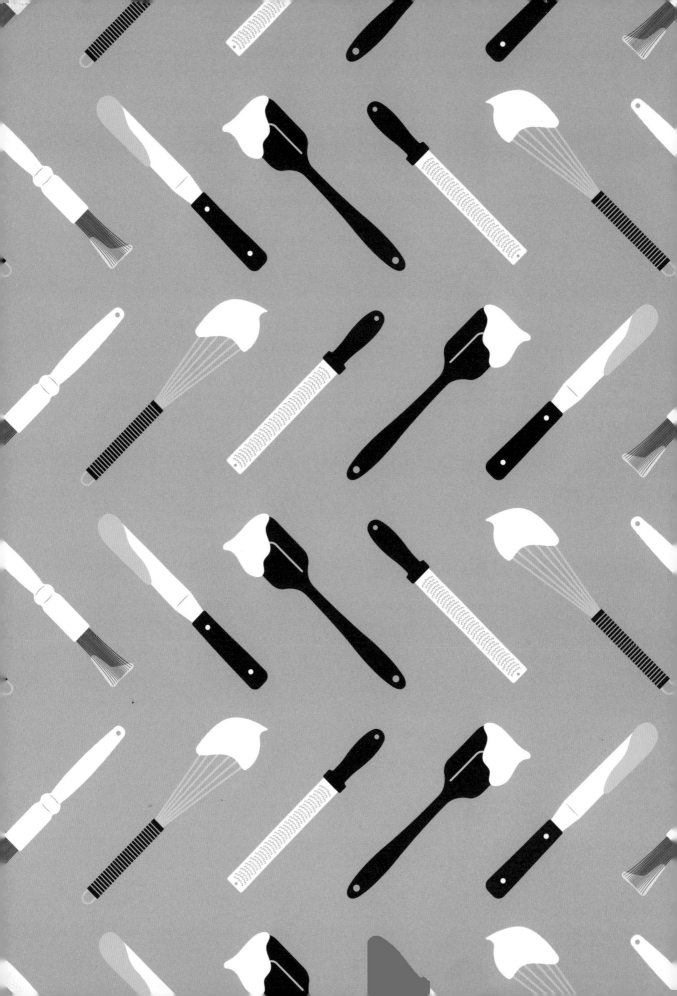